Hezbollah

Hezbollah

The Political Economy of Lebanon's Party of God

Joseph Daher

PlutoPress
www.plutobooks.com

First published 2016 by Pluto Press
345 Archway Road, London N6 5AA

www.plutobooks.com

Copyright © Joseph Daher 2016

The right of Joseph Daher to be identified as the author of this work has
been asserted by him in accordance with the Copyright, Designs and
Patents Act 1988.

British Library Cataloguing in Publication Data
A catalogue record for this book is available from the British Library

ISBN   978 0 7453 3693 0   Hardback
ISBN   978 0 7453 3689 3   Paperback
ISBN   978 1 7837 1997 6   PDF eBook
ISBN   978 1 7837 1999 0   Kindle eBook
ISBN   978 1 7837 1998 3   EPUB eBook

Typeset by Stanford DTP Services, Northampton, England

Simultaneously printed in the European Union and United States of America

Contents

List of Tables

Acknowledgements

I am very much indebted in the writing of this book to my family (my parents, my brother and my wife) for their support and love through these past years. I would like to thank especially my mother Juliet and my wife Paola, who supported and encouraged me constantly in my work. I would also like to thank my daughters, Yara and Tamara, who without knowing it calmed me in times of stress by their presence and lovely smiles.

I owe a debt of gratitude to the two direct supervisors of my doctoral dissertation (on which this book is based), Dr. Adam Hanieh and Professor Gilbert Achcar, for their assistance, comments and time. Their precious advice and support have truly touched me and have guided this work.

I would like to thank my friends of the Socialist Forum for the help they gave during my year in Lebanon and afterwards in my research, especially Walid Daou, Camille Dagher, Ghassan Makarem, Farah Kobeissi and the late Bassem Chiit. I would like to pay tribute through this book to Bassem who passed away in October 2014. His activism and writings were inspirational.

I also thank David Shulman, editor at Pluto Press, for his help in publishing this book and all the team that contributed to this process.

Finally, I would like to dedicate this book to my father Nicolas, who passed away in September 2014, with all my love and gratitude. He always has been a true inspiration for me and continues to be in my daily life. His great humanism, large heart, generosity, courage, honesty, humor and knowledge have very much influenced me in my various activities and works. By dedicating this book to him, I cannot but also dedicate this book to the people of Syria, from where our family originally comes. They have suffered enormously since the beginning of the revolutionary process in March 2011, from massive destruction and displacements and grave human rights violations. My deep thoughts are with them.

Introduction

Hezbollah was formed in 1985 during a period of intense political crisis characterized by the Lebanese Civil War and the invasion of Lebanon by Israel in 1982. It was established as an Islamic political group, based in Shi'a-populated areas in Lebanon, with an emphasis on armed resistance against Israel. Over the years, Hezbollah came to be seen by many—in both Lebanon and the wider Arab world—as the only viable force able to resist Western and Israeli encroachment on the country. Following the various wars of aggression on Lebanon by Israel, most notably the 2006 invasion, Hezbollah was celebrated for its apparently well-disciplined military and propaganda capabilities, and its ability to effectively resist the Israeli state. Portraits of Hassan Nasrallah, the movement's General Secretary, could be seen in demonstrations in the major capitals of the Arab world. Even in the Gulf Arab states, where ruling regimes have traditionally expressed hostility towards Hezbollah, following the 2006 Lebanon War, prominent individuals such as the wealthy Kuwaiti businessman Nasser al-Kharafi have publicly praised the group (Farid 2001 and Wehbe, B. 2011).[1]

In addition to its armed capabilities and standing in the Arab world, Hezbollah has become one of the most important political actors in Lebanon, holding a large parliamentary bloc of no less than ten deputies since the first post-Civil War legislative elections in 1992, and a minimum of two ministers in every Lebanese government since 2005. Hezbollah has confirmed its popularity by winning many municipal elections and now controls the most significant Shi'a-populated areas in the South of Greater Beirut, South Lebanon and the Bekaa Valley. The organization is a mass movement, with an extensive network of charities and other institutions that meet needs and provide services for the population. Indeed, Hezbollah's social and political influence among the Shi'a population is much more significant than its ally Amal.

Hezbollah's ideology is a Shi'a-inspired version of an Islamic political movement. Islamic political movements are found across the world—from the Muslim Brotherhood in Egypt and elsewhere, the *Jamaat-i-Islami*, the multiple Ulema associations, and the movement of Iranian Ayatollahs. In all these cases, Islam is erected as an absolute principle to which all demands, struggles and reforms are to be subordinated. The common denominator of all of these Islamic political movements is "Islamic fundamentalism," according to Gilbert Achcar, "in other words a will to return to Islam, the aspiration of an Islamic Utopia that is not limited to one Nation and that should encompass all the Muslim peoples, if not the whole world" (Achcar 1981: 2). This definition can be seen reflected in the words of Muhammad Khairat al-Shater, the former Deputy Guide of the Egyptian Muslim Brotherhood:

> The Ikhwan are working to restore Islam in its all-encompassing conception to the lives of people, and they believe that this will only come about through the strong society. Thus the mission is clear: restoring Islam in its all-encompassing conception; subjugating people to God; instituting the religion of God; the Islamization of life, empowering of God's religion; establishing the Nahda of the Ummah on the basis of Islam […] Thus we've learned [to start with] building the Muslim individual, the Muslim family, the Muslim society, the Islamic government, the global Islamic state.
>
> (Amal al-Ummah TV 2011; Bargisi, Mohameed and Pieretti 2012)

Religious fundamentalism is not limited to the Islamic religion, and we can see common elements among various religious fundamentalist movements throughout the world. It is important to note, however, that despite the call to return to an earlier age, fundamentalisms should not be seen as fossilized elements from the past. While they may employ symbols and narratives from earlier periods, fundamentalisms are alive, dynamic and representative of major contemporary trends, designed to satisfy cultural needs (Marty 1988: 17). Their emergence must thus be fully situated in the political, economic and social context of the contemporary period.

In the Middle East, the rise of both Shi'a and Sunni Islamic political movements took place in a period—through the 1980s and 1990s—in which the left and nationalist forces were considerably weakened for various reasons: setbacks for Arab nationalism; US support to the Saudi Kingdom, which, in turn, helped foster various Sunni Islamic fundamentalist movements, most particularly the Muslim Brotherhood, as a counterweight against Arab nationalism; regional events starting with the 1973 oil boom that allowed Gulf monarchies to increase their regional funding; weakening of the progressive forces in the early 1970s, with the intense repression by Arab regimes such as Egypt, Syria and Iraq that abandoned their previous radical social policies and increasingly adopted a rapprochement with the Western countries and the monarchies of the Gulf; weakening of Palestinian and Arab national progressive forces by the multiple attacks against the Palestinian national movement by both the Arab states and Israel; and the establishment of the Islamic Republic of Iran in 1979.

This was the regional context in which Hezbollah was formed. Hezbollah's popular social base among the Lebanese Shi'a population, which was first concentrated among the relatively poor Shi'a and some petit bourgeois components, was then extended to encompass all social classes. Today, the party has significant political and social support among a growing Shi'a bourgeoisie, located both inside the country and in the diaspora.

Given this process of integration into the political system, and the extending social base of the organization, a range of questions can be raised about the nature of Hezbollah as a political party and as a social force. How can we explain the politics and practice of Hezbollah in relation to the political economy of Lebanon and the country's Shi'a population? How has it been able to build such a widespread base of support amongst Shi'a in Lebanon? What is the nature of the relationship between Hezbollah and the Islamic Republic of Iran (IRI)? What role do Hezbollah's military capacities play in its hegemony over Lebanese Shi'a populations? How can we explain the political and social evolution of Hezbollah?

The answers to these questions are significant both in terms of the insights they offer into Political Islam as an ideology, as well as their implications for understanding the broader political economy of Lebanon and the Middle East.

The objective of this work is to understand Hezbollah through a historical and materialist understanding of Political Islam, tracking the evolution of the organization's structures and relationship within the wider political system, and locating this evolution within the changing class and state formation in Lebanon. In this manner, this book moves the debate beyond the typical focus on ideology as a means of identifying and understanding the policies of Islamic political movements. The book argues that while the "Islamic way of life" may be the professed goal of Hezbollah, its actual practices can best be understood as harmonious with—and reflective of—the nature of the capitalist environment in which it operates.

In addition to helping conceive the evolution of Hezbollah and its place within the contemporary politics of the region, we seek to counteract a prevailing Orientalism within much of the study of the Arab world. This Orientalism tends to hold up the region as being beyond the grasp of social scientific frameworks typically employed to understand processes of political change elsewhere in the world. In this regard, this book concurs with the conclusion of Arab writer, Aziz al-Azmeh, that: "the understanding of Islamic political phenomena requires the normal equipment of the social and human sciences, not their denial" (Al-Azmeh 2003: 39).

Structure of the book

This book is organized into seven main chapters.

Chapter 1 looks at the origins of sectarianism in Lebanon from the time of the French Mandate (1920) through to the end of the Civil War (1975–1990). It traces the position of different sectarian communities over this period, and analyses the impact of the Civil War on the political and social conditions of the Shi'a population in particular. This period coincides with the establishment of Hezbollah in 1985, and provides important insights into its subsequent evolution. Throughout this chapter, sectarianism is viewed as a tool used by the Lebanese bourgeoisie to intervene ideologically in the class struggle, strengthening its control of the popular classes and keeping them subordinated to their sectarian leaders (Amel 1986: 323, 326–27). Sectarianism needs to be seen as constitutive, and reinforcing, of current forms of state and class power. Along these lines, we consider sectarianism as a product of modern times and not a tradition from time immemorial. As the Lebanese–Palestinian scholar Ussama Makdissi has noted, "sectarianism is a modern story, and for those intimately involved in its unfolding, it is the modern story—a story that has and that continues to define and dominate their lives" (Makdissi 2000: 2).

Chapter 2 studies the evolution of the Lebanese political economy from 1990 to 2016, the period covering the end of the Civil War until today. It focuses in particular on the Shiʿa population, whose political and socio-economic status was significantly lower than other Lebanese religious sects at the end of the Lebanese Civil War and has since changed considerably. We will see the changes in the position and stratification of the Shiʿa population as a result of neoliberal policies, and the connection of these changes to the development of Hezbollah as a political organization. These neoliberal policies led to the deepening of the historically constituted characteristics of the Lebanese economy: a finance and service oriented development model in which social inequalities and regional disparities were very pronounced. The chapter discusses the consequences of these characteristics as they developed through the neoliberal period, and the subsequent political orientation of the Hezbollah towards both economic policy and the sectarian political system. It concludes with a survey of three specific case studies in areas where the Hezbollah has significant influence and control: (1) the management of urban policy in the municipal neighborhood of Ghobeyri; (2) attitudes towards rent-control laws in Beirut; and (3) agricultural policy in the Bekaa Valley.

Having established these developmental trends over the neoliberal period, Chapter 3 examines their implications for Lebanon's class structure, in particular amongst the Shiʿa population. The chapter demonstrates that the neoliberal period saw the emergence of a new Shiʿa bourgeoisie within various sectors of the economy, and the resulting re-balancing of sectarian power across the country. This process, however, was not evenly distributed, and many Shiʿa remain marginalized throughout significant urban and rural areas. The chapter then turns to a concrete mapping of the new Shiʿa bourgeoisie through an analysis of the largest Shiʿa business groups and their relationship to the Hezbollah itself. These factors are then brought together in an analysis of the changing social base of the party.

Chapter 4 traces the growth of the party as a mass movement and attempts to understand how the party has managed to achieve a position of hegemony in Shiʿa areas, despite the tensions arising from the nature of its social base. This chapter examines in detail the internal organization of the party and its large network of institutions. The latter has played an important role in diffusing the ideas of the party through the Shi'a community and extending its hegemony through the provision of much-needed services. The chapter analyses how the success of Hezbollah's network of organizations, managed mostly from Hezbollah's Executive Council, has allowed it to strengthen its position amongst the population, focusing in particular on four critical sectors: (1) social support, (2) religious institutions, (3) media and culture, and (4) education/youth work. The chapter explores the ideological content of Hezbollah's work in these sectors, emphasizing the role that two concepts—*hāla islāmiyya* (the Islamic milieu) and *iltizām* (personal commitment)—have played in building allegiance to the party. It also analyzes the distinctively gendered characteristic of these ideological underpinnings of the party's work.

Chapter 5 turns to Hezbollah's orientation towards the Lebanese labor movement. Beginning with the history of the trade union movement through the Civil War period, the chapter examines the various social and worker protests that continued through the 1990s and into the contemporary period. It shows how the General Confederation of Lebanese Workers (known as the CGTL), the main trade union confederation, was progressively weakened by the main bourgeois and sectarian political forces and subordinated to their interests, because they feared the CGTL's capacity for mobilization. In this regard, Hezbollah's behavior towards various economic demands, strikes and the organization of labor is analyzed. The chapter thus provides a link between the political economy analyses provided in Chapters 2 and 3, and the socio-political analysis of Chapter 4. In this manner, it offers an important illustration of the tensions that have arisen in the organization as a result of its claim to represent the struggles and needs of the poorer ranks of the Shi'a population, concomitant with its changing social base.

Chapter 6 analyzes a crucial aspect of Hezbollah's organization: its military activities and armed apparatus. The chapter begins by examining Hezbollah's military struggle against the State of Israel, followed by its coercive activities towards other Lebanese actors during the Lebanese Civil War and, later, in 2008, when it led military operations against the March 14 coalition. Hezbollah's use of its military capacities to guarantee its power and security in the region is also analyzed.

Chapter 7 looks at Hezbollah's behavior regarding the popular uprisings in the Middle East and North Africa, which started in December 2010 and January 2011 with the overthrow of dictators in Tunisia and Egypt and which are still unfolding. This chapter will particularly examine Hezbollah's involvement in Syria, and the ways its involvement has exacerbated sectarianism within Lebanon. We will also see the consequences of the Syrian uprising on the relationship between Hezbollah, Iran and the Palestinian Islamic movement Hamas. The concluding chapter brings together the overall analysis in both a theoretical and political sense.

A Note on Sources

This study draws upon a wide range of academic writing in the fields of politics, political economy, sociology and development theory. As the following chapter will outline in greater detail, its basic theoretical framework is based upon Marxian and other critical analyses of Lebanon and the Middle East. In addition to the academic literature, research for the book has involved a detailed textual analysis of many books, newspaper articles, reports, political pamphlets and written interviews of key political personalities in Lebanon. My fluency in English, Arabic and French has enabled me to conduct interviews and consult primary material in the language of the sources and documentation used to establish the findings of this book.

In addition to the insights gained from these written materials, I spent over twelve months in Lebanon conducting fieldwork, from August 2011 to September 2012. During this time I was able to travel extensively throughout Beirut, the Bekaa Valley, and the southern and the northern regions of the country. This research period, which included wide-ranging consultation with activists, trade unionists, workers, students, members of political parties and academics was a valuable complement to my previous experience in the country. More than forty people were interviewed in Lebanon (in Arabic, French and English depending on the circumstances), and I also learnt from countless "off the record" discussions with individuals and groups involved in Lebanon's political scene. Moreover, my time in Lebanon allowed me the opportunity to consult various libraries, archives and research centers.

Given the political environment of Lebanon, this fieldwork was faced with numerous obstacles. First, accessing Hezbollah officials has become more difficult than in the past because of internal security measures within the party and the secrecy of the organization. I nevertheless obtained some interviews with Hezbollah-affiliated intellectuals and party representatives in the organization's mass fronts and research institutes. I also met with rank-and-file sympathizers and members of the party. Throughout this process, I had to take into account the highly sectarian atmosphere of the country when assessing the information I gathered. My long involvement with and knowledge of Lebanese politics helped me assess the more ideological and biased claims made by some sources.

Finally, my own personal vantage point contributed greatly towards the writing and framing of this book. I am a Swiss citizen of Syrian origin. I have spent long periods in Syria and in the region since my childhood. My family and close friends have been affected by the ongoing events in Syria, and a large number of them have had to leave the city of Aleppo (where we are originally from), for other safer parts of the country or to neighboring states. My interest in Hezbollah long pre-dates the party's involvement in Syria, but the events of recent years have helped me to corroborate and refine many of the arguments made below.

1

Sectarianism and the Lebanese Political Economy
Hezbollah's Origins

In September 1920, after the demise of the Ottoman Empire, the country of Greater Lebanon was established under the authority of the French Mandate. The territory of the new country included Mount Lebanon, which had gained a semi-autonomous status under Ottoman rule through the interferences of European foreign powers in 1860, and also the regions of the Bekaa Valley, *Jabal 'Amil* (South Lebanon), Akkar, Beirut, Saida and Tripoli. These latter regions had been, until 1918, part of the two Ottoman *wilāya* of Damascus and Beirut. At this time, Lebanon was composed of seventeen religious groupings that each had particular geographical and social characteristics.[1] Christians, who composed 55 percent of the total population of the country in 1920, were mainly concentrated in Mount Lebanon. The Christian population was divided into various sects, the main ones being Maronite, Greek Orthodox and Greek Catholic.[2] Muslims—Sunni, Shi'a, Druze and Ismaeli—were a majority in the new territories incorporated into Greater Lebanon: the Bekaa Valley, *Jabal 'Amil*, Akkar, Beirut, Saida and Tripoli. In these regions, Muslims formed a majority of 200,814 against 117,332 Christians (Picaudou 1989: 57).[3]

The French Mandate in Lebanon and Syria was a means of furthering France's political and economic interests in the Middle East (Khoury 1981: 452; Makdissi 1996). Lebanon and Syria were controlled by two sets of French companies called "*Intérêts communs*" and "*Sociétés concessionaires*." These two companies had a monopoly over public services and controlled the main sectors of the economy. Lebanon's role as an economic intermediary towards Syria was also confirmed during French occupation (Owen 1976: 24), with Beirut continuing to act as the main port for the Syrian interior (Traboulsi 2007: 91). Beirut's role as a regional warehouse was strengthened by the Mandate's policy of reserving the large Syrian market for Beirut merchants in exchange for higher tariff protection for agriculture and industry, which was more important to the Syrian hinterland economy (Gates 1989: 14).

These projects consolidated the Christian bourgeoisie's power linked to European capitalism and the tertiary sector—notably banking and finance (Gates 1989: 16). The large landowners of the periphery, who constituted the local notabilities, also benefited from the French Mandate. Projects of agricultural development and government aid in the Akkar, the South and the Bekaa principally benefited the large landowners supported by French governors (Traboulsi 2007: 92).

A principal means through which France dominated the country was the encouragement of sectarian patterns of rule, particularly its strategic alliance with the Maronite population. Under French control, elections for a representative council took place in 1922 followed four years later by elections for the Chamber of Deputies. These two elections were conducted along sectarian lines and were boycotted by the country's Sunni Muslim population, who were generally opposed to the partition of Syria and the formation of Greater Lebanon.[4] Sunni Muslim leaders complained that 83 percent of the fiscal revenues came from territories with a Muslim majority, in which 380,000 people lived, while 80 percent of those revenues were spent in Mount Lebanon that held only 330,000 inhabitants (Traboulsi 2007: 81). Furthermore, in the new Greater Lebanon under French rule, Maronite Christians from Mount Lebanon constituted a majority of state politicians and civil servants, as opposed to the previous *wilāyat* of Beirut, which were mainly Sunni Muslims and Greek Orthodox (Traboulsi 2007: 93).

Within the uneven political economy dominated by French capitalism, the Maronite population played a principal intermediary role involving themselves in international import and foreign trade, finance and the representation of European firms. For this reason, the announcement of the French Mandate was supported by the Maronite Patriarch Huwayk, and those sections of the Maronite population linked to (and dependent upon) French rule. Other smaller Christian denominations were less inclined to the Mandate, partly because they were more closely linked to regional trade networks—especially trade between Beirut and Damascus.[5]

Muslim populations, particularly the Sunni community, were on the whole opposed to the French Mandate (Firro 2003: 67). In addition to their marginalization within the political structures established by the French, Sunni notables feared threats to their position within intra-regional trading networks, including trade between the different ports of the Ottoman Empire, the export of agricultural products from the Syrian interior and the local trade in grain (Issawi 1982: 58). For these reasons, Sunni elites tended to support the political and territorial unity of Syria.

Throughout the 1930s, however, differences between the Sunni and Maronite elites began to narrow in favor of independence for both Lebanon and Syria (as two separate countries), albeit with strong political and economic links.[6] Some Muslim leaders, notably Riyad al-Solh from Saida, argued for an alliance with Christian-led political forces that were supportive of the separation of Lebanon and Syria (while remaining opposed to the French Mandate).[7] Initially this position was not widely supported within the Sunni population and led to a distancing between Solh and the dominant Muslim pro-union factions. Nevertheless, this opposition did not last, especially following the signing of the Franco-Syrian Treaty of Independence in 1936 in which the Syrian representatives of the National Bloc dropped their annexionist demands concerning Lebanon in return for France's integration of the Druze and Alawite autonomous zones into the Syrian Republic (Traboulsi 2007: 101).

In addition to this, opposition to the French Mandate and harsh social and economic conditions spread throughout Lebanon. The bourgeoisie from across sectarian tendencies increasingly favored the independence option and supported the various workers and popular strikes and protests challenging the rule of the French Mandate. The opposition of the bourgeoisie targeted the economic privileges of the Mandate, as demonstrated by the monopolies exercised on behalf of the French concessionary companies, their fiscal exemptions and the export of their profit to France. Even the Maronite church, a traditional ally and supporter of the French in the country, joined the opposition to the French Mandate for reasons very close to those of the bourgeoisie (Traboulsi 2007: 105).

Lebanese independence was achieved in 1943. The National Pact, an unwritten understanding between Maronite and Sunni notables, and the new Constitution of 1943, would establish the founding principles of the newly sovereign Lebanon. Both documents confirmed political representation along sectarian lines and entrenched the domination of the Maronite community within the top echelons of the state. The President, according to Constitution, was required to be Maronite, and had extensive powers, while Christian deputies also had a majority in the parliament in a 6:5 ratio to Muslims (Salibi 1971: 83; Faour 1991: 631). The Sunni elite, however, was nevertheless promised greater participation in state affairs and decision-making, including the position of Prime Minister, than during the mandate period.

In contrast to their Maronite and Sunni counterparts, the political and socio-economic situation of the Shi'a population was significantly weaker at the time of independence. They had the lowest social indicators with illiteracy rates reaching 68.9 percent in 1943, compared to 31.5 percent in the Catholic Christian community (Nasr 1985). Eighty-five percent of Shi'a were concentrated in two main regions: South Lebanon (with the exception of the coastal city of Saida, which was predominantly inhabited by Sunni) and North-Eastern Lebanon, particularly the Baalbek-Hermel region (Nasr 1985). The Shi'a population was also largely rural—a characteristic which in subsequent decades would change dramatically with very significant implications as we shall see. Indeed, the urban-based Shi'a constituted no more than 10 percent of the whole community in 1948 (Nasr 1985).

The reason for the condition of great sections of the Shi'a population was that they were located—as much as 85 percent of them—in the periphery of Lebanon (Bekaa, North and South Lebanon). At the time of independence, Lebanon's periphery was characterized by large private properties owned by wealthy landowners. These properties accounted for three-quarters of the best land in the Shi'a countryside, and enabled the quasi-feudal exploitation of private sharecroppers (Nasr 1985). The Shi'a population had not yet experienced the social disruption, peasant revolts or rapid expansion of export farming that had already transformed the Maronite majority area of Mount Lebanon as it was integrated into the world capitalist economy.

The Shi'a were also largely marginalized within the political system, despite the agreement (as part of the National Pact) that they would hold the position of Speaker in the National Assembly (Hazran 2010: 533). They had the lowest level of political representation of all communities, with very few Shi'a holding a position of state official before 1974 (Daher 2014: 43). Empirical studies indicate that in 1946 only 3.2 percent of the highest civil service posts were held by Shi'a, increasing to just 3.6 percent by 1955, although Shi'a were then 18 percent of the Lebanese population (Hazran 2010: 533). In 1962, only 3 percent of Class I posts in the state administration were held by Shi'a, who constituted 19.2 percent of the population at that time. In addition, similar figures were revealed for Class II and III governmental posts in the late 1960s (Halawi 1992 cited in Hazran 2010: 534).

Notabilities of important Shi'a families typically governed the Shi'a population during this period with political power monopolized by six "notable families": the As'ad, Zein and Osseiran in southern Lebanon, and the Hamadeh, Haydar and Husseini families in Baalbek and Byblos (Firro 2006: 750–51; Nasr 1985). These *zu'āma*, as they were called, were generally large landowners who acted as intermediaries to access services for the vast majority of poor Shi'a. This relationship meant that the Shi'a population was heavily characterized by clientelism and patronage. Harel Chorev describes these characteristics as follows:

> (1) control of landed families over their sharecroppers; (2) capital of merchant families; (3) control over the allocation of national resources; and (4) ability to mediate between the public and the authorities. All of these made it possible for a *za'īm* to provide his clients with protection and employment, and help them in their contacts with the authorities. This patronage-based socio-political structure was presented as being all-encompassing, characterising not only the relationships between the *za'īm* and the public, but also between senior *zu'āma* and *zu'āma* of lower standing.
> (Chorev 2013: 308)

This *zu'āma* system was not limited to the Shi'a population, and was also present among Christian and Sunni populations.

1945–1975: From Independence to Civil War

Following Lebanon's independence in 1943, control of the state and the country's economy continued to be concentrated in the hands of a narrow oligarchy. Between 1920 and 1972, deputies in the parliament represented some 245 of Lebanon's most prominent families. By 1972, and after nearly fifty years of parliamentary life, 359 MPs had been elected of whom slightly more than 300 had inherited their seat because of family ties (Khalaf 1979: 196). State policies reflected the interests of these political and economic elites, who aimed to maintain and strengthen Lebanon's position as a key financial intermediary between the Arab world and Europe (Gates 1989: 32).

Due to this intermediary position between the West and the Arab world, the Lebanese economy in the first two decades after independence was largely dominated by the service sector, which in 1976 constituted 72 percent of the Lebanese economy (Dubar and Nasr 1976: 67; Owen 1988: 32). Within this sector, banking was dominant.

Alongside the predominant weight of finance and services, industrial production was limited, growing only minimally from 14.52 percent of GDP in 1950 to 16.7–18 percent in 1974 (Dubar and Nasr 1976: 76; Traboulsi 2007: 157). Lebanese industry followed a typical path of a dominated economy of the Third World (or the periphery), with most production concentrated in low-wage light industry (Dubar and Nasr 1976: 80).

The dominant position of the commercial and financial bourgeoisie, linked closely to Western capital, also imposed itself on the structure of the agricultural sector. In addition, government policies supported the interests of large landowners, who received the large majority of the Ministry of Agriculture's assistance, while small farmers were neglected (Dahir 1974 cited in Nasr 1978: 10).

This situation had important consequences for the structure of social relations in rural areas. Most significantly, agricultural production became increasingly dominated by large farms located in areas such as the Bekaa Valley, Akkar and the southern coastal plains. These farms were frequently owned by urban elites, who forced traditional share-croppers to leave the land. The proportion of sharecroppers in the active population fell from 25 percent in the 1950s to 5 percent in the 1970s (Dahir 1974 cited in Nasr 1978: 6). After being displaced from their traditional livelihoods, former sharecroppers were forced to either move to Beirut, migrate abroad or to become agricultural wage laborers.

Smallholder farmers, who constituted 57 percent of the active agricultural population in the early 1970s, faced similar pressures to sharecroppers but were able to survive the increased pauperization by engaging in more than one type of activity. More than half of all farmers at the end of the 1960s worked in a secondary, usually non-agricultural job (Gaspard 2004: 91; Nasr 1978: 6). The relative share of agriculture in the national economy declined from 20 percent of the GDP in 1948 to less than 9 percent in 1974, while the share of the active population working in the sector decreased from 48.9 percent in 1959 to 18.9 percent in 1970 (Mallat 1973: 6; Nasr 1978: 13). The agrarian sector lost more than 100,000 active members in less than two decades (Dubar and Nasr 1976: 100).

In this context, Lebanon experienced large-scale rural to urban migration during the two decades following independence, with the urban population rising sharply from 25 percent of the overall population in 1950 to 65 percent in 1975 (Nasr 2003: 148). Most of these internal migrants came predominantly from Shi'a rural areas. By 1973, 63 percent of Shi'a were living in cities, including 45 percent in Greater Beirut (Harb 2010: 42). These newcomers found jobs in the service sector, where they were subjected to severe exploitation in terms of wages and working conditions. These trends were reinforced by the lack of work opportunities in services and public administration for new graduates. The level of unemployment grew from 70,000 people in 1969, about 10–13 percent of the workforce, to 120,000 people in 1974, representing 15–20 percent of the workforce (Nasr 1978: 3). Great disparities remained between the center (Mount Lebanon and Beirut) and the periphery (the suburbs of Beirut, South Lebanon, Akkar and the Bekaa). The annual per capita income in Beirut was estimated at $803 in the early 1970s, while in South Lebanon it did not exceed $151 (Traboulsi 2007: 160). Rapid urbanization meant that Beirut was surrounded by a massive poverty belt in which 400,000 people out of a total population of 1 million lived on the eve of the Civil War in 1975 (Traboulsi 2007: 161).

Class and Sectarian Divisions

By the early 1970s, Lebanese society was characterized by pronounced social, regional and sectarian inequalities. It was estimated in 1959–1960 by the French mission of inquiry IFRED (Institut Français de Recherche et d'Études du Développement) that 4 percent of the "very rich" were taking 33 percent of the national income, while the poorest 50 percent of the population received only 18 percent (cited in Farsoun and Farsoun 1974: 95–96). A study conducted by Bishop Grégoire Haddad stated that 79 percent of the Lebanese population received less than the monthly minimum income, which was $135 in 1975 (Haddad 1975 cited in Traboulsi 2007: 162). Another indicator of these inequalities was that 84 percent of the total savings were undertaken by 3–4 percent of households until the mid-1960s (Gaspard 2004: 76).

Overlaying these inequalities were clear sectarian and regional distinctions. Prior to independence, the Maronite bourgeoisie held a position of dominance. In 1973, the Christian fraction of the bourgeoisie owned 75.5 percent of total commercial companies, 67.5 percent of total industrial companies and 71 percent of the total of Lebanese owned banks (Labaki 1988b: 166). At the same time, the Shi'a popular classes were relatively deprived. In terms of secondary education, 15 percent of Sunni and 17 percent of Christians had finished their secondary education, while the percentage of Shi'a did not exceed 6.6 percent (Norton 1987: 17). In 1971, the average Shi'a family's income was L£4,532 in comparison with the national average of L£6,247 (Norton 1987: 17) (L£3 = US$1). The Shi'a represented the highest percentage of families earning less than L£1,500. They were also the most poorly educated, with 50 percent of Shi'a having no schooling (compared to 30 percent nationwide). In 1974, the Shi'a-dominated South received less than 0.7 percent of the state budget while the region held 20 percent of the national population (Norton 1987: 18).

Despite these differences, it is important to note that the gap between the Christian and Muslim populations had nonetheless narrowed and it would be wrong to ascribe class position solely on the basis of affiliation to sect. According to Nasr (2003: 151), the upper class was divided between 65 percent Christians and 35 percent Muslims in 1975. The percentage of professionals in banking who were Muslim jumped from zero in 1950 to 35 percent in 1982–1983, while during the same period the percentage of Muslim professionals in industry increased from 33 percent to 44 percent (Labaki 1988a: 145). Similar trends could be seen within the poorer classes. One 1974 survey of 7,070 workers in twenty-six of the largest industrial factories in an eastern suburb of Beirut found that the breakdown of the workforce was almost evenly divided between Muslims and Christians (54.96 percent and 45.04 percent respectively) (Dubar and Nasr 1976: 88–90). The sample interviewed in this survey represented nearly 10 percent of total employment in factories where more than five workers were employed, and around 40 percent of workers in large industry. The results indicate that, at that time, a substantial number of Christian workers were found within the Lebanese labor force.

Despite its generalized impoverishment, the Shi'a population had undergone significant changes in the period following independence, particularly under the presidency of Fuad Chehab (1958–1964). Chehab had attempted to integrate parts of the Shi'a population into the political administration of the country, and moderated regional inequalities through the development of economic, transport, electricity and water infrastructure.

His government imposed stricter quotas on the recruitment of civil servants and military personnel, which benefited Shi'a who were hitherto largely under-represented (Deeb, L. 2006: 73). Indeed, by the early 1970s, Shi'a represented 22 percent of Class I Civil Service posts (31 of 139 positions), up from just over 3 percent in the 1960s (Hazran 2010: 533). Increased state intervention in education also benefited the Shi'a, who did not have a large network of private schools like the Maronite population. Thus in South Lebanon and the Bekaa (mostly populated by Shi'a), the number of pupils in primary and secondary schools increased from 62,000 in 1959 to 225,000 in 1973 (Nasr 1985). Similarly, the development of the Lebanese University, which was national and free, opened access to higher education for young Shi'a from poorer backgrounds. One indication of the impact of these reforms was the number of Muslims working in the state administration, which reached 47.32 percent in 1978—up from 41.3 percent in 1943 (Labaki 1988b: 175).

Another very significant trend affecting the development of the Shi'a population was the impact of international migration (as it had been for the Maronite population a century earlier). The growth of a Shi'a diaspora had begun during the French Mandate, with Shi'a from villages and small towns migrating to West Africa. In the 1950s and 1960s, these flows were redirected towards the Arab oil countries (Labaki 1988b: 175). By 1975, 50 percent of Shi'a in the Bekaa and 65 percent in South Lebanon had abandoned their villages. Some three-quarters, according to Salim Nasr (1978: 10), had settled in Lebanese cities and the remainder went abroad, chiefly to Africa and the Gulf.

The growth of an increasingly educated, younger middle class and a relatively prosperous Shi'a diaspora had begun to transform power relations in the community. Older established leaders of that community, the *zuʿama*, and the clerical leaders associated with them, were increasingly marginalized by migrants who used their remittances to purchase land and orchards, establish channels of commerce and carve out spheres of socio-political influence (Nasr 1985). This new layer of the Shiʿa population initially directed its economic activities towards relatively minor sectors such as small-scale real estate, citrus cultivation, leisure businesses and trade with Africa (Nasr 1985). By the early 1970s, however, it had expanded into banks, industries and large commercial enterprises. This new elite, formed through the pathway of migration, could be seen in clerical institutions (Imam Sadr), the political sphere (MPs such as Y. Hammoud, S. Arab, H. Mansour), and financial activities (A. Jammal, H. Mansour) (Nasr 1978: 10).

It was in this context that a key Shiʿa-based party emerged in 1974, known as the movement of the *Mahrumīn* (later known as Amal), around the leadership of the cleric Moussa al-Sadr. Sadr was born in Iran and arrived in Lebanon in the early 1960s with significant funds to launch social projects for the Shiʿa population. He sought to capitalize on the institutionalized discrimination of the Shiʿa and to build a movement that would rival the left, which was influential amongst the Shiʿa at the time (Chorev 2013: 309; Abisaab and Abisaab 2014: 114). In order to achieve this goal, Sadr built alliances with important families such as the Beidun, Bazzi, Osseiran and Zein (the latter controlled the *al-ʿIrfan* newspaper which served as a platform for Sadr's political project) (Chorev 2013: 309–10), while opposing specific traditional *zuʿama* (Deeb 1988: 683)[8] families such as the Asʿad.

It was under Sadr's initiative that the Shiʿa were organized into a more coherent voice, codified in the creation of the Higher Islamic Shiʿa Council (HISC) in 1967 that had the goals of defending the rights of the community and improving its social and economic conditions, including the distribution of relief funds to the Shiʿa. Not long after HISC's establishment, the Lebanese government disbursed US$10 million in aid to it (Traboulsi 2007:178). In May 1969, Sadr was appointed to chair the Higher Islamic Shiʿa Council. This Council was primarily conceived as a forum for the rising and increasingly influential Shiʿa middle class and bourgeoisie and newly influential political Shiʿa personalities, who in the past were blocked from political power and social influence by traditional Shiʿa *zuʿama* (Sachedina 1991: 445).

Sadr was able to mobilize a great majority of the Shi'a population behind his movement. The movement drew their strength from peasants, workers and the urban middle classes who directly experienced the frustration caused by the under-representation of the Shi'a in a political system dominated by the Maronite and Sunni bourgeoisie. Wealthy overseas Shi'a also supported him as they sought a place in this system, as well as a social status that corresponded to their newly acquired wealth (Daher 2014: 46–47; Abisaab and Abisaab 2014: 115–16). Sadr wanted the state to act as a guarantor of the interests of the new and emerging Shi'a bourgeoisie and to enable it to achieve a higher status in the administration and ministries (Abisaab and Abisaab 2014: 115–16). Although Sadr did not challenge the sectarian basis of Lebanon's political arrangement, he was critical of Maronite domination and accused the various governments of neglecting the South and the Bekaa, rendering the Shi'a a "disinherited population in Lebanon" (Norton 1987: 42). This nevertheless did not prevent Maronite bourgeois leaders in search of a Muslim ally to seek relations with Moussa Sadr as a counterbalance against the majority of Sunni leaders allied to Nasserism and Palestinian national organizations (Mikaelian 2015: 157). This was all the more significant given the substantial demographic changes in Lebanon at the time, with the Muslim population estimated at 55–60 percent of the Lebanese population by the early 1970s (Picard 1985: 1000). Moreover, the Shi'a constituted the largest single confessional group in Lebanon on the eve of the Civil War, with an approximate population of 30 percent (equivalent to around one million people) (Norton 1987: 17).

The Lebanese Civil War 1975–1990

The Lebanese Civil War began in 1975, and had profound consequences for these trends and for the character of the sectarian system in the country. A full discussion of the causes of the Civil War is beyond the scope of this book, but it is important to highlight some of the political and social changes that were occurring in the country at the time as part of situating the roots of Hezbollah's formation and the character of its relationship to the Shi'a population.

Foremost amongst these changes was the increasingly fractious debate opened up by the growing presence of the Palestinian resistance in Beirut and southern Lebanon. In addition to the 100,000 Palestinian refugees already located in Lebanon from the time of the 1948 *Nakba* (Norton 1987: 8), South Lebanon had become the main geographical base of Palestinian armed groups following the events of "Black September" in 1970 in Jordan and the repression of Palestinian organizations by the Hashemite Kingdom. At the onset of the Civil War, the number of Palestinians living in Lebanon had reached around 260,000, of which more than half resided in refugee camps (Kassir 1994: 74). Palestinians living in the camps were largely excluded by Lebanese law from full integration into Lebanese society,[9] while those who lived outside of the camps generally had higher socio-economic standing. Many Palestinians in the camps were incorporated into Palestinian armed political organizations, mostly as military recruits (Kassir 1994: 208). It should be noted as well that a great number of the Lebanese Shi'a joined Palestinian armed organizations during this period (Norton 2007: 16).

Political forces in Lebanon were increasingly divided over support to the Palestinian resistance and the large Palestinian presence in the country—questions that intersected with the future of the sectarian system described above. The Phalange party and its allies, organized in the Lebanese Front and led by Maronite notables (Traboulsi 2007: 187), criticized the resistance and sought to maintain the domination of the Maronite community in Lebanon's political and economic life. In opposition to the Lebanese Front, the Lebanese National Movement (LNM)—led by the Druze leader Kamal Jumblatt of the Progressive Socialist Party (PSP) in alliance with other leftist and nationalist movements—supported the Palestinian resistance and called for an end to the sectarian political system.

Within this constellation of forces, Lebanon's Shi'a saw increasing divisions between the poorer populations in Beirut and southern Lebanon and the community's leadership represented by Sadr's *al-Mahrumīn*. In the early stages of the Civil War, Shi'a areas had been the targets of attacks by Phalangist forces, including the infamous massacre of "Black Saturday" on December 6, 1975, in which numerous Shi'a were killed.[10] In this context, *al-Mahrumīn* initially participated in the LNM and held a strong relationship with Palestinian organizations, from 1975 the latter provided training bases, instructors and arms to the newly established movement's military organization *Afwāj al-Muqāwama al-Lubnāniyya* (known by its acronym *Amal*) (Nasr 1985). In May 1976, following the Syrian entry into Lebanon in support of the Lebanese Front against the

LNM, Amal began to distance itself from the Palestinian resistance and eventually left the LNM (Norton 1987: 42).[11] This shift was criticized by large sections of the Shiʿa population, which in its majority supported the LNM and the Palestinian resistance. Moreover, continued attacks by Phalangist forces against Shiʿa areas—notably the agreement between the Kataeb[12] and Amal, which in July 1976 led to the expulsion of 100,000 Shiʿa residents from the neighborhood of Nabaʿa—further accentuated the divisions between the population as a whole and the stance of the Amal leadership (Daher 2014: 49). Following the disappearance of Moussa Sadr in Libya in September 1978,[13] Amal entered into fierce battles with different forces of the LNM, particularly the Lebanese Communist Party (LCP) and the pro-Iraqi Baʿth party. These battles reflected a competition over the political leadership of the Shiʿa population, with the LCP and Baʿth holding a strong base of support in the Shiʿa suburbs of South Beirut (Kassir 1994: 104).

In addition to the regional dimensions that underlay the root causes of the Civil War, the conflict also indicated profound social discontent with the political and economic situation in the country. Deepening social inequalities had given birth to a growing trans-confessional social and political movement struggling for better working and salary conditions, freedom of trade unions, democratization and a secularization of the Lebanese system. On the political level, the challenge to the political and economic elites coalesced under the LNM. Since 1967, leftist and nationalist forces had increased their strength in different social struggles, trade unions and other institutions (Dubar and Nasr 1976: 326). The results of the legislative elections in 1972 and the regional elections in the South in 1974 registered a growth in support for leftist candidates as well as candidates of the Amal movement—both forces challenging the power of the traditional elites.

Despite the widespread anger at the socio-economic situation, indicated by numerous individual and collective acts directed against symbols of wealth and power during the Civil War (industries, large stores, warehouses) (Traboulsi 2007: 234), its political expression tended to fall back onto sectarian lines. This was partly the result of a weakness in the organization of the urban workforce, which related to the disproportionate size of the unorganized informal sector linked directly to sectarian organizations (Dubar and Nasr 1976: 332). The rate of union membership in the mid-1970s did not exceed 6 percent (Gaspard

2004: 65). The weakness of organized labor undermined attempts to build across sectarian lines, although mobilizations by the CGTL in the later years of the Civil War did represent an important counterpoint to sectarianism (see Chapter 6).

In addition to this underlying social structure, the ideological orientation of the LNM and some sections of the left reinforced the increasingly sectarian turn of the Civil War. It was at this period indeed that the concept of "community class," which was developed by two prominent intellectuals associated with the Organization of Communist Action in Lebanon (OCAL), Mohsen Ibrahim and Fawwaz Traboulsi, expanded from its origins among a small circle of left intellectuals to become one that was widely held among key left organizations in Lebanon—notably the LCP and the progressive front, the LNM.

According to this theory, the predominant weight of Christians in Lebanon's business elite meant that Christians could be understood as constituting the bourgeoisie, while Muslims (particularly Shiʿa) made up the vast majority of the working class and poor. From this perspective, the struggle of a particular sect—in this case the Shiʿa—represented a form of class struggle. In Fawwaz Traboulsi's words, the left needed "to confront the religion of the rulers with the religion of the governed, the religion of the satiated with the religion of the hungry" (Traboulsi 1988 cited in Daou 2013).

The LNM deepened its alliance with Muslim elites and some Islamic groups, leading it to increasingly abandon socio-economic demands and the goal of secularizing political structures (Picard 1985: 1014; Chiit 2009b; Daou 2013). Traboulsi described the LNM's position as increasingly defensive by dropping its reform program and adopting an increasingly Arab nationalist discourse with sectarian themes, in which sects were divided between "patriotic" and "non patriotic ones" (2007: 214). In this manner, the positions of the LNM and some sections of the left paved the way for increased sectarianism and the facilitation of foreign interference in the internal politics of the country (Picard 1985: 1016–17; Chiit 2009b; Daou 2013).

These trends confirm the prognosis of Mehdi Amel (1986: 212), who argued that the bourgeoisie would attempt to give a confessional aspect to the class struggle in order to maintain its own dominant position. The confessional inflexion of class struggle reflected the ability of the bourgeoisie to impose itself as the representatives of subordinated classes, making the latter dependent on its political and confessional representation (Amel 1986: 125).

Amel was actually one of the most vocal critics of the concept of "community class." He argued against any attempt to ascribe and equate class position according to membership in a particular sect, and as a result, to then build alliances on the basis of sectarian affiliation. Such alliances would, according to Amel, further entrench the sectarian dynamic inherent to the system and thus strengthen the position of those in power. At a theoretical level, the community class concept was mistaken, in Amel's (1986: 242) belief, because it resulted from an amalgam of the political (the sectarian system) and the economic (the social relations underlying capitalist society). Instead, Amel advanced a position that highlighted the contradictory class nature of different sect communities, one in which the role of sectarianism helped to obscure relations of power and domination within the community itself.

The departure of the Palestinian political and armed forces—in addition to thousands of civilians—from Lebanon in late August and early September of 1982 also constituted a big blow for the progressive and national forces of Lebanon.[14] The progressive and national forces of Lebanon lost an important political and military ally and were now on their own against the rest of the Lebanese bourgeois and sectarian forces, even ex-allies such as Amal who had increasingly begun to oppose the presence of Palestinian forces. At the end of the 1970s and the beginning of the 1980s, the Amal movement, headed by Nabih Berri alongside other traditional Muslim leaders, led the opposition to the Palestinian mini state,[15] demanding the halt of military operations from Lebanese territory and the return of Lebanese authorities to the South (Traboulsi 2007: 214). In the two years preceding the Israeli invasion of June 1982, frequent clashes occurred between Amal on one side, and the Palestinian organizations and LNM on the other.

The LNM, which had lost many political forces since its establishment in 1969, such as the pro-Syria Ba'th branch, the Amal Movement and an important Syrian Social National Party (SSNP) faction which left the movement or halted their participation as its relations deteriorated with Damascus, was dissolved following the 1982 Israeli invasion, increasing the process of sectarianization in the Lebanese political scene. In addition to PLO forces, the Israeli forces targeted the Lebanese nationalist and progressive organizations that had members from various religious sects, weakening them considerably, politically and militarily. All this while the Lebanese sectarian political forces, among them Druze, Christian and Shiʿa, were not the object of Israeli attacks, or only marginally so (Achcar and Chomsky 2007: 52).

The Lebanese National Resistance Front (LNRF), commonly known by its Arab acronym as *Jammul*, was established in 1982 by the LCP, the OCAL, the Arab Socialist Action Party Lebanon (ASAP-L) and the Syrian Social National Party (SSNP). This new coalition had the objective of replacing the LNM, but above all to resist the Israeli occupation. By the spring of 1985, the LNRF had succeeded in driving the Israelis out of the western Bekaa, Rashaya and other large areas in the South. The leadership of the Front then decided to bring the fight to the Israelis by attacking targets inside the "security belt," the highly militarized strip of territory along Lebanon's southern border that the Israelis used as a buffer zone (Diab 2012). Nevertheless, this period was the beginning of the end of the LNRF, which was the target not only of Israel, but also of the Syrian regime following the refusal of the LNRF's leadership to submit to the demands of "coordination" with Syria (Diab 2012). In addition, from 1984, economic assistance to the LNRF from the USSR and Arab countries was ceased (Daher 2014: 103).

Over the next few years, the LNRF's leadership was subject to a wave of assassinations that were attributed to Islamic forces close to Hezbollah (as we will see), and also to Amal. At the same time, according to Elias Atallah (then the LNRF's top commander), Amal and Hezbollah would frequently inform the Syrians of any LNRF plans they caught wind of. The LNRF's resistance attacks became less frequent and less successful (Nash 2008).

The internal fighting between leftist groups—including the remaining PLO elements and the Druze PSP—and Amal in the Lebanese capital in 1987 also weakened the LNRF, while the entry of Syrian forces into West Beirut increasingly prevented the LNRF's frame of actions.

After Amal suspended most of its resistance activities following Israel's first withdrawal in 1985, and because the Syrian regime progressively prevented with all its capacities all of the LNRF's resistance activities, Hezbollah gradually became the sole resistance movement, strongly supported by the Syrian and Iranian regimes (Traboulsi 2007: 230). The Taʾif Agreement then acknowledged Hezbollah as the sole resistance actor. The Islamic party with its close ties to Tehran would therefore carry the resistance torch, but only if it coordinated closely with Damascus.

Following the Israeli invasion of Lebanon in 1982 and a growing turn towards sectarian politics, basic survival for much of the population—particularly in the capital, Beirut—was increasingly linked to the control of resources by various militias. Political, economic and administrative functions in Beirut were divided between ten militia-controlled territories, largely built around illegal ports. Militias took over most of the state's income generating functions, including customs duties and indirect taxes, and the collection of a "protection tax" from families in areas that they controlled (Traboulsi 2007: 232; Chiit 2009b). Militias were also involved in: arms and drug trafficking, contraband sale of commercial goods and livestock, piracy and attacks on banks and ports. These groups maintained trade relations between themselves because none of them could achieve full economic independence in the neighborhoods under their authority. After 1983, the main militias took control over a major part of the import trade and all distribution of fuel and flour. They would develop into large business enterprises, which not only invested their revenues in the war effort, but also in a number of "holding companies" registered in Lebanon (Traboulsi 2007: 237).

The Civil War also brought considerable social dislocation. Fifteen years of conflict resulted in the deaths of 71,328 people, with a further 97,184 injured (Traboulsi 2007: 238). The demography of Lebanon was modified during this period as the sectarian cleansing of the various militia cantons led to the displacement of 670,000 Christians and 157,500 Muslims (Abou Rjeili and Labaki 1994: 256; Nasr 2003: 146). This meant an increasing homogeneity of the various districts and a corresponding segregation of the population along sectarian lines—patterns that would endure in the post-Civil War environment. No more than 30 percent of the displaced were to return to their homes after the Civil War (Nasr 2003: 150). Moreover, nearly a third of the population of Lebanon, estimated at 894,717 people, left the country during the Civil War (Abou Rjeili and Labaki 1994: 256). As a result, the bulk of the Lebanese workforce became employed abroad; the structure of the economy leaned even more in favor of the tertiary and rentier activities at the expense of the productive sectors, which suffered most of the destruction (Traboulsi 2007: 238).

Hezbollah's Establishment

Although officially established only in 1985, Hezbollah was active militarily and politically from mid-1982, operating under the banner of the "Islamic Resistance" (Traboulsi 2007: 229–30). The emergence of the organization was associated with several factors in the context of this fractured state increasingly dominated by militias. First, since the early 1960s, young *ulema* of Lebanese origin came back from Najaf in Iraq and tried to re-establish—each on his own—the political and social role of the theologians (Qassem 2008: 25–26). Muhammad Hussein Fadlallah, Muhammad Mahdi Chamsedine and Moussa al-Sadr were the most prominent, and are mentioned by Naim Qassem (2008: 25–30) and Hezbollah MP Dr. Hassan Fadlallah (2015: 74) as key actors in the Shi'a population and in the origins of Hezbollah. Moussa Sadr was the most influential. The political culture fostered by his *Mahrumīn* movement, and the communitarian awakening he provoked, played an important role in the formation of Hezbollah. The members of Hezbollah today, like its current Secretary General Hassan Nasrallah, Naim Qassem and others such as Hussein Mussawi, were originally members of the *Mahrumīn* (Charara and Dromont 2004: 86).

Although he was never a member of the party, Muhammad Hussein Fadlallah also played a major part in the origins of the Islamic movement, and he is often portrayed as the spiritual father of the Hezbollah (Mervin 2008b: 277). Without occupying an official position in the party, he was in many ways its leading ideologue throughout the 1980s. His speeches were published in Hezbollah's newspapers (*al-'Ahed*), and he encouraged the members of the *al-Dawa*[16] Lebanese branches to merge with Hezbollah (Mervin 2008b: 278).

Fadlallah first engaged politically on the side of Muhammad Baqir al-Sadr, who was the main spiritual guide of al-Dawa party in Iraq, where he was born and raised (Mervin 2008b: 278). In 1966, he went back to the popular neighborhood of Naba'a in Lebanon, which was inhabited in the majority by Palestinians and Lebanese Shi'a. He opened a *husayniyya*, a dispensary called the "Usra al-Tākhī" (Fraternity Family) and a *hawza*,[17] the Islamic Legal Institute (*al-Ma'had al-char'ī al-islāmī*), which was a unique institution in Lebanon for advanced religious studies modeled on the seminaries of Najaf (Charara 2007: 63–71; Blanford 2011: 26). In 1966, *al-Ittihād al-Lubnānī lil-talaba al-Muslimīn* (The Lebanese

Union of Muslim Students), which was the first Shi'a Islamic student organization in Lebanon, was established under Fadlallah's influence and patronage. The organization's students used to follow the religious courses of Fadlallah in the Islamic Legal Institute in Naba'a (Charara 2007: 88; Mervin 2007: 311). Many young people were attracted to Fadlallah and some gravitated around him, distinguishing themselves later on in Hezbollah, such as Ali Fayyad (Hezbollah MP) and Muhammad Said al-Khansa (Hezbollah Mayor of Ghobeyri) (Harb 2010: 239).

Fadlallah was first supportive of the Islamic Republic of Iran (IRI) and of the concept of *Wilāyat al-Faqīh*[18] (Mervin 2008b: 281). In the middle and late 1980s, he became more critical of the Islamic Movement in Iran and of the Iranian state (Mervin 2008b: 282), and in the early 1990s his relation with Iran and Hezbollah became more distant (International Crisis Group (ICG) 2003: 13), as we will see in Chapter 5.

The establishment and development of the Hezbollah must also be understood in the framework of the political dynamics and developments of the IRI. As we will see, the Hezbollah has been politically, socially and financially supported by Iran since its official establishment in 1985 and even earlier in the case of the activities of groups linked to it. In the ten years following the overthrow of the Shah and the establishment of the IRI, the regime's foreign policy was dominated by the two main ideological foreign policy principles of the revolution: "Neither East nor West" and the "Export of the Revolution" (Rakel 2009: 113). The policy of exporting "the revolution" was particularly promoted during the first years of the revolution by the conservative factions of the new state.

In the summer of 1982, the IRI sent 1,500 soldiers from the Iranian Revolutionary Guard Corps (IRGC), known as Pasdaran,[19] to training camps set up in the Syrian city of Zabadani and in the western Bekaa district (with Syria's authorization) (Norton 1987: 19).[20] According to Norton (2000: 11): "the contingent quickly became the nodal point for the Iranian training, supply, and support of Hezbollah under the watchful eye of Ali Akbar Mohtashemi, then Iran's ambassador to Damascus."[21] At the same time as establishing these training camps, Iran sponsored the establishment of a "Shura Lubnān," the Council of Lebanon, in which two representatives, Ali Akbar Mohtashemi (Iranian ambassador in Syria) and Ahmad Kan'ani (head of the Pasdaran in Lebanon), out of the five were Iranians. The Council had as a role to organize and oversee the activities and programs of Hezbollah within Lebanon and to operate as a nodal connection between Iran and Lebanon.

According to the Hezbollah MP Dr. Hassan Fadlallah (2015: 88–89), the Shura held its first meeting on January 23, 1983, in which was drafted the outline of its overall policies and it was decided that the Shura would be the main point of reference for decisions made by the leadership of the Islamic movement in Lebanon. Three days later, the Shura held its second meeting and they determined their overall principles, including: the reliance on mass Islamic work and far from the spirit of narrow "partisan work," the necessity of a political movement that expresses a political position and has the legitimacy required; the organization of work through the establishment of committees according to necessity in various areas; the separation of the security committee and the military apparatus from the rest of the committees; and the establishment of a direct relationship between these committees and the Shura. Following this second meeting, the organizational structure of the party was constructed according to these principles with establishment of the committee of Jihad (in charge of collecting information, observation, equipment and operations), the committee of Ulema, and the Central Committee (in charge of policies, culture, media, finance, social issues, planning, Mosque affairs, popular mobilization, follow-up and coordination of various affairs).

The attempt by the new Iranian leadership to export the Islamic revolution was further accompanied by the imposition of religious practices and discourses following Khomeini's ideology in the regions where the IRGC and Hezbollah were present. Upon their arrival, IRGC soldiers spread Khomeini's theories on Islam in Baalbek and the surrounding villages, while pictures of Khomeini and Iranian flags became much more prevalent in the region. In addition, the main square in Baalbek was renamed after Khomeini; more women were wearing full-length black chador and alcohol was removed from many shops and hotels (Blanford 2011: 45).

Between 1984 and 1986, Hezbollah and groups linked to it attempted to impose Sharia rule and conservative social codes in the areas it controlled (Daher 2014: 116), notably in some areas of West Beirut and in villages of the Bekaa, such as Machghara. Owners of grocery stores were forbidden to sell alcohol, while others were deliberately attacked. Shops and restaurants had to close on religious days. In some cases they also forbade Christians in the Ras Beirut neighborhood, close to the American University of Beirut and Hamra, to perform their own religious celebrations (Charara 2007: 356–57). Hezbollah was also accused of plastering posters of Khomeini on walls in Beirut, harassing women who were said to be immodestly dressed and bombing shops selling alcoholic beverages (Jaber 1997: 51–53). As Hezbollah became ever more entrenched in the South following Israel's withdrawal to the Israeli–Lebanese border and the establishment of the "security zone" (a 15-km wide strip of land paralleling the border) in June 1985, it banned the sale of alcohol, parties, dancing and mixed swimming on the long beaches of Tyr, and closed down cafés (Chehabi 2006: 226). In some villages in the Bekaa Valley, Christians were reported to have left their villages because of the atmosphere of fear and threat imposed by Hezbollah (Charara 2007: 356–57).

The very close link between Iran and Hezbollah was reflected in the declarations during this period by the group's leaders. *Sheikh* Hassan Trad, Imam of the mosque of the Imam Mehdi in Ghobeyri at the time and Hezbollah member, said that: "Iran and Lebanon are one people and one country" (1986 cited in Charara 2007: 250). Ali Akbar Mohtashemi, Iran's ambassador to Syria from 1982 to 1986, who played a pivotal role in the establishment of Hezbollah: "we will support Lebanon as we support militarily and politically our Iranian provinces" (cited in Charara 2007: 250); Sayyid Ibrahim al-Sayyid, at the time Hezbollah's spokesman: "We do not say that we are part of Iran, we are Iran in Lebanon, and Lebanon in Iran" (1987 cited in Charara 2007: 250).[22]

Another key element in the emergence of Hezbollah was Israel's invasion of Lebanon in 1982, which saw support for Amal plummet as the organization was widely perceived as having offered tacit endorsement of the June invasion (Norton 2000: 9). In July 1982, the Amal Deputy head and official spokesman of the party, Hussein Mussawi (who later co-founded the Hezbollah and who was attracted to the model of the IRI), accused Amal's leadership of blatant collaboration with Israeli occupying forces (Norton 1987: 88). Another point of contention of Amal members was the participation of Amal leader Nabih Berri in the National Salvation Committee (NSC). The NSC was created by the Lebanese President Elias Sarkis to foster dialogue between the most powerful militia leaders including Bashir Gemayel, who was viewed as an Israeli ally during the Civil War. Therefore, the NSC was described by many of Amal's youth as an "American Israeli bridge" (Norton 1987: 105). Indeed, according to Norton, Amal leaders, notably Nabih Berri and Daoud Sulayman Daoud, were seeking a modus vivendi with Israel and the United States. They assumed that the latter was now the major power in Lebanon (Norton 2000: 13). Norton argues (1987: 50): "there is no doubt that Berri's willingness to contemplate a deal that would privilege Syria's enemies provoked Damascus to lend support to Hezbollah as a counterweight to Amal" and led to the Syrian regime accepting the establishment and development of Hezbollah during this period in the regions of Lebanon under the authority of Damascus (Lamloum 2008b: 95).

The initiative to establish Hezbollah had come mostly from Amal members at odds with the leadership of Nabih Berri, who had become Amal's leader following Sadr's death.[23] These Amal members formed an organization called Islamic Amal (led by Hussein Mussawi), and allied themselves with other Shiʿa groups such as the al-Dawa party, which had constituted organizations such as *al-Ittihād al-Lubnānī lil-talaba al-Muslimīn* (The Lebanese Union of Muslim Students), armed organizations, and other "cultural committees active in neighborhoods of Dahyeh, the Bekaa and the South (Fadlallah 2015: 81), and the *Ulema* assembly of the Bekaa. These organizations represented a geographical base of the Shiʿa Islamic leadership from Beirut to the Bekaa Valley. Following cooperation and joint activities between 1982 and 1985, they produced a joint document titled "Manifesto of the Nine,"[24] and advanced the following objectives:

- Islam is the comprehensive, complete and appropriate programme for a better life. It is the intellectual, religious, ideological and practical foundation for the proposed organisation.
- Resistance against Israeli occupation, which is a danger to both the present and future, is the ultimate priority given the anticipated effects of such occupation on Lebanon and the region. This necessitates the creation of a jihad structure that should further this obligation, and in favour of which all capabilities are to be employed.
- The legitimate leadership is designed to the Guardianship of the Jurist who is considered to be the successor to the Prophet and the

Imam. The Jurist Theologian draws the general guiding direction for the nation of Islam. His commands and proscriptions are enforceable.

(cited in Qassem 2008: 32)

These groups dissolved their existing organizations in favor of a single new party, which later came to be known as Hezbollah.

An important part of Hezbollah's legitimacy in its early days was the military struggle it waged against the Israeli occupation. During this period, groups acting under the banner of the "Islamic resistance" also pursued military operations against the US presence in Lebanon, notably through an attack against the US embassy in April 1983 and against the US Marine barracks in October 1983, which led to the departure of the American marines from Lebanon (Norton 2000: 1). Both attacks were widely considered to have been carried out under the order of the IRI (Norton 2007: 71).

Following the withdrawal of Israel from Beirut in 1983, Hezbollah engaged in an active recruitment campaign in Beirut's southern suburbs with a view to expand into Amal's heartland of South Lebanon (Shanahan 2005: 115). In 1984, the party established its political bureau and its weekly newspaper al-'Ahed, which expressed support for the IRI during the Iran–Iraq War and praised the aid brought to Hezbollah by the IRGC (Lamloum 2008a: 23). This was followed a year later by the publication of "Hezbollah's Open Letter to the Downtrodden of Lebanon and the World," a political manifesto that formally declared the existence of the movement. The manifesto (Al-risāla al-maftūha allati wajjahaha "Hizb Allāh" ila al-mustad'afīn, 1985) held up the 1978–1979 Iranian Revolution as an inspiration to action, a proof of what could be accomplished when the faithful gather under the banner of Islam. It stated the movement's belief in Ayatollah Khomeini as the "single wise and just leader," in line with Khomeini's own vision of Wilāyat al-Faqīh. The manifesto outlined Hezbollah's rejection of Israel on the grounds that it had occupied Muslim land and had an expansionist agenda. It also expressed Hezbollah's opposition to Western nations, particularly the United States, due to their support for Israel (Al-risāla al-maftūha allati wajjahaha "Hizb Allāh" ila al-mustad'afīn, 1985).

Reflecting its origins, Hezbollah's members were mostly drawn from young clerics who were opposed to Amal's non-clerical leadership and its accommodation with Lebanese clientelism and the political system. The party's unequivocal opposition to both the Israeli invasion and the Lebanese political system thus drew supporters away from Amal and into its own sphere of influence.

Significant levels of financial support from Iran was another factor that allowed the party to grow to the detriment of Amal, with Hezbollah able to "offer not only the virtue of ideological simplicity and authenticity, but the rewards of hard cash as well" (Norton 1987: 106). Hezbollah fighters were well paid and guaranteed to receive a regular monthly salary from Iran, while Amal's members were dependent on the Shiʿa of Lebanon for their funds. Hezbollah could afford full-time gunmen and possessed an extensive system for the payment of pensions to the families of martyrs, while many Amal cadres were part-time and volunteers (Norton 1987: 106). By the middle of the 1980s, members of Hezbollah received $300 per month, compared to $100–150 in other militias including the Israel-sponsored South Lebanon Army (SLA) (Picard 2000: 198).

The rivalry between the two organizations was most sharply expressed in the southern suburbs of Beirut, where the two groups fought each other over leadership of the Shiʿa population. Hezbollah and Amal waged a struggle against leftist parties and intellectuals in these areas and the South of Lebanon, most significantly against the LNRF (Lebanese National Resistance Front, see Chapter 7).

The suburbs are strategically localized at the entry of the capital Beirut on the road that leads to the South. In this area, Hezbollah's political activities were mostly concentrated in Dahyeh—particularly the neighborhood of Ghobeyri—where they launched what was described as "Islamic work" through committees operating in mosques and hussayniyyāt (public meeting rooms dedicated to the Imam Hussein, the third Imam in Shiʿa Islam) (Harb 2010: 59).[25] Dahyeh was home to half a million Shiʿa, many of whom had been displaced there following the Israeli occupation of southern Lebanon or attacks by Christian militias on eastern Beirut suburbs such as Nabaʿa and Sin el-Fil. The concentration of the Shiʿa population in this area means that it came to provide an important power base at the national level (Harb 2010: 78). Finally, the southern suburbs lacked basic and necessary services for a population in need, and thus presented great potential for investments in institutions and services by the political actor controlling this space or its supporters (Harb el-Kak 1996).

Hezbollah's growth in these areas was further facilitated by the expansion of its charitable, medical and educational activities—funded principally by Iran.[26] As Picard (2000: 308) notes, in deprived areas such as the Bekaa and Beirut's southern suburbs Hezbollah strengthened its popular base by establishing "local branches of numerous Iranian foundations created during the Iran–Iraq War to provide aid to various groups of the injured (orphans and the wounded) and for reconstruction, or for the support of social services." In practice, the organization set up its own social services independently from the state, structured around a set of autonomous organizations operating in networks and providing a complete range of assistance to Shiʿa (discussed in Chapter 5) (Qassir 2011). During the Civil War, Hezbollah guaranteed the distribution of electricity to the population of Dahyeh during power outages through its own generators, and took care of garbage collection and repair of the water and sewage pipes (Harb 2010: 77). They also provided jobs to youth who were by and large unemployed during the Civil War, and for whom the only alternative was to become member of a militia. Those employed in Hezbollah institutions were not required to join the party, but had to respect its Islamic ideology including Islamic dress codes (Harb el-Kak 1996).

This large social support network, and the on-going growth of the Shiʿa population in the southern suburbs of Beirut, South Lebanon and the Bekaa, massively expanded the constituency of the party. It enabled Hezbollah to position itself as a massive welfare provider with the support of Iran, transmitting the political and ideological beliefs of the Iranian Islamic Revolution to the poor Shiʿa families and larger sectors of the Shiʿa population.

Hezbollah appeared and presented itself increasingly to the Shiʿa popular masses as the party that continued the struggle for the Shiʿa cause, which had been betrayed by Amal, and as the savior of the violated rights of the Shiʿa in the continuity of Imam Sadr. Hezbollah was also able to recruit members and supporters from wealthier layers of the Shiʿa population, many of whom had lost confidence in Amal (Khatib, Matar and Alshaer 2014: 50–52).

The Lebanese Civil War finally ended in 1989–1990, following the signing of the Ta'if Agreement in Saudi Arabia. The agreement reconfigured the sectarian system in the country and, as will be discussed in later chapters, codified Hezbollah's new ascendant position within the political system by allowing Hezbollah to maintain its armed wing. In the same year as the Ta'if Agreement, negotiated settlements under the auspices of Iran and Syria also endorsed the military domination of Hezbollah in Dahyeh (Chehabi 2006: 229).

Conclusion

The political economy of Lebanon has been largely characterized by its intermediary role in the regional system, dominated by finance and services. Within this structure, sectarian patterns of governance have played a critical role, symbolized in the dominance of a Maronite- and Sunni-linked bourgeoisie over the main levers of the country's politics and economy.

Despite its historical marginalization, the Shi'a population has undergone significant changes since Lebanon's independence. The period prior to the Civil War witnessed a progressive change in the socio-economic status of some parts of the Shi'a, signified in the rise and formation of a new Shi'a middle class that is relatively well-educated, ambitious and seeking to challenge the peripheral position of their community. This was initially indicated in the rise of Amal and further accentuated through the fifteen years of Civil War. The conflict had two main consequences for the Shi'a population: first, the political disappearance of the traditional *zu'ama* leadership of the community, who had already been significantly weakened in the years prior to the Civil War. Second, the establishment of Hezbollah in 1985. Hezbollah has since become the most prominent voice of the Shi'a population, surpassing Amal in the process. This position of prominence was reached through Hezbollah's position as a welfare and services provider to the Shi'a population, and as the main actor in the military resistance against Israel. In both cases, this was made possible though the financial support of Iran, through which Iranian capital along with the political and ideological beliefs of the Iranian Islamic Revolution were transmitted and diffused among the Shi'a.

This account confirms the early insights of Mehdi Amel regarding the relationship between class formation and the sectarian system in Lebanon. The deepening of sectarian identity is a function of the political intervention of the Lebanese bourgeoisie and the Lebanese state (Amel 1986: 326–27). As Amel has observed, the latter is particularly important: "communities are not communities unless through and by the state [...] and the Lebanese state guarantees the sustainability of the dynamics that reproduce communities as political structure, which only by the state becomes institutions" (Amel 1986: 29). For this reason, laws such as the electoral and personal status laws—which are regulated along religious and sectarian lines—are critical to the maintenance of sectarian identity. As Makdissi has pointed out, "to be Lebanese meant to be defined according to religious affiliation" (Makdissi 1996).

Viewed from this perspective, the Lebanese Civil War was not simply a sectarian crisis; it was, according to Amel (1986: 330), a crisis of the political system in its current form, in other words as the system of the domination of the Lebanese bourgeois class. In the case of the Shi'a population, the crisis of the traditional *zu'ama* leadership began before the Civil War and became accentuated during and after the Civil War. This crisis has resulted in the re-articulation of sectarian patterns of rule, first through the rise of Amal, and subsequent to that of the Hezbollah.

The other fundamental cleavage that established itself in the political and social spheres of Lebanese society since 1967 was the level of implication of Lebanon in the Arab–Israeli War and the attitudes towards the Palestinian resistance. The departure of Palestinian fighters in 1982 increased the sectarianization of the Lebanese Civil War considerably.

Amel's perspective points to the importance of understanding the changes in the class structure of the Shi'a itself, beyond homogenizing interpretations that equate sect with class. Instead, as the analysis above has confirmed, the political expression of the Shi'a community has been shaped by the ongoing class differentiation within the Shi'a. This can be seen first in the rise of Amal, and later with the formation of the Hezbollah. In both cases, these Islamic movements have rested upon a contradictory class base that reflects both the growth of poorer layers of Shi'a (largely dispossessed from rural areas and concentrated in the southern suburbs of Beirut) as well as their linkages to the relatively prosperous layers that emerged through the Civil War and in the Shi'a diaspora. The Hezbollah has attempted to resolve the tensions arising from this contradictory class base through its emphasis upon a sectarian and religiously structured identity rather than any kind of consistent representation of the poorer layers of Shi'a society. This religious identity has become one of the means through which the organization has managed to deepen its hegemony within the Shiʿa population, as Chapter 5 will show in further detail.

The tensions arising from within the social base of the Hezbollah have been further accentuated in the neoliberal period that followed the end of the Civil War. Lebanese neoliberalism has promoted the increasing class differentiation of the Shiʿa in Lebanon, and Hezbollah's response to this process has been to move closer to the interests of the emerging Shiʿa bourgeoisie. The following two chapters demonstrate and analyze this trend in greater detail, and indicate their implications for Hezbollah's standing in the Shiʿa population.

2

Hezbollah and the Political Economy of Lebanese Neoliberalism

Emerging from the end of the Civil War, Lebanon's political economy was marked by a fractured sectarian system dominated by a growing Sunni bourgeoisie led by Rafiq Hariri alongside various militias that ruled over much of the country. The political arrangements codified in the Ta'if Agreement[1] entrenched this sectarianism while strengthening the position of the Sunni and Shi'a in the Lebanese political system. Political changes included the weakening of the position of president (required to be a Maronite Christian) and the commensurate increase in the Prime Minister's powers (a Sunni Muslim).[2] Moreover, the ratio of Muslims to Christians in the new Lebanese Parliament rose to 6:6, up from 5:6. The term of speaker of the parliament, held by a Shi'a, was also increased to four years (and constitutionally protected from being voted out during the first two years) (Traboulsi 2014: 72). In addition, the Ta'if Agreement granted Syria de facto hegemony over the country, a situation that was supported by the USA in 1990 following Syrian participation in the US/ UN-led operation against Iraq in that year (Nizameddin 2006: 95).

The Ta'if Agreement was not only the basis of a new political consensus between the Lebanese elite, but also put the country on the path of economic liberalization measures that had been pursued elsewhere in the Middle East since the 1980s, with an emphasis on increased integration into the global economy and private sector growth (Baroudi 2001: 71). This reform plan worked to re-establish Lebanon's financial position in the Middle East, particularly in the context of an expected increase in regional cross-border capital flows as a result of the 1992 Oslo Accords between Israel and the Palestine Liberation Organization (PLO) (Perthes 1997: 17; Bali and Salti 2009: 252).

Reconstruction plans began to take significant steps forward following Rafiq Hariri's accession to the prime ministership in 1992. As a wealthy businessman benefiting from regional and international support, Hariri's appointment occurred in the wake of the strikes and demonstrations that swept the Karama government, and then forced the departure of the Solh government (May 1992–October 1992).[3] Hariri had deep connections with the Kingdom of Saudi Arabia, and had amassed a large fortune in the Saudi construction and public works sector. In Lebanon itself, he established an independent network of services and charitable activities, including the provision of education, healthcare, jobs, food and financial aid, targeting mainly Sunni but benefiting other communities as well (ICG 2010: 2). This business network gave him an important social base in the country's predominantly clientelist system.

Hariri's vision for Lebanon's political economy was centered upon the liberalization of capital flows and the deregulation of the tax system as means to entice foreign capital to invest in economic infrastructure (ICG 2010: 3; Young 1998: 5).[4] In this context, the character of neoliberalism in Lebanon was heavily oriented towards opening up the economy to foreign investment flows, primarily aimed at the banking, financial and real estate sectors, further deepening the heavily financialized nature of the Lebanese economy.

Politically, Hariri's rule was characterized by:

The support of the Syrian regime, which handed him control of the economy, outsourced the anti-Israeli resistance to Hezbollah and left politics and security in the hands of General Ghazi Kanaan, Syria's High Commissioner in Lebanon. Secondly, Hariri had the cooperation of militia leaders and those who had accumulated their wealth from War and emigration, and was surrounded by associates, party members and security officials, who covered the entire political spectrum [...] in addition to a large coterie of technocrats and lawyers, graduates of international financial institutions and private companies. One of the most noteworthy measures he took to entrench his power was his indefatigable and costly effort to gain control of the media.

(Traboulsi 2014: 23)[5]

Hariri's economic agenda was financed by both his personal fortune and his international contacts.

The main outlines of the Hariri government's reconstruction plan were detailed in a document titled *Horizon 2000, for Reconstruction and Development*, a sectorial and regional expenditure program of $14.3 billion that extended over the period from 1993–2002. In 1994, the budget of the program was raised to $18 billion over a thirteen-year period stretching from 1995–2007 (Makdissi 2004: 119). The geographic distribution of reconstruction funding was characterized by the same regional inequalities as before the Civil War, with the bulk of investments concentrated in Beirut and Mount Lebanon—around 80 percent of the total—and the remainder outside of these areas. These projects were marked by the blurring of lines between public and private property and helped to consolidate Hariri's increasing political and financial power. The best example of this is the case of the private company Solidere, in which the Hariri family was the major shareholder and the driving force in the company's lobbying. The Solidere Company was given exclusive rights to rehabilitate infrastructure and develop the downtown business area in Beirut, and was accused by property owners of forcibly purchasing their properties at less than their market value (Makdissi 2004: 83).

Focusing on these liberalization measures, successive governments failed to tackle other economic and social problems such as unemployment, low wages, poverty (particularly in the regions of the Akkar and the Bekaa Valley), increasing corruption and the poor quality of social services (Baroudi 2002: 64).

By the late 1990s and early 2000s, a new set of neoliberal policies was put in place to address the heavy fiscal burden of rising public debt and a relatively high debt service. Beginning in 1996, government wages were frozen and automatic wage increases were ended; real wages thus tended to decline significantly due to rising inflation (prices increased by about 120 percent from 1996 to 2011) (Zaraket 2014).[6] At the same time, increasing levels of foreign debt were accumulated (Baroudi 2002: 68). In 2002, the public debt reached 173 percent of GDP, while the payment of the debt represented 18 percent of the GDP, which amounted to 80 percent of the budget income (Nasnas 2007: 86).

Privatization was accelerated in the early 2000s with a new law, which established a Higher Privatization Council that aimed at the further sell-off of public sector enterprises (Makdissi 2004: 121; Nasnas 2007: 90). During this period, the reorganization of the state television station and Middle East Airlines (MEA) was carried out, leading to the lay-off of 2,000 employees (Makdissi 2004: 121; Nasnas 2007: 87). In addition, a new VAT rate of 10 percent was introduced on goods and services.

Moreover, in 2001 the government reduced the share paid by employers to the National Social Security Fund (NSSF) from 38.5 percent to 23.5 percent.[7] As part of the Hariri government's attempt to encourage Foreign Direct Investment (FDI), a new law on investments was adopted in 2001 that established a "One stop shop" for private investors (Nasnas 2007: 87). Another law was aimed at attracting "bien fonds," or property funds, by lifting restrictions on property ownership and setting taxes for foreign investors at the same level as Lebanese citizens.

These measures did little to reduce the public debt or revitalize the economy. The need for further external support led to the Paris I Conference on February 23, 2001, which was organized with the support of international institutions such as the World Bank, European Investment Bank and the European Commission. At this meeting, 500 million Euros were provided to Lebanon in accordance with pledges by the Lebanese government to stimulate the economy by liberalizing and facilitating trade, containing public expenditure, privatizations, attracting FDI and modernizing the tax system (Sherry 2014).

A further meeting was called in Paris by the then French President Jacques Chirac in November 2002. In preparation for this conference, the Lebanese government put forward a budget for 2003 that incorporated further expenditure cuts and revenue enhancing measures, including new taxes and fees. The measures envisioned in the document submitted to the Paris II conference planned to fully privatize the cellular phone system and energy sectors, and to transform the fixed phone system and power sectors into commercial entities (Makdissi 2004: 122). At this conference, donor countries and institutions finally provided a total package of financial and developmental assistance of $4.4 billion. The IMF was also given an important role in supervising financial assistance and the implementation of neoliberal measures in the country. In 2004 and 2005, the privatization of the water sector, ports and airports through concession arrangements was agreed (Nasnas 2007: 96).

These plans were disrupted following the assassination of Rafiq Hariri on February 14, 2005, which was followed by the Israeli war on Lebanon in summer 2006. The Israeli attack resulted in the death of more than 1,100 people, the displacement of over a quarter of the population, and an estimated $2.8 billion in direct costs with more than 60 percent of the damage affecting the housing sector (United Nations Development Programme [UNDP] 2009: 42). This crisis was further reinforced by political instability that followed the resignation of Hezbollah ministers and their allies from the government in November 2006.[8]

At the Paris III Conference on Assistance to Lebanon on January 25, 2007, the international community pledged $7.6 billion in financial assistance in the form of loans and grants to the Lebanese government. The bulk of these loans, especially those provided by international institutions such as the World Bank and the IMF, were accompanied by strict conditions and were based on the implementation of the neoliberal reforms announced by the Prime Minister Siniora at the beginning of the month.

Nevertheless, because of internal political conflict, a number of privatization processes were delayed.

Social Outcomes of Neoliberalism in Lebanon

By the end of the first decade of the 2000s, the political economy of Lebanon was marked by the highly polarized outcomes of neoliberal reform. In 2008, it was estimated that 28 percent of the population was categorized as poor and living on US$4/day or less (the upper poverty line), while 8 percent were extremely poor, living on US$2.4/day or less (the lower poverty line) (UNDP 2008a: 11). Unemployment levels were also significant, with only an estimated one-third of the working-age population actually in employment (UNDP 2008a: 14). Between 40–50 percent of Lebanese residents did not have access to the NSSF or any other public social security. Temporary foreign workers, whose numbers are estimated to reach more than one million, lacked all social protection.[9]

Alongside this widespread poverty, inequality levels remained extremely high. The richest 20 percent of the population received 43.55 percent of the national income between 2004 and 2005, while the poorest 20 percent received 7.07 percent (UNDP 2009: 63). It has been estimated that only 800 bank accounts, belonging to less than 200 families, contained approximately 20 percent of total deposits worth nearly $14 billion in 2007. Credit Suisse's Global Wealth Databook 2013 notes that at least 48 percent of Lebanon's privately held wealth is held by some 8,900 citizens, just 0.3 percent of the adult population (Credit Suisse 2013 cited in Executive Magazine 2013). In this context, ownership and control of capital is highly concentrated, with half of Lebanon's domestic markets considered oligopolistic to monopolistic and a third dominated by a single firm with a market share above 40 percent (Ministry of Economy and Trade [Lebanon] 2003 cited in Berthélemy, Dessus and Nahas 2007: 4). The banking sector, which had a size equivalent to 350 percent of GDP in 2009 (The Daily Star 2010) is particularly marked by a concentration of ownership—five banks (Bank Audi, Blom Bank, Byblos Bank, Fransabank and BankMed) controlled about half the volume of total deposits in 2002 (Gaspard 2004: 194).

These pronounced levels of inequality are closely related to the rentier and financialized nature of the economy, which has been reinforced by the neoliberal measures outlined above. Wages and social contributions, for example, accounted for only 23 percent of GDP in 2009, while the share of interest payments accounted for 10 percent of GDP or a third of government expenditures in 2011 (Matabadal 2012: 5). As the purchasing power of Lebanese citizens decreased due to rising inflation, the importance of rent derived from interest was accentuated through policies that encouraged banks and high-income earners to purchase Lebanese treasury bills with high interest rates. In 2002, when the general debt reached $30 billion, $22 billion went to the banks in the form of interest on Treasury bonds (Traboulsi 2014: 25). The banking sector benefited particularly from these policies, increasing its capital from $103 billion to $966 billion between 1990 and 2007, with deposits growing from $6.6 billion in 1992 to $58 billion in 2005 (Traboulsi 2014: 25).

By the end of 2013, the Gross Public Debt had reached $63.46 billion, representing 140 percent of the GDP while the payment of the interests of the debt represented 40 percent of the total revenues and 28 percent of the total expenditures. (Republic of Lebanon, Ministry of Finance 2013: 1). Between 1993 and 2008, Lebanon paid $38 billion on debt, or an average of $9,500 per person over this period (Traboulsi 2014: 25).

The rentier features of the economy are also indicated by the weight of the service sector, which made up 79–81 percent of GDP in 2010, while agriculture and industry constituted 5.1 percent and 13–15.9 percent respectively (BIC 2012: 6). Services hold around 60 percent of the total labor force (Nasr 2003: 153), while the industrial sector accounted for 15 percent, construction 8.6 percent and agriculture 7.6 percent in 2007 (UNDP 2008a: 143).

This weakness in the production sectors is reflected in the dependence on foreign capital inflows and remittances from the Lebanese diaspora.

The share of FDI in GDP reached 15 percent in 2009, and was mostly concentrated in real estate and tourism-related investment (70 percent and 22 percent respectively of total inflows) (Investment Development Authority of Lebanon (IDAL) 2011: 14). Another significant source of foreign capital came from Lebanese expatriates, with remittances constituting 22 percent of GDP in 2011 ($7.6 billion) (The International Bank for Reconstruction and Development and the World Bank 2011: 14).

The implications of these processes for the relative balance of different regions and—in a closely related sense—the economic weight of Lebanon's sectarian communities, will be explored in Chapter 3. We will see that one important outcome was the promotion of a number of newly emergent groups in Lebanon that came to rival the commercial and financial bourgeoisie, who had left during the course of the Civil War. As a result, a new bourgeoisie formed through the fusion of different sections of capital: wealthy "Gulf entrepreneurs" who amassed large fortunes in the Gulf (the most prominent being Rafiq Hariri), rich émigrés returning to the country (especially Shiʿa from West Africa), and some war profiteers and new wealthy layers who were associated with the militias (Nasr 2003: 151). At this stage, however, it is necessary to turn to Hezbollah's response to these policies at both the political and economic level.

Hezbollah's Changing Attitude towards the Sectarian State

One of the striking features of Hezbollah's evolution through the neoliberal period is its changing attitude towards sectarianism and its growing integration into the structures of the state. In its early days, the party was highly critical of the existing political system and the entrenched privileges of both Maronite and Sunni political classes. The 1985 founding manifesto of the party named the existing political system and its sectarian privileges as the root cause of Lebanon's problems (Al-risāla al-maftūha allatī wajjahaha "Hizb Allāh" ila al-mustadʿafīn 1985). As an alternative, Hezbollah advocated an Islamic form of government in the framework of Ayatollah Khomeini's vision of Wilāyat al-Faqīh, stating the movement's belief in Khomeini as the "single wise and just leader" (Al-risāla al-maftūha allatī wajjahaha "Hizb Allāh" ila al-mustadʿafīn 1985). Despite this call for a theocratic state, the party was nevertheless aware of the concerns that many Lebanese might have, adding that its foundation would only be possible "on the basis of free and direct selection of the people, not the basis of forceful imposition, as some people imagine" (*Al-risāla al-maftūha allatī wajjahaha "Hizb Allāh" ila al-mustad'afin* 1985).

This initial position against the sectarian status quo began to change following Hezbollah's acceptance of the 1989 Ta'if Agreement. While Hezbollah would note that Ta'if failed to eliminate the shortcomings of the old system, stating that it "maintains the Maronite system and reinforces the Israeli occupation" (*Al-Ahed* 1989 cited in Khatib, Matar and Alshaer 2014: 57), it began to emphasize the importance of civil peace and state and institutional reconstruction rather than any fundamental change in the system. This acceptance was partly due to the organization's greater weight in the political process—codified in the Ta'if Agreement—as well as its official recognition as a resistance movement that allowed it to remain armed while other militias were disarmed (Zigby 2000: 41).

The party was also affected by the changes in the IRI, its main political, military and economic ally. It signed the Ta'if Agreement only after it had received permission from the Iranian government (Khatib *et al.* 2014: 57). The end of the Iran–Iraq War and the death of Ayatollah Khomeini in 1989 led to a more pragmatic foreign policy in the IRI. The Iranian leadership, led by its new president Rafsandjani and the new Supreme Leader Khamenei, was more preoccupied by socio-economic problems in Iran, and the rise of the USA as a single great power following the demise of the USSR. The Iranian leadership was therefore trying to adjust its policies in accordance with the new unipolar balance of power (Rakel 2009: 117–18).

Since this period, the IRI witnessed improvements in diplomatic relations with the monarchies of the Gulf, the European Union, China, India, central Eurasia, Russia and the United States, while the main currents arguing for the "Export of the Revolution" lost influence in the highest echelon of the state (Rakel 2009: 113). This was reflected in 1989: first, by the fall from favor of Ayatollah Hussein Ali Montazeri, after he protested against the liquidation of 30,000 members of the People's Mujahedin (this was a few months before the death of Ayatollah Khomeini, despite having been the designated successor of Khomeini for years); and second by Ali Akbar Mohtashemi's removal as Minister of Interior (Daher 2014: 117). The "revolutionary" tendency was sidelined.

At the same time, this evolution in the Iranian political sphere was accompanied by a policy of socio-economic liberalization, which included invitations to Iranian investors and managers who had left during the Iran–Iraq War to return to their country (Tehranian 1993: 354).

The pragmatic turn of the Iranian leadership, and the end of the willingness to export the "revolution" at the end of the 1980s and early 1990s, pushed Hezbollah to attenuate and even cease its rejection of the Lebanese political system and seek increasing integration.

The election of Abbas al-Mussawi in May 1991 as Secretary General, instead of Tufayli, represented this evolution. The election of Hassan Nasrallah as Secretary General, following al-Mussawi's assassination in 1992 by the Israeli army, confirmed the path of "*infitāh*" (opening). Tufayli was considered to be too close to the currents of the "Export of the Revolution" camp, which was no longer welcome by the new Iranian leadership, led by Rafsandjani and Khamenei. Al-Mussawi and Hassan Nasrallah were considered to be ideologically closer to these leaders and had a more conciliatory attitude towards integration in the Lebanese political system (Daher 2008: 273–74). It was in this period that the last Western hostages were released and the Islamic movement allowed the army to deploy to their strongholds in the Iqlim al-Touffah region of South Lebanon (Blanford 2011: 95).

Moreover, the increasing political and military domination of Lebanon by Syria, the intermediary through which arms and Iranian aid had to go through, also played a role in pushing for Hezbollah's integration into the Lebanese political system (Blanford 2011: 95). Therefore, Hezbollah had to accommodate Syria's own geopolitical calculations and diplomacy, in other words, it had to take into account Damascus' political interests when planning their military attacks or retaliations against Israel's occupation forces (Salloukh 2012: 100).

Iran and Hezbollah nevertheless continued to have strong relations throughout the 1990s. The link between Khamenei and Hezbollah was strengthened and formalized, as the Iranian Supreme Leader was adopted by the party as their *marja'*, or religious guide (considered the most senior rank in the Shiʿa clerical hierarchy), in 1995, and Hassan Nasrallah and Muhammad Yazbeck were designated as his representatives in Lebanon in 2000 (Mervin 2008a: 83).

In this context, Hezbollah's participation in the 1992 legislative elections provoked a range of heated debates within the organization, with two schools of thought emerging. A very small minority within Hezbollah, led by the ex-Secretary General *Sheikh* Tufayli, opposed any integration into the political system, while the bulk of the leadership argued for a more pragmatic orientation (Blanford 2007b). Eventually the matter was submitted to Ayatollah Sayyed Ali Hosseini Khamenei for judgment, who issued a *fatwa* supporting the decision of the majority of the leadership to participate in the elections (Khatib 2014: 24).

Disagreements between Hezbollah and Tufayli gradually grew, especially following the 1996 "Hunger Revolt" in the Bekaa and the call to overthrow the government in 1997. Tufayli was definitively expelled from the Islamic movement after he organized a separate demonstration from Hezbollah's official march on Jerusalem Day in 1998 (Harb 2010: 195; Daher 2008: 274–75). He later became one of the most outspoken critics of Hezbollah and the leadership of the IRI, accusing both of corruption and of selling out the ideals of Iran's 1979 Islamic Revolution (Blanford 2007b).

The Tufayli episode did not stop Hezbollah's policy of *"Infitāh"* and the Islamic movement has participated in all parliamentary and municipal elections since then. From 1992 to 2009, the party controlled the largest legislative blocs in the National Assembly. Their elected positions were twelve seats (in 1992), ten seats (1996), twelve seats (2000), fourteen seats (2004), eleven seats (2005) and twelve seats (2009) out of a total of 128 seats. In the various municipal elections, Hezbollah has also demonstrated its popularity, winning eighty-seven municipalities out of 142 in the South (61.2 percent), thirty-six municipalities out of thirty-eight in the Bekaa and all of the six municipalities in the suburbs of Beirut (100 percent) in 2000 (Hamzeh 2004: 132–33). This domination was confirmed once again in the municipal elections of 2016 with nearly similar results, although since 2005, Hezbollah has been running in elections in coalition with Amal. In the 2016 elections, however, this coalition faced greater opposition, with the LCP and its allies either winning some or all the municipal council seats in seventeen towns and villages across the South Lebanon and Nabatieh governorates (The Daily Star 2016c).

This period of *"Infitāh"* was also characterized by a growing collaboration between Hezbollah and the Syrian-backed Lebanese Army and its security agencies, particularly following the election of General Emile Lahoud, the former commander of the army, as President of Lebanon in

1998. This relationship was further cemented following the nomination of Major General Jamil al-Sayyid to the leadership of General Security (Hodeib 2013b). In the words of Abd al-Halim Fadlallah (2012a), the Director of the Hezbollah think-tank CCSD (Consultative Center for Studies and Documentation), and Dr. Hassan Fadlallah, a Hezbollah MP, Emile Lahoud's arrival to power in 1998 began an alliance with the state on a strategic level and he was described as a partner of the resistance (Fadlallah 2014, cited in Bassam 2014; Nassif 2014).[10]

In addition to this, a number of analysts have pointed out the presence of Hezbollah in the state structure, especially in securing key positions in the security apparatus. Several critical army posts are currently headed by individuals with ties to Hezbollah or its allies (ICG 2014: 13), and the General Security Director of the Interior Ministry (one of the two state security agencies[11]) Major General Abbas Ibrahim, and the head of security at Beirut's airport, Wafiq Shuqayr, are known to be close to Hezbollah (Khoury 2013a; ICG 2008: 3).[12]

This gradual acceptance of the sectarian political system was reflected in the new Manifesto of the party in 2009. Although it confirmed the position of the 1985 Manifesto, that political sectarianism was a major problem "which thwarts Lebanon's reform and development" (Manifesto 2009), the new Manifesto postponed any change to the system until a non-determined future date. Until that point "homogenous democracy"—a term used to describe the sectarian system—would remain "the fundamental basis for governance in Lebanon, because it is the actual quintessence of the spirit of the constitution and the core of the Charter of the co-existence" (Manifesto 2009). In this contradictory sense, political sectarianism was described negatively but the sectarian system itself was upheld as the basis of co-existence. Previous to the Manifesto, Naim Qassem expressed a similar position declaring that "the suppression of political sectarianism was the best and healthiest way to alleviate the burden of the confessional system in Lebanon," but at the same time "there is a need of an objective and calm debate, based on proofs and dialogue, to elaborate an adapted project and its mechanism of implementation, even on the long term" (cited in Qassem 2008: 287).

Likewise, Abd al-Halim Fadlallah, the Director of Hezbollah's development think-tank, the CCSD, has argued that the Lebanese sectarian system allowed a sectarian balance in political representation, adding that the nominations of senior officials should continue to respect this balance, while at the lower levels, the cancellation of administrative sectarianism could be discussed (Fadlallah 2010). In an interview, Fadlallah stated that: "Hezbollah made a tactical position towards the sectarian system, considering that it was now possible to change the system slowly from within through reforms." Only through a consensus of Lebanese political parties could a solution be achieved, argued Fadlallah (2012a), adding that Hezbollah could not ignore the fears of large sections of the Christian population, that the end of the sectarian political system might lead to a diminution of Christians' political representation in parliament. Fadlallah (2012a) also agued that the Hezbollah had to take into consideration some Christians' fears that any improvement in the conditions of Palestinian refugees would alter Lebanon's sectarian balance in favor of the Sunni (Palestinian refugees in Lebanon are overwhelmingly Sunni). The Hezbollah's timidity, even inaction, in advancing the issue of Palestinian refugees civic rights in Lebanon can be better understood in this context, along with the opposition of some sections of the Shiʿa population to the nationaliza- tion of Palestinian refugees. The Lebanese Shiʿa Islamic movement has not commented or replied to the repetitive racist statements of its close ally the Free Patriotic Movement (FPM) against Syrian and Palestinian refugees,[13] nor has it done anything in government or elsewhere at the level of institutions against the repeated and multiple abuses faced by Syrian refugees in Lebanon.

Similarly, this rather unclear position towards the sectarian political system was reflected in the debate around the proposal by Nabih Berri for the formation of a national committee to discuss the elimination of sectarianism. Berri, head of the Amal movement and Chair of the Lebanese Parliament since 1992, in which Nasrallah, who supported this initiative, argued that "this committee or body may continue its dialogue for five, ten, twenty or even thirty years" (cited in Shapira 2009).

The Hezbollah viewed with suspicion the attempts to challenge the sectarian system from outside the parliament. The Hezbollah did not participate or mobilize its members to take part in the demonstrations at the beginning of 2011, calling for an end of the sectarian regime, which started in February and at first numbered more than 3,000 people. The mobilization then grew to 10,000 and 25,000 people on March 6 and 20 demonstrations respectively (Abi Yaghi 2012). On the contrary, Hezbollah, as well as other political forces, warned their members not to participate (Chiit 2011; Daou 2011). The Islamic movement also did not participate in the protest by around 300 people outside the parliament to protest against the "Orthodox law" on February 19, 2013 (Al-Akhbar English 2013b). The electoral "Orthodox Gathering" Law, which was promoted by Hezbollah ally, the FPM, and endorsed by all of Lebanon's Maronite leaders, entrenched Lebanon even further into sectarianism by allowing people exclusively to vote for candidates that were from their confession (Qifa Nakbi 2011). At that time, Hezbollah, although supporting officially and rhetorically an electoral law based on a single constituency and proportional representation that maintains the same sectarian representation (Qassem 2008: 260; Fadlallah 2010; Fadlallah 2012b; Orient le Jour 2012b), supported and voted in favor of the electoral "Orthodox Gathering" Law in joint parliamentary committees (Orient le Jour 2013a). The law was nevertheless finally abandoned.

The party would adopt a similar approach to the popular mobilizations that began at the end of the summer 2015 around the "campaign you stink," which originally was triggered after a waste management crisis and then increasingly radicalized itself to challenge the whole sectarian and bourgeois Lebanese political system. In addition, the Hezbollah, although it rhetorically supported the protests, initially accused protesters of being controlled by foreign actors and said that the struggle against *Takfiris*[14] and the Zionist state are the most important issues. Hassan Nasrallah argued that the party had adopted a "neutral position towards the movement because we don't know its leadership, its project and objectives" (Al-Ahed News 2015g). The Lebanese Islamic movement supported the dialogue called by the Chair of Parliament Nabih Berri as a way of solving the crisis, as well as the election of Michel Aoun, head of the FPM, as President of the Republic, propositions that completely maintained the existing framework of the sectarian and bourgeois system of the country (Orient le Jour 2015d).

Hezbollah went from being a radical, anti-systemic party in the 1980s to a party participating at all levels of the Lebanese political system. This is not in contradiction with the fact that Hezbollah never stopped declaring that an Islamic state was its preferred option. Hassan Nasrallah declared in 1994:

> The solution, in our opinion, is the establishment of an Islamic state in Lebanon and beyond [...] but I do not wish [to impose this] by

force or violence, rather we prefer to wait for the day that we succeed in convincing our countrymen—by means of dialogue and in an open atmosphere—that the only alternative is the founding of an Islamic state.

(*Al-Ahed* 1994, cited in Wärn 2012: 23)

In 2004, Hezbollah's declaration "Identity and Goals" stated that one of its ideals is the establishment of a "pure" Islamic state (cited in Alagha 2006: 245–46). The party's Deputy Secretary, Naim Qassem (2008: 47), has also written that the preferred option for Hezbollah is an Islamic state, as stated in the Manifesto of 1985, but this should not be imposed against the will of the population and therefore is not an option today in Lebanon as a majority would refuse it. He reiterated this position in an interview in 2016 (Al-Mayadeen 2016), while the Hezbollah Minister Dr. Hassan Fadlallah (2015: 38) expressed a similar opinion saying that the Lebanese Shi'a Islamic party believes in an Islamic state as a preferred option but its implementation in the current circumstances of Lebanon today does not allow it because of political and sectarian diversity. Hezbollah's leadership has indeed been keen to stress that this objective was not a practical option in the near future given Lebanon's confessional and sectarian make-up. In addition, no mention of establishing an Islamic state has been made in the municipal and parliamentary elections programs since 1992 (Alagha 2007: 104). Despite the absence of the establishment of an Islamic state in the Manifesto of 2009, this remains a fundamental and founding principle of Hezbollah. Nasrallah admitted during the presentation of the new Manifesto that it was essentially a "political document," which did not touch on "matters of creed, ideology or thought" (cited in Blanford 2011: 480). He said, for example, that the Islamic movement's view on the *Wilāyat al-Faqīh* "is not a political stand that can be subjected to revision" (cited in Blanford 2011: 480).

The Hezbollah's downplaying of the enforcement of an Islamic state has not prevented the Islamic movement from opposing several propositions regarding the secularization of the state. The Hezbollah has indeed declared its opposition to any kind of possible personal status civil law alongside Islamic status law, and declared such propositions as being anti-Islamic (Qassem 2008: 288; Orient le Jour 2011b), while the MP Ibrahim Amin al-Sayyid associated the promulgation of civil marriage with "an implementation of atheism" (Mikaelian 2015: 171).

This evolution of the Hezbollah's position towards the political system has important implications for the party's relationship to Lebanese neoliberalism. Most particularly, its increasing participation at all levels of the political system since 1992, including in national and municipal administrative bodies, has meant that the party has become directly responsible for implementing many of the reforms advocated by the Lebanese elite and international institutions. Even whilst in opposition, the party has increasingly subordinated opposition to these reforms to its growing interests within the political system. The tensions this has generated within the organization can be seen through a closer examination of the Hezbollah's economic program as we will see.

In addition to the formal role that the Hezbollah plays in Lebanon's political economy, its integration into the system has also encouraged forms of clientelism and corruption. Even close allies of the Hezbollah have raised this issue. Zyad Abs,[15] for example, a member of the FPM and one of the main actors behind the Memorandum of Understanding between Hezbollah and the FPM, has criticized the fact that "it is in Hezbollah controlled regions, such as the southern suburbs, that we saw the development of mafias of motors, of forgery networks, kidnapping for ransom and taxes collected illegally on certain businesses" (Orient le Jour 2012c). In 2010, the Hezbollah faced a corruption scandal following the collapse of a pyramid scheme allegedly led by one of the richest men in South Lebanon, Salah Ezzedine. Ezzedine had close ties to the party and its leadership. He owned the Dar al-Hadi publishing house, which handles many of the Hezbollah's publications and is named after Nasrallah's son who was killed in 1997 in battle against Israel (Blanford 2011: 475). Ezzedine's fall resulted in the loss of $300 million to $1 billion for some 10,000 Lebanese Shi'a. After the collapse, Ezzedine was dubbed the "Lebanese Bernie Madoff" by Lebanese newspapers, while bankers declared that it was the biggest fraud of its kind the country had ever seen (The Star 2009; Worth 2009; Hersh 2010). Hezbollah has also been accused of importing hundreds of untested medications into the country. Those involved include Abdul Latif Fneich, the brother of the Hezbollah Minister Muhammad Fneich, and four companies linked to the organization (Khraiche 2012; Now Lebanon 2012; Orient le Jour 2012d; El-Cheikh and Saghyieh 2013a).

The journalist Nicholas Blanford, reporting at the beginning of 2015, noted the increasing allegations of corruption within Hezbollah following the decline of financial assistance from the IRI due to falling oil revenues and the consequences of international sanctions against Iran. He wrote that the Hezbollah-run Rasoul al-Azam Hospital in Beirut's southern suburbs, which has treated hundreds of casualties evacuated from the Syrian battlefields, had started to pay its suppliers every six months, instead of every three months, and with an Iranian official flying in specially to handle the transfers so as to prevent pilfering of funds (Blanford 2015). Hezbollah has also been accused of being involved in illegal transnational activities as a source of funding for the Islamic movement, such as bank frauds, currency counterfeiting, drug trafficking,[16] the manufacture and sale of fake goods, intellectual property piracy and the trade in African "blood diamonds" (Blanford 2011: 356).

In the municipal elections of 2016 in the South, growing grievances against the Amal–Hezbollah coalition were expressed by voters. These emphasized the "favoritism" towards incompetent entrepreneurs and the theft of land with the blessing of the municipalities. For a growing number of voters, to contest Hezbollah's local policies did not equate with the betrayal of the resistance (Orient le Jour 2016).

Hezbollah's Response to Neoliberal Reform

Throughout three decades of neoliberal reform, Hezbollah continued to portray itself as the party of the "oppressed," which opposes deprivation and champions the rights of farmers, the poor, workers and the homeless (Harb 2010: 16). From its manifesto of 2009:

> Savage capitalist forces, led by the USA and Western countries and embodied mainly in international monopoly networks of companies that cross nations and continents, networks of various international establishments especially the financial ones backed by superior military force have led to more contradictions and conflicts—of which not less important—are the conflicts of identities, cultures, civilizations, in addition to the conflicts of poverty and wealth.
>
> (Hezbollah Manifesto 2009)

Despite this militant tone, the Hezbollah's theoretical conception and policy orientation have not presented any systematic alternative to neoliberalism in Lebanon. Instead, the organization's overall attitude has been an attempt to balance its professed social justice goals with consistent support for neoliberal measures such as liberalization, privatization and fostering the growth of the private sector. We can find this contradiction in the political thought of previous important figures of Shiʿa Islamic fundamentalism such as Muhammad Baqir al-Sadr (1935–1980) and especially Ayatollah Khomeini (1902–1989).

Among his many books, Al-Sadr wrote two books with the aim of confronting Marxism and secular thought: *Falsafatunā* (*Our Philosophy*) in 1959 and *Iqtisāūnā* (*Our Economics*) in 1961 (Baram 1994: 539). In *Falsafatunā*, he wanted to show that Islam is the source of a philosophy superior to other currents of thought, particularly Marxism. He advocated that the best solution to the plight of the population is the Islamization of society and the establishment of an Islamic state (Mallat 1988: 707).

The second book, *Iqtisāūnā*, is structured along similar lines, extensively criticizing Marxism and attempting to demonstrate that Marx underplays spiritualism in favor of economic reductionism. Al-Sadr promoted an Islamic economic system, which consists of private and public property, while refuting both socialism and capitalism (Mervin 2007: 304–305). In his view, socio-economic problems are the result of the misconduct of man (Aziz 1993). The solution is therefore to be found in religion. He argues that an Islamic state, which would implement an Islamic economic system, would set the direction of economic activities while giving individuals the right of private ownership to achieve a social goal. He adds that the government's role in an Islamic state is to oversee and regulate economic activities, while adding that an Islamic government is free to adopt a wide range of economic policies from full control of the economy to free enterprise in order to achieve its social goals (Aziz 1993).

Meanwhile, Khomeini developed various economic discourses according to the particular political period, adapting these according to the interests of the Islamic movement. In 1979–1982, at the height of Iran's revolution and popular mobilization, Khomeini had presented Islam through the lens of social justice, praising the oppressed (who were equated with the poorest sections of society) and condemning the oppressors understood as the rich, the greedy palace dwellers and their foreign patrons (Abrahamian 1993: 133). This radical rhetoric was instrumental in mobilizing the urban populace against the Pahlavi monarchy. But after 1982, during the consolidation of the new Islamic regime of Khomeini and the associated repression of the opposition (especially the left and progressive forces), he increasingly equated Islam with respect for private property and depicted the bazaar (market place) as an essential pillar of society. He now progressively delineated three main classes: an upper class (*tabaqeh-e bala*) constituted of the remnants of the old wealthy families; a middle class (*tabaqeh-e motavasset*) formed by clerics, intellectuals, civil servants, merchants, shopkeepers and tradesmen; and a lower class (*tabaqeh-e payin*) composed of laborers, peasants and slum dwellers (Abrahamian 1993: 51). The "oppressed" ceased to be an economic category describing the deprived masses, becoming instead a political label for the new regime's supporters and including wealthy bazaar merchants (Abrahamian 1993: 53). The class-struggle rhetoric was significantly diminished with Khomeini arguing that Islam sought harmonious relationships between factory owners and workers, and between landlords and peasants, while warning that: "if these class antagonisms are not alleviated, their inevitable explosion would destroy the whole Islamic Republic" (cited in Abrahamian 1993: 51).

Other Islamic political movements have also tended to profess a rhetorical concern for social justice aspirations (to be largely fulfilled through charitable means), whilst on the other hand, defending market-led principles and economic liberalization. As the Tunisian Islamic leader Rached Ghannouchi noted in 1992: "we [the Islamic political movements] are the guarantor of a particular social order and of a liberal economic regime" (1992 cited in Toscane 1995: 95). Ghannouchi has also declared that: "foreign investment is welcome in Tunisia, companies must make profits and unions have sometimes been excessive in their demands, including the General Union of Tunisian Workers [known as the UGTT]" (cited in Sereni 2014). Indeed, Ghannouchi has accused the UGTT of being a heritage of the French colonial period and of not being a natural institution of Muslim society (cited in Sereni 2014).[17]

The scholar Patrick Haenni (2005: 65) has written that Islamic political movements have witnessed an increasing "embourgeoisement" in the process of Islamization of society in different countries, especially among its leadership and cadres. He speaks of an "Islam de Marché" (Islam of the Market) that is sympathetic to neoliberal policies while combining it with moral conservatism. He writes that this "Islam de Marché" was promoted by the rising and newly pious bourgeoisie from the beginning of the 1980s.

Throughout the world, conservative religious movements have actually supported neoliberal policies while advocating increased charitable work, leading some scholars to talk of "a smooth alliance between neoliberals and religious fundamentalists," which could be characterized as "religious neoliberalism" (Hackworth 2013: 100). Confirming this trend, various religious conservative movements support the idea that Faith Based Organizations (FBO) could replace the state's public services because they are more efficient. The American religious leader Marvin Olasky, for example, argues that government-based welfare is an abject failure because it is wasteful and does not emphasize personal responsibility. Therefore, he argues, welfare states should be dismantled and replaced with locally based religious systems that are funded by biblical tithes. He adds: "such programmes would not burden the federal government and would be able to sort the 'deserving' from the 'undeserving' poor" (Hackworth 2013: 104–105). Olasky's political views have had a strong influence on the US Republican Party; he was a close advisor to former President George W. Bush in the 1990s. Based on this idea of less state and more independent FBOs, Olasky promoted the idea of "compassionate conservatism" (Hackworth 2013: 105). In the Middle East context, Islamic fundamentalist movements have also adopted this form of "compassionate conservatism," combining neoliberal policies and conservative moralism (Haenni 2005: 104; Roy 2002: 150–52). The Egyptian Muslim Brotherhood, for example, has supported increased religious compliance and the work of charity organizations (Freedom and Justice Party 2011: 9), while also advocating neoliberal policies in which the private sector would play a leading role in the economy (Freedom and Justice Party 2011: 26). Hassan Malek, a businessman and ranking Muslim Brotherhood figure, actually went so far as to say in 2012 that the principles guiding economic policies followed under Mubarak were sound and on the right track, but corruption and nepotism marred their implementation (Reuters 2011).

In much the same way as al-Sadr and Khomeini, Hezbollah's economic thought has consistently upheld the market and the defense of private property as a key tenet, despite also professing allegiance to social justice goals.[18] Throughout the neoliberal period in Lebanon, this theoretical orientation has meant that Hezbollah's support for measures such as privatization, liberalization and opening up to foreign capital inflows, has not been viewed by the organization as contradicting its commitment to addressing poverty and inequality. Understood within a calculus of strengthening the party's political position and clientelist networks, Hezbollah may have expressed a limited rhetorical opposition to specific policies and their outcomes, but it has not presented any consistent or principled opposition to the overall trajectory of neoliberal reform in Lebanon.

These characteristics are most clearly articulated in the work of Hezbollah's development think-tank, the CCSD (Consultative Center for Studies and Documentation), which has organized several large conferences on economic and social issues, including a 1999 conference titled "The Economic and Social Crisis in Lebanon, and Alternatives," and a 2012 meeting around the theme of "Reform of Social Policies in Lebanon: From Selective Subsidy towards Welfare State." Although the conference's introductory document noted that: "it is necessary in a country such as Lebanon to seek unifying social policies ensuring community security and guaranteeing welfare," its major emphasis echoed the neoliberal language of Lebanese policy makers, highlighting "motivating growth" and facilitating "the established monetary and financial objectives [of the state]" as the key goals (CCSD 2012). Muhammad Raad, head of the Hezbollah's Deputy bloc in parliament, summed up this orientation in his introductory speech, declaring that:

> the objective of social policies are to guarantee social peace, achieve well being and stimulate development in Lebanon [...] the mission of this conference is to find a formula that conciliates between achieving this objective and preserving the competitiveness of the economic sectors.

> (Raad 2012)

This balance between ameliorating the impact of neoliberal reform while promoting growth and private sector development is also found in the writings of two prominent Hezbollah thinkers, Ali Fayyad (a former director of CCSD and currently an MP for Hezbollah in the Lebanese parliament) and Abd al-Halim Fadlallah (the current director of CCSD), alongside the collective works undertaken by the CCSD under their leaderships. Both authors are critical of some aspects of globalization and the implementation of various economic agreements, including those with the IMF and the Euro-Mediterranean partnership (Fayyad 2008a: 15). The CCSD, in a collective work (2009: 16) and Fadlallah (2008: 13), also condemned the liberalization of trade in 2001 because it hurt small enterprises which were not strong enough to compete with foreign products. It also criticized the reduction of public social spending and the increase in indirect taxes (CCSD 2008a: 24). In addition, the lack of transparency and equity in development policy are recurrent criticisms of CCSD works (Fadlallah 2008: 13).

Despite these criticisms, however, both authors continue to place a primacy on the support of the private sector based upon "non-ideological motivated choices that enjoy a general consensus and guarantee the interests of all the parties and sectors of the society" (Fadlallah 2008: 16; Fayyad 2008a: 13). They argue that economic and social decisions should not be taken at the expense of the private sector (CCSD 2009). In this regard, budget rationalization is put forward as necessary in areas such as health and basic education (CCSD 2009: 42). Along similar lines, both Fayyad and Fadlallah (CCSD 2008a: 62) have supported the privatization of the state electricity company, Electricité du Liban (EdL), and praised this as a positive outcome of the Paris III agreement that could help the general finances of the state. Indeed, the Hezbollah Minister Muhammad Fneich was an important actor in the ongoing privatization of EdL (Verdeil 2008) as Minister of Energy and Water between July 2005 and November 2006, arguing for the possibility of private companies to provide their electricity to the network (Verdeil 2009). Fneich called for the full privatization of electricity production stating that experience showed that the "state is an unsuccessful merchant" (cited in Habib 2008), while declaring in addition that the government "should not be involved in any commercial activity, adding that the private sector should be given a bigger role in some of the public departments' affairs which have commercial nature" (cited in Habib 2008). According to Fneich, the private sector should be responsible for the operation and maintenance of power plants, as well as importing fuel oil (Habib 2008).

Even Hezbollah-affiliated trade unionists have supported this privatiza-tion, with one noting that privatization "might open new opportunities for workers" and could "settle the problem of electricity [regarding the problems of provisions of the EdL and to secure stable jobs to its employees]" (Zeid 2012).

The attempt to balance social justice goals with neoliberal reform is further indicated in comments by Abd al-Halim Fadlallah. He affirmed that: "the economic direction of the party leans towards the social market economy, neither open liberalism nor socialism." He added that he is in favor of the free market, because there is no alternative to it in Lebanon. He nevertheless emphasized the need for a stronger state, and not an economy that impoverishes the poor for the benefit of the rich (Fadlallah 2012a). He has also said that Hezbollah does not oppose a liberalized economy or the privatization of public enterprises if this process is transparent and respects social and economic balances. He declared that social justice is possible through a liberal economy if it is well regulated and the productive economy plays a role in it (Fadlallah 2010).

In reality, however, this orientation towards a "social market economy" has tended to be eclipsed by Hezbollah's consistent support for neoliberal measures. This has been the case whether the organization has been in opposition or part of the ruling government. Following the 2003 Paris II Conference, while Hezbollah was part of the opposition, it did not take a position or offer any assessment of the social consequences of privatizing state assets including Middle East Airlines (MEA) (Abla 2003; Nsouli 2007), a company that employed several hundred Shiʿa, who were subsequently made redundant. The privatization of MEA led to considerable protests against the prospect of 1,200–1,500 workers losing their jobs (Al-Bayyan 2001). Ali Taher Yassin, the current head of the Hezbollah-linked al-Wafa trade union (see Chapter 6), was involved in the negotiations around the lay-offs as a representative of the workers. In an interview, he claimed that the proposed privatiza-tion was not necessarily against the interests of the workers or the wider population (Yassin 2012). Moreover, he stated that Hezbollah has no principled positions against privatization, but that each case must be studied to determine whether it has positive or negative implications for the country's economy (Yassin 2012). He explained that:

the company used to lose money every year and was a burden on the Lebanese society [...] Privatisation became a necessity and the state was still able to keep the majority of shares of the company. This solution was the least harsh solution for the workers. We protected a number of workers and eased the pressure on them, but at the end of the day we have to make a balance between the interests of the workers and the needs of the Lebanese economy. I don't want to protect the rights of the workers and then the company dies. It does not make sense.

(Yassin 2012)

Since the Hezbollah's participation in successive Lebanese governments from 2005, no additional funds were allocated to sectors like education and health or the productive sectors of economy. There was no attempt to implement progressive taxation. On January 4, 2007, the parliament, including the Hezbollah, adopted the plan conducted by then Prime Minister Siniora, which included: austerity measures aimed at bringing the debt down from 180 percent to 144 percent of GDP in 2011, a VAT increase from 10 percent to 15 percent, privatization of the mobile telephone sector, elimination of the budget deficit in five years, initiatives to attract foreign investors and fiscal reform of the administration (Vivien 2007).

Even when the Hezbollah and its allies of the March 8 movement dominated Miqati's government between 2011 and 2013, it did not challenge Hariri's policy legacy. They continued the process of privatization in the electricity company EdL, promoted a project to liberalize the system of house rent, which could force more than 180,000 families out of their homes (see below) and rejected a program by Charbel Nahas[19] to increase wages and social benefits including universal health coverage of workers and transport indemnities (discussed in detail in Chapter 6).

Budgets for the productive sectors have not seen any increase, except for a very small increase in the Ministry of Agriculture—and, in this case, only to expand its bureaucracy (see below). In the 2012 budget, the accounts of the CDR as well as some other accounts were kept off the budget, which meant that the supervision and governance of public spending would remain unchanged. This is in spite of Hezbollah's previous demands for more transparency (Saif 2012).

In the 2013 draft budget of the Miqati government, supported by Hezbollah, a number of provisions raised taxes on many everyday items while creating loopholes and work-arounds for banks, real estate developers and sectarian institutions. The draft notably included an increase in the VAT from 10 to 12 percent, which would raise the poverty rate to 32 percent (Chaaban and Salti 2009: 7). Five-year tax exemptions (beginning from the date of the law's issuing) were given to hotels in areas that the state wishes to develop. Tourist establishments built in the last three years would also be exempted from taxes on profits for the next five years (Zbeeb 2012c). In 2014, with the establishment of a new national unity government led by Prime Minister Tamam Salam, the Hezbollah member Hussein Hajj Hassan (the newly appointed Minister of Industry) thanked the Parliament for decreasing tax on exports by 50 percent and congratulated industrialists for this long awaited accomplishment (National News Agency [NNA] 2014a). He added that this was the first step in support of exports (NNA 2014a).

In summary, while the Hezbollah has periodically condemned the outcomes of capitalist development in Lebanon at a rhetorical level, it has been a willing participant in the elaboration of neoliberal policies through successive Lebanese governments. As the first section of this chapter observed, these policies have particularly concentrated on urban renewal and reform, linked to the financialization of the economy—and have led to the ongoing marginalization of other sectors such as agriculture. For this reason, a more detailed understanding of Hezbollah's orientation to these processes is best illustrated through an examination of three key areas that lie at the juncture of these outcomes: (1) Municipal urban policy in Hezbollah-controlled areas; (2) Debates around the liberalization of the housing rental market; and (3) Agricultural development. In each of these areas, we can discern Hezbollah's support for neoliberal reforms, coupled with the organization's attempts to strengthen its clientelistic networks and influence in Shi'a dominated areas.

Municipal Policies: The Case of Ghobeyri

In Lebanon, municipal councils are accorded a great deal of influence over urban planning, zoning regulations and housing policy. In this context, the municipality of Ghobeyri, in southern Beirut, constitutes a particularly instructive example of Hezbollah policies at the local level. Ghobeyri occupies a large part of Dahyeh, and is the location of the headquarters and associations of Hezbollah.[20] Mona Harb has noted that, in Ghobeyri, "the largest municipal committees (those of work, education, health, financial and social) are in the hands of Hezbollah executives or individuals who worked with the party through its social associations" and, for this reason, it provides "a microcosm of the operation of Hezbollah on the field" (Harb 2010: 7). In Ghobeyri, and Dahyeh more widely, Hezbollah's urban restructuring policy has closely followed the main precepts of neoliberal reform—the prioritization of private, individual ownership of real estate and the marginalization of existing residents. It is a policy that, according to Mona Fawaz, has acted to: "consolidate spatial segregation, the privatization of public spaces, the gentrification of its areas of intervention, and further delegation of communal or public services to private channels of provision" (Fawaz 2014: 922–23).

One of the consequences of this policy has been the increasing polarization of wealth in the municipality. On the one hand, the area is home to a number of expensive hotels and developments for tourists, including BHV-Monoprix, Mariott, Summerland and the Coral Beach (Harb 2002: 133). At the same time, large numbers of poor residents live in dilapidated and informal housing arrangements. This includes the Palestinian refugee camp of Shatila, the site of an infamous massacre by Phalangist forces in 1982.

Muhammad Said al-Khansa, who is a founding member of the Hezbollah and who has been active in the various party social organizations, has been the mayor of the municipality of Ghobeyri since 1998. He comes from a large and respected clan that dominates the busy trade in automobile parts, according to Norton (2007: 104). He adds that the "Al-Khansa are represented across a rich variety of business" (Norton 2007: 104).

With increased powers as a result of the 1997 Law, Al-Khansa, the mayor of Dahyeh, has followed a municipal development policy that is in close synergy with the urban renewal schemes launched under Hariri. Most saliently, this policy has focused on attracting private capital flows and speculative investment into real estate property, while marginalizing and dispossessing poor communities who have long been resident in the area (Harb 2009).

In an interview, Al-Khansa confirmed this orientation and his prioritization of private real estate development in Ghoberyi. He cited numerous examples, including two large malls directly linked to the liberalization of financial and real estate markets through the 2000s—the Beirut Mall (2006),[21] funded by Saudi investors and BHV (1998), a large French multinational company. In addition, Al-Khansa has overseen the development of commercial tourist resorts (Summerland, funded by Saudi and Lebanese investors, and Coral Beach), luxury hotels (Monroe and Mariott) and the Cité Sportive (a sport center) (Harb 2002: 137; Al-Khansa 2012). The Mayor explains his support for these developments through the taxes they pay to the municipality, and characterizes them as an example of "progress" that responds to the consumer demands of the residents of Dahyeh (Harb 2002: 137; Al-Khansa 2012). They were provided with numerous incentives, including fast track permits, construction subsidies and the development of associated infrastructure (Al-Khansa 2010, 2012). In an interview, Al-Khansa commented that: "the region of Dahyeh has witnessed an urban renaissance over the past years, and it is not surprising that there are luxury apartments in the area of Ghobeyri ranging between 800,000 dollars to one million dollars" (Al-Khansa 2010).

While expressing pride in this ongoing construction boom and real estate investments from wealthy Shi'a businessmen of the diaspora and from Arabs in the Gulf, Al-Khansa has another project planned called "New Dahyeh." This new neighborhood aims to attract diplomatic buildings, large malls, retailers, businessmen and investments from the Shi'a diaspora. Al-Khansa explained that this project is aimed at keeping the most prosperous Shi'a classes in Dahyeh, who might otherwise depart for other areas of Beirut (Al-Khansa 2012).

While these developments are planned, the Shatila refugee camp and informal neighborhoods in Ghobeyri, including Sabra, Horch al-Qatil and Jnah, are provided with only minimal and ineffective urban services (Harb 2009). The mayor commented in his interview that he would like to see the residents of these informal neighborhoods sell their lands and leave the area in order to build new buildings for middle-class families—a goal first suggested by Rafiq Hariri in his incomplete 1996 Elissar Project, which aimed at restructuring the residential profile of Beirut through an expansion of highways and the removal of poorer residents (Al-Khansa 2010, 2012). More precisely, the project cited the western coastal sections of Dahyeh that are an area of informal settlements with myriad unsettled property rights issues (Deeb and Harb 2013: 233). Indeed, Al-Khansa has expressed his support for the Elissar Project, claiming that it was a strategic choice that would enable increased tax collection from residents in the area. In 1996, at the beginning of the Elissar project, the Hezbollah actually "convinced," as explained by Lara Deeb and Mona Harb (2013: 233), residents to accept Elissar's financial compensation and leave their homes in order to facilitate the highways needed to complete Hariri's reconstruction of downtown Beirut. They add that this clearly showed the Hezbollah's prioritization of national political maneuverings and alliances over its constituents' rights (Deeb and Harb 2013: 233). Mona Harb, however, has countered "that Hezbollah is interested in the Elissar model as a way to ensure that 'the seashore is liberated' for lucrative real estate development, which will benefit the class of bourgeois developers in its constituency" (cited in Ohrstrom and Quilty 2007).

Al-Khansa's goal of spatially transforming Ghobeyri through the removal of informal communities is further indicated on the municipality's website, which records destruction of "illegal settlements" and lauds the joint efforts of the municipality, the police and the army to demolish poorer, unregistered housing in order to preserve the "interests of all" (Ghobeyri municipality 2013). The Union of Municipalities of the Suburbs (Dahyeh) has echoed this orientation in declarations against informal dwellings—condemning them as violations of private property rights—and calling on the municipality and security agencies to remove all such housing from the area (Slab News 2013). In implementing these policies, Hezbollah has adopted a discourse that sees public space as a potential site of disorder (*fawda*). In addition to the privatization of these areas, they have been earmarked for trash disposal sites (Fawaz 2007: 22–23). These kinds of representations echo contemporary neoliberal language that justifies intensified securitization and control over public access and use of municipal space (Fawaz 2007: 22–23).

Lebanon's Housing Rental Policy

The municipal development model embraced by the Hezbollah in Ghobeyri confirms the organization's embrace of policies aimed at restructuring the urban space in line with the interests of capital accumulation. This same orientation can be seen in Hezbollah's attitude towards a new liberalization law for residential rents that was eventually passed by the Lebanese Parliament in May 2014.

In 1992, following the end of the Civil War, two laws were passed in Lebanon (Rent Acts nos 159 and 160) which froze all housing rental agreements signed before this date and thus helped to protect poorer communities from rent inflation and the possibility of eviction (Marot 2012). In 2012, however, a new law was proposed by the Administration and Justice Parliamentary Committee—a committee that included Hezbollah—to liberalize these pre-1992 house rents so that they would rise over a period of six years to current market levels. The projected rise in house rents is very high, and most tenants would not have been able to cope with it (Andraos 2012).[22] The new law also gave owners the right to evict tenants in the case where they could not afford to pay at the new level (Abou Zaki 2012b).

These proposals raised considerable fears that the 180,000 families currently renting at pre-1992 levels would face the loss of their accommodation. A large proportion of this number is made up of elderly people, and it is estimated that 65 percent of those affected live in poverty.[23] As Rana Andraos has noted, the significant gaps between income and rents means that people on "a minimum wage of around $500" would find it difficult to obtain housing in a situation where the "average annual rent is between $7–10,000 in the capital and suburbs" (Andraos 2012). Bruno Marot predicted:

> the rapid deletion of House Rent Acts n°159 and 160—meaning the liberalization of the whole housing stock—will confront many households with a housing market they cannot afford. Massive evictions towards the periphery should be feared and could result in the rise of social and territorial inequality between gentrified central urban areas and peripheries coping with a substantial influx of pauperised families. This process would be far from being harmless in a society where the socio-sectarian fabric is still largely contentious.
>
> (Marot 2012)

Despite these fears, the proposed law was met with acclaim by banks and real estate developers who predicted a large increase in land prices following the removal of rent caps (Abou Zaki 2012b). One business magazine noted:

With buildings being vacated and renovated, and others being torn down for new projects [...] $50 billion could be pumped into the economy in the coming years. A back of the envelope calculation of 30,000 buildings being re-developed at an average of $500,000, would generate $15 billion and potentially billions more in associated services.

(Cochrane 2012)

The head of the National Federation of Trade Union of Workers and Employees in Lebanon (known as FENASOL) and LCP member, Castro Abdallah, argued in an interview that:

The new law regarding house rents is in the interests of the big companies, foreign investments and banks. The most important investments are made in the real estate sector. They want to liberalize the rents because the price of lands went up, this concerns 180,000 renting families that they want to take out in the next 6 years and put them in other regions. They want to create new demographics on the ground. Want to push people back in their sectarian regions. They want to achieve what they were not able to do during the Civil War. Sectarian cantons.

(Abdallah 2012)

On the main beneficiaries of this law, Hisham Ashkar has argued:

In sum, property owners are the main beneficiaries, since this reform allows them to have total control on their properties, and to maximize the capitalization on them. Tenants are the real losers, since they lost all their privileges, and most of them will be forced out of their homes. As for the real-estate investors/developers, they do not really benefit from this reform, since it strengthens property owners' negotiation position, in a sector already characterized by the scarcity of its prime resource: land. A situation that will force investors/developers to compromise, to share a bigger part of the perceived profit with property owners, thus cutting down their own profit.

(Ashkar 2014a)

In the context of this highly contested debate over the rental laws, Hezbollah has been a prominent supporter of the new changes. In an interview for this book, Abd al-Halim Fadlallah (2012a) from the CCSD stated that he was in favor of the new law and considered the fixed low rents a problem and unsustainable for the owners, although he added that total liberalization of the sector may not be the best solution because of its probable negative consequences on the 180,000 families concerned. Once again, we see the Hezbollah's general support for market reform coupled with an expression of social justice concerns.

At the level of practical intervention, however, these concerns around the possible implications of the law have not led the Hezbollah to engage in any opposition to the law. The union leader Castro Abdallah (2012) stated in an interview that the Hezbollah did not participate in any demonstrations against the law and has not supported the Association of the Owners of Rental Buildings, which defended the tenants. In April 2014, the law to liberalize the pre-1992 rent contracts was voted in the Lebanese parliament, and all the Hezbollah deputies voted in favor with the exception of Walid Sukkarieh, the Hezbollah MP, who criticized the law as a gross violation of the rights of the tenants (Noujeim 2014). A proposal by the Follow-Up Committee of the National Conference of Tenants to include a new housing plan for the poor was not included in the bill.[24] In response to the passing of the bill, activists have continued to mobilize against the expected eviction of tenants and the gentrification of Beirut and Mount Lebanon. The Hezbollah, however, has not participated in these protests (NNA 2014b).[25]

The Bekaa Valley

As Chapter 1 detailed, the agricultural sector has been one of the most neglected economic sectors in Lebanon since the independence of the country. On some occasions, the Hezbollah has organized a series of workshops on the Bekaa economy and engaged in some small investment plans in the region, particularly after the revolt led by Tufayli in 1997 in which some protestors accused the Hezbollah of acquiescing to the policies of the Hariri's government and dismissing the Bekaa's grievances (Abisaab and Abisaab 2014: 134). The Islamic movement has also claimed to support more investment for poorer and marginalized farmers, but its presence in government since 2005 has not seen this take place, despite the fact that the party was in charge of the Ministry of Agriculture between 2009 and 2014. Instead, the Hezbollah has continued to advance the interests of large landowners from which it draws political and clientelistic support.

The Hezbollah's governance has come under attack, for example, by farmers of the Bekaa region for its reliance on large landowners and powerful clans (Daher 2012: 421). Indeed, cannabis farmers have criticized the Hezbollah for "conspiring to keep people dependent on them" by refusing to support low-cost irrigation or the building of dams and instead supporting the interests of large landowners (Hodeib 2013a).[26] In an interview conducted for this book, Jihad al-Mualim, President of the Federation of Workers and Employees in the Bekaa, noted that large landowners are the ones benefiting from Hezbollah's agricultural policies in the Bekaa. He argued that these landowners are being assisted financially by the ministry and being granted the vast majority of loans from private banks (Al-Mualim 2012). As a result, the inequalities among farmers are very large, with 5 percent of farmers' controlling 47 percent of total cultivated lands, while half of the farmers own only 8 percent of the total cultivated lands (Nasnas 2007: 178).

For this reason, Al-Mualim's federation has reiterated its demands for the establishment of a bank of development for agriculture, in an attempt to redress the inequality in funding for smaller farmers. Despite an agreement between the Ministry of Agriculture and private banks to facilitate loans to small and middle farmers, this has not translated into reality because high risks and low benefits do not encourage banks to lend (Al-Mualim 2012; Nassif 2012; Mohieddine 2012). The need for a bank of development for agriculture has been a constant demand of the Federation of Agriculture since the end of the Civil War, alongside the provision of social insurance in the agricultural sector and the establishment of a High Council of Agriculture including federations, unions, professionals and the ministry, to discuss development policies in the sector (Nassif 2012; Mohieddine 2012).

Al-Mualim further notes that no consistent or sustainable projects to improve the irrigation of lands—especially in the Bekaa and the South—have been undertaken. Lebanon still relies upon foreign agricultural imports while national products are not protected (Al-Mualim 2012). At the same time, despite the rhetorical support of Hezbollah's former Minister of Agriculture to tackle the problem of cartels and monopolies in the sector, no measures limiting their influence have been implemented.

The large landowners and retailers still dominate the market (Al-Mualim 2012; Mohieddine 2012).

The budget of the Ministry of Agriculture has been slightly increased under Hezbollah's administration, but most of this has been used for the recruitment of new employees and not to promote development projects. According to Youssef Mohieddine, President of the Federation of Agriculture, the new development projects are mostly linked to international financial assistance and projects, and not from the government. Funding is distributed to further reinforce clientelist and sectarian interests of the Hezbollah (Mohieddine 2012).[27] Mohieddine claimed that:

Until today, May 2012, no development project has been suggested by the Ministry despite the fact that we had a conference at the Ministry of Agriculture where we agreed on a common strategy for the agricultural sector and we agreed on a structure of a committee, which would gather all the unions and federations and Ministry to discuss and work on projects of development. All these decisions taken by this conference were not taking into account and not implemented, and the Ministry continued to work on partisan base and work with Jihad al-Bina [Hezbollah's construction wing] [...] the Minister favours its own people and institutions, by providing them first and foremost with the largest international funding development projects. The Minister Hussein Hajj Hassan is the one who controls the distribution of aid as minister. He favours the people in his party or close to it.

(Mohieddine 2012)

In the same vein, Alfred Nassif, President of Federation of Proprietors of Kermel in the Bekaa, and Secretary President of the Federation of Agriculture in Lebanon, stated that, "Yes, the budget of agriculture was raised, but we have not seen anything change, and when they distribute financial assistance, it's first to [Hezbollah's] public and people" (Nassif 2012). This clientelism further extends to claims that the Hezbollah has attempted to marginalize and divide the main agriculture unions, by establishing new structures in the Bekaa:

[Hezbollah's former Minister of Agriculture] gave licences to numerous new associations and cooperatives in the country, and especially in the region of the Bekaa, in which they had only a poor presence. They were also provided with financial assistance. He gave a lot of assistance to others but not our unions [...] He did not give to the general Federation as well [...] There is a clear discrimination [...] the Ministry provides more services and assistance to [Hezbollah-affiliated] federations and unions, such as Federation of farmers in Lebanon (known as INMA), a federation linked to Hezbollah, while filling its administration with Hezbollah members and making Jihad al-Bina [Hezbollah's construction firm] an auxiliary institution of the Ministry.

(Nassif 2012)

Antoine Hayek, the President of the Lebanese Association of Agriculture, has echoed these criticisms, declaring that a series of recommendations, endorsed by all political parties, were suggested in February 2009 at the socio-economic forum organized by the Commission of the European Union. The propositions were part of a comprehensive strategy to support the agricultural sector, which notably included a project of loans to the sector, the development of appropriate national banking laws and the modernization of insurance policies related to hazards and natural disasters. All these propositions were then submitted to the Council of Ministers in 2009, but were not taken into consideration (cited in Orient le Jour 2014a). Hayek (Orient le Jour 2014a) also accused the Hezbollah of not seeking stricter controls on imports in order to better protect national production. The former Minister of Agriculture Hajj Hassan, he said, has "failed to alleviate the problems of the sector. Agriculture has remained vulnerable to natural disasters, to all kinds of obstacles and corrupt practices, all generating high risk" (Orient Le Jour 2014a).

In addition to all this, the Islamic movement has also adopted a laissez-faire attitude regarding the lawless northern Bekaa, where drug barons have small private militias to protect their cannabis fields and where stolen cars are traded and counterfeit money is printed (Blanford 2011: 476–77). The Hezbollah especially turns a blind eye to the cultivation of plants for hashish and marijuana because it is unwilling to antagonize the powerful clans and tribes who take part in this illicit business (Blanford 2011: 477) and to maintain their influence in the region. As an example of these links between the Hezbollah and these clans, Noah Zaiter, a well-known drug dealer[28] from a famous family clan of the Bekaa and who has been subjected to several arrest warrants, was seen on pictures published on social media visiting Hezbollah fighters in the Syrian region of Qalamoun in mid-September 2015. In the past, he had also made his marijuana-cultivated fields available to Hezbollah to transform them into training areas for young recruits (Orient le Jour 2015e).

After his departure of the Minister of Agriculture, Hajj Hassan said bluntly that: "those who think that an alternative to hashish exists are wishful thinkers" (Mucci 2014).

In general, the consensus among all the farmers and agriculture rep-resentatives and trade unionists interviewed for this book indicated that they felt sidelined from any real control or influence over agricultural policy, while the Hezbollah has continued to prioritize its relationship with large landowners and its goal of strengthening its clientelist networks.

Conclusion

Lebanon's neoliberal reform process, which began in the early 1990s following the end of the Civil War, was accelerated under Rafiq Hariri, and has been consistently followed by all subsequent Lebanese governments. These policies have particularly aimed at attracting financial flows from outside with a focus on urban reconstruction as a main sectoral pivot of economic growth. This orientation confirms the way in which the outcomes of war and conflict have been used to deepen the trajectory of neoliberal reform. It is a trajectory supported by all main political actors in Lebanon, international institutions such as the World Bank and the IMF (coordinated through the successive Paris aid conferences) and regional investors (particularly from the Gulf states). These policies have accentuated the spatial and social inequalities in Lebanon and are closely linked to the heavily financialized nature of the country's political economy and the marginalization of important sectors, such as agriculture and industry.

In this context, the Hezbollah has not distanced itself from the process of neoliberal reform. Whether in opposition or participat-ing in government, the Hezbollah has continually supported these policies including on issues such as privatization, tax reform and urban development. In the management of the municipalities that it governs, as well as in the urban sphere more generally, the Hezbollah has promoted policies that encourage capital accumulation at the expense of poorer and marginalized residents. In agriculture, the Hezbollah Minister has not made any significant changes to previous policies and, moreover, has sought to strengthen its clientelist ties in areas such as the Bekaa Valley. We can see in the Hezbollah's Minister, and more generally in the party's policies regarding economic and social issues, no willingness of the party to challenge existent power structures and their entrenched institutional manifestations.

Hezbollah's sources of funding also explain the lack of opposition to the capitalist system and rather conservative economic program. The Islamic movement is founded on financial support from the Lebanese Shi'a middle class and bourgeoisie, the IRI, and the alms (*zakāt*) collected by the Hezbollah on behalf of Khomeini. According to Hamzeh, the party in addition to the massive funding of the IRI relies on "donations from individuals, groups, shops, companies, and banks as well as their counterparts in countries such as the United States, Canada, Latin America, Europe and Australia," and on the Hezbollah's own business interests, which take "advantage of Lebanon's free market economy" with "dozens of supermarkets, gas stations, department stores, restaurants, construction companies and travel agencies" (2004: 64). The Hezbollah's Foreign Relations Unit, which was established in 1985 and is currently led by cleric Ali Daamoush, is actually responsible for maintaining and developing relations with the Lebanese-Shi'a communities around the world. Its main objective is fundraising for the Islamic movement, and managing religious and political propaganda on behalf of the Hezbollah. The Unit is mostly composed of clerics and businessmen who are known in the Shi'a communities and are publicly associated with the Hezbollah. The Unit is active in Europe, Africa, the USA and Asia (Terror Control 2014).

The Hezbollah's role in these processes confirms that it does not present a fundamental challenge to the current political economy framework of Lebanon but, on the contrary, has been integrated into this system as a political fraction tied to the sectarian bourgeoisie. In this sense, the early assessment made by Mehdi Amel on the behavior of the Islamic bourgeoisie in the 1980s can in many ways be observed in the Hezbollah's evolution regarding the Lebanese political system:

the aspiration of fractions of the Islamic bourgeoisie to strengthen their positions in the power structure, or rather to modify the place they occupy within the confessional political system, in order to better share the hegemony and not to change the system [...] through its participation it will lead to a strengthening and an anchoring of the confessional political system and not to its change or its suppression. This solution is not actually a solution, it will lead only to a worsening of the crisis of the system.

(Amel 1986: 337–38)

Chapter 3 will further extend this analysis through a mapping of the evolving position of the Shi'a fraction of the bourgeoisie in Lebanon. It will show that the Hezbollah's links to this class fraction—particularly in the key sectors of urban renewal, construction and real estate—have been strengthened through the neoliberal period. The remaining chapters of the book will complement this analysis through an examination of how the Hezbollah has nonetheless managed to deal with the contradictions arising from these policies: building a hegemonic position within the wider Shi'a population (Chapter 5); acting to demobilize labor movements in the country (Chapter 6); and its behavior and interventions in revolutionary processes in the region (Chapter 7).

3

Lebanese Class Structure Under Neoliberalism

As noted in Chapter 2, the post-Civil War era saw an increasing influence of the Sunni business community over various sectors of the Lebanese economy.[1] The Christian fraction of the bourgeoisie lost much of its power to a Muslim-Sunni capitalist section, which benefited from foreign ties and lucrative connections to diaspora communities, particularly in the Gulf (Pearlman 2013: 120–21). Today, the two richest families in Lebanon are from the Sunni community: the Hariri family (three brothers and one sister) and the Miqati family (two brothers).[2] Together their estimated wealth is $14 billion—some 15 percent of all private wealth in the country (Executive Magazine 2013).

The banking sector, for example, is made up of more than seventy banks (Association of Banks in Lebanon 2014a), predominantly managed by founding families (although they are not always the major shareholders). The sector is largely dominated by the country's twelve "Alpha" banks,[3] banks with deposits over $2 billion (Cochrane 2010). At the end of 2008, Alpha banks held $95 billion in consolidated assets, or 88.3 percent of all banks' consolidated assets, and $77.3 billion in customer deposits (83.7 percent of total deposits) (Cochrane 2010).

The Christian fraction of the bourgeoisie dominates the leadership of many of these Alpha banks, without necessarily holding the majority of shares. These are often in the hands of foreign actors. This includes the largest bank in Lebanon, the Audi-Saradar Bank, which is chaired by Raymond Audi, and the third largest bank, Byblos Bank, established by the Bassil Family.

The Christian and Sunni fractions of the bourgeoisie are also involved in other sectors such as trade (both imports and exports)[4] and real estate development/construction through large family-owned conglomerates. This sectoral distribution of economic interests is linked to the form of neoliberalism discussed in Chapter 2. It has also been marked by a strong interpenetration of both the political and economic spheres, with these large families straddling high-ranking positions in both commerce and government. In construction, for example, H. Ashkar has pointed out that in post-war Beirut, amid the reconstruction process, the presence of economic elite, emerging from the real estate development sector, in the political arena intensified (Ashkar 2011: 70).

The main business associations—the Beirut Traders Association (BTA), the Association of Banks in Lebanon (ABL), the Association of Lebanese Industrialists (ALI) and the Chamber of Commerce and Industry of Beirut (CCIB)—are also dominated by these conglomerates.[5]

Importantly—and again linked to the particular form of neoliberalism in Lebanon—foreign capital inflows have helped to strengthen the position of both these Sunni and Christian conglomerates. Most significant in this respect has been foreign investment from the GCC countries. Further confirming the link between the Lebanese government and the Gulf region (particularly under Hariri's leadership), around 60 percent of FDI from 2002 to 2007 originated from the GCC. More than half of this Gulf FDI was in real estate, and the remainder in services and the banking sector (Association of Banks in Lebanon 2012). As a consequence of these FDI flows, Gulf capital has become a major shareholder in key Lebanese banks—including Audi Bank,[6] Blom Bank[7] and Credit Libanais.[8] In real estate, the Blom Investment Bank has documented that land held by GCC investors rose to "2 Million square meters (sqm) in 2005, up from 0.5 Million sqm in 2002 and increasing steadily since then" (Blom InvestBank report 2010: 11).[9]

Alongside these capital flows from the Gulf, political relationships between the GCC and the Sunni bourgeoisie have also strengthened. Perhaps the clearest example of this is the Hariri family, which, as Adam Hanieh has noted:

could be considered a subcomponent of Khaleeji (Gulf) Capital—its accumulation is centered in its ownership of the Saudi-based construction company Saudi Oger, and the family holds Saudi citizenship. In this sense, the neoliberal trajectory of the Lebanese government—and the country's economic penetration by Khaleeji Capital—are directly linked to the GCC's political influence.[10]

(Hanieh 2011: 160)

Poverty and Lebanon's Sectarian Mix

The political and economic dominance of Sunni and Christian elites, however, has not been extended to all layers of both communities. Indeed, one of the striking characteristics of the last two decades has been the increased prevalence of poverty in some key Sunni- and Christian-dominated areas. While Beirut and Mount Lebanon continue to be the centre of most economic growth, the previously marginalized Shi'a areas of South Lebanon, southern Beirut and the Bekaa Valley (although this latter area still has a high level of poverty) are no longer the poorest regions of the country. Poverty is today the most acute in some areas of northern Lebanon, in particular the city of Tripoli and its surrounding suburbs.

The most recent demographic study conducted by Informational International, a Beirut-based research firm, showed that of the country's 4.8 million Lebanese citizens in 2011, 34.8 percent were Christian and 65.1 percent were Muslim. The Shi'a population is concentrated in the northern half of the Bekaa, Baalbek and Hermel, which have a population of more than 75 percent Shi'a, in southern Beirut and southern towns such as Bint Jbeil and Nabatieh (Corstange 2012). The Sunni mainly live in Beirut and in northern areas, such as Tripoli and the Akkar, as well as in the central Bekaa and in the southern city of Saida. Various Christian communities are located in Beirut, Mount Lebanon, Zahle and Jezzine, with smaller numbers living in the Bekaa, the South and the North (Lebanese Election Data 2014).

Regarding the socio-economic situation of each region, from 1997 to 2005, the two governorates of Mount Lebanon and the North saw a relative decline in their mean per capita expenditure. The decline was nevertheless far more significant for the mostly Sunni-populated North, which witnessed a major deterioration in its mean per capita ranking— from the third highest in the country to the lowest in 2004–2005 (UNDP 2008b: 16–17). In this same period, Beirut saw the highest growth rate in per capita consumption, 5 percent annually, as a result of investments and widespread job creation witnessed in the city after 1997. Growth rates in consumption expenditures were around 4 percent higher than the national average in Shi'a-populated areas such as Nabatieh, the Bekaa and the South (UNDP 2008b: 17). Mount Lebanon and the North had a growth below the national average, with the Northern governorate observing an insignificant annual growth of 0.14 percent (UNDP 2008b: 17). The Shiʿa-dominated Nabatieh governorate witnessed the country's highest level of growth in per capita private consumption between 1997 and 2004 with a figure of 5.82 percent (UNDP 2008b: 46). This growth was most likely the effect of worker remittances from abroad, and a strong network of non-governmental organized support around recon-struction (for further discussion, see Chapter 4) (UNDP 2008b: 46).

In 2005, the mean per capita consumption was highest in Beirut (more than 150 percent of the national average), and lowest in the Sunni-dom-inated North (75 percent of the national average) (UNDP 2008b: 46). These figures were reflected in the North's increased poverty levels (a 52 percent poverty headcount using the upper poverty line and 17.5 percent using the lower poverty line) (UNDP 2009: 151). The North makes up 20.7 percent of Lebanon's population, but 46 percent of the "extremely poor population" and 38 percent of the entire poor population, which is the aggregate of the extremely and moderately poor population (UNDP 2008b: 48). At the same time, the "extremely poor population" represented in Beirut is 0.87 percent, Mount Lebanon 18.94 percent, the Bekaa 17.16 percent, the South 15.38 percent and Nabatieh 1.62 percent (UNDP 2008b: 111).

Households in the North are four times more likely to be poor in comparison with those that reside in Beirut. There are, moreover, substantial differences in poverty within the North governorate: Tripoli city and the Akkar region, mostly populated by Lebanese Sunni, have the highest percentage of overall poverty rates, with extreme poverty reaching 20.61 percent in Akkar and 23.17 percent in Tripoli, and overall poverty rates of 62.98 percent and 56.72 percent respectively (UNDP 2008b: 48). The economic and employment conditions of Akkar were particularly hard hit by the 2006 Israeli war on Lebanon, and later as a result of the destruction of the Palestinian refugee camp of Nahr al-Bared camp in the summer of 2007.[11] In contrast, the Koura, Zgharta, Batroun and Bcharre regions, mostly populated by Lebanese Christians, have relatively low poverty levels with 24.7 percent of overall poverty and 4.5 percent extreme poverty (UNDP 2008b: 48).

In terms of infrastructure and economic activities, the differences are also significant. According to the Central Administration for Statistics (CAS), there are only 17,000 [commercial] establishments in the North Lebanon governorate, compared to 73,000 in Mount Lebanon and

72,000 in Beirut (Abou Zaki 2012a). Beirut and Mount Lebanon are also the main centres of tourism and hold 75 percent of the country's hotels (Ministry of Tourism 2004 cited in UNDP 2009: 129). Moreover, Beirut and its suburbs, which include nearly 38 percent of the total population of Lebanon, had at the end of 2004 nearly 70 percent of all commercial bank deposits and were receiving more than 80 percent of total bank loans (Nasnas 2007: 46). In contrast, the northern city of Tripoli's share of bank loans to the private sector did not exceed 2–3 percent (Abou Zaki 2012a).

These figures show that the most impoverished regions are now concentrated in Sunni majority areas of the North[12] rather than the previously excluded Shi'a areas of the southern suburbs of Beirut and South Lebanon. Over the past two decades, the regions with a majority Shi'a population have actually moved from a position of marginalization and poverty to one of increased economic and political weight, while the northern areas mostly constituted of the Sunni population, have seen their position worsen.

At the same time, inequalities are important within Shi'a-populated areas, just as they are in the rest of the Lebanese society. This can be seen in the very high intra-regional poverty rates for those areas where the Shi'a form a high majority: in the Baalbek Hermel region, comprising more than 70 percent Shi'a, the percentages of the lower and upper poverty lines represented respectively 13.4 percent and 32.54 percent in 2005; in Tyr (around 84 percent Shi'a), they were 8.96 percent and 36.41 percent respectively (UNDP 2009:147); in Nabatieh (more than 95 percent Shi'a), they were 1.05 percent and 11.37 percent respectively; in Bint Jbeil (more than 87 percent Shi'a), they were 3.09 percent and 25.51 percent respectively (UNDP 2008b: 110; Lebanese Election Data 2014). These figures indicate that poverty remains very high within Shi'a areas, despite the fact that the position of the community relative to other sects has improved. In other words, there has been a widening gap and differentiation within the Shi'a population itself.

The polarization of wealth inside the Shi'a population is perhaps best observed in Dahyeh, a stronghold of the Hezbollah and populated in the majority by Shi'a (around 80 percent of its 750,000 inhabitants) (Wehbe, M. 2013b). The journalist, Muhammad Wehbe, has described the increasing social inequalities of Dahyeh as follows:

Overpopulation has put pressure on public services and infrastructures, resulting in the strengthening of illegal individual initiatives, such as electricity generators and water tanks. The poor live side by side with the middle and high class in the same geographic location populated by one same sect. There is little development taking place in the suburbs, and the crime rate is increasing. The children of parents, who had come to Dahyeh in search of security and an income, are now leaving Lebanon in search of a decent job. The scene shows the numerous class contradictions within the walls of each religious sect. In the Hay al-Sellom neighborhood of Dahyeh, expensive SUVs share the road with small cars, taxicabs and motorbikes. In Haret Hreik and Hay al-American (the Americans' neighborhood) also in Dahyeh, it is not odd to find shops renting for as high as $3,000 a month, in contrast to other places in the southern suburbs like Souk al-Jammal in Shiah and Souk al-Burj, where rents do not exceed, at most, $600 [...] The difference in the price of a square meter of a built-up area between Hay al-Sellom and Haret Hreik can reach up to 30 percent. Similarly, an apartment in Hay al-American can cost more than $500,000, compared to a maximum of $170,000 for an apartment in Hay Al-Sellom.

(Wehbe, M. 2013b)

The head of the CCSD, Abd al-Halim Fadlallah, classified the residents of Dahyeh as lower middle class or upper lower class (Wehbe, M. 2013c), while others have spoken of the rise of a "Shi'a middle class" after the Ta'if Agreement which spread over wider areas of Dahyeh (Mohsen 2012). This rising middle class has been experiencing, according to journalist Ahmad Mohsen,

an upward movement not only physically, with a construction boom, but also economically and socially. This encouraged investors to set up amenities to suit this new class, which grew on the margins of the changes taking place during the Hariri era.

(Mohsen 2012)

In addition to this, in the wake of the Liberation of the South in 2000 from Israeli occupation, private investments and real estate development schemes privileging middle- and high-end consumers have multiplied in Dahyeh (Deeb and Harb 2013: 53). The area is, in other words, not simply a zone of poor slums as it is often presented, but rather a zone giving an indication of the increasingly significant class changes and differentiation within the Shiʿa population itself.

According to one estimate, Dahyeh holds more than 30 percent of Lebanon's total domestic purchasing power (Wehbe, M. 2013c). The area's business activities have increased following the 2006 Lebanon War. A study carried out by Lara Deeb and Mona Harb published in 2009–2010, under the title "Cultural Activities of Arab Youth," showed that 64 percent of Dahiyeh's cafés and restaurants appeared between 2006–2008, and the number of bank branches in the area increased from 64 in 2009 to more than a hundred in 2013, according to some bankers (cited in Mohsen 2012).

In summary, the last two decades have seen the emergence of a layer of the Shiʿa population that has risen to an important position within Lebanon's class structure. Taken as a whole, the Shiʿa are marked by an increased polarization of wealth between this layer—which profited from neoliberal reform and the recalibration of the sectarian system following the Taʾif Agreement—and poorer layers of the population which populate Shiʿa suburbs in Beirut, the Bekaa and the South. The following section explores in greater detail the composition of this emerging Shiʿa fraction of the bourgeoisie and its connection to Hezbollah.

Mapping the Shiʿa Fraction of the Bourgeoisie

As Chapter 2 outlined, one of the distinctive features of neoliberal reform in Lebanon has been the emphasis on the liberalization of capital inflows, particularly aimed at the reconfiguration of urban space through new housing and tourist developments and other construction projects. Much of this has targeted Shiʿa-majority areas in Greater Beirut and the South of Lebanon under Hezbollah control. These construction activities have been supported through parallel state funding, which has leveraged a growing volume of investments from the Lebanese Shiʿa diaspora living in Africa and North and South America (Nasr 2003: 155). The emerging Shiʿa fraction of the bourgeoisie has converged around these capital flows, utilizing them as a means of deepening their accumulation opportunities.

As part of the initial rise of Amal documented in Chapter 2, Nabih Berri played an instrumental role through the post-Civil War period in supporting this process. Fawwaz Traboulsi describes his role succinctly:

Berri needed the post (Speaker of Parliament) to become a focus for economic interests, especially the real estate, banking, trade and other concerns of Shiʿa diaspora in Africa and the Gulf. During the Civil War, Berri had formed what was termed "the Shiʿa Holding Company," and when fighting forced the closure of Beirut's commercial center and economic activity had become divided between Jounieh and Kaslik in East Beirut and Hamra and Verdun streets in the West, Berri came to oversee a new real estate zone in Ain el-Tineh and Verdun that constituted the second biggest arena for African investment after that of Mazraa. Following the 1975–89 Civil War he oversaw Intra Invest Company (IIC) and the Finance Bank through its chairman Hassan Farran, as well as infrastructure developments projects in the South.

(Traboulsi 2014: 71)

One indication of the presence of this growing Shiʿa fraction of the bourgeoisie is its increased representation in the main business associations. As Baroudi (2000: 92) has noted, the number of members representing the Shiʿa fraction of the bourgeoisie never held more than two out of twenty-four seats in the *Jamʿiyyat Tujar Beirut* (Beirut Traders Association [BTA]) board prior to the Civil War. This number was to double to four in 1998, following negotiations between Rafiq Hariri and Nabih Berri (the head of Amal) with the Shiʿa members nominated by Shiʿa merchants in consultation with the Shiʿa dominated *Tajamu' al-Iqtisādiyyin al-Lubnāniyyin* (the Association of Lebanese Economists) (Baroudi 2000: 92). The number of members of the Shiʿa fraction of the bourgeoisie on the BTA has remained at this level until today (Beirut Traders Association 2014).

In the Chamber of Commerce, Industry and Agriculture of Beirut and Mount Lebanon, the representation of the Shiʿa fraction of the bourgeoisie on the Board of Directors increased from 11 percent before the Civil War, to 21 percent after the Civil War (Baroudi 2000: 96). Muslim members of the Board were now equally divided between Sunni and Shiʿa. In the Association of Lebanese Industrialists, there is now parity on the board between Muslim and Christian, while in 1975 it was composed of two-thirds Christian and one-third Muslim (Baroudi 2000: 96).[13] The representation of the Shi'a fraction of the bourgeoisie has now reached five members, up from two in 1988 and none before 1975 (Association of Lebanese Industrialists 2014).

The only business association where this shift is not found is the Association of Lebanese Banks, which was formed in 1959 and has held a large Christian majority on its Board of Directors until the 1990s, reflecting the domination of Christians over the banking sector in the country. After the Ta'if Agreement, representation on the Board was distributed equally between Christians and Muslims. Four Sunni nevertheless dominate the representatives for the Muslim community, whereas there is only one Shi'a and one Druze (Baroudi 2000: 98). In 2014, the only Shi'a representative was Tanal Sabah, President of the Lebanese Swiss Bank (Association of Banks in Lebanon 2014b). The weakness of Shi'a representation indicates the particular character of class formation in the Shi'a community (for further details, see below), specifically their absence in commercial banking; only four banks are controlled by Shi'a: the Lebanese Swiss Bank, owned by Tanal Sabah; Middle East and African Bank (MEAB), owned by the Hejeij family; the Fenicia Bank, owned by the Achour Group; and the Jammal Trust Bank (JTB) owned by Anwar Ali Jammal.

A more micro-level analysis confirms these trends. The Appendix provides an overview of some of the key Shi'a-owned companies and individuals that constitute an important segment of this bourgeoisie. The groups listed have been identified by their representation on the industry councils noted above, as well as through discussions with business analysts and individuals in Lebanon. The data indicates three salient characteristics: First, these business groups are clustered around two main economic activities: construction/real estate activities and the import/export trade. One example of this is the Shar Metal Company (SMC), which is owned by the Shahrour family. SMC is the largest ferrous and non-ferrous scrap metal exporter and processor in the Middle East, and is thus a good example of how trade liberalization has helped to underpin the development of Shi'a trading activities. SMC's CEO, Fadi Ali Shahrour, has strongly supported neoliberal reform in Lebanon in his position as vice-president of the BTA since 1998 and is also close to Nabih Berri.[14] The Shahrour family has important investments in multiple sectors of the Lebanese economy including trade, industry and real estate (March 14, 2010; Shar Metal Company 2013; Metal Bulletin Company Database 2013). In the real estate sector, the Jaber Group provides an illustrative example of an important Shi'a-controlled conglomerate. The Group has built numerous luxury apartment buildings in downtown Beirut and also operates three major hotel chains. In addition to its real estate development activities, Jaber produces and exports LPG gas cylinders (Jaber Group 2013). A member of the Jaber family, Yassin Jaber, was Minister of the Economy and Foreign Trade between May 1995 and November 1998. In this position, he supported the Hariri government's liberalization of trade (Baroudi 2001: 89).

Another important characteristic of these new Shi'a-based conglomerates is their international connections. While these groups are largely based in the core areas of Hezbollah's influence—Dahyeh, the Bekaa Valley and the South of Lebanon—they also have very strong links with Shi'a communities in the diaspora (particularly Africa). Pearlman describes this phenomenon well:

A long history of migration linked South Lebanon to Africa, where developing economies, minimal competition, and scant regulation enabled entrepreneurial migrants to make great profits with little formal education. Observers noted that, given these dimensions of African countries as destinations, émigrés maintained close ties and returned to Lebanon more than migrants to Europe or the Americas. Some returned to become a "nouveau riche" in the South, where they bought land and built commercial enterprises [...] Émigrés invested capital in banks, industries, real estate, and other business ventures. In some towns and villages neglected by the state, returned migrants assumed leadership over socioeconomic development.

(Pearlman 2013: 117)

These links with the Shi'a diaspora have provided important opportunities for the community's emerging bourgeoisie. Indeed, the exceptions just noted for Shi'a involvement in the financial sector arose largely as a result of these diaspora links. Both the JTB and the MEAB were initially based in Africa, where prosperous Shi'a businesspeople opened banks to provide services to expatriate communities, and also financed trade to Lebanon itself.

The former owner of the MEAB bank, Kassem Hejeij, was the target of US Department of the Treasury sanctions under the allegations of "supporting Hezbollah's Financial Operations and Terrorist Activities" in June 2015. Hejeij was accused of maintaining:

> direct ties to Hezbollah organizational elements. In addition to his support to Adham Tabaja [see below, Hezbollah member and CEO of Inmaa Group] and his affiliated companies in Iraq, Hejeij has helped open bank accounts for Hezbollah in Lebanon and provided credit to Hezbollah procurement companies. Hejeij has also invested in infrastructure that Hezbollah uses in both Lebanon and Iraq."
>
> (US Department of the Treasury: 2015b)

Hejeij was sanctioned as an individual but the bank was not mentioned. He nevertheless resigned from his position, despite denying the accusations, and his son Ali Hejeij has become the new chairman of the bank since then.

These three characteristics of the emerging Shiʿa fraction of the bourgeoisie—an emphasis on real estate and trade, a relative weakness in the financial sector and linkages with Shiʿa diaspora populations—have been further accentuated by economic policies supported by the Hezbollah in its areas of influence. The majority of the companies listed in the Appendix, for example, have their headquarters in the Hezbollah-controlled municipalities such as Ghobeyri. In these areas, they have benefited from the types of neoliberal urban redevelopment models discussed in Chapter 2. Moreover, the Hezbollah's ministerial representatives have promoted economic policies, particularly concerning trade, that have facilitated the activities of Shiʿa-controlled conglomerates—most recently in 2014 when the Hezbollah Minister Hussein Hajj Hassan was the main actor pushing for an eventually successful 50 percent decrease in export tax (NNA 2014a). Through policies such as these, Hezbollah has facilitated the accumulation of opportunities for the Shiʿa conglomerates discussed here. Moreover, the Hezbollah has increasingly emphasized the strengthening of links with the Shiʿa diaspora, especially in Africa, where it now provides loans for young entrepreneurs to establish businesses (Leichtman 2010: 281).

While the main levers of Lebanon's economy remain under the control of conglomerates of the Sunni and Christian fractions of the bourgeoisie, the emerging Shiʿa economic fraction is a striking development that has paralleled the rise of the Hezbollah as a political force.

Hezbollah's Own Economic Development

In addition to these privately owned Shiʿa conglomerates, another significant feature of business activity in Lebanon is the increasing prominence of companies under Hezbollah's direct influence. Already in the beginning of the 1990s, Mona Harb el-Kak (1996) had noticed that the associations and organizations linked to the Hezbollah often dealt with private architectural offices and companies whose officials were sympathizers of the Islamic movement. The Lebanese scholar, Fawwaz Traboulsi (2014: 48), argued that a major base of the party's social support rests upon Shiʿa businesspeople who profited from the Civil War or commercial activities in the diaspora, as well as the upper middle classes linked to new education and migration opportunities.

As with the conglomerates listed in the Appendix, these companies have tended to focus upon construction and real estate, as well as tourism and recreational activities aimed at a growing Shiʿa fraction of the middle class.[15] In many cases, these companies have been involved in real estate development targeting prosperous Shiʿa migrants as far afield as Michigan or Australia (Beydoun 1989 cited in Pearlman 2013: 123). South Lebanon, in particular, has experienced a booming real estate market that a report described as "village after village [of] palatial-looking villas," despite the fact that "many of them [were] empty" (Integrated Regional Information Networks [IRIN] 2013). Most of these villas were built by Lebanese in the diaspora as monuments to their successes abroad (Pearlman 2013: 123). Hezbollah is well aware of the economic power of the growing Shiʿa fraction of the middle class as is demonstrated by the following words of a prominent Hezbollah member interviewed by M. Harb and L. Deeb: "We are a big powerful consumer movement that attracts big investors" (Deeb and Harb 2013: 55).

There are four companies under the Hezbollah's direct influence that provide an excellent illustration of these trends. The first of these is Tajco, a real estate development company owned by the Shiʿa businessman Ali Tajjedine. The Tajjedine family has operated real estate, diamond export, supermarket and food processing businesses across Angola, Gambia, Sierra Leone and the Congo for many years.[16] Ali Tajjedine is a former

Hezbollah military commander who worked in trade and real estate in these countries before becoming owner of Tajco (Traboulsi 2014: 90). One of the main missions of Tajco is to act as an intermediary for Hezbollah to purchase lands and it is also involved in construction and civil engineering works.[17] In 2007, Tajco purchased a 2.2 million-square-meter farm near the villages of Rayhan and Al-Qatraneh close to the city of Jezzine (Farrel 2012), which will welcome a new community called Ahmadiyeh with houses and shops surrounding a stone quarry owned by Tajjedine (Blanford 2007a). The current Minister of Industry and Hezbollah member Hussein Hajj Hassan declared at the time that this would accommodate the "natural growth" of Lebanon's Shi'a population and buttress "resistance" against Israel (Williams 2007). Tajjedine has also bought lands in Dalhamiyeh, in the Bekaa Valley, with the goal of launching further residential projects (Farrel 2012).

A second large construction company linked to the Hezbollah is the Al-Inmaa group, which has been involved in the construction of numerous Hezbollah projects and one of the partners of the company is Amin Chirri, who was the Hezbollah's MP in parliament between 2005 and 2009 (Deeb and Harb 2013: 71). Inmaa defines itself as an "Engineering & Construction company and a leading investment group in Lebanon" (Al-Inmaa Engineering and Contracting 2013a), which has more than 1,200 employees spread across different branches. Its projects are concentrated in Shi'a-populated regions, especially in Dahyeh (notably Bir Hassan, Haret Hreik, Shiah) and South Lebanon. The company's subsidiaries include Al-Inmaa Engineering and Contracting, which operates in Lebanon and Iraq, as well as Lebanon-based Al-Inmaa for Entertainment and Leisure Projects. Lara Deeb and Mona Harb (2013: 88) explain that the company started its activities in the beginning of the 1990s building relatively affordable housing complexes in Dahyeh and then progressively began catering to more affluent customers, with middle- and high-end buildings in Dahyeh's neighborhoods.

The close linkages between Al-Inmaa and Hezbollah's political structures is confirmed by its CEO, Adham Tababja (Janoubia 2012), who is also the Mayor of the Kafr Tabnit municipality and is affiliated to the Hezbollah (Bint Jbeil 2010; Nejm 2010). He has been the target of sanctions from the US Department of the Treasury for his links with Hezbollah (US Department of the Treasury 2015b). Moreover, Tababja is Vice-President of the Al-Ahed football club (Al-Akhbar 2011), which is sponsored by the Hezbollah (Daher 2014: 170), and a shareholder of the Lebanese Media Group, Hezbollah's parent company for Al-Manar Television and Al-Nour Radio (for more description of these media groups, see Chapter 4) (Wikileaks 2009). The director of the Al-Inmaa group in South Lebanon is Ali Tababja, who is also the President of the Employers Association of Restaurants, Parks and Tourism Companies in the South (Al-Ainin 2008), and the Vice-President of the Lebanese Federation of Tourism unions (Ittihād al-Wafā': 2012). Mona Harb and Lara Deeb (2013: 88) also state that kinship relations with Hezbollah members have facilitated the company's contracting work and growth over the years.

The scale of Inmaa's construction activities and its linkages with the reworking of urban space in Hezbollah-controlled areas can be seen in the company's project portfolio. In Dahyeh, the group built an amusement park (Fantasy-World), which includes restaurants and coffee shops targeting a pious clientele. The Hezbollah Mayor of Ghobeyri participated in the planning and facilitated the legal processes necessary for the project's implementation (Deeb and Harb 2009: 199). Inmaa has also built restaurants and amusements centers in the Bir Abed neighborhood (Family House), Saida (World of Joy), Tyr (City of Joy), Hadath (New Land), Baalbek (Restaurant al-Rawabi), Bint Jbeil (Family Park) and Nabatieh (Joy) (Al-Ainin 2008). These projects include gyms, pools, saunas and massage rooms (Deeb and Harb 2008). In the city of Taybe in Baalbek, Inmaa has built a summer tourist resort aimed at attracting religious families on vacation (Le Thomas 2012b: 290). It has also built the Hezbollah-controlled al-Mehdi school in Hadath (Al-Inmaa Engineering and Contracting 2013b), the Hezbollah radio building (Radio Nour) in Haret Hreik (Al-Inmaa Engineering and Contracting 2013c) and a number of residential buildings. In recent years, Inmaa has been involved in operating international projects, including the Maxime Restaurant in Dubai (Al-Inmaa Engineering and Contracting 2013d) and in oil and construction development projects in Iraq through the Iraqi branches of Al-Inmaa Engineering and Contracting (US Department of Treasury 2015b).

Another important Hezbollah-linked company is Meamar Engineering and Development, which was founded in 1988 (Meamar 2014). Since that time, Meamar has been involved in more than 150 projects including: sporting facilities, Shi'a religious institutions, schools and hospitals. For these projects, Meamar's clients are almost exclusively organizations linked to Hezbollah, such as the Islamic Health Society, the Iranian Committee for the Reconstruction of Lebanon (ICRL), the Mehdi Scouts, the Shahid Association, the Islamic Religious Education Association (IREA) and municipalities controlled by Hezbollah Mayors (such as Ghobeyri and Bint Jbeil). At the celebration of the company's 25th anniversary, many Hezbollah members were present including Muhammad Raad, head of the Hezbollah Deputy bloc in parliament, Muhammad Fneich, Minister of Administrative Development, and the two Deputies Ali Fayyad and Ali Mekdad (Meamar 2014).[18] The event was prominently covered on Hezbollah's Al-Manar TV (2014) and in the party's magazine (Al-Amal al-Baladi 2013: 42).

The final enterprise linked to the party is the Arch Consulting Company, which was previously part of Jihad al-Bina (Hezbollah's construction organization) but became an independent company in 2005 (Nasr 2011). Arch is registered under the name of Walid Ali Jaber (Arch 2014), who was a Hezbollah-supported candidate in the Burj al-Barajneh's municipal elections in 2004 (Al-Ahed News 2004). As with Meamar, Arch has built hospitals, schools and religious institutions in the Hezbollah-controlled areas in Beirut, South Lebanon and the Bekaa (Arch 2014).[19] It is also involved in tourism, infrastructure, and hydraulic projects. Internationally, Arch company built the Abidjan Islamic Cultural Centre in the Ivory Coast managed by al-Ghadir Association (Arch 2014), a Shi'a religious association established by a supporter of Hezbollah (Mieu 2009; Pompey 2009).

These companies offer important insights into the nature of the Hezbollah's economic activities. Each of them is privately owned and operated, and thus help to enrich a narrow layer of the Shi'a community who control them. At the same time, they are very closely linked to the party itself; all four companies are headed by Hezbollah members and supporters, including electoral candidates for the party. Their projects are largely based in the Hezbollah-controlled areas with clients mostly drawn from Hezbollah's educational, media and schooling institutions. Hezbollah officials frequently praise these institutions in publicly organized celebrations.[20] Indeed, the close links between the Hezbollah and these companies have led to public concerns being expressed around clientelism and patronage stemming from the party's position in the state apparatus.[21] The explicit and open nature of their relationship with the party is one further indication of the network of private sector institutions that have arisen around construction and real estate activities in Shi'a-populated areas, and points to the emergence of a bourgeoisie linked to the Hezbollah.

The investments in the construction and real estate sectors of Hezbollah-affiliated companies or under its influence in Lebanon corresponds and reflects the nature of an adventurous, speculative and commercial capitalism that dominates the region, which is characterized by short-term profit seeking as explained by Gilbert Achcar (2013a: 102). The construction and real estate sector, which is a successful economic branch in the region, is at the crossroads of land speculation, driven by: (1) the search for shelter investments in real estate; and (2) an economy of commercial and touristic services funded greatly by the regional oil revenues, both by the capital and consumers alike from rentier states.

The Changing Character of Hezbollah's Social Base

The preceding discussion provides confirmation of the expanding social base of the Hezbollah. From its roots in the poor Shi'a populations of Lebanon, the Hezbollah has become a party whose membership and cadres increasingly reflect the growing Shi'a fraction of the middle class and bourgeoisie—especially in Beirut.[22] In the southern suburbs of Beirut, many members of wealthier families and most of the merchants have been integrated into Hezbollah (Abisaab and Abisaab 2014: 133), while the party's activities and institutions (particularly those connected to tourism and leisure) cater to middle-class Shi'a.

This transformation is reflected in the profile of party cadres, who are no longer composed of clerics from a lower middle-class background as at the time of the party's foundation in 1985, but are now largely drawn from a professional class, who hold secular higher education degrees. One illustration of this is the party's increasing weight in professional associations (Qassir 2011). The Order of Engineers and Architects, for example, has been dominated by the Hezbollah since 2008 when the party won the most votes in the association's elections (Bou Dagher 2008). The Hezbollah estimated that at least 1,300 engineers were members of the party in 2006 (Al-Akhbar 2006). The high numbers of engineers in the Hezbollah is linked to the reconstruction of the South and Dahyeh following the various wars, especially after the end of the

Civil War and the 2006 Lebanon War and the development of the real estate projects in these regions.

In the Medical Doctors Association, the Hezbollah was represented on the winning list in the 2013 elections (Shibani 2013). Likewise, in the Lebanese Dentist Association, the Vice-President, Muhammad Kataya, is supported by the Hezbollah (Now Media 2011; Lebanese Dentist Association 2014). In the Lebanese Pharmacist Order, which has 7,000 registered members (El-Shark Online 2012), a Hezbollah representative narrowly missed out from winning leadership of the union in the 2012 elections—losing by only 131 votes to a Future Movement-backed candidate (Hamdan 2012). The only exception to this trend is the Lawyer's Association, where despite expanding numbers and an increasing challenge to the Amal lawyers, Hezbollah has not managed to become dominant over these latters (Mortada 2010).[23]

Similarly, Hezbollah's political leaders are typically drawn from well-educated and wealthy layers of the Shi'a community. In the national elections of 2009, for example, five of the ten elected Hezbollah deputies held doctoral degrees and at least four others were involved in prominent Lebanese businesses.[24] The longest serving Hezbollah Deputy, Ali Ammar, comes from one of the wealthiest families in Burj al-Barajneh (Karim 1998: 211).[25] At the municipal level, these patterns are repeated, with the Hezbollah electoral candidates selected from powerful Shi'a families such as Al-Khansa, Kazma, Kanj, Kumati, Farhat, Rahhal and Slim (Harb 2010).

Even at the supporter and sympathizer levels these same trends can be noted. Today, heterogeneous layers of society perceive the Hezbollah in different ways. Judith Palmer Harik (1996: 55), a professor at the American University of Beirut (AUB), has examined this social diversity of Hezbollah support. She found that beginning in the mid-1990s, supporters of the party could be found throughout all social classes, and were no longer largely restricted to the poorer, pious layers of the Shi'a population. This trajectory continued through the 2000s, as indicated by the party's very high results in the 2009 legislative elections from areas that were not traditionally poorer Shi'a communities, such as Nabatieh and Jbeil.[26] In an interview for this book, Abd al-Halim Fadlallah (2012b) also confirmed that a large number of youth from the middle and higher classes of the Shi'a population now support (or have joined) the party—including tribal elites in the Bekaa Valley who were traditionally opposed to Hezbollah.

In its educational network, the changing characteristics of Hezbollah's social base is indicated by the very high tuition fees required to attend its al-Mustapha schools under the control of the Hezbollah leader Naim Qassem. According to Catherine Le Thomas (2012a: 179), these schools are aimed at the children of the party's leadership, as well as upper- and middle-class fraction of the Shi'a population. The al-Bathoul school, a girls' school that forms part of the al-Mustapha network, has annual fees of around $1,600, an amount that is unaffordable for the majority of Lebanese (Le Thomas 2012a: 179). Le Thomas concludes that:

> the al-Mustapha network of schools, which can be considered as being part of the upper middle class category of Hezbollah schools, provide a service to the wealthy Shi'a class and spread the political ideology of the party under Naim Qassem's supervision.
>
> (Le Thomas 2012a: 142–43)

In addition to this, other Hezbollah institutions are oriented towards wealthier layers of the Shi'a population. One example is the hospital Rassoul al-Aazam, which provides VIP and "Super Suites" rooms for patients (Al-Rassoul al-Aazam 2014).

Another element pointing to the growing integration and linkage between Hezbollah and Lebanese Shi'a capitalists is the number of businessmen being the targets of sanctions by the US Department of the Treasury for their links with the party: Kassem Hejeij, former CEO of MEAB; Ali Tajjedine, CEO of Tajco company; Adham Tabaja, CEO of Inmaa Group; Husayn Ali Faour, one of the owners of Car Care Center based in Dahyeh; Ali Youssef Charara, Chairman and General Manager Spectrum Investment Group Holding SAL (US Department of the Treasury 2016);[27] Mustapha Fawaz and Fouzi Fawaz based in Nigeria,[28] majority shareholders (70 percent) of Amigo Supermarket Limited, and owners of Wonderland Amusement Park and Resort Ltd,[29] and of Holding Kafak Enterprises Limited (US Department of the Treasury 2015a); Abd al-Nur Shalan,[30] Lebanese businessman (US Department of the Treasury 2015b); Kamel Mohamad Amhaz and Issam Mohamad Amhaz, owners of Stars Group Holding (US Department of the Treasury 2014),[31] etc...[32]

These characteristics of Hezbollah's political representation and social base indicate that while the organization continues to draw support from people from all levels of society, its priorities are increasingly oriented to the highest strata. The Hezbollah MP, Ali Fayyad, acknowledged this trend in 2010, when he remarked that:

> Hezbollah is not a small party anymore, it's a whole society. It is the party of the poor people, yes, but at the same time there are a lot of businessmen in the party, we have a lot of rich people, some from the elite class.

> (Hersh 2010)

The Hezbollah leader, Hassan Nasrallah, also provided indirect confirmation of these trends in a September 2009 speech, in which he urged members to quit the "love of luxury," and called on them to adopt belief in God simply because of "fear of the end" (Al-Insaniyyah 2009).

This situation was nevertheless still present or at least felt by some sections of the population in Dahyeh as shown in an interview in the beginning of 2016 by Lebanese journalist Hanin Ghaddar of an 18-year-old ex-Hezbollah fighter, who served as a soldier in Syria, was wounded and left the party a few weeks after suffering his injury. He said that stark disparities in Dahyeh in the standards of living are raising serious discontent among people and that:

> most of the young folks in Dahyeh do not have cars or proper access to public transportation, while most Hezbollah officials' sons are driving brand new expensive cars. We see this every day. Their houses, cars, clothes etc [...] are all in our faces every single time we go out.
>
> (Ghaddar 2016)

Conclusion

The post-Civil War period witnessed the growing political and economic importance of the Shi'a population in Lebanon. This chapter has shown that Shi'a dominated regions are no longer the most impoverished in the country (although poverty is still present in these areas), but rather the Sunni-populated regions in the North have been the worst affected by the deepening of neoliberalism. In Dahyeh, South Lebanon and the Bekaa Valley, an emerging Shiʿa fraction of the bourgeoisie grew in conjunction with the opportunities presented by neoliberal reform and the reconstruction funds that followed in the wake of 2006. This was indicated by an expanding presence of the Shiʿa fraction of the bourgeoisie in various business associations.

The Hezbollah, as the most important representative of the Shiʿa population in Lebanon, was influenced by these socio-economic transformations in three respects. First, by the development and increasing presence of cadres coming from more privileged backgrounds and educated in secular universities, in contrast to the situation prevailing when the party was founded by religious clerics and people from a lower socio-economic background. Second, the party has formed close connections with the wealthier layers of the Shiʿa population and elite families, indicated through its political alliances in elections in places such as Dahyeh. Third, the Hezbollah has itself become an important economic actor in Lebanon, with multiple business interests that provided employment to thousands of people in addition to its network of organizations.

The analysis of the context and the changes in the Lebanese economic and social structures are key elements to an understanding of the Hezbollah's behavior and policies. They indicate that the party itself has undergone a profound transformation from an organization firmly rooted in poorer Shiʿa areas to one that increasingly represents the interests of a wealthier Shiʿa constituency and that competes with Amal to best serve the interests of the Shiʿa fraction of the bourgeoisie. There is indeed an increased competition between Amal and the Hezbollah to attract the wealthiest sectors of the Shiʿa fraction of the bourgeoisie and best represent its interests in Lebanon.

4

Hezbollah and Shi'a Civil Society

Hezbollah has managed to achieve a position of hegemony among Lebanon's Shi'a population through a balanced combination of consent and coercion, based on the one hand through its provision of much needed services to large sections of the Shi'a popular sector, and, on the other, through repressive measures directed against those who step outside the norms established by the party.

These intertwined factors of consent and coercion are facilitated through Hezbollah's wide-ranging network of organizations, which has helped it to disseminate its ideas and to deepen its support base within the Shi'a population. The Hezbollah's parliamentary Deputy, Dr. Ali Fayyad, has claimed that: "the organisations of Hezbollah were established to build a solid relation between the party and its public; they are one of the essential elements in its strategy of mobilisation" (1998 cited in Harb 2010: 97).

Hezbollah's organizations can be seen as part of what Gramsci described as the "multi-layered associations and voluntary groups" that constitute civil society: associations, educational and religious institutions, the media, and so forth (Fontana 2008: 93). These institutions constitute a "hegemonic apparatus [...] a complex set of institutions, ideologies, practices and agents (including the 'intellectuals')" (Thomas 2009: 225), through which the Hezbollah has engaged its opponents in the struggle for political power by intervening in civil society. As Peter Thomas has noted, the struggle for political power depends not simply on "the ability of a class's initiative in political society," but is also related to whether it can:

relate adequately to its "social basis" in civil society [...] Political power is immanent to the hegemonic projects by means of which classes constitutes themselves as classes (relations within classes)

93

capable of exercising political power (as opposed to an incoherent mass of corporative interest confined to the terrain of civil society).

(Thomas 2009: 226–27)

The Hezbollah's institutional network also deserves a Gramscian description of "hegemonic apparatus" because it operates to a very pronounced degree as a coherent interlocked whole. There is significant rotation of leadership among the institutions, which also provide employment to the cadres and popular base of the party.[1] This network means that individual institutions reinforce each other's activities— the construction wing of the party Jihad al-Bina (see below) builds the organization's schools, while the Hezbollah religious centers and institutions provide them with books and instructors. The party's media wing publicizes the organization's reconstruction activities and religious message. Its research unit helps to plan social interventions and provides employment for graduates from its educational institutions. In this manner, the Hezbollah's institutions represent a unified and coherent intervention into Lebanese civil society.

One striking aspect of this coherence is the ideological framework propagated through the organization's network of civil society institutions. The principal element of this framework is the ongoing and deepening Islamization of the Shiʿa population, which has been vital to strengthening the Hezbollah's hegemony. The Hezbollah's socialization structures have been primarily aimed at strengthening the religiosity of its social environment, thereby fostering an adherence of the community to the organization as the embodiment of Islamic values (understood, as discussed below, through a particularly distinctive variant of Islam). Islamization has been both promoted by Hezbollah organizations, while, simultaneously employed as a means of disciplining elements of the Shiʿa population that have resisted this process. It is through these twin elements of consent and coercion, mediated through the vehicle of Islamization, that the Hezbollah has developed its hegemonic position amongst Lebanese Shiʿa.

Hezbollah's Structure and Relationship to Civil Society

An important facet to understanding Hezbollah's intervention in civil society, and the Shiʿa population more generally, is the organization's internal structure. This structure is defined by an extreme centralization and concern with hierarchy and discipline (ICG 2003: 2), features that enable the ideological and political orientation of the party to be consciously and systematically transmitted to its wider social environment. This structure is also marked by the predominance of religious clerics in its upper leadership, further confirmation of the significance that specific religio-ideological conceptions have on the organization's political practice (Hamzeh 1993: 325).

The highest decision-making body of the party is the "Decision Making Consultative Council" (*Majlis Shura al-Qarār*) known as the Shura, which is composed of seven members: the Secretary General Hassan Nasrallah, the Vice-Secretary Naim Qassem, and five other cadres. In the Shura, decisions are usually reached by consensus and only occasionally through a formal vote. Resulting directives are binding on the movement's constituent bodies (ICG 2003: 2). The Shura is elected every three years, not by the party rank-and-file members, but by the General Convention (*al-Mu'tamar al-'ām*), which gathers according to different sources between 200–250 high cadres, and includes heads of various sections, geographical regions and units of work (Daher 2014: 195). The last General Convention was held in 2008–2009, with the 2012 meeting postponed due to the conflict in Syria (Al-Monitor 2013). In addition to electing the Shura, the General Convention discusses general policies of the party regarding the party's daily operations in Lebanon, and its relations with Shi'a constituencies and other Lebanese political forces.

The Shura forms the main core of the party's strategic intervention in civil society and its wider political orientation. This role is carried out through five councils, each headed by one of the Shura members, who are joined by other key cadres. Daher (2014) describes these councils as follows:

- The Executive Council (EC), composed of twelve members. The EC defines the public action of the party together with its foreign policy. The members of the EC are generally regional party leaders and/or members in charge of specific sectoral policies (media, health, social, education and so forth).
- The Political Council (PC), which is in charge of communication and coordination with the other Lebanese political and

social actors. The PC analyses the general political situation and provides analysis and recommendations to the Shura. In addition to conjunctural political debates, the PC administers permanent "files" on subjects such as relationships with Christian and Islamic parties, Palestinian factions and Arab countries.

- The Jihad Council (JC), which runs the military resistance and the security apparatus of the party. The JC is responsible for the security of the members of the resistance and its arms, notably through the surveillance of alleged collaborators.
- The Judicial Council (JudC), which brings together different clerics from the various regions of Lebanon and passes rulings on aspects of religious law.
- The Parliamentary Work Council (PWC), which gathers Hezbollah members of parliament to coordinate their political interventions and the communication of decisions. A sub-council was added to this in 2005, the Government Work Council, which includes consultants specialised in certain sectors.

(Daher 2014: 193–95)

In turn, these councils oversee a further tier of committees that involve other party cadres tasked with implementing selected policies. In addition to these councils and committees, two new organizations were established in 2004: (1) the CCSD (Consultative Center for Studies and Documentation), the Hezbollah-affiliated think-tank based in Beirut, responsible for social, development and economic research and programs; and (2) the Federation of Hezbollah Municipalities, an organization that links together the Hezbollah municipalities in order to strengthen coordination between them (Harb 2010: 88).[2]

These nationwide structures are complemented at the regional level by district councils, called the Regional Shura Councils, which are supervised by members of the Shura. Their main responsibility is to follow up on the daily activities and needs of the district (Hamzeh 1993: 327). In each district, Hezbollah members are organized in groups (*majmu'āt*) of between 30–35 people, based in individual neighbor-hoods. These groups coordinate through factions (*fasā'il*), networks of 4–5 groups that represent a small city or set of villages and report to the Regional Shura Council (Daher 2014: 191).

At the same time the ideology of the *Wilāyat al-Faqīh* plays an important role in the internal coherence and discipline of the party. Membership in the Islamic movement is conditional on allegiance to the *Wilāyat al-Faqīh* and respect for the implementation of its decision among the leadership and its cadres (Daher 2014: 216).

The picture that emerges from this structure is of a tightly organized and highly hierarchical party, which clearly transmits decisions and their implementation from the top to the individual member. In an interview conducted for this book Abd al-Halim Fadlallah (2012a), the Director of CCSD, confirmed this conclusion. He described the party as a pyramidal organization in which debate is limited to the highest ranks of the party. Decisions are communicated to members through the official structures described above, and cadres are also responsible for meeting with sympathizers in order to explain the official positions of the party (Fadlallah 2012b).

This pyramidal structure—organized at its core by the Shura—is thus the sole origin of the party's policy and strategic orientation towards the wider Shi'a population. This orientation, however, is mediated through a range of civil society activities that enable the party to interface with supporters and non-members. The most important of these activities: social support, religious institutions, media/cultural activities and education/youth work are discussed in the following section.

Social Support Activities of Hezbollah

A vital element in Hezbollah's support among the Shi'a population has been its attempts to support the civil population following conflict and war, demonstrated, most notably, in the aftermath of the 2006 Lebanon War with Israel (Alagha and Catusse 2008). The direct beneficiaries of the party's resources and services, including employees and members in Beirut alone, are estimated to reach up to 40,000 people, according to some sources (Harb 2010: 91; Traboulsi 2014: 80).[3] Others have estimated the figure to be between 60,000 and 80,000, when factoring in the security and military apparatus (Nakhoul 2013).[4] In addition to this, the party offers a range of social support to a wider layer of non-members and supporters in the Shi'a population. The Imdad organization for example, established in 1987, provides health care, education and recreation services, support for orphans, emergency relief, income-generating programs and a small amount of financial aid for impoverished families (Al-Imdad 2014).

This support includes direct financial aid through the organization's "good loan institution" (*mu'assasa Al-Qard al-Hassan*), which was established in 1982 and distributes loans without interest according to Islamic religious law (Alagha and Catusse 2008). This institution has twenty-three branches and around 300 employees distributed between Beirut, the Bekaa and the South (Al-Qard al-Hassan Association 2014c). According to its website, *Al-Qard al-Hassan* has lent more than $245 million since 1983, in a total of over 700,000 loans, including 110,000 in 2013 alone (Al-Qard al-Hassan Association 2014b). These loans are funded through donations, religious taxes, administrative fees and subscriptions to the institution (Al-Qard al-Hassan Association 2014b). In 2012, the association had 150,000 subscribers who benefited from preferential loans in exchange for paying a monthly subscription of L£10,000 ($6.66), and 35,000 people who contribute to the organization (Al-Qard al-Hassan Association 2014b).[5]

Much of the Hezbollah's financial support aims at the provision of welfare to the most vulnerable and poor Shi'a populations. The researcher Melani Cammett (2014: 16) shows that Hezbollah charities are mostly located in low-income areas. More than half of Hezbollah's institutions are today located in communities that are more than 98 per cent Shi'a, while the party is generally less eager to establish agencies in mixed areas (Cammett 2014: 105).

An interesting means by which Hezbollah provides its welfare support is "discount cards," which can be purchased for a small fee and then entitle the holder to significant price reductions in Hezbollah-affiliated shops and community services. The card, al-Amir, for example, is distributed by the association "La Famille,"[6] whose general director is Imad Wehbe, a graduate of Hezbollah's Mahdi school.[7] The card costs $1, and provides discounts of up to 50 percent in a wide range of institutions such as "cooperatives, clothing shops, libraries, medical centers, sport centers, furniture house, electronic and electricity shops, and recreational centers, (including restaurants and coffee houses)" (Anon 2012a; Hassan 2014; La Famille 2014). In this manner, the Hezbollah not only reduces daily living costs for Shi'a families, but also provides support to local businesses (often Hezbollah-affiliated).[8] The card was first launched in Dahyeh in 2004–2005, and has now expanded to the South and the

Bekaa, with around 75,000 people using the card by 2014 (Hassan 2014). Moreover, Hezbollah also distributes these cards as gifts to Shi'a families who regularly attend the organization's cultural events, as well as military training (Now Media 2008b). A 2014 ceremony for the card was held under the auspices of the Hezbollah Minister of Industry Hussein Hajj Hassan (Al-Ahed News 2014).

Other kinds of discount cards are only available to Hezbollah members. One example of this is the al-Nour card, which can be obtained by members for a L£20,000 ($13) monthly subscription. According to a wife of a Hezbollah member interviewed for this book, the al-Nour card allows its holders to benefit from price reductions in various Hezbollah-affiliated shops and warehouses, furniture shops, entertainment locations, kindergartens, restaurants throughout the country and organized hajj pilgrimages (Anon 2012a; Shams el-Din 2012; El-Cheikh and Saghyieh 2013a).

Alongside these welfare activities and financial support to poorer Shi'a populations, perhaps the most striking example of the social support offered by the Hezbollah has been its building efforts within Shi'a areas, particularly following the destruction of 2006. The implementing body for these building projects was the aforementioned Jihad al-Bina foundation, which was created in 1985 to assume responsibility for reconstruction during and after the Civil War (Hamzeh 2004: 50–51). Between 1988 and 2002, Jihad al-Bina led the construction of seventy-eight buildings and the rehabilitation of another 10,528 structures (including homes, schools, shops, hospitals, infirmaries, mosques, cultural centers and agricultural cooperatives), most of them in South Lebanon (Hamzeh 2004: 50–51). Jihad al-Bina relies on financial assistance from its Iranian sister organization as well as from Islamic charitable sources. In addition to reconstruction, the organization also helps provide water and electricity to Shi'a populations where the state is weak or absent. From 1988 to 2012, the Foundation distributed 8,095,055 barrels of water to 113 reservoirs in all regions of the southern suburbs, drawing periodically from a reservoir in Burj Abi Haidar (Jihad al-Bina Development Association 2013).

A few days following the 2006 Lebanon War, Hezbollah distributed millions of dollars in cash for building purposes to thousands of families, a process described by Jihad al-Bina as follows:

the housing compensations were paid according to the initial surveys of demolished buildings, which Jihad al-Bina was capable of accomplishing in an unprecedentedly short period of time. Compensation was settled without any complications to $12,000 in Beirut (representing $4,000 for rent allowance for the year, and $8,000 for the furniture), $10,000 in the South ($2,000 for rent allowance for the year and $8,000 for furniture). They settled the documents essential to identify the individuals and their demolished buildings, and in one month, compensations were paid to more than 12,000 individuals.

(Jihad al-Binā᾽ Ma'an nabnī wa nuqāwim 2014)

The party's Executive Council was in charge of this distribution, which took place in offices situated in schools and other buildings throughout the bombed neighborhoods of the southern suburbs, South Lebanon and the Bekaa. Hundreds of volunteers helped expedite the process, covering 75 percent of the requests in forty-eight hours (Harb 2007: 229).

Most of this activity focused on reconstruction of the Dahyeh neighborhood, the principal urban base of the organization. To this end, Jihad al-Bina established the project "Wa'd" (Promise), which specifically targeted building in Dahyeh. According to the CCSD (2008b: 67), Wa'd arose following numerous meetings between the residents of Dahyeh, whose homes had been destroyed during the war, and Hezbollah cadres, in which 80 percent of the residents of destroyed homes decided to entrust Hezbollah and its teams of engineers with the reconstruction of the zone. The Hezbollah leader Hassan Nasrallah explained how the process occurred in a speech on May 11, 2012 to commemorate the conclusion of Wa'd:

I met with the people—the owners of the residential units—[…] following the war. I presented to the people the decision as it is. There is no possibility that the state rebuild your houses. It will pay the compensations for the residential units and you have two choices:

The first choice is that residents of every building form a committee and agree among themselves to build the building and we are at your service. We will also help with financing and paying the differences and also improving the building because the money which will be paid by the state is not enough even to reconstruct the building as it was, and as well from building it better than it was. Of course we are at your service and we will not withdraw.

The other choice: we have a project and the institution will be charged on your behalf, by consulting you and cooperating with you, to reconstruct these buildings.

So we were before a democratic project, which is based on dialogue. No one has obliged anyone to do anything. No one imposed anything on anyone.

(Al-Manar 2012b)

Nasrallah's account, however, is challenged by Mona Harb, who was a member at the time of the Reconstruction Unit at the AUB (Harb 2007: 229; Fawaz and Harb 2010: 22). The members of this group tried to initiate a public debate on the reconstruction options in the neighborhood of Haret Hreik (in Dahyeh), but their propositions were rejected by the Wa'd team (Fawaz and Harb 2010: 2). Harb and another Beirut-based scholar, Mona Fawaz, have argued that Hezbollah controlled the reconstruction process completely; they involved only selected actors from its own apparatus. They claim that Hezbollah operated outside public institutions and even isolated the Haret Hreik elected local government from its decision-making structures (Fawaz and Harb 2010: 30–31). In this manner, the Hezbollah took responsibility for the reconstruction of Dahyeh and at the same time asserted its domination over this section of the city. The Wa'd project had the advantage of maintaining, and legitimizing, the geographical integrity of the Hezbollah's power base, while reinforcing the party's prestige because it was implemented by the party's development wing. Fawaz and Harb note:

Dahyeh is Hezbollah's capital, the site of its institutional headquarters and of its governing councils. Its location in the city of Beirut gives it tactical weight and significant visibility that is capitalized upon in the party's mobilisation strategies and political decision making. Its reconstruction is thus an opportunity to reassert the party's dominance, especially amid acute life threatening challenges such as those unfolded in summer 2006. In Dahyeh, more than elsewhere, the act of reconstruction was hence an act of defiance and survival for Hezbollah. This largely explains the party's swift mobilization in the process.

(Fawaz and Harb 2010: 21)

The Waʿd project indicates the way in which reconstruction has been utilized by the Hezbollah as a major element in building a popular base of support in key Shiʿa areas. Not only were the residents of Dahyeh supplied with desperately needed housing, but the reconstruction activities provided thousands of jobs in a community that consists of half a million Shiʿa Lebanese. According to Maher al-Hajj and Hassan Said Jashi, respectively spokesperson and director of the Waʿd project, more than 400 engineers and around 15,000 to 20,000 workers as a whole were employed in the Waʿd project (cited in Leroy 2015: 38), while twenty-three contractors and fifty engineering companies were involved in the project, in addition to seven companies supervising the implementation (Yaghi 2012). Moreover, the organization's high profile activities in the area provided it with an enormous propaganda victory in the wake of the war. In this manner, reconstruction represented a potent symbol of the party's claims that it was the principal defender of the rights of the Shiʿa community in Lebanon.

Nonetheless, despite the important social role that Waʿd (and reconstruction in general) has played in Shiʿa areas, it is important to note that the model envisaged by Hezbollah continued to emphasize market-driven and private property-based conceptions of urban space (Fawaz 2014: 922–24). Mona Fawaz has highlighted this feature of Waʿd in Haret Hreik, pointing to the fact that the project was centered upon the assumption that the beneficiaries would be "property owners in the area, those who can produce a substantiated claim for property ownership" (Fawaz 2011: 60). She notes that to view Haret Hreik:

> as only the sum of 200 private individual apartments is nonetheless quite problematic [...] the neighbourhood was also, for example, the centre of economic and educational activities [...] many other dwellers and visitors should be entitled to bring claims and participate in articulating a communal vision for what the neighbourhood was and the potential it has.
>
> (Fawaz 2011: 60)

The residents' desire for an increased and better utilized public space—including "better sidewalks, more open spaces, playgrounds, less [traffic] congestion" (Fawaz 2011: 60)[9]—were ignored in the reconstruction plans, which instead emphasized the interests of retailers and owners of companies and institutions (CCSD 2008b: 131–35). Moreover, in line with the arguments made in the previous two chapters, these reconstruction activities not only helped to consolidate Hezbollah's social base in Dahyeh (Fawaz 2009: 332–34), but also acted to enrich those large construction conglomerates that were close to the party itself— companies not linked to the party were excluded from the lucrative contracts (Irving 2009).[10]

Mosques, *Hawzāt* and Religious Institutions

As noted earlier, the political elites of the Shi'a population, the *zu'āma*, were significantly weakened during the Civil War as a consequence of the political and military strength of Amal and the Hezbollah. In this context, new religious institutions were an important site of challenge to those existing elites who had typically monopolized religious learning and scholasticism. These new institutions included Hezbollah-affiliated mosques and *hawzāt* (religious seminaries), which provided space for previously marginalized youth to enter religious vocations while simultaneously helping to disseminate Hezbollah's particular worldview and ideology. According to Rula Abisaab, the new *hawza*:

> posed a challenge to elitist and family-transmitted scholastic traditions in Jabal Amil and brought about a status reversal for displaced Shi'a youth from working-class backgrounds whose lives lacked the educational stability or socio-economic growth necessary for self-actualization. The seminary students who identify with Hezbollah are largely drawn from lower social classes and families that lack the traditions of Shi'a scholasticism. This challenge to the older traditions of learning must be seen against the background of overall socio-economic changes. An incremental process of rural deterioration in the Shi'a regions, combined with demographic change and marginalization at the hands of the Lebanese state, popularized new modes of thought, of which the Islamist cultural and political revolution represented by Hezbollah is one. The production of Islamist ideas, in turn, led to the emergence of new forms of economic activity, wage labour and professions tied directly to the institutions, seminaries, schools, organisations and overall mobilization activities of Hezbollah.
>
> (Abisaab 2006: 231)

The main sites of public religious activity in the early years of Hezbollah were the mosques of Bir al-Abed (*al-Imām al-Rida*), Ghobeyri (*al-Imām al-Mahdi*) and Airport Road (*al-Rasul al-'Azam*), all located in the southern suburbs of Beirut, and the *hawza* of Baalbek founded in 1978 by Abbas al-Mussawi (second Secretary General of the party, 1991–1992). The sermons and religious formations provided in these institutions were highly politicized. Their diffusion was also helped by recorded audiotapes, which had proven an effective means of propaganda during the years of the Iranian revolution (Lamloum 2009a). Important Hezbollah "*Hawzāt*" are found today in Siddikin in South Lebanon *Hawza al-Imām al-Mahdi*, the *Hawza al-Imām al-Muntazar* in Baalbek, *Hawza al-'almiyya al-dīnniyya* in Tyr and *al-Rasul al-Akram*'s in the southern suburbs of Beirut. Other institutions linked to Hezbollah diffusing the religious and political message of the Islamic movement are the Centre for Youth Education in Jibsheet (South Lebanon), the Educational Hawza in Brital (Bekaa), the Iranian Religious Centre in Tyr and the Centre for Islamic Martial Arts in Kabrikha (South Lebanon) (Hamzeh 1993: 327).

Hezbollah has also established very strong relations with three clerical associations, which are the *Hay'at 'Ulamā' Jabal 'Amil* (the Committee of *Ulema* of Mount Amil), directed by Atif al-Nabulsi,[11] (not a member of Hezbollah but very close to it and supportive of its policies), the *Tajamu' al-'Ulamā' al-Muslimīn fi Lubnān* (Association of Muslim *Ulema* in Lebanon), headed by Sheik Hassan Abdallah (*Tajamu' al-'Ulamā' al-Muslimīn fi Lubnān* 2014), and the *Tajamu' al-'Ulamā' al-Muslimīn fil-Biqā'* (Association of Muslims *Ulema* in the Bekaa) (Charara 2007: 4).

In the *hawzāt*, *sheikhs* train other *sheikhs* whose role is to spread support for the Islamic way of life (see below) and the policies of Hezbollah. Women and men are trained separately, and go on to pass their religious knowledge to the immediate and extended family unit (Harb 2007: 225). Through these institutions, Hezbollah promotes a certain popular conception of religion that links support for the party with the fulfillment of religious obligations. Hezbollah-affiliated *sheikhs* in *hawzāt* and mosques can be viewed as organic intellectuals whose role, in a Gramscian sense, is to elaborate a particular project for the Shi'a population by organizing it in both ideological and practical terms. The role of the *ulema*, or more generally religious clerics, as a vanguard is also symbolized by Khomeini's slogan: "the *Ulema* are the leaders" (cited in Charara 2007: 65). An important aspect to this religious work is the institutionalization of religious celebrations and ceremonies, which are used to bind Hezbollah's members and supporters around a common ideology and conception of collective action (Harb 2010: 173–75). In this sense, the form of Hezbollah's religious activities is highly political—a link that is clearly demonstrated during election periods. At these times, religious ceremonies are used to mobilize popular support for the party. At the same time, the *Sheikh*s play a key role in relaying *fatwa*s from the Hezbollah or religious leaders close to the Islamic movement, for example in imposing a moral obligation to vote for the list supported by the Hezbollah during the various elections summed up in the party slogan: "your vote is a duty (*amāna*) on which you will be judged at the end of your days" (Al-Hajj 2002: 176).

All religious holidays give rise to activities and celebrations prepared by Hezbollah through the *Jam'iyya al-Ta'līm al-Dīnī al-Islāmī*, the Islamic Religious Education Association (IREA), an educational organization linked to the Hezbollah (Le Thomas 2012a: 157–58).

All of these institutions and religious occasions are thus used by the Hezbollah to develop a wider religiosity within the Shi'a population and a separate sense of identity set apart from the wider Lebanese society. In this manner, as Mona Harb (2010: 173) has noted, Shi'a Islamic belief—reinforced and institutionalized by the Hezbollah in religious holidays, ceremonies and processions—allow the Hezbollah to accumulate "symbolic capital," thus guaranteeing the reproduction and the legitimation of the party itself. She adds that the investment of the movement in these types of activities, called demonstratives, "constitutes a form of legitimate self assertion by which power is known and recognized," in the words of Pierre Bourdieu (1980 cited Harb 2010: 173).

Media and Production of Culture

Since its establishment, the Hezbollah has placed a particular emphasis on developing its media network. This dates back as early as 1982, when formal media institutions were first developed by groups of people who would officially establish the party in 1985. First, they published a newsletter called *al-Mujtahid* (*The Struggler*), which had a peculiar Iranian inspired rhetoric and style by carrying reports about Iran and local developments related to Iran, as well as the activities of the Islamic

Committees and speeches by Iranian and Lebanese clerical leaders (Khatib, Matar and Alshaer 2014: 9).

The publication of this newsletter was stopped following the Israeli invasion of Lebanon in June 1982, and was replaced by a four-page leaflet called *Ahl al-Thugur* (*The People of the Outpost*), which maintained its focus on Iranian affairs and the battle between the Islamic Nation and the Israeli enemy (Khatib *et al.* 2014: 9).

According to Abbas al-Mussawi, the second Secretary General of the party, who was assassinated by Israeli forces in 1992, "When the stands of the mosques will associate themselves with the modern stands that are television and video, it is at this moment that we will be able to create the Ummah" (Lamloum 2008a: 22). Naim Qassem has also noted that Hezbollah's "visual media is an efficient arm because it transmits the event without any need of comments" (cited in Lamloum 2008a: 26).

Hezbollah's media network has three main components: First, the television channel Al-Manar, established at the beginning of the 1990s at the initiative of businessmen close to the party. The television channel is now under the total domination of the party (Qassir 2011). Second, websites, magazines and newspapers such as the weekly *al-Intiqad* (*The Critical*) formerly known as *al-'Ahed* (*The Pledge*), which is the party's main mouthpiece and was established in June 1984, *Baqiyyat Allāh*, a monthly cultural magazine focusing particularly on issues relating to Islamic Shiʿa Law, which is distributed to around 17,000 cadres and members of Hezbollah (Lamloum 2008a: 33) and the magazine *al-Amāna* of the association *al-'Amal al-Baladī* (the municipal work), which concentrates on municipality issues. Last, the radio station al-Nour (Harb 2010: 99) established in 1987, which is now one of the largest and most listened-to radio stations in Lebanon. It also broadcasts abroad (Qassir 2011). Each of these institutions play a key role in diffusing the vocabulary and the imagery of Hezbollah's worldview through shows, documentaries and games addressing themes of resistance, Islam, Palestine and Zionism (Harb 2010: 110). Hezbollah also has other resources to spread its messages such as musical groups (including al-Wilāya and Waʿd), publishing houses (Lebanese Cultural Centre, al-Hadi Publishing) and film and production houses (Ressalat and Dar al-Manar) (Lamloum 2009a).

Until the mid-2000s, all the communication activities of the party were supervised by the Central Information Unit (*Wahdat al-Iʿlām al-markazī*) (CIU), which was managed by a member of the *Majlis al-Shura* and directly submitted to the authority of the President of the Executive Council (Lamloum 2008a: 24). The CIU combined the regional units (Bekaa, Beirut and the South), the unit of foreign relations managing relations with national and international media, the committee of information activities in charge of graphics, banners, chants and placards, in addition to the directors of the *al-'Ahed* newspaper, the directors of al-Manar television and al-Nour radio station (Lamloum 2008a: 24). The CIU was also in charge of collaboration with municipalities governed by Hezbollah to rename squares and decorate them with specific pictures and banners. New names were attributed to some specific squares for example: Jerusalem avenue, Khomeini avenue, Hadi Nasrallah avenue and Resistance avenue (Harb 2010: 163). As explained by the director of the CIU in an interview in 2004: "we want to create a specific urban décor, pedestrian streets, monuments on squares that reveal the identity of the neighbourhoods, which show that we are here now, in this location" (cited in Harb 2010: 163).

In 2004, the party's 7th Congress decided to place even greater priority on cultural issues and their link with popular mobilization (Harb 2010: 87). This led to the establishment of the Artistic and Media Unit, attached to the EC, which was placed in charge of graphic means of communication (posters, paintings and slogans) that would be spread throughout Shi'a areas (Daher 2014: 200). In this manner, Hezbollah aimed at reproducing a specific identity in the territories it controlled, where party references would be materialized in space through banners and pictures installed in the streets, objects positioned on public squares and regular commemorations (Harb 2010: 163). This panoply of images is a striking confirmation of Gramsci's observation that a movement seeking hegemony must never tire of repeating its ideas: "repetition is the best dialectic means for working on the popular mentality" (cited in Thomas 2009: 340).

In this framework, Al-Manar television held a particularly important place due to its large audience as the second most watched television channel in the Arab world (after Al-Jazeera with an estimated 10 million viewers in 2001) throughout the 2000s (Harb 2010: 153). Al-Manar has nevertheless probably lost some sections of its audience following its military involvement in the Syrian revolutionary process alongside the Assad regime, which has proven hugely unpopular among the people of the region. According to a survey conducted in March 2013 by Pew Research Center, Hezbollah was widely unpopular in the region (Drake 2013). Hezbollah was actually viewed unfavorably in Egypt by 75 percent, in Turkey by 73 percent, in Jordan by 72 percent and in Lebanon by 59 percent. Views are mixed in the Occupied Palestinian Territories where 49 percent have an unfavorable view of Hezbollah, while 43 percent have a positive one. Views of Hezbollah in the Palestinian territories have nevertheless turned significantly more negative since 2011 when 61 percent saw the militant group positively and 37 percent had an unfavorable view. And a similar trend was observed among Palestinians in Lebanese refugee camps. There, increasingly negative views of the Hezbollah were on display for example in May 2013 when Palestinians in the Ain al-Hilweh refugee camp burned humanitarian aid donated by the party, citing its role alongside the regime in Syria's civil war with one banner saying: "We don't want assistance soaked in the blood of the Syrian people" (Zaatari 2013). In Tunisia, 38 percent have an unfavorable view of the Hezbollah and 35 percent have a positive one, with 27 percent expressing no opinion. Within Lebanon about nine out of ten Shi'a (89 percent) view the Hezbollah favorably while 94 percent of Sunni and 60 percent of Christian regard the Hezbollah unfavorably (Drake 2013).

According to station officials in the mid-2000s, Al-Manar's annual budget stood at approximately $15 million (Krayem cited in Jorish 2004). It employs around 350 people, including twenty foreign correspondents (Lamloum 2009b). Its organization consists of six departments,[12] including a department in charge of its Internet website which alone has ten employees. As Olfa Lamloum (2009b) has argued, the first mission of Al-Manar was to build a space of legitimacy for the armed resistance against the Israeli occupation, whose ultimate reference point is Islamic and Shi'a symbolism. The channel has also filled two other major functions:

> It is first to weld and reproduce the Shi'a popular basis of Hezbollah structured in a political community through the "mis en scene" or demonstration of the power of the party, especially in times of crisis and of intense inter-communitarian conflicts. Al-Manar therefore operates as a mediator of the identity of Hezbollah and of all its attributes of legitimation to its Shi'a popular base. It participates in the reproduction of its system of representation, which draws its

references in the collective memory of the Shi'a martyrology. It boasts its cadres of frames of perception and allows the public to locate, perceive, identify, classify the events of (his or her) environment, their experiences and the world. It systematically transmits the different religious and political ceremonies and ritual celebrations organized by the party [...] which characterises the time of the community and maintain a space of familiarity between its members. Social programs publicise the merits of Hezbollah's social actions and valorise them as a source of legitimation. Sports and children programs and soap operas offer a fun but virtuous entertainment.

(Lamloum 2009b)

One example of Al-Manar's broadcasting was the series *al-Ghālibun*, which traces the history of the Hezbollah from 1985 to 1992. *Al-Ghālibun* was broadcast by Al-Manar in the summer of 2012, during Ramadan, and cost $2 million to produce (Calabrese 2013). The series was explicitly crafted to portray the Hezbollah as the principal resistance movement against Israel through the 1980s and early 1990s. It relates a fictional account of its main protagonist, Nasser, who begins as a secular fighter but finally decides to join the Hezbollah because "it is stronger and more effective [than other parties] because of the faith of its members" (Calabrese 2013). In shows such as this, Al-Manar's programming projects a historical narrative that upholds the party's claims to be the sole and most effective representative of the Shi'a population, while simultaneously tying this to its religious principles.[13]

Dina Matar and Farah Dakhlallah argue in a similar vein that:

Al-Manar has continued to promote Hezbollah's culture of resistance, considered an integral aspect of the party's Iranian-inspired Islamic milieu in Lebanon, and, which along with its constituent resistance identity and culture, are essential products of Hezbollah's institutions which operate today as a holistic and integrated network which produce sets of values and meanings embedded in an interrelated religious and political framework—that of *Wilāyat al-Faqīh*.

(Dakhlallah and Matar 2006: 31)

They add that Al-Manar particularly emphasizes its role as the communal voice of Shi'a in Lebanon during its coverage and religious programming of the Shi'a holy months (Dakhlallah and Matar 2006: 31).

The specific religious principles of the party are also imposed on the employees of the channel in regards to their personal appearance on air. The management places restrictions on which headscarves can be worn by female presenters, insisting that the head covering had to be a dark uniform color (Zaraket 2012). The employees are also ordered by Al-Manar management to avoid the appearance of unveiled women on the station's programs, restricting their appearance to news bulletins and reports, where for example, people on the street are asked for their opinion (Zaraket 2012). As Huda Rizk has noted, "from a media perspective, i.e. externally, the party is open to unveiled women and accepts them because it needs them to show an image of openness in the Arab and Western worlds and it needs their political support" (cited in Merhi Z. 2012). Nonetheless,

> the party wants to make sure that people who are socially different from it are not hostile to it. But if you are an unveiled Shi'a woman, then it's a different story. Such a woman can not be brought into prominence in the party because she can not be a role model.
>
> (cited in Merhi Z. 2012)

Al-Manar therefore adheres fully to the role assigned to television by Imam Khomeini: a public university whose pedagogic role is to guide the population towards a pure society, uncorrupted by the West (Chelkowski and Dabashi 2000: 262–64). The IRI, since the victory of its own revolution, actually emphasized the role of media in the dissemination of the Islamic culture. This is demonstrated by the law of 1982, which approved the constitution of Iranian radio and television, stating that "mass media, radio, television, must be at the service of […] the dissemination of Islamic culture" (Rajaee 1993: 121).

In addition to its media network, Hezbollah has developed a specific attitude towards the production and control of art. In 2004, the party centralized its direct involvement in these processes through an affiliated professional organization called the Lebanese Association for the Arts (LAA) or *al-Jam'iyya al-Lubnāniyya lil-Funun* (Deeb and Harb 2011: 17). The newly established LAA was in charge of designing and implementing cultural projects commemorating the resistance and other themes, centralizing previously dispersed efforts in this sphere (Deeb and Harb 2013: 67–70). The LAA produced exhibitions, videos, billboards and other media narrating the key ideals of the "resistance society," celebrating political and religious events and commemorating the party's successes and achievements. In 2006, following the war, the LAA was the institution in charge of the campaign in three different languages (French, English and Arabic) praising the divine victory of the Hezbollah (Fawaz and Harb 2010: 25). It was the LAA as well that launched the campaign "Values" with slogans such as "order is from the faith" and "my family is my happiness," which wanted to raise awareness about "order" and "family values" as the Hezbollah considered there was a general decline in values that led to growing "social problems" (divorce, selfishness and drug addiction).

The LAA showed the increasing importance given by the Hezbollah to the notion of "culture," understood as a holistic concept, as it gathered professionally trained artists, graphic designers, and architects.[14]

In 2010, the LAA was separated into two associations that are in charge of different domains of cultural production. *Ressalat* (messages) became the organization responsible for media campaigns. The Association for the Celebration of the Tradition of Resistance, "*Jam'iyya Ihyyā' Turāth al-Muqāwama*," manages the construction of large-scale structures including the Khiam and Mleeta sites, the memorial garden in Marun al-Ra's in southern Lebanon, the memorial museum for martyred Hezbollah Secretary General Sayyid Abbas al-Mussawi in the Bekaa Valley, as well as the Resistance Museum in the southern suburbs of Beirut (Deeb and Harb 2013: 239). The conscious attempt to build popular hegemony through the use of these sites has been noted by one of their designers:

> You can control people by narrating a specific heritage and memory. This is what the Israelis do. We are fighting their culture by providing a counter-culture. We want to fix our memory through architectural and design language. Few people read books but many people come to visit a building, a museum or a heritage site.
>
> (cited in Deeb and Harb 2009: 203–204)

Within this cultural emphasis, the control of the memory of the Hezbollah soldiers killed on the military field against the Israeli army is highly significant. Hezbollah institutions involved in this include the "Tribute to Martyrs," a foundation that honors the martyr's family and assists them by, for example, taking care of the maintenance of the tomb (Daher 2014: 149). Another center, "Memories of the Martyrs," was established in 2004 with the objective of enhancing and preserving the legacy of the Islamic resistance and particularly of martyrs (Markaz Athār al-Shuhadā' 2014).

In all of these activities, it is evident that the Hezbollah expends a conscious and considerable effort in shaping how the wider Shi'a population perceives the historical narrative of resistance and the party's role in it. This narrative is heavily linked to—and reinforced by—the religious symbolism associated with the Shi'a faith. It is revealing, for example, how the contemporary themes of resistance, persecution and martyrdom are continually situated in reference to pivotal moments in Shi'a history (notably Ashura, which commemorates the martyrdom of the Imam Hussein in 680, during the Battle of Karbalā'). The construction of this narrative through the Hezbollah's intervention in the media and cultural field thus helps to legitimize the Hezbollah as the authentic expression of Shi'a identity today. It also acts to strengthen the norms associated with Hezbollah's religious message, an important aspect of the consensual and coercive features of Hezbollah's hegemony explored further below.

Education and Youth

A fourth major priority of the Hezbollah's intervention in civil society is the education and youth sector. The Educational Institute (*al-Mu'assasa al-Tarbawiyya*, founded in 1991) of the Hezbollah is the institution that supervises the educational sector and is aimed at recomposing Shi'a society (*āda siyyāgha tarkiba al-mujtama'*) by producing "a new 'mentality' for a society participating actively in its own reconstruction, in resistance and in economic rebirth" (Harb and Leenders 2005: 187). An important feature of this "rebirth" is the inculcation of the values of *iltizām* (religious commitment)—a notion that is discussed in greater detail below (Interview of the Vice-President of the Islamic Institute, 1998, cited in Harb and Leenders 2005: 187).

To this end, the party has established and directly operates a network of private schools including al-Mahdi (13,500 students), al-Mustapha (8,300 students) and Imdad (3,500 students). The al-Mahdi schools have expanded rapidly to fourteen schools in Lebanon (seven in the South, four in the Bekaa and three in Dahyeh) as well as one institution in the city of Qom in Iran (Le Thomas 2012a: 92). The total number of students in the Hezbollah's network of schools reached nearly 30,000 in the mid-2000s (Le Thomas 2012a: 85). According to one researcher, between 70 percent and 80 percent of students in al-Mahdi schools had a family member affiliated to the Hezbollah (Osseyran 1997: 142). The Hezbollah also runs technical institutes established by independent foundations linked to the party, such as the al-Shahid technical institution linked to the al-Shahid hospital. In the mid-2000s, around 23,000 children were beneficiaries of the financial support system for education established by the Islamic movement, according to Lebanese researcher Nizar Hamzeh (2004: 57).

There are two main institutional links between the party and this network of schools. First, the organization has a Student Mobilization Unit, which is in charge of student related issues. Catherine Le Thomas notes that the Unit: "is the interface between the party and its institutional environment (including its private schools and the public schools under its domination)" and through this Unit the party: "seeks to promote Hezbollah's interests in the sector, by pursuing as far as it can a cultural, social and political action on the public and private education establishments located in the Shi'a majority populated regions" (Le Thomas 2012a: 97). To this end, the Student Unit organizes students affiliated to the movement through student committees. The movement also provides scholarships for students to complete their university studies.

The second key institutional link to the education sector is the IREA mentioned above. IREA provides Islamic religious teaching, which is the main objective of the association and is widely known to be linked to the Hezbollah. Naim Qassem was a founding member and the organization's president from 1974, the year of its establishment, to 1988 (Le Thomas 2012a: 85, Jam'iyya al-Ta'līm al-Dīnī al-Islāmī 2012).

The association has 1,300 employees and manages the al-Mustapha schools. Through the 2000s, about 60 percent of the public schools in the Shi'a-dominated regions were using IREA services, particularly in Beirut and the Bekaa (Le Thomas 2012a: 85). The association provided its services to about 135,000 students in 507 schools, both private and public, in 2002–2003 (Le Thomas 2012a: 85). It was around 141,260 students in 2012 (Jam'iyya al-Ta'līm al-Dīnī al-Islāmī 2012). The Hezbollah's influence is therefore not limited to its own schools but to other public schools as well.

The iconography deployed in the schools reinforces the religious and political content of images visible in the streets of Dahyeh, with a prevalence of Shi'a religious images and portraits of Khomeini and Khamenei (Le Thomas 2008: 156). The Hezbollah's Information Unit, which is in charge of displaying this iconography, aims to propagate a message conveying the religiosity of the school environment that is seamlessly connected to the surrounding streets (Harb and Leenders 2005: 190). Teachers are selected on the basis of their religious commitment, and are expected to take mandatory religious lessons of thirty hours per year, with an exam at the end of the year (Le Thomas 2008: 155). Catherine Le Thomas argues that:

> schools are an essential tool in the societal perspective of Hezbollah, because they represent a matrix to consolidate and expand the popular basis of the party and to form a new generation of youth—all-rounded Shi'a—holders of its project of society.
>
> (Le Thomas 2008: 149)

In addition to formal schooling, Hezbollah also seeks to mobilize youth through extra-curricular activities. One of the most important institutional examples of this is the al-Mahdi scouts, which help to socialize youth aged from 6–18 years old into Hezbollah's belief system. In 2015, more than 76,000 youth were members of the organization, which also had close to 4,000 scout leaders, according to the General Commissioner of the association Nazih Fayyad, who has been at the head of the al-Mahdi scouts since its establishment in 1998 (Ayub 2015). The al-Mahdi scouts are not limited to the Hezbollah's network of schools, but also include Islamic establishments and villages in Shi'a dominated regions. Numerically, they are the most important scout group in Lebanon (Le Thomas 2012b: 288). The al-Mahdi scouts organize a number of activities, but with a specific emphasis on religion, notably by teaching to follow the *Wilāyat al-Faqīh* (Le Thomas 2012b: 299) and the culture of religious commitment (Harb 2010: 111). The General Commissioner of the association Nazih Fayyad explains that the scouts are educated in the Islamic method and that the objective of the association is first to teach individuals to be self-reliant, second, to serve the people and the society, third, to defend the motherland, and finally to promote education and *ijtihād* (Ayub 2015). Scout activities are spread throughout the year and link up with activities of other Hezbollah organizations. Sporting events are an important focus of scout involvement, and the Hezbollah owns seven sport fields in Dahyeh, as well as a sports club of around 120 teams (Harb 2010: 110). The driving principle of these activities is clearly expressed by the head of the youth and sport division in the Hezbollah:

> From 1982, the party wanted to diffuse a sport culture and a work among the youth to mobilise them [...] The sport work unifies the opinions and allows the control of moral corruption. This latter has increased, we must teach people religion, and try to reform the individual religiously. Sport educates the mind.
>
> (cited in Harb 2010: 110)

Hāla islāmiyya: Consent and Coercion

This survey of the Hezbollah's network of social, cultural, religious and educational institutions confirms the importance attached by the organization to building a base of support in the Shi'a areas of Lebanon and the ways in which hegemony has been constructed through the party's intervention in the various spheres of civil society. A common theme that runs through all of these spheres is a pronounced emphasis on a particular religious conception of the world. As noted earlier, this conception is consciously articulated from the top of the organization's hierarchy (the Shura Council) and runs through all subsequent institutional tiers. Members of Hezbollah are expected to follow a strict religious education, including acceptance of the *Wilāyat al-Faqīh* doctrine (Fadlallah 2012b). The party's work in the areas of culture, media, schooling and youth has a strong emphasis on religious symbolism and is generally directed by religious figures (Daher 2014: 200). Even its social support services are conceived of in religious terms.[15]

The ideological framework guiding this religious framework is, however, distinct and relatively unique.[16] It is encapsulated in two important notions: the *hāla islāmiyya* (the Islamic milieu) and *iltizām* (commitment), which have as their aims an increase in the level and the atmosphere of religiosity among both society and individuals.

The *hāla islāmiyya* expresses a totalizing, collective identity that embodies a vision of "Islam as an ideology (*'aqīda*) and system (*nizām*), as an idea (*fikr*) and government (*hikm*)" (Qassem 2008: 34–35). The adhesion to the *hāla islāmiyya* produces a collective identity generating a strong sense of belonging, which gives meaning to the individual. Lara Deeb (2006: 36), for example, explains that for the *hāla islāmiyya* to be fully accomplished, each person is responsible for carrying out informed choices based on religious knowledge. The *hāla islāmiyya* is therefore conceived as a collective product, with solidarity and a sense of voluntarism as essential keys to its development. Harb and Leenders emphasize that "Hezbollah's institutions make sure to promote the significance of solidarity and community work through a variety of religious narratives and symbolic references" (Harb and Leenders 2005: 192).

Within this collective identity, *iltizām* refers to individual norms and practices (Harb 2010: 190). Lara Deeb (2006: 102–103) describes *iltizām* as obligations, for example, the *hijāb* (headscarf) is part of the *iltizām* for women, drinking alcohol is forbidden for the committed (*multazimīn*). *Iltizām* ranges from the contractual to those obligations that are linked to a personal sense of duty. There are many ways to express *iltizām*, as Deeb explains: "a socially inclined person might distribute food to the poor, a politically inclined person might collect donations for Hezbollah resistance fighters, and a religiously inclined person might pray and fast regularly" (Deeb 2006: 36).

A key characteristic of these notions is the role of the Hezbollah authority figures in circumscribing the norms of social behavior. As one observer has noted in regards to the Hezbollah schools in Dahyeh,

> The Islamic school cultivates particular ways of life consistent with the Islamic ideal, which is defined by the religious figures and persons of authorities in the community or the network it belongs. It (the Islamic school) seeks to draw for its users the right paths, moral, social, religious, political and offer figures that embodies the highest level of the ideals and thoughts that it promotes.
>
> (Le Thomas 2012a: 151)

A notable and important feature of this religious perspective is the way in which social passivity and difference are stigmatized. All social practices that do not fit within the framework defined by the Hezbollah are thereby branded as being unlawful (*harām*), corrupted (*mafsudīn*) or shameful ('*ayb*) (Harb 2010: 185). In this manner, Hezbollah propagates a worldview that encourages support and engagement with the party's activities (as a necessary requirement of religious piety), while simultaneously ostracizing those who deviate from these norms. Social behavior thus adapts itself to the worldview of the Hezbollah, and leads to high levels of conformity within the Shi'a populations.

The Hezbollah's vision of these religious codes and norms also sets itself up as "authentic" Islam, which Lara Deeb (2003: 2) defines as an Islam that has a modern interpretation based on knowledge and understanding, in contrast to a traditional, unquestioned Islam that is followed blindly by the older generations. This is a further reflection of the transformation within the Shi'a population itself, between old and new elites (Deeb 2003: 2–3).

A distinctive feature of this "authentic Islam" is a specific Shi'a identity that is demarcated from Sunni and Christian populations. One illustration of this is shown in the content of school textbooks used in Hezbollah schools. In the history textbook "*Nahnu wa Tārīkh*" (*Us and History*), for example, the history of Islam is taught in a manner that is highly sectarian and Shi'a oriented (Le Thomas 2012a: 229). The Umayyad government is described as corrupt and unjust, while the penetration of Shiism in Lebanon in the region of the *Jabal 'Amil* is characterized as the real or authentic territory of belief. This particular status of *Jabal 'Amil* is specific to Hezbollah's schoolbooks and is not present in other history books of Lebanon. The Abbasid Caliphates are also portrayed very negatively in showing their cruelty and injustice and presenting them as the assassins of the descendants of Imam Hussein, and Jaafar Sadiq (the sixth Imam of Duodeciman Shiism). The decline of the Abbasid Caliphates are explained as the logical consequence of their injustice and their taste for pleasure. Catherine Le Thomas argues that: "although the story always condemns personalities and dynasties, and not a religion or a particular sect, this nevertheless contributes to underline the boundaries and limits between Shi'a and Sunni and to trace the founding moments establishing this boundary" (Le Thomas 2012a: 229).[17]

This particular variant of Shiʿa Islam—articulated through the notions of *hāla islāmiyya* and *iltizām*—is consistently promoted by the Hezbollah through the institutional networks described in this chapter. Ideologically, it is a key element to Hezbollah's construction of consent and coercion within Lebanese Shiʿa areas. The consensual aspects of this have been discussed here and include the various social services provided by the Hezbollah and the socialization of youth into the *hāla islāmiyya* through the organization's network of kindergartens, schools, scouts, leisure parks, summer camps, organized trips, television programs and so forth. All these institutions and experiences contribute from a young age to the learning and acquiring of religious, social and political values linked to the *hāla islāmiyya*. Media and cultural networks of the party further strengthen the acquisition and internalization of these values (Harb 2010: 182).

It is critical, however, not to ignore the coercive aspects of this particular ideological framework. Precisely due to the high levels of social conformity and the strict policing of any deviation from the dominant norms, any behavior that steps outside these norms is likely to be very costly to the individual on both a social and material level. This prospective threat is utilized as a form of coercion.

One example of this is Hezbollah's network of neighborhood committees for "enjoining virtue and forbidding vice," which are active in party-dominated areas, particularly Dahyeh. The activities of these committees include decorating city blocks during Ramadan and informing the party about "improper" activities occurring in their neighborhoods (Deeb and Harb 2011: 16). The party is able to exercise social and economic pressure in order to forbid activities that fall outside its understanding of appropriate moral behavior. If a business does not reform (which, for example, can include abstaining from serving alcohol or exerting greater control over mixed-sex interaction in the establishment), Hezbollah will initiate a boycott and put the café or restaurant out of business by ruining its reputation (Deeb and Harb 2011: 16–17). In one example, in the town of Hula in 2012, members of Hezbollah attempted to close a shop providing alcohol and wounded two members of the LCP who came to the help of the owner of the shop (Orient le Jour 2011d; Noujaim 2012). In October 2009, a Brazilian samba show was banned and torpedoed in the southern city of Tyr after about 100 Shiʿa clerics under the chairmanship of *Sheikh* Ali Yassin, a powerful

Hezbollah follower, met and issued a *fatwa* forbidding it and declaring it sinful (Bejjani 2009). Hezbollah militants have also disrupted events such as ceremonies called *zajal* (improvised poetry competition) in some areas of the South (ICG 2007: 20). In the August 2002 edition of Hezbollah's magazine *Baqiyyat Allāh*, Khamenei's *fatwa* on music was published, which characterized any music that takes a human being into a state of euphoria as *harām*, and dictated that one should only listen to cassette tapes registered and approved by the Islamic Council. According to Deeb and Harb (2013: 137), Hezbollah follows this understanding by deeming as *harām* any music conducive to dancing or that excites the sexual instincts. Following the municipal elections in May 2016, municipalities in southern Lebanon (Aitarun, Jibshit and Khiam), under the control of the Hezbollah, issued a series of decisions to prevent women from frequenting mixed swimming pools, mixed Internet cafés and mixed sports activities (Al-Barzi 2016).

Mona Harb recounts another case of an ex-Hezbollah member who became a communist and was subsequently stigmatized by his neighbors in the Hay al-Sellom neighborhood. His ostracism was articulated through the notions of *hāla islāmiyya*/*iltizām* and their emphasis on conformity; being a communist was characterized as heresy, and led to his social exclusion and eventual departure from the neighborhood (Harb 2010: 183). Even members close to the leadership can feel these disciplining elements—in 2003, the director of Al-Manar was fired for having published unconventional views on Ashura and for implicitly questioning the doctrine of the *Wilāyat al-Faqīh* (ICG 2003: 14).

Hezbollah also uses forms of coercion and consent when individuals attempt to utilize certain ideological concepts outside of the party's tutelage. One example of this is the case of a Shi'a entrepreneur who launched a children's magazine independently from Hezbollah, in which he featured prominently the concepts of resistance and *Wilāyat al-Faqīh* (Harb and Leenders 2005: 197). The individual was quickly approached by Hezbollah members, who informed him that he would either need to partner with Hezbollah and place the magazine under the supervision of the party, or cease publication (he chose the latter course) (Harb and Leenders 2005: 197).

Hezbollah has also used its financial influence to pressure institutions to conform to the principles of the *hāla islāmiyya*. The Shqif Club for example, which had previously played a prominent social and cultural role all over the South and served alcoholic drinks and hosted dancing parties, was forced to ban alcoholic drinks and dancing after the club experienced a financial deficit and Hezbollah took over its cafeteria through one of the party's financiers (El-Cheikh and Saghyieh 2013b). The same thing occurred with the Qasr al-Muluk, which was "rescued" by Hezbollah money and ceased serving alcohol (El-Cheikh and Saghyieh 2013b).

On a political level, any dissenting Shiʿa voice or critic of Hezbollah faces the threat of violent intimidations from the party, its supporters and even its allies. *Sheikh* Muhammad Hussein Fadlallah, for example, was the target of violent condemnations from the followers of the *Wilāyat al-Faqīh* and the Hezbollah after he proclaimed himself a *"marj'iyya"* (religious reference) in 1994, following the death of the Imam Al-Khui' in Iraq of whom he was the representative in Lebanon. Flyers and graffiti condemning him were placed the following evening on the walls surrounding his house and his mosque in Haret Hreik. For some Hezbollah members and followers of the *Wilāyat al-Faqīh* the self-proclamation by Fadlallah as a *"marj'iyya"* was considered a challenge to Khamenei and the IRI. Fadlallah argued for the plurality of the *"marj'iyya,"* but also of the *Wilāyat al-Faqīh* (Mervin 2008b: 283). The Hezbollah nevertheless intervened quickly to prevent any further violent outbreak, fearing dissension among the Shiʿa population as Fadlallah was a very popular cleric and a religious reference (*marj'iyya*) for many (Harb 2010: 239).[18]

The aftermath of the 2006 Lebanon War strengthened Hezbollah's refusal to tolerate criticism from other organizations and actors in the public sphere. Members and supporters of the Hezbollah engaged increasingly in a *takhwin* discourse (accusations of treachery) against the Shiʿa who criticized or expressed reservations about the practices of the Hezbollah. Such individuals were denied certain social and economic services, with the community as a whole subject "to greater pressure to conform to the expectations of Islamist clerics about religious observance, dress code, and social conduct" (Abisaab and Abisaab 2014: 143).

There are several recent illustrations of the increased use of coercive measures against those critical of Hezbollah. For example, the members and supporters of the Lebanese Option Party (LOP) (formerly called the Lebanese Option Gathering) have been the target of numerous attacks. Established in 2007 and headed by Ahmad al-Asʿad, the son of the well known As'ad feudal family in the South, the LOP is an independent Shi'a political party opposed to March 8, and more particularly to the Hezbollah[19] and Amal. The car of Ahmad al-As'ad was burned in 2009 (Khatib, Matar and Alshaer 2014: 32). Moreover, Hezbollah members attacked protesters from the LOP and killed the head of the party's student wing Hachem Salman (19 years old), after shooting him in the abdomen during a protest against the Hezbollah's involvement in Syria (Naharnet 2013; Orient le Jour 2013c).

In interviews conducted by the International Crisis Group on the situation of the political opponents of the Hezbollah in Dahyeh, several individuals complained of political intimidation against them and spoke of an atmosphere hostile to all critics of the party. One journalist said that:

> when you live in Dahyeh and are opposed to Hezbollah, you must accept to lead a difficult life. You will probably feel isolated. If you oppose, or simply don't follow Hezbollah, you can't run a business. Party members, partisans, supporters will just boycott your shop.
>
> (cited in ICG 2014: 20)

In May 2014, the journalist Hanin Ghaddar faced a violent campaign from Hezbollah media and its allies after criticizing the Hezbollah's intervention in Syria to assist the Assad regime (Ghaddar 2014). In July 2014, in the city of Saida, a member of the Lebanese Resistance Brigades (LBR), which are affiliated to the Hezbollah, attacked and threatened to kill the journalist Abdel Basset Tarjman, who directs a website (Saida Gate) which is critical of the Hezbollah (Orient le Jour 2014c). Ali al-Amin, a journalist and editor-in-chief of the Janoubia website, which is critical of the Hezbollah, was also the target of various social media campaigns by Hezbollah supporters against him, notably accusing him of having directly corresponded via email with Israeli Occupation Forces spokesperson Afikhai Adrei (Now Media 2016).

Hassan Nasrallah attacked independent Shi'a figures who are opposed to the Hezbollah in a speech in May 2015 accusing them of being "the Shi'a of the American embassy" and "traitors, agents and morons" (Abdallah 2016).

The *"takhwin"* discourse was once more used during the 2016 municipal elections, as well as other intimidation techniques. The

Hezbollah encouraged campaigns that accused some candidates who challenged the party's lists of not respecting the blood of the "martyrs of the resistance," of opposing "the resistance," and of siding with the "takfirist" in the Baalbek and Hermel area and in Dahyeh (Khalifa: 2016); or, in the case of the election of the municipality of Baalbek, the Hezbollah member Mr. Ibrahim Amin Sayyed said that the party would not hand over the municipality of Baalbek to Daesh (Islamic State), as a way to scare the population of a possible victory of the rival list, which is not affiliated to Daesh, and to discredit its opponents in the elections. In the villages of Labweh and Kasr in the Baalbeck-Hermel area, Hezbollah armed men intimidated voters and candidates from rival lists (Amhaz 2016; Noujeim 2016). Similar pressures were exerted on rival lists in Burj al-Barajneh and Ghobeyri municipalities. A social media campaign was launched by members of the party which linked the May 2016 killing of a Hezbollah military commando in Mustapha Badr al-Din, Syria (see Chapter 6), to the municipal elections, by accusing opponents of Hezbollah's and Amal's lists of standing with the murderers, in other words the Sunni jihadists, while promising the expulsion and prosecution of each voter for the rival lists (Khalifa 2016).

Gendering Hegemony: The Role of Women in Hezbollah's Worldview

The intertwined features of coercion and consent, expressed through the Islamization of Shiʿa populations, also have a specific gendered component. In many ways, Hezbollah's promotion of a particular role for women in society is a central aspect of the way that its hegemony is projected. Following the position of Khomeini, women are seen as the main transmission mechanism for the collective inculcation of religious norms embodied in the *hāla islāmiyya* and *iltizām*. As mothers, according to Khomeini, women hold a "sensitive role [...] in the upbringing of their children and consequently in the rectification or degeneration of society" (Khomeini 2001: 38 and 81).[20] Similarly, the Hezbollah *Sheikh* Naim Qassem (2008: 291–93) has characterized the primary role of women as mother, sister, wife and daughter.

This perspective can be seen in Hezbollah's school textbook, *Al-Islām Risālatunā*, published by the IREA, which has a chapter titled "The Position of Woman in Islam." This book is taught to children prior to high school level, and outlines the role of women according to the Hezbollah's interpretation of Islam. While upholding the right of women to work and to be educated, it emphasizes what it describes as "female work": teaching, sewing, nursing and so forth. Most significantly, the manual notes that: "Islam states that the work of a woman should not be done at the expense of the family, because to educate the future generations is the most important for Islam" (Le Thomas 2012a: 206).

In line with this emphasis on the transmission of values to future generations, women form a major strategic interface between the party and its surrounding social environment. They are typically organized in specific women's councils, distributed through mosques and neighborhoods, which help mobilize for social and cultural events called for by the party (Qassem 2008: 86). Some women of the Hezbollah have run for office in Lebanese city councils, but none have in parliamentary elections.

In most cases, the Hezbollah's institutions are led by a small number of male cadres, alongside a large number of women volunteers who interact with its wider constituency. The party's Social Affairs wing, for example, is organized through the structure of *"al-akhawāt al-mutatawwi'āt"*—sisters' volunteers—who target beneficiaries of the Hezbollah's social work.[21] The network of social workers is composed of five to six men working full time, and more than one hundred female volunteers. Men hold fixed employment and work schedules, and their role is to process loans and allowances for beneficiaries. Women volunteers, on the other hand, have no fixed timetable, contract or office space. The recruitment of these volunteers is based on two criteria: to live in the neighborhood where she works and to believe in the Hezbollah's ideology, including Islamic values and support for the resistance (Fawaz 2004: 358–59).

As volunteers, they make a weekly visit to families in their neighborhoods of residence to check on those receiving benefits and who have other needs (Fawaz 2004: 358–59). One of their key tasks during these visits is to strengthen the party's links with families and to monitor the households' commitment to the Hezbollah's political perspective as well as conformity to the *hāla islāmiyya* and *iltizām* (Harb 2010: 176). If the volunteers detect any behavior deemed to lie outside the norms established by the party, it could lead to the termination of social support (Le Thomas 2012a: 142). In this manner, female volunteers play a central role in transmitting the particular values associated with the party to its wider social milieu, while also mediating the coercive aspects of the Hezbollah's hegemony.

In consolidating this particular position of women in the organization, the Hezbollah places considerable emphasis on building adherence to fixed gender roles. Once again, this is closely related to religious symbolism and reference to historical moments within the Shiʿa faith. In the Ashura commemorations, for example, clerics stress the differently gendered roles of *Ahl al-Bayt* (the Prophet's family)—men are said to have participated in fighting while women looked after the children and provided moral support (Boumet Beirut 2013). Males are presented as chivalrous and strong; women are modest, patient and supportive. The cleric usually explains that these roles complement each other and that therefore, men and women must take on these roles in contemporary struggles. Men must be *"Hussayniyyūn,"*[22] and women must be *"Zaynabiyyāt."*[23] This is the way, according to the Hezbollah's rhetoric, to strengthen the nation, achieve victory and guarantee their places in heaven (Boumet Beirut 2013).

The differently gendered roles of Hussein and Zaynab translate into the appropriate types of contemporary social activism promoted by the Hezbollah. Lara Deeb (2009: 249) notes that men are encouraged to work and volunteer with organizations such as Jihad al-Bina in roles such as engineering, management and construction, while women are expected to engage in social welfare voluntarism. In this way, Zaynab provides the model for the ideal Shiʿa woman—a pious individual whose voluntarism in health, education or welfare serves as her contribution to the community's development.

Within this gendered division of labor, the headscarf and other sartorial codes are given an important place in marking how women are expected to appear and behave. The headscarf is presented as the equivalent of weapons wielded by men in combat. Men resist by their strength, while women protect themselves and society through wearing the headscarf and veil. Again, this is closely related to the individual norms of *iltizām*. The committed woman is known as the *multazima*, and she is expected to wear the veil and a long dress that covers her body. The colors that she wears should be dark in order not to attract attention.[24] The veil expresses both a religious and political commitment, in contrast to the traditional headscarf usually worn in Lebanese villages (Chaib 2008: 297). The boundaries between men and women are strictly codified—*multazimāt* are expected not to shake hands or mix with men and schools segregate girls and boys starting from the age of nine (girls are also taught different subject matter) (Deeb 2006: 107; Le Thomas 2012a: 256). These practices should not be seen as merely an attempt to return to tradition, but rather to re-work supposed religious norms as an integral part of what is conceived as "modernity" (Deeb 2006: 32–33). Gendered roles are particularly important in this respect, because the explicit dress and behavioral codes assigned to women become central markers of modernity.

The Hezbollah has adopted many of these customs aimed at fixing gender roles from similar practices in Iran. A significant example is the celebration of the *taklīf*, widespread in all schools in Iran and known as the Day of Prayer (Paivandi 2006: 132). This ceremony is aimed at nine-year-old girls who are said to have reached the age of responsibility (accountability), and encourages them to undertake certain religious obligations, such as praying and fasting, and to begin wearing the headscarf and veil (Le Thomas 2012a: 377). *Taklīf* was initiated at the end of the Civil War, first in the Hezbollah's network of schools and then with the al-Mahdi scouts (Le Thomas 2012a: 300 and 377).

Another example of the defining of gender roles is the restriction placed on mixed-sex interaction on social media. At the beginning of 2014, the Hezbollah Deputy Hussein Mussawi defended the *fatwa* of Imam Khamenei prohibiting "chat" between men and women on Facebook and warning those who participate in social networks by declaring:

> to those who commented on the fatwa of one of our references that prohibited a particular mode of social networks that lead to moral corruption and to the fall of the safeguards of society, we say God bless those who know their limits and respect them.
>
> (Orient le Jour 2014b)

In line with these attitudes towards women's role in society, the Hezbollah has not supported legislation at the national level aimed at ensuring equality for women in the family. In 2010, for example, women's rights activists submitted a draft bill regarding the protection of women, including the criminalization of marital rape. This draft bill was completely modified by the parliamentary subcommittee at the urging of the Hezbollah's Minister, Muhammad Fneich (Merhi N. 2012). In particular, the text was changed to remove the key clause legislating against marital rape (Merhi N. 2012). The subcommittee maintained Article 26, which states that women can only bring cases of domestic and family violence to the civil courts if permitted by religious courts—institutions known to be patriarchal in considering the male as the head of the household and the family unit as sacrosanct (Khoury 2013b). As a result, while active in the Miqati government (2011–2013), the Hezbollah deputies resisted attempts to move marriage and divorce rights into civil courts rather than religious jurisdiction (Khoury 2013b). In March 2014, the whole parliamentary bloc of Hezbollah deputies refused to respond to a petition from the National Coalition for a Law to Protect Women from Domestic Violence, which would have criminalized marital rape (Majed 2014).

In summary, the Hezbollah's involvement in Shi'a civil society has distinctly gendered characteristics that are reflected in the organization's structure and political orientation. The norms set out in the *hāla islāmiyya* and *iltizām* ascribe fixed gender roles and, as part of this, women are expected to play a central position in the transmission of the Hezbollah's ideological tenets to its wider social base codified in their role as mothers, educators and carers. This "gendering of hegemony" is reinforced through historical allegory and reference to Shi'a religious traditions (Deeb 2009: 350–53). It is demarcated through detailed sartorial codes and modes of behavior, which also help to reinforce social norms through mechanisms of consent and coercion.

Conclusion

The Hezbollah's growing hegemony within the Shi'a population originated in the context of a society ruled by militias and a weak Lebanese state during the Civil War. In the absence of a functioning state, the Hezbollah has built a highly visible social base in these areas during the 1980s and 1990s. A key reason for the Hezbollah's success is the result of its deep penetration of civil society, expressed through its wide network of social institutions and extensive cultural apparatus. The weakness of the Lebanese state in the post-Civil War period, whether in terms of its role as a service provider or even as a guarantor of civil peace, has enabled the Hezbollah to develop its domination of the Shi'a population concomitant with its military resistance against Israel. The party has utilized the reconstruction projects associated with the aftermath of the Civil War and the Israeli invasion to provide the much needed social services to the Shi'a populations. Much of this activity has focused on key power centers of the Hezbollah's rule, notably Dahyeh.

All of these activities have displayed aspects of both consent and coercion, understood in a Gramscian sense. Underpinning this consent and coercion has been a specific religiously inspired conception of the world, captured in the notions of *hāla islāmiyya* and *iltizām*. An important place has thus been accorded to religious, media, cultural and educational institutions, which form an overarching "hegemonic apparatus" that operates as a key site of cultural acquisition for the Shi'a population. In this regard, party cadres and activists in the institutions of this apparatus can be seen as Hezbollah organic intellectuals.

Through all these mechanisms, the Hezbollah's civil society organizations help to promote a coherent worldview that is able to incorporate a variety of individual and collective interests within the Shi'a population.[25] The construction of a Shi'a identity is not static and fixed but is an ongoing process that is mediated through the Hezbollah's institutional networks. Through the conscious application of the notions of *hāla islāmiyya* and *iltizām*, this process of identity formation delineates the borders of the Shi'a's belonging, in both its coercive and consensual aspects. It is also distinctively gendered, promoting a particular role for women in Hezbollah organizations as the key mediating link in the transmission of the party's ideology. The diffusion of the Hezbollah's ideology via its network of organizations facilitates the continuation and the reproduction of its power over all sectors of the Shi'a population.

Nonetheless, while the Hezbollah has utilized these institutions as a means of building popular consent and support (always circumscribed by the borders of coercion), their vision should not be understood as a complete, anti-systemic vision of society as a whole.[26] The Hezbollah's process of engagement with civil society has not challenged contemporary hierarchies within Shi'a society, nor has it encouraged any form of independent self-mobilization from below. Instead, popular activities have been utilized to further inculcate the religious values associated with the *hāla islāmiyya*, and are typically carried out in a top-down fashion from the executive levels to the social base. The next chapter explores this tension within the Hezbollah's practice of social engagement through the lens of the labor movement.

5

Hezbollah and the
Lebanese Labor Movement

During the Lebanese Civil War, trade unions played an important role in organizing various demonstrations and civil resistance against the continuation of the conflict, the sectarian division of the country, the power of militias and the Israeli occupation during the 1980s (Al-Amir Najde 2012; Dirani 2012). In the interviews conducted for this book, labor leaders and activists spoke proudly of this record.

Adib Bou Habib, head of the Printing Press Employees Federation, founder of the Lebanese Observatory of the Rights of Workers and Employees (LORWE) and an ex-member of the LCP, recounts that:

> federations and trade unions continued during the Civil War to play a role for the workers by fighting for increased wages and inflation adjustment, as well as access to social insurance. The trade union movement was the conscience of the people.
>
> (Bou Habib 2012)

A distinctive feature of this role was the attempt by federations and unions to organize across the sectarian lines that were becoming increasingly entrenched. Ahmad Dirani, a member of the LORWE and an ex-member of OCAL, highlighted this characteristic of labor work, noting that:

> during the Civil War, the trade unions organized demonstrations in 1987 and 1988 that gathered workers from both sides of Beirut for the unity of the country. This was important because it existed outside of the dynamics of the Civil War, and against the system of militias.
>
> (Dirani 2012)

Between 1985 and 1989, more than 114 collective protests took place in opposition to the Civil War.[1] The increasing number and diversity of demonstrations during these years expressed the frustration of the population with increasing socio-economic difficulties such as the remarkable 400 percent inflation rate of 1987 (Sleibe 1999: 156–57), as well as their anger with the activities of militias.[2] These protests also took place during a period of intense internal conflicts within political organizations of the same front, such as the battle between the Kataeb and Lebanese Forces (LF), or the disputes between Amal, the PSP and LCP (Sleibe 1999: 160–61). In this context, the role of the CGTL and other trade unions took on growing importance.

The CGTL mobilized throughout the Civil War around the issues of sectarianism and the specific concerns of workers; notably the declining real value of wages (as a result of inflation) and the provision of social insurance to all workers (Bou Habib 2012). The CGTL was the only significant, nationally organized force that had cross-sectarian representation and emphasized the unity of the country and opposition to the Civil War. Between 1983 and 1991, its leadership was dominated by members or sympathizers of the LNM, which included most nationalist and leftist forces (Sleibe 1999: 64).

In the years following the end of the Civil War, this social weight continued to be asserted in demonstrations and strikes throughout the country. In 1992, for example, the CGTL organized strikes and demonstrations in protest against inflation, the high cost of living and the management of the economic crisis. Despite threats by the Syrian Vice-President Abdel Halim Khaddam, who declared that "they (the Syrian regime) did not want strikes in the country, because it threatens national security" (Al-Haf 2012), against CGTL leaders—who had been summoned to Damascus by the Syrian regime—the strikes lasted for three days (Bou Habib 2012; Dirani 2012, Al-Muntada al-Ishtirākī 2012: 4–8).[3] The movement was able to paralyze the country by obstructing roads from the North to the South of the country, with eighteen cases of burning tires positioned on the highway in Beirut and Tripoli alone (Al-Haf 2012). Eventually the CGTL called off the strikes, but nonetheless, the Karama government resigned in face of the social mobilizations and new elections were organized (Al-Muntada al-Ishtirākī 2012: 4–8).

Following the election of Hariri in 1992, the CGTL presented the new government with a list of demands that included wage increases, expansion of workers' fringe benefits, consumer price regulations, rent controls, respect for the autonomy and independence of the labor movement, and the incorporation of the views of federations and unions into the reconstruction and economic recovery plans (Baroudi 1998: 536). Despite the union movement's demonstrated capacity to mobilize, these demands were not addressed by Hariri. As a result, further national strikes and demonstrations were called in 1994 with essentially the same demands as the 1992 strikes (in addition to concerns around the lack of publicly owned social services) (Baroudi 1998: 537).

On July 19, 1995, a further general strike was called that was stopped only following the deployment of the army and security services against striking workers (Sleibe 1999). The government enforced a ban on demonstrations that had been imposed by the government in 1993. The security forces reportedly beat some of the demonstrators and arrested about 200 participants including CGTL leaders, members and journalists in Beirut, Saida and Nabatieh. Many were detained for days before being released without charge, but seventy were tried in Beirut and Saida on charges of violating Article 346 of the Penal Code, which prohibits gathering for the purposes of inciting riots and disorder. About half of those tried were acquitted while the rest were sentenced to one month's imprisonment, which was immediately commuted to a fine (Amnesty International 1997).

Social struggles nonetheless continued throughout 1995 and 1996, particularly following the government's refusal to increase public sector wages. During these two years, public school teachers suspended the grading of the official baccalaureate high school exams to pressure the government for wage increases. Their actions were particularly effective because the fate of about 60,000 students hung in the balance. Likewise, university professors launched a strike in February 1996, and further strikes were called by the CGTL (Baroudi 1998: 537). In response, the government declared a state of emergency and sent security forces to break the strikes (Baroudi 1998: 538). Despite this repression, some gains were won through the mid-1990s strike wave, including a threefold increase in wages between 1993 and 1996. Real wages, however, continued to fall, as the government refused any indexation to inflation (Baroudi 1998: 544).

Demobilization and Co-option

As this 1990s wave of strikes unfolded, a clear strategy to undercut the power of the CGTL and associated federations and unions became evident. According to Adib Bou Habib, this strategy was jointly elaborated by the main political elites in Lebanon at the time (despite their different interests and rivalries): the Hariri government, Hezbollah, Amal and other Syrian regiment aligned forces such as the Ba'th party and SSNP (Bou Habib 2012; Dirani 2012). The latter parties played a critical role in this process, since all the Lebanese Labor ministries between 1993 and 2005 were controlled by political forces close to the Syrian regime. In the main, this strategy rested upon two essential pillars: (1) establishing rival federation and union bodies organized along sectarian lines or/and submitted to political forces drawing its power from the Syrian regime; and (2) the intervention in the internal affairs of the CGTL itself. Through these means, the Lebanese political elite attempted to weaken the ability of the CGTL to mobilize across sectarian lines, and to subordinate the labor movement to the priorities of the government's economic reform measures. The objective was to eliminate the main obstacle in the implementation of neoliberal policies and a possible political rival to the sectarian and bourgeois political elite.

At the same time, we can add the interferences of the Syrian regime which was present militarily in Lebanon and, until its military withdrawal in 2005, collaborated with various Lebanese governments to repress and weaken the CGTL and its activities. For example, in the general strike called by the CGTL in July 1995, the Syrian authorities supported the decision of Prime Minister Hariri to ban all demonstrations, and the order of the army and Internal Security Forces to implement the ban. They were therefore allowed to deploy themselves in Beirut and other cities to crack down on protests. The Syrian regime had the double objectives of stabilizing Lebanon following the Civil War and containing criticism against its own presence (Osoegawa 2013: 134).

State intervention in the CGTL started as early as 1993 when the Minister of Labor Abdallah Amin, a member of the Ba'th party, attempted to revive an older trade union body, the Federal Confederation of Sectoral Unions. He planned to bring in new legislation that would permit the involvement of the state in CGTL affairs (Bou Habib 2012; Dirani 2012; Abdallah 2012; Gharib 2012). This initiative failed and, in its place, the Minister of Labor began to issue licenses for the creation of new federations and unions, mostly divided along sectarian lines and with little real presence on the ground. In 1993, forty-one new trade unions and five new federations were licensed, a very significant jump on the sixty-two trade unions and twenty-two federations that existed the year before (Bou Habib 2012; Dirani 2012; Abdallah 2012; Gharib 2012). These new labor bodies, as Ghassan Sleibe noted in an interview for this book, "were designed to compete with existing trade unions and to limit the autonomy of the union movement" (Sleibe 2012). Most importantly, they also impacted on the nature of decision making in the CGTL because representation in the Executive Council of the CGTL was not based on a union's membership size—rather, each union was automatically granted two seats. Moreover, the Executive Council elected the CGTL's Political Bureau, composed of twelve members (Bou Habib 2012; Dirani 2012). In this manner, the newly licensed unions linked to political parties close to the Syrian regime (Hezbollah, Ba'th and the SSNP) invariably gained increasing weight in the CGTL.

Despite these attempts to undermine the CGTL, the strategy of Lebanon's political elite met with significant resistance from the federation's leadership and rank-and-file workers. From 1993 to 1998, a series of intense political struggles emerged within the CGTL between non-sectarian and leftist forces, on the one hand, and the government and Syrian-linked forces on the other.[4] It was in the context of these struggles that the Hariri government promulgated the 1993 law against "unapproved" public demonstrations (see above) and, in 1997, arrested the CGTL's President and Vice-President because they had refused to allow seven new unions established by Amal and the Ba'th to join the federation and participate in its elections (Bou Habib 2012; Sleibe 2012). Before the 1997 elections, other incidents of arrests of trade union leaders were reported. A report by Amnesty International stated that:

> on 13 April 1997, police reportedly surrounded the CGTL headquarters in Saida while new elections were being organized, arresting 26 trade unionists. Those detained, who included journalists, were released without charge the same evening. Police also reportedly surrounded the CGTL headquarters on the election day (24 April 1997) and arrested three union officers, apparently to prevent them from voting.
> (Amnesty International 1997)

The 1997 elections proved to be an important turning point, seeing a contest between Elias Abou Rizk (one of those arrested by the government), supported by the left and democratic trade unions, and

Ghanim al-Zoghby, supported by the Ministry of Labor and the SSNP, Hezbollah, the Baʿth party and Amal. Zoghby won the election but was only in office for one year, unable to decisively defeat the support base of Abou Rizk (Abdallah 2012; Al-Muntada al-Ishtirākī 2012: 4–8). When Abou Rizk returned to office between 1998 and 2001, attempts were made to unite the CGTL across party and sectarian lines and to mobilize against the policies of the new Hoss government. However, with the increased weight of pro-Syrian federations and trade unions in the CGTL leadership (who supported Hoss), Abou Rizk's attempt to renew labor mobilizations proved unsuccessful (Bou Habib 2012; Sleibe 2012). This was despite the intensification of neoliberal policies through this period (see Chapter 3), while thousands of workers were also laid off in 2000 from failing economic establishments (Baroudi 2000: 88).

By 2001, the Lebanese state had achieved virtually full control of the leadership of the CGTL following the election as President of Ghassan Ghosn, affiliated with SSNP and a protégé of Nabih Berri. Ghosn's candidacy was supported by the government and political forces close to the Syrian regime, including the Hezbollah, Amal, SSNP and the Baʿth. The election of Ghosn also marked the entry of Usama al-Khansa of al-Wafa federation (see below), the Hezbollah's labor unit, to the CGTL's executive council (Salloukh 2015: 76).

Ghosn and the new CGTL's leadership were criticized by workers and trade unionists on many occasions in the following years for being linked to these sectarian political forces, especially the Amal leader and President of Parliament, Nabih Berri (Abdul-Hussain 2003a).[5] The CGTL's demonstration on Labor Day in 2002 was for example held under Berri's auspices and in the presence of several MPs (Salloukh 2015: 77). Numerous critics also accused the leadership of the CGTL of only rhetorically claiming to protect worker's interests, while usually compromising the rights of workers, especially on the issue of wage adjustment. They blamed the CGTL for its inability to face challenges from the state policies and repressions against workers and representatives of trade unions (Abdul-Hussain 2002a, 2002c).

In the decade following Ghosn's election, the CGTL was progressively restructured along sectarian lines. At the time of writing, Ghosn remains in the presidency, and ten out of twelve members of the CGTL's leadership are affiliated with the March 8 Alliance.[6] On the Executive Council, March 8-allied members hold a wide majority of seats as well

(Anon 2012b). A number of independent and left-wing federations have deserted the CGTL (whether by leaving completely the CGTL or by not taking part in its meetings) due to its sectarian character and its submission to the sectarian and bourgeois political and economic elite.[7]

Hezbollah's Intervention in the Labor Movement

The Hezbollah's prominent position in the CGTL leadership reflects its willingness to create new rival and sectarian federations and unions as a means of building a base in the CGTL structures. To this end, the party has established numerous federations and trade unions across different sectors whose leadership is composed solely of Shi'a members and who are politically dominated by the Hezbollah. The most important example of this is the al-Wafa federation (which was first established in 1988 as al-Wafa Bekaa federation as it was only composed of trade unions from this region)—mostly bringing together workers in agriculture, construction, and hospitals (Yassin 2012a).[8] In 2000, only five trade unions were linked to al-Wafa with around 400 members in total (Bedran and Zbeeb 2000: 223). But over the last decade, it has expanded to Beirut and South Lebanon, bringing in a wider range of economic sectors (Ittihād al-Wafā' 2014a). There are currently eight trade unions affiliated to al-Wafa,[9] representing around 2,500 workers according to its current head, Ali Taher Yassin (Yassin 2012a).

Ali Taher Yassin is now on the executive body of the CGTL representing the Hezbollah. He explained that the role of al-Wafa is to protect the rights of the workers, but added that the union is "linked to Hezbollah and follows its line. We belong to Hezbollah." The main reason that Hezbollah first established new trade unions in the Bekaa, according to Yassin, was that trade unions in the region were not linked to the party, despite the fact that the region was dominated by the Hezbollah and was a majority Shi'a area. Most of the heads of federations and trade unions linked to the Hezbollah are members of the party, and are required to follow the party ideologically, religiously and politically (Yassin 2012a). The executive council of al-Wafa is composed of Shi'a members only (Ittihād al-Wafā' 2014a).

In addition to al-Wafa, the Hezbollah has also established rival federations in the agricultural sector,[10] the health sector[11] and the transport sector.[12]

In this latter sector, the first taxi drivers' federation was set up in 1969 by a group of leftist taxi drivers with the support of Kamal Jumblatt, Minister of the Interior and leader of the Progressive Socialist Party (PSP). It succeeded in negotiating the affiliation of taxi drivers to the National Social Security Fund (NSSF) in 1982 (Abi Yaghi 2012). However, the federation was weakened during the Hariri government when the Minister Abdallah al-Amin (1992–1995) granted Amal a license to create a new federation in the sector. The appointment of the Hezbollah ally Trad Hamadeh as Minister of Labor in 2005 then led to the granting of another license to a third transport sector federation (Abi Yaghi 2012),[13] "the Loyalty Federation" (al-Wala'), which is affiliated to Hezbollah according to its head Abdallah Hamadeh (2012). The al-Wala' Federation brings together four unions: the General Trade Union for the Drivers of Public Minibuses in Lebanon, the Trade Union of Transport Drivers and Workers in Lebanon, the Trade Union of Van Drivers of Schools and Universities in the Bekaa and the Union of Drivers for Student Transport in the South (Ittihād al-Wafā' 2014b). The executive council of al-Wala' is solely composed of Shi'a members and is politically dominated by the Hezbollah (Ittihād al-Wafā' 2014b).

The party organizes its work in these affiliated federations and unions through its Trade Union and Workers' Unit (TUWU) headed by Hashim Salhab (Ittihād al-Wafā' 2013). The orientation of the TUWU closely echoes the "social market" approach explained in Chapter 3. While claiming to prioritize the defense of workers, its public statements and annual reports tend to call for harmonious economic development and a dialogue that unites business owners and employees towards the greater national interest of Lebanon (Wahdat al-niqābāt wa al-'ummāl al-markaziyya fī Hizb Allāh 2008). The TUWU displays no principled opposition towards neoliberal measures such as privatization—as evidenced in the significant case of the MEA sell-off (see Chapter 3)—calling rather for the balancing of interests and the judgment on a case-by-case basis of instances of privatization.[14] At the same time, while employing this cross-class discourse, the TUWU also specifically emphasizes Shi'a religious reference points—including the commemoration of historic Shi'a martyrs (such as Imam Mahdi) as well as that of Hezbollah political and military figures (Wahdat al-niqābāt wa al-'ummāl al-markaziyya fī Hizb Allāh 2008, 2009). Workers' celebrations organized by the TUWU, such as Labor Day, are also held in religious institutions controlled by the Hezbollah.

A Renewal of Labor Struggles: 2004–2011

As demonstrated in Chapter 3, the early 2000s marked an important moment in the consolidation of Lebanese neoliberalism following the IMF-led negotiations around the Paris I and II Agreements from 2001–2003. Despite the significant economic changes that occurred in the wake of these agreements, opposition by the CGTL to government economic reform was largely absent. A new wave of labor mobilization would emerge, however, which lay largely outside the structures and initiative of the CGTL. The full implications of the progressive weakening of the CGTL—and its subordination to the Lebanese Ministry of Labor and political forces close to the Syrian regime—would be demonstrated throughout this renewal of the country's labor struggles. Moreover, the Hezbollah's orientation towards these new movements has been characterized by prevarication and an unwillingness to encourage independent mass struggles. At all decisive conjunctures, the Hezbollah has prioritized its own sectarian interests, frequently counterposing these to a cross-denominational labor movement.

In May 2004, the CGTL, under the pressure of popular and trade union mobilizations and protests, called for a one-day general strike throughout the country against high fuel prices but also more generally against rising prices, the lack of social services and the harsh social situation in the country which was facing approximately 30 percent unemployment (Al-Sharq al-Āwsat 2004; Al-Mustaqbal 2004; Indymedia Beirut 2004). Al-Amir Nadje and Bassam Tleiss, President of the Lebanese Federation of Drivers of Public Transport and transport interests in Lebanon, called May 27 "a first step in increasing progressively the actions of the movement [which were to] continue until the first of next July" (Al-Mustaqbal: 2004). According to the President of the Federation of the Public Transport Drivers, Abdel al-Amir Nadje (2012), the CGTL's leadership bureaucracy, under pressure from the political elite, limited the strike to one day, despite the fact protesters and trade unions, especially in the transport sector, opposed this decision and called for the strike's continuation (Chiit 2009b; Al-Amir Nadje 2012).

Most trade unions and other labor associations had announced their support for the strike call. These included the public and private school teachers, bank employees, transport workers, the workers of the national electricity company, Electricite du Liban, Lebanese university staff, farmers, agricultural workers, the water authority workers in Beirut and the North, construction workers, the workers of Trans Mediterranean Airlines and the civil servants who held a five-minute solidarity strike (Al-Sharq al-Āwsat 2004; Al-Mustaqbal 2004).

On the day of the strike, there were anti-government demonstrations and protests throughout the country (Al-Manshour 2004). Already early in the morning, the taxi service and van drivers had started their strike action. Taxi drivers blocked the road to the South-East of Beirut. The same situation was reported at Nabatieh, in Tripoli, in Saida and other cities. Schools and public transport were paralyzed nationwide. Beirut airport was brought to a total standstill for at least three hours (Al-Sharq al-Āwsat 2004; Al-Mustaqbal 2004). Outside the cabinet headquarters, there was a sit-in, again with banners against the high petrol prices, but also against corruption, government fiscal policies and the high levels of unemployment.

The country was paralyzed by these mobilizations. A turning point would come around midday, with the deadly repression of protesters by the army in the neighborhood of Hay al-Sellom, one of the poorer Shi'a neighborhoods of southern Beirut.

The army opened fire on demonstrators and strikers, who were gathered in Hay al-Sellom, killing five protesters and injuring dozens, while arresting more than 130 people (Indymedia Beirut 2004; Adada 2015). Protesters, mostly taxi and mini-van drivers who had gathered originally at 5am in the neighborhood, were attacked by the army when they were heading towards the main demonstrations in the Council of Ministers' headquarters. As soon as the clashes began, the CGTL, which had called for the strike, called on protesters "to stop demonstrating and to remain peaceful and civil and refrain from breaking the law" (Libcom 2004).

The neighborhood Hay al-Sellom was turned into a closed security area by the army, preventing people from entering and exiting it and conducting a vast campaign of arrests (Indymedia Beirut 2004). Following the killing of protesters in Hay al-Sellom, protests spread to several areas of the southern suburbs in the neighborhoods of Burj al-Barajneh, Al-Mreije, Al-Ouzaai, Al-Kafaà, on the Highway Hadi Nasrallah, Shiah and Shatila roundabout. At the same time, the Labor Ministry was burned down by protestors. The Lebanese army then spread in the areas of clashes from Ouzaii to Gallery Semaan, and roads were blocked by military on one side, and burning tires on the other side. Troops shot at protesters, injuring some, while others were arrested (Indymedia Beirut 2004).

The main Lebanese sectarian political parties supported the army, saying: "The army is the red line," while most of the media portrayed the strike as a "barbaric attempt to attack the army" (Chiit 2009b). A few days later in a press conference, the Hezbollah leader Hassan Nasrallah accused individuals linked to the US Embassy of instigating violence between protestors and the army and that "after the shooting in Hay al-Sellom area, groups linked to the embassy worked to spread chaos and violence in other regions in the southern suburbs" (El-Ghoul 2004). He added that the instigators had acted with the aim of undermining the close relationship between the government and the Hezbollah, and he denied claims the Hezbollah had any interest in seeing Premier Rafiq Hariri leave office, while he insisted that his party "was not involved in Thursday's rioting over gasoline prices in Hay al-Sellom" (El-Ghoul 2004).

In an interview, Ali Taher Yassin (2012b), the Hezbollah trade unionist, and Abdallah Hamadeh (2012), the head of the federation of al-Wala' linked to Hezbollah, both characterized the events of Hay al-Sellom in 2004 as an attempt to create instability and chaos in the country by some parties and provocateurs that had nothing to do with the demonstrators and unions' strikes. While regretting the repression and acknowledging that some people had legitimate demands, Yassin (2012b) nevertheless went on to say that what happened in Hay al-Sellom's neighborhood was due to a unique local situation, with particular family and tribal dynamics, instead of the wider social dynamics created by the strikes and the demands of the people (Yassin 2012b). The Hezbollah's official line of 2004 was not challenged.

Following the withdrawal of Syrian forces from Lebanon, a new government was formed by Fouad Siniora on July 19, 2005. This government included Hezbollah representatives for the first time in Lebanese history, including Trad Hamadeh as the Minister of Labor. The Lebanese government had to face a major mobilization for the defense of public services by the teachers' union in May 2006, which gathered at least a quarter of a million people and forced the government to reverse some of its decisions such as: "diminishing the pensions, increasing VAT from 10–12 percent, raising fuel prices by 30 percent and imposing short term contracts on government workers and teachers" (Chiit 2006; Gharib 2012).

The Hezbollah participated in these protests, alongside the FPM and the LCP (Qualander 2006). The ruling parties of March 14 attacked the movement, saying it was mostly Shi'a orchestrated and was infiltrated by Syrian workers. The Siniora government claimed that the demonstrations were not workers' demonstrations but an attempted coup planned by the Shi'a to take power—this was despite the fact that the demonstration brought together workers from all denominations according to one participant interviewed for this book (Chiit 2009a; Gharib 2012). The CGTL was again not a leading force in the mobilization.

In January 2007, a demonstration called by the CGTL against the Paris III agenda gathered only 2,000 people. One of the reasons for this small size was the fact that the March 8 forces, including the Hezbollah who were in the opposition at the time, did not mobilize for the protest. While critical of some aspects of the Paris Conference, the Hezbollah explained that they did not want to jeopardize its outcomes (Achcar 2007). Indeed, the Hezbollah parliamentary deputies, despite their resignation from the government in December 2006, supported the reform program presented by Prime Minister Siniora to the conference itself (Catusse and Abi Yaghi 2011: 73). Nonetheless, following this small demonstration in January and the increasing tensions between the opposition and the government, the March 8 Coalition including Amal, Hezbollah and FPM, called for a general strike on January 23, 2007.[15] Although this began as a largely bureaucratic initiative, it turned rapidly into a popular uprising with the main roads of transit in the country blocked. This situation overwhelmed the strike's initiators and they decided to end the strike declaring that it might "create confessional tensions" (Chiit 2009a). The Hezbollah agreed to this termination of the strike, refusing suggestions by General Aoun to launch a rally in front of the government headquarters (ICG 2007: 2). According to radical left activist, Bassem Chiit (2009a), the March 8 coalition feared that this popular movement was moving towards taking up socio-economic issues across sectarian lines, and the Hezbollah preferred to emphasize only the interests of the Shiʿa.

One of the characteristics of Hezbollah's orientation towards these social and labor struggles, particularly those that were to emerge through 2008, was its unwillingness to support large-scale, independent mass mobilizations of workers, preferring to rely instead upon small-scale, armed actions against its political opponents. In this sense, the Hezbollah has reinforced a sectarian dynamic within these struggles, undercutting any cross-sectarian impulse that they may have potentially channeled. A good example of this is found in an aborted general strike of May 2008, which was called for by federations and trade unions of taxi drivers, teachers and farmers, demanding an increase in the minimum wage, higher public wages (which had been frozen since 1996), and measures against the country's runaway inflation (Catusse 2009).[16] The strike, initially called for May 7, did not take place following the outbreak of street fighting between opposing political forces. The March 14 political forces, which at the time held governmental power, raised the threat of shutting down the Hezbollah's telecommunications network. In response, the Hezbollah declined to mobilize for the general strike and instead launched armed attacks on neighborhoods in Beirut that were known to be support bases of March 14. These fights broke popular mobilization in the streets and any possibility of joint worker struggles across sectarian lines (Catusse 2009).[17] As explained by the trade unionist Ahmad Dirani, the Hezbollah's military intervention was "aimed against the possibility of a large trade union and workers mobilisation taking the lead against the government in a democratic way. Hezbollah did not favour this option" (Dirani 2012). Dirani argued that such a mobilization would not only have achieved social gains around economic issues but could also have addressed the threat to the Hezbollah's telecommunication system.

In June 2011, a new government led by the March 8 forces and headed by Najib Miqati as Prime Minister was formed. The Hezbollah held two ministries in this government: the Ministry of Agriculture (Hussein Hajj Hassan) and a Minister of State (Muhammad Fneich). The experience of the Hezbollah in this government is instructive, as it indicates the party's unwillingness to support significant reform measures aimed at addressing the situation of workers in Lebanon. Debates around these measures focused particularly on an initiative advanced by the Minister of Labor Charbel Nahas, soon after the formation of the new government. Nahas' initiative contained a number of significant social reforms, particularly the goal of establishing a "social wage," which would adjust the salaries of workers and private sector employees in line with the rate of inflation, and also expand the range of subsidies (Traboulsi 2014: 51 and 55). These measures would be funded by higher taxation on finance and other rentier activities and, in this respect, would have represented a reversal of the weakening of labor vis-à-vis capital that had been characteristic of the previous years (Lebanese Observatory of the Rights of Workers and Employees [LORWE] 2013b: 6–7). The initiative also proposed that transport allowances be included in salaries, and the establishment of a universal health care system (LORWE 2013b: 6–7).

Nahas' initiative was opposed by a range of different political forces. Initially, the inclusion of universal health coverage in a social wage was rejected by Amal's Minister of Health, Ali Hassan Khalil, who opposed the plan because he believed it encroached on his domain of responsibility (Nahas 2012). This was despite the fact that the NFSS came under the Labor Ministry, and therefore was the responsibility of Nahas not Khalil (Traboulsi 2014: 55). The Lebanese journalist Muhammad Zbeeb and the trade unionist Adib Bou Habib both argued that Khalil's opposition was due to the fact: "that the Ministry of Health and Social Security are part of Amal and Berri's share in the pie and they wanted to use the universal health coverage for their own political and clientelist interests" (Zbeeb 2012a; Bou Habib 2012). Following pressure from Amal and Hezbollah in October 2011, Nahas agreed to separate the universal health coverage from its wage reform project (Traboulsi 2014: 55–56). The latter would become the new line of battle inside the government.

Nahas' first wage initiative included a rise in the minimum wage to L£890,000 ($593) per month, plus transport allowances. This proposition, however, was firmly rejected by private sector employers, who instead reached an agreement called the "Consensual Agreement on Wage Reform" with the leadership of the CGTL and the Prime Minister Najib Miqati (LORWE 2013b: 6–7). This agreement was less advantageous to workers as it did not include transport allowances and would only raise the minimum wage to L£675,000 ($450) (Orient le Jour 2012a). The private sector argued that adding transportation allowances to the basic salary would increase costs to an unsustainable level and damage the private sector in particular (The Daily Star 2012a).

The Consensual Agreement (CA) was adopted by the government in December 2011, with the two Hezbollah ministers, Muhammad Fneich and Hussein Hajj Hassan, voting to support it rather than the Nahas initiative. In reference to the role of the CGTL, Fneich argued: "workers and employees reject the wage adjustment plan proposed by the Minister of Labour Charbel Nahas" (Orient le Jour 2011e). Hezbollah's position, however, was strongly marked by the contradictions inherent to its "social market" standpoint and the different demands emanating from its social base. The day after the vote, following widespread popular criticisms against the position of its ministers, Hezbollah shifted its position to support a strike and demonstration organized against the CA. The Hezbollah ministers explained that their earlier vote in favor of the CA was the result of a lack of coordination with Nahas, and not in opposition to the plan itself (Al-Akhbar 2012).

The Hezbollah, however, declined to support a demonstration in support of the Nahas Plan on December 15, which drew more than 6,000 people in Beirut (Al-Akhbar English 2011).[18] At this demonstration, many protestors expressed their opposition through placards, chants and group discussions about the role of the CGTL.[19] One activist, Farah Kobeissi (Al-Akhbar English 2011), in an interview with *Al-Akhbar* newspaper, accused the CGTL of collusion with the government, while adding that the CGTL's decision is not taken democratically by the workers, but by a group of bureaucrats that are very close to the employers, the government and the political forces in power, therefore hindering its ability to be truly representative of workers (Al-Akhbar English 2011). Indeed, not only did the CGTL oppose Nahas' plan, they also filed a complaint against him with the International Labor Organization, accusing him of fragmenting the trade union movement in Lebanon (LORWE 2013b: 15).

A final round of parliamentary voting on the CA and the Nahas initiative took place in mid-January 2012. In the debate prior to the vote, Nahas proposed a minimum wage of L£868,000 ($578.60) plus transport allowances (Traboulsi 2014: 55). Despite numerous meetings between Nahas and the Hezbollah, Amal, and the Prime Minister, no agreement was reached. His plan was eventually rejected in favor of the CA, and he resigned from the cabinet in February of 2012 (Traboulsi 2014: 56). The Hezbollah trade unionist Ali Taher Yassin justified the vote and CGTL's refusal of the Nahas plan, stating that:

The CGTL did not want to hold the responsibility of putting in danger the stability of the country. The national and regional political scene does not allow all these changes, especially when you have the other party (March 14) trying its best to create instability.

(Yassin 2012a)

Yassin was to echo these sentiments at the CCSD conference, "Reform of Social Policies in Lebanon: From Selective Subsidy towards Welfare State" in March 2012 (which the author attended), arguing that it would be difficult for workers to raise further demands around wages due to the lack of stability in the country, and the potential damage that may arise to the Lebanese economy. While declaring that "humane" salaries are necessary, Yassin argued that these should be reached through negotiation with employers. At the conference, he defended the leadership of the CGTL from the complaints of audience members that the federation no longer represented the interests of workers (Yassin's intervention in the Conference Reform of Social Policies in Lebanon: From Selective Subsidy towards Welfare State 2012). Pointedly, Yassin's intervention followed that of Nicolas Elie Chammas, President of the Beirut Traders Association, with whom he shared the same panel. Chammas attacked Charbel Nahas for promoting a "Marxist discourse" and an "atmosphere of class struggle" in the country, adding his support for the CA. Yassin did not respond either directly or indirectly to Chammas. Other trade unionists linked to the Hezbollah, Akram Zeid and Abdallah Hamadeh (head of the al-Wala transport federation), also argued that the party could not support the Nahas initiative because of economic reasons and the potential for instability in the country (Zeid 2012; Hamadeh 2012).

At the end of 2015, the increase in wages promised in the CA had not yet been implemented and the mechanisms to fund them are still being discussed in commissions in parliament. The Hezbollah, although rhetorically supporting the CA agreement, has joined the "technical accountant" discourse shared by March 14 and March 8, as argued by researcher Raed Sharaf (2014), to explain the difficulties in implementing the wage increase as set out in the original agreement. Political parties, including the Hezbollah, explain that they have to maintain the existing financial policy, and warn of the danger of economic collapse if the wage increase is implemented according to the existing plan and without some sacrifice on the part of workers.

In summary, the period 2004–2011 provides a useful illustration of the orientation of the Hezbollah towards labor movements in Lebanon. The period witnessed a significant upsurge in labor militancy, marked particularly by the call for general strikes in 2004 and 2008, and the fierce debate around the Nahas initiative in 2011. These struggles revealed the tensions inherent within the Hezbollah's claim to represent the poor and marginalized layers of the Shiʿa population, alongside its integration into the political elite and increasing linkages to the emerging Shiʿa bourgeoisie. At all major points, the Hezbollah has expressed a rhetorical concern with issues such as privatization, the implications of agreements such as Paris III and the decreasing value of real wages. At the same time, it has strongly resisted attempts to mobilize its mass base in a manner that would support independent initiatives across sectarian lines. In general, these tensions have been resolved in favor of neoliberal reform, particularly in those periods in which the Hezbollah has held governmental positions.

Alternative Labor Movements in Lebanon?

The 2011 mobilizations around the Nahas plan marked a significant moment in the Lebanese labor movement not least because they indicated the emergence of new organizational structures that have attempted to renew the earlier, cross-sectarian orientation of the CGTL. One important example of this is the founding of the Union Coordination Committee (UCC) (*Hay'at tansīq niqābiyya*).[20] The UCC brings together more than forty independent trade unions and between 140,000 and 176,000 members, mainly employed in the civil service or as public and private school teachers (Gharib 2012; LORWE 2013b: 8). The league of teachers of primary (Public Primary Schools Teachers League in Lebanon [PPSTLL])[21] and secondary schools (the Public Secondary Schools Teachers League in Lebanon [PSSTLL]),[22] which consist respectively of 65,000 and 40,000 members (Catusse and Abi Yaghi 2011: 81), have been the driving force of the organization. Mainly consisting of public employees of the state, the UCC is not legally recognized as a federation or a trade union,[23] but it is nevertheless registered by the Ministry of Culture where its offices are located (Gharib 2012). This status does not officially allow the UCC to organize strikes, but has not prevented it from striking and placing itself at the head of social mobilizations. Leaders of the UCC, such as Hana Gharib (until 2015), who is also a member of the LCP, and Mahmoud Haidar, have nevertheless expressed that one of their objectives was to transform the leagues of teachers into trade unions and the UCC into a federation of trade unions in the public sector (LORWE 2013a; Al-Hajj 2014a). According to activists interviewed for this book, the UCC's democratic organizational structure has helped protect it from attempts by the state and political forces to undermine or intervene in its political affairs as had occurred with the CGTL (Bou Habib 2012; Gharib 2012; Sleibe 2012; George al-Hajj 2012). Indeed, the opposition to the CA was led primarily by the UCC, including the aforementioned demonstration on December 15, 2011. We will see that the democratic structures of the UCC were nevertheless not enough to resist the efforts of sectarian bourgeois political parties, despite their rivalries, to dominate and control it in order to stifle its cross-sectarian mobilization capacities and its challenge to the sectarian and bourgeois political system.

The growth of the UCC took place in the context of continued labor struggles throughout the country in 2012 and 2013.[24] In spring and summer 2012, for example, protests erupted by more than 2,500 contract workers at the electricity company, EDL, demonstrating against the privatization plans of the government.[25] The workers claimed that the Ministry of Energy and Water (MoEW) had failed to provide them with permanent employment, social security, a decent monthly salary and job security (Abou Zaki 2012c). The majority of EDL workers are daily subcontracted workers ("*muyāwimīn*") whose numbers increased from approximately 500 to 2,400 between 1995 and 2011 (Civil Society Knowledge Center, Lebanon Support, 2016).[26] These workers do not enjoy any social security, pension, insurance or benefits, and are banned from forming unions or going on strike (al-Saadi 2015). At the time of the protests, the Minister in charge, Gebran Bassil, a FPM member and nephew of General Aoun, refused to meet the contract workers and described them as troublemakers and outlaws (Abou Zaki 2012c). He also sent in the security services to prevent the strikers from reaching their sit-in. His restructuring plan envisioned that 1,800 of these workers would be made redundant. The Hezbollah, who had been in charge of the Ministry from July 2005 to November 2006 under Minister Muhammad Fneich, supported the privatization process;[27] first endorsing Bassil's plan in Cabinet (Al-Akhbar English 2012a), and then voting in favor of a draft law allowing contract workers at Lebanon's state-run electricity company to become full-time employees. During this period, the Hezbollah did not criticize Bassil's vocal and sectarian attacks on the workers' mobilization, despite the fact that the vast majority of affected workers were Shiʿa.[28] The CGTL was also absent from supporting the workers, only intervening on the 93rd day of the strike in which they took the side of EDL administration and pressured strikers to end their action (LORWE 2013b: 12).[29] In the end, the EDL workers were able to obtain temporary contract employment for all daily-workers in the three new subsidiary companies, and the promise by the Ministry of Energy and Water of a full-employment schedule after the contracts end in 2016 (Civil Society Knowledge Center, Lebanon Support, 2016).

In February and March 2013, massive demonstrations and open-ended strikes were called by UCC-led teachers demanding the implementation of a decision to increase salaries that was passed by the Minister of Education in 2012. Tens of thousands of teachers demonstrated throughout the country and the strikes lasted for more than three weeks. Public schools and some private schools participated in the strikes, except the Catholic schools and those schools in Beirut's southern suburbs affiliated with Amal and the Hezbollah (Salloukh 2015: 203). The UCC was a major force behind these mobilizations, which have continued throughout 2014 due to the continued failure to implement the wage increase. The UCC has resisted calls by the government to fund the salary increase by shifting the burden onto the poorer layers of society, including via suggested measures such as new indirect taxes, a reduction of benefits for teachers, cuts to retirees' pay and an increase in contractual employment (Orient le Jour 2013b; Andraos 2013).[30] In the summer of 2015, the UCC was still pressuring the government for the implementation of the policy that had been agreed more than two years prior.[31]

After summer 2015, the UCC nevertheless witnessed a lower level of protests and opposition against the Lebanese government following the victory in January 2015 in the elections for the Association of Public Secondary Education teachers' administrative committee, which has played a leading role within the UCC, of the list headed by Abdo Khater. Khater is a member of the FPM, who was supported by all the sectarian political parties of both March 8 and 14, and he won against the list headed by Hanna Gharib, who was only supported by independents and the LCP.[32] The list supported by March 8 and 14 forces swept up sixteen of the administrative committee's eighteen seats (Salloukh 2015: 86). This occurred despite promises of the new head of the League of Teachers, Mr. Khater, not to give up the fight started by Hanna Gharib for the implementation of the salary increase (Orient Le Jour 2015b). The coalition between March 8 and 14 forces, whose common list was called the Union's Consensus, against the list of Gharib, gathered under the name of the Independent Union's Movement, also won the February 2015 elections for the Beirut, Mount Lebanon, the South and North regional branches and all but two seats in the Bekaa branch (Salloukh 2015: 87). These elections were reminiscent of the earlier episodes when sectarian political forces acted to undermine the role of the CGTL. On his side, Hanna Gharib, still a popular figure among a wide section of the labor movement, became the new Secretary-General of the Lebanese Communist Party at the elections of the 11th National Congress in April 2016 (The Daily Star 2016a). Upon his election, he promised a "rebirth" of the party, calling on all communists outside of the party to return to its ranks (The Daily Star 2016b). In mid-June, Hanna Gharib launched a scathing attack against the country's ruling political class, saying that Lebanon's "authoritarian leaders were ravaging its capabilities and its natural resources, using sectarianism to impose its authority and dictatorship, practices status quo and is united over the exploitation of workers, teachers, farmers and the poor" (The Daily Star 2016d).

Other struggles that emerged in 2013 should also be noted, such as attempts by the Federation of Unions of Banks' Employees to defend the last remaining collective agreement in Lebanon, protests by employees of the Spinneys supermarket chain to defend their right to organize, and mobilizations by contract workers and those without fixed contracts in the education sector who were seeking protection and continuity of employment. The UCC was again prominent in solidarity with these struggles, for example through its petition for a million-person rally, built by campaigning across the country and in meetings with local popular organizations. The EDL strike continued into 2014, including a strike on April 15. Workers at EDL have expressed their agreement with the UCC's attempts to increase the salary scale (Wehbe, M. 2012). At the end of summer 2014, a new massive strike began at the EDL headquarters, as workers called for full-time employment. EDL had announced that when its three private service providers' contracts expire in 2016, that EDL would continue to employ only 897 of the nearly 2,000 contract workers. Daily-workers all throughout Lebanon joined the strike and blocked roads. In December 2014, the end of the four-month strike at EDL headquarters was announced after the company's board and workers along with representatives of political parties reached a deal about the establishment of public limited competitions to enter a full-position employment in EDL (Civil Society Knowledge Center, Lebanon Support, 2016). Strikes and sit-ins however continued after the announcement of the end of the protest by the EDL workers throughout 2015 and into beginning of 2016. By summer 2016, the EDL workers were still pressuring the authorities and employers to heed their long-standing demands through demonstrations, sit-ins and strikes (The Daily Star 2016e).

The teacher's struggles through 2013 and 2014 indicated several salient and inter-related features of the Lebanese labor movement. First, they demonstrated the unwillingness of Hezbollah to support any independent mobilizations of workers, particularly given its participation in government. During these strikes, Hezbollah refused to take a stance within government in support of the salary increases and did not mobilize its membership in the UCC-led actions. On several occasions, Hezbollah representatives actively opposed these strikes. In November 2013, during a meeting of the southern branch of the Public Secondary Schools Teachers League in Lebanon, Hezbollah (and Amal) representatives argued against a UCC strike planned for November 26, while a majority of the remaining participants voted in favor (Sharaf 2014). Furthermore, Hezbollah teachers did not participate in open-ended strikes called by the UCC, and refused the calls of Hanna Gharib for escalation of the protests (Sharaf 2014). Likewise, during a marking boycott called by the UCC in summer 2014, Hezbollah representatives called for an end to the boycott and supported a parliamentary decision to automatically pass all students in an attempt to break the action (Al-Hajj 2014b) and undermine the UCC in public opinion, as well as to divide the ranks of the UCC. Nonetheless, the UCC decided to continue the boycott and to join further strikes called by various sectors of the public administration to implement an increased salary scale (Orient le Jour 2014d; Al-Hajj 2014b). But this decision was reached after a long discussion in which public secondary school teachers—except those affiliated with Amal and the Hezbollah—and their colleagues in the technical school voted to maintain the boycott, while private school teachers and primary public school teachers voted to overturn the decision under the pretext of rescuing the UCC's public image (Salloukh 2015: 85). The first breaches in the UCC and Gharib's leadership appeared, with consequences as we have seen.

Despite its large base of teachers and network of schools (as outlined in Chapter 4), only a small number of Hezbollah teachers participate in the UCC while many have let their membership in the organization lapse.[33] The Hezbollah has argued that this was due to the UCC's strategy of militancy, rather than their preferred course of consensus and dialogue (Zoghbi 2013).

In addition to the Hezbollah's abstention from these strikes, the teachers' strike further confirmed the marginalization of the CGTL, which had been undermined by the erstwhile attempts to bring it under state control. Instead, the prominent role of the UCC pointed to the emergence of a new institutional configuration within the trade union movement.

Today, the CGTL is facing significant problems. Its funding is now completely tied to the discretion of the Labor Ministry, which places considerable constraint on activity as the federation does not receive dues from its membership (Wehbe, M. 2012; Anon 2012b). The federation's leadership has resisted any reform in the structure of the CGTL, which is still organized through a federal structure that gives equal representation to a member organization of more than 8,000 members (such as the Federation of Unions of Banks' Employees) and one composed of forty-two members (such as Federation of the Trade Unions of Mount Lebanon) (Bedran and Zbeeb 2000). The large growth in these small federations is indicated by the fact that the CGTL consisted of more than fifty federations and between 580 and 640 unions in the beginning of the 2010s, up from twenty-two federations and sixty-two unions in 1992— concurrent with a significant reduction in the proportion of workers covered by the federation (now standing at between 4–7 percent of the country's work force) (Bou Habib 2012; Abdallah 2012; Sleibe 2012; Salloukh 2015: 77).[34] This structure has entrenched the control of the March 8 forces over the CGTL, which now represent more than half of its component federations (Dirani 2012). Moreover, the leadership of the CGTL, notably its President Ghassan Ghosn, has been accused of corruption (Wehbe, M. 2012). According to Ali Taher Yassin, the CGTL's

Council of Delegates (*Majlis al-Mandubīn*), which is in charge of verifying the federation's accounts, has not met since 2001 (Yassin 2012a).[35]

The decline of the CGTL is further reflected in the increasing public opposition to the federation expressed by worker activists. In May 2012, a meeting called "The Consultative union meeting for a democratic and independent trade union movement" was organized at the initiative of the Lebanese Center for Trade Union Training. Numerous federations opposed to the CGTL participated in this meeting, including the Printing Press Workers' Federation, National Federation of Workers, the Federation of Chemical Workers and the Federation of Construction and Timber Workers (LORWE 2013b: 15). The gathering expressed its support to the UCC and criticized the economic direction of the state. The most important outcome was the goal of building a democratic and independent trade union movement, autonomous from the decisions of political parties and the leadership of the CGTL. In response to threats to its authority, the CGTL leadership issued a statement in December 2012, accusing anyone establishing an independent trade union outside of the CGTL of seeking to: "atomize, dismember, and divide the trade unions and abandon the workers in order to serve the Zionist project calling for constructive chaos" (Zbeeb 2012d).

At a conference held in October 2013 to discuss the CGTL's record, many labor activists argued for the establishment of an independent, combative and democratic trade union movement, as an alternative to the current federation (Al-Hajj 2013). Charbel Nahas declared at the conference that: "the CGTL's leadership are little more than agents of big business" and that: "their role is tantamount to keeping a lid on the labor movement and signing off one concession after another" (Al-Hajj 2013). Ghassan Sleibe pointed out that the great majority of trade unionists in the CGTL are linked to the sectarian political parties who pay their wages, adding that: "these officials, in most cases, do not even belong to the sector they represent, thus severely limiting their ability to represent the rank and file" (Al-Hajj 2013). This growing opposition has also been manifested in demonstrations held on May Day in 2012 and 2013 in front of the CGTL's headquarters, in protest against the federation's policies. The slogan "The People Want to Overthrow the Confederation," has been written several times on the walls of its headquarters, while graffiti campaigns by young activists on the streets of Beirut were organized for May Day in 2012 to express their rejection of the institution, which they see as a "traitor that does not represent the interests of workers, but those of the government" (Al-Kantar 2013).

Conclusion

Historically, the Lebanese labor movement has played a prominent role in encouraging cross-sectarian mobilizations in support of worker and other social struggles. This record extends back to the period of the Civil War—when the CGTL organized demonstrations and strikes across the various areas of Beirut—and continued through the mobilizations against the neoliberal policies of Hariri and subsequent governments, whether led by March 8 or March 14 forces. These struggles have been viewed by all sections of Lebanon's elite as presenting a potentially serious challenge to the status quo, including the sectarian division of the political system. In response to the challenge posed by the labor movement, Lebanese governments have attempted to undermine the CGTL through establishing rival, sectarian-linked federations and trade unions as well as direct intervention in the affairs of the CGTL itself. By the early 2000s, this process proved relatively successful.

The Hezbollah, along with other political forces supported by the Syrian regime, has participated in this weakening of the labor movement. The party has formed separate, Shiʿa-based federations and trade unions in agriculture, transport, construction, printing, press, the health sector, cooperatives and electricity. This proliferation of federations and trade unions has enabled it to win significant power in the CGTL, in which the majority of leadership seats are controlled by Amal and the Hezbollah. Today, the CGTL is unable and unwilling to mobilize workers, despite the intensification of neoliberal policies over the recent period. As many of the interviews conducted for this book indicated, the CGTL has instead become a vehicle for the political agenda of the Hezbollah, Amal and the other smaller Syrian-allied parties (Bou Habib 2012; Dirani 2012; Gharib 2012; Sleibe 2012).

This shift in the composition of the CGTL leadership has created a transformation in the discourse of the Lebanese labor movement—away from an orientation based on cross-sectarian mobilization, towards one that identifies sectarian goals as paramount and projects a unanimity of interests of different class fractions within sectarian communities. In this sense, the Hezbollah (and likewise Amal's) influence in the official structures of the labor movement corresponds to the changing class composition of the Shi'a community as a whole, and an alignment with the elites of the Shi'a community.

This record, in regards to social and workers struggles, appears to confirm that the party's interests are more aligned with those of the elites of the Shi'a community than with those of workers or poorer populations. It is apparent that the Hezbollah, much like the other political parties in Lebanon, acts in practice to prevent the emergence of a cross-sectarian popular movement in Lebanon, which would be able to confront deeper social and economic issues. The potential emergence of such a class dynamic could challenge the sectarian system and the position of the dominant political parties, including that of the Hezbollah.

6

Hezbollah's Military Apparatus

The Hezbollah's military apparatus is governed by the Jihad Council (JC) (*al-Majlis al-Jihādī*), which, according to various sources (Daher 2014: 195; Blanford 2011: 101), is presided over by Hassan Nasrallah. The Jihad Council is under the authority of the *Majlis Shura al-Qarār*, which as Chapter 5 noted, wields all decision-making power and directs several subordinate functional councils. The *Majlis Shura al-Qarār* views all elements of the group's activities, including its political and military wings, as part of one holistic entity (Qassem 2008: 91). According to the Hezbollah's top officials, this unity of purpose among the group's diverse activities is essential to its success. Qassem told a Lebanese newspaper in 2000 that "If the military wing were separated from the political wing, this would have repercussions, and it would reflect on the political scene," adding that "Hezbollah's Secretary General is the head of the Shura Council and also the head of the Jihad Council, and this means that we have one leadership, with one administration" (cited in Levitt 2013).

The Jihad Council nevertheless enjoys a strategic ambiguity according to the American researcher Matthew Levitt. Levitt argues that neither the majority of Hezbollah officials nor the party's elected parliamentarians are aware of the details of their party's covert military activities, which are decided on by the most senior leadership of the party and of the Jihad Council (Levitt 2013).

The Jihad Council runs three different units called the Islamic Resistance, the Security Organ and the External Security Apparatus (ESA).

Islamic Resistance

The Islamic Resistance's historic role since its establishment has been military confrontation with Israel. As was noted in Chapter 2, 1,500 Pasdaran established the Islamic Resistance in summer 1982, setting up training camps in the Syrian city of Zabadani and in the western Bekaa district (with Syria's authorization) (Norton 1987: 19). At this time, Abbas al-Mussawi encouraged his students and followers to undergo military training in the camps located in the West Bekaa. According to Subhi Tufayli, more than 1,000 youths were trained during the summer of 1982, and clandestine groups were constituted and sent to the South where the first military operations of the party were launched against Israeli's occupation (cited in Daher 2014: 80).

Today, the exact number of Hezbollah soldiers is difficult to estimate, but is believed to range from 5,000 (Daher 2014: 295) to 7,500 full-time soldiers with some 20,000 reservists (Nakhoul 2013). The Hezbollah recruits usually follow a specific course of military training, which generally takes places in Iran in the various training camps run by the Qods Force of the IRGC and sometimes in Syria. Recruits into the Hezbollah's Special Forces unit, the most elite element in the military organization of the party, go through an intensive three-month course divided into two forty-five-day programs with a five-day break in between. The Special Forces cadres are full-time soldiers who train continuously, while most of the Hezbollah combatants are part timers with day jobs or college students (Blanford 2011: 120–21).

While receiving formal orders from the leadership, the military apparatus of the Islamic movement is very autonomous in their implementation. To this end, the Hezbollah has purposely reduced inter-mediaries between the top military leadership and local commanders on the ground (Berti and Gleis 2012: 64–65). Naim Qassem (2008: 98–100) has stated that once the green light for a military operation is given, the small command involved in its planning, execution and tactics handles all the decision-making.[1] In this manner, Hezbollah's command structure is less pyramid-like and more horizontal in nature (Berti and Gleis 2012: 65). Timur Goksel, the former spokesman of the United Nations monitoring force in South Lebanon, has confirmed this—noting that Hezbollah fighters "don't work in military hierarchies or military command levels. There is one leader in Beirut and all the other units in the field are autonomous, they know what they are doing [by themselves]" (cited in Asia Times 2006).

Security Organ Unit

The Security Organ Unit is responsible for the security of the members of the Hezbollah and its arms in Lebanon, notably through the surveillance of alleged collaborators (Daher 2014: 195; Blanford 2011: 428–32). It is in charge of the Hezbollah's four territorial commands covering the South, Dahyeh, the Bekaa Valley and the Mediterranean coastline (Blanford 2011: 346). In these regions, the Security Organ monitors the entry and activities of visitors, including journalists and photographers (Blanford 2011: 428–32).

The Security Organ Unit has been quite effective in the protection of Hezbollah members since the establishment of the Islamic movement. This was particularly visible during the 2006 Lebanon War: not a single high-ranking cadre of the Hezbollah was killed during the thirty-three days of war despite numerous attempts by the Israeli army, including the dropping of twenty-two tons of bombs on a bunker in Beirut allegedly used by senior members of the Hezbollah (Democracy Now 2006) or the failure to kidnap twice the *Sheikh* Muhammad Yazbeck in the city of Baalbek and its surroundings (Daher 2007: 45).

The Security Organ Unit, with the cooperation of the ICRG, was responsible for the discovery of the most significant security breach in the party's history—a Mossad agent located in the leadership of Hezbollah Unit 910 (a unit that coordinates the group's foreign operations, see below). This double agent, Muhammed Shawraba, worked with four other members of a Mossad team. The Hezbollah security apparatus has detained and interrogated Muhammed Shawraba and his four colleagues since November 2014, after placing them under surveillance for six or seven months. Shawraba was tried for treason after he tipped off Israel about five operations to avenge the killing of the Hezbollah's top military commander Imad Mughniyah, leading to their failure (The Daily Star 2014d). He allegedly also passed to Israeli secret services information that led to the 2008 assassination of the high-ranking Hezbollah official Imad Mughniyah and the 2013 killing of Hassan al-Laqqi (Middle East Eye 2014). This was not the first time that spies had penetrated the ranks of the party. In 2011, the Hezbollah leader Sayyid Hassan Nasrallah acknowledged that at least two Hezbollah members had confessed to working for the US Central Intelligence Agency (The Daily Star 2014d).

The Security Organ Unit, despite its efficiency, has nevertheless not prevented the assassination of seven Hezbollah commanders by Israeli armed forces. The first was *Sheikh* Ragheb Harb, one of the founding fathers of the Hezbollah, who was gunned down in the Nabatieh town of Jibchit in southern Lebanon in 1984 (The Daily Star 2013). The last one was in December 2013: Hajj Hassan al-Laqqis, who was, according to Lebanese journalist Radwan Murtada, the "head of Hezbollah's air defence division, and one of the resistance's most important 'electronic minds'" (Murtada 2013), and was killed outside his home in the southern suburbs of Beirut.

In addition to these functions directed against external threats, the Security Organ Unit is an important part of the repressive apparatus of the Hezbollah within Lebanon itself, and has frequently been compared to a "quasi-state apparatus" in the regions under the Hezbollah's domination. This has been illustrated on numerous occasions where the Security Organ Unit has overruled the authority of Lebanese government institutions. In September 2010, for example, SUVs with tinted windows and no license plates, belonging to the Hezbollah, entered the grounds of Lebanon's international airport to provide security to the former head of the General Security in Lebanon, the retired General Jamil Al-Sayyid (Khaddaj 2010b).[2] He was greeted by the Hezbollah MPs and allies in the VIP lounge of the airport, in an attempt to prevent his arrest by the security services. The Lebanese judiciary had earlier issued a memorandum to the Central Criminal Investigations Department to bring Al-Sayyid in for questioning for allegedly threatening the Prime Minister of Lebanon, Saad Hariri. The Hezbollah, however, called on the judiciary to revoke the decision (Lynch 2010; Khaddaj 2010b). Against the accusations of "violation of a public facility" and undermining the "authority of the state" following the airport incident, the Hezbollah MP, Nawaf al-Mussawi, responded that "the authority of the state is already violated," and added that: "what happened, will happen every time we want it to happen" (cited in Khaddaj 2010b).

The Hezbollah has further demonstrated its quasi-state capacities through displaying its own security forces in Dahyeh and some other Shi'a-populated regions in spring 2013, after they were the target of several planned explosions and attacks from jihadist groups. These groups justified their attacks as an act of retaliation for the Hezbollah's involvement in Syria.[3] In response, Hezbollah's soldiers implemented tight security measures and put up multiple checkpoints throughout Shi'a-populated areas. Although these checkpoints were later taken over by Lebanese soldiers, the Hezbollah continued to deploy security units and also deepened its coordination with the army.[4] Throughout 2014, particularly around the Ashura religious events, the Hezbollah again utilized its own security units to patrol and police Shi'a areas—further confirming its ability to take the place of the state in regions under its control.[5] Indeed, regions under the Hezbollah's influence were left out of the 2015 security plan of the Lebanese Interior Ministry, with the Minister stating that Dahyeh, South Lebanon and Bekaa, were part of Hezbollah's defensive framework and therefore no deployment of state security forces would take place (Orient le Jour 2015a).

Tight security measures are also adopted in the South regarding the activities of Palestinian armed groups acting against Israel outside the framework of the Hezbollah. This situation has been observed on several occasions since the 1990s. In March and April 2002, for example, during the "second" Palestinian Intifada, some small Palestinian factions from Lebanese refugee camps fired several Katioucha rockets from South Lebanon. The Hezbollah, who denied any involvement in these attacks, chased the authors of the attacks and participated most probably in their arrests by the Lebanese authorities a couple of weeks later (Harik 2004: 189). The Hezbollah, until today, controls the South and especially the areas close to the border and tries to prevent any action that is outside its framework. In June 2011, for Naksa Day,[6] the Lebanese army wanted to prevent new clashes at the border with Israel, not to repeat the protests on Israel's borders that had occurred on Nakba Day a few weeks before and which resulted in eleven protesters being killed (Zaatari 2011). The Lebanese army strengthened its presence around the camps, especially in the South where dams were installed on the road to the border, while Lebanese officials, including Hezbollah members, held meetings with Palestinian leaders to encourage them to back down. The Palestinian refugees, cancelled the march of the Naksa, and instead held sit-ins and marches in the refugee camps (Issacharoff, Khoury and Pfeffer 2011; Orient le Jour 2011c).

External Security Apparatus (ESA)

Finally, there is the External Security Apparatus (ESA), which is the unit in charge of operations conducted by the Hezbollah outside of Lebanon.[7] The ESA was reportedly led by Imad Mughniyah until his assassination in February 2008 in Damascus. His successor is his brother-in-law Mustapha Badr al-Din, who has filled a series of military and security positions in the organization (Terror Control 2014). In May 2016, he was killed in a large explosion near Damascus airport in Syria, where he was fighting alongside the Assad regime forces, "carried out by takfiri groups [in other words Syrian opposition armed groups] in the area," a statement by the Hezbollah said (cited in Barrington 2016).

The most-known part of the ESA is Unit 1800, which is responsible for conducting operations in Israel and the Occupied Palestinian Territories (OPT). Unit 1800 establishes contact and coordinates with Palestinian groups including the Islamic Jihad, Hamas and others, in military operations against Israeli targets (Berti and Gleis 2012: 65). The unit provides military training, expertise and funding to Palestinian groups and has also recruited Palestinians to conduct operations directly under its control (Berti and Gleis 2012: 65). The unit also supervises the creation of cells and networks in the OPT and within Israel; it trains Palestinians at camps in the Bekaa Valley, or sends them to Iran for advanced training (Blanford 2011: 357).

Through this Unit, the Hezbollah has reportedly assisted some Palestinian armed factions during the Second Palestinian Intifada (2000–2005), despite the fact that it prevented the launching of any military operation from Lebanon against Israel by anyone other than the Hezbollah and its allies.[8] The Hezbollah has also helped with the smuggling of arms and ammunition to the Gaza Strip by sea directly, or through tunnels dug under the Gaza–Egypt border. Technical data was also allegedly transferred to some Palestinian armed factions for bomb-building techniques or rocket design (Blanford 2011: 351).

Unit 1800 has also been involved in the countries surrounding Israel: Jordan and Egypt. In Egypt, a Hezbollah cell was discovered by the Egyptian security services. Muhammad Yusuf Ahmad Mansur, who served as an Egypt-based leader of a Hezbollah cell, along with a number of his fellow operatives was arrested for planning to carry out terrorist operations against Israeli and other tourists in Egypt. In November 2009, the Hezbollah Secretary General, Hassan Nasrallah, publicly acknowledged that Mansur was a Hezbollah member involved in transporting arms and equipment to Palestinian militants. In April 2010, an Egyptian court sentenced Mansur to fifteen years for his involvement in the cell, which was subordinate to Hezbollah's Unit 1800. Muhammad Qabalan was the Lebanon-based leader of Unit 1800, and Mansur's superior, coordinating the Egyptian cell's activities from Lebanon. For his involvement, he was sentenced in absentia by the Egyptian court to life imprisonment (US Department of the Treasury 2013). In late January 2011, during the beginning of the Egyptian revolutionary process, the imprisoned members of the Hezbollah cell escaped and Mansur returned to Lebanon. In February 2011, Mansur appeared on Lebanese television with Hezbollah officials at a Hezbollah rally in Beirut (US Department of the Treasury 2013).

Following the American and British military-led invasion of Iraq in 2003, Hezbollah also established the Unit 3800, formerly known as Unit 2800, to support the training and operations of the Mahdi Army and other Shiʻa political groups under the guidance of IRGC (Orléans 2014). These groups were mostly involved in combatting Western occupation forces and Iraqi Sunni-sectarian groups, but attacked Iraqi Sunni civilians as well (Blanford 2011: 357; Deghanpisheh 2014). Unit 3800 drew on expertise from Hezbollah's Unit 1800. According to a 2010 Pentagon report, Unit 3800 provided these Iraqi Shiʻa sectarian militias with "the training, tactics and technology to conduct kidnappings [and] small unit tactical operations," and to "employ sophisticated improvised explosive devices (IEDs)" (cited on Orléans 2014). The individual in charge of Hezbollah's Iraq activities and relations with Iraqi political movements is the Lebanese cleric Muhammad Kawtharani, who is a member of Hezbollah's Political Council and was a former protégé of Muhammad Baqir al-Sadr (Rayburn 2014: 18).[9] According to some sources, the Hezbollah's Unit 3800 commander Khalil Harb has also been spotted in Yemen in 2012 training Houthi rebels in Yemen and has been accused of facilitating the movement of large amounts of currency to them (Orléans 2014).

Hezbollah and Armed Resistance

As is clear from the above account, the formation and development of these parts of the Hezbollah's armed apparatus have been closely connected to the organization's resistance activities, particularly against Israel. The 1989 Ta'if Agreement legitimized the Hezbollah's military wing as a resistance actor against Israel, and the organization was not required to disarm, unlike all other factions. The Hezbollah's attacks against Israel steadily increased following the Ta'if Agreement reaching 644 operations against the Israeli armed forces and South Lebanese Army (SLA) in 1994 and 908 in 1995 (Blanford 2011: 145).

In September 1997, a week after the death of Hadi Nasrallah (the 18-year-old eldest son of the Hezbollah leader Hassan Nasrallah alongside two other Hezbollah soldiers in a clash with the Israeli army), the Islamic movement announced that the Hezbollah was forming a new resistance unit, the *Sarāya al-Muqāwama al-Lubnāniyya* or Lebanese Resistance Brigades (LRB). The LRB would be open to all volunteers regardless of their religious sect (Blanford 2011: 197). This new unit would be trained and guided by the Hezbollah cadres. The Sarāya launched their first attack against SLA outposts six months after their establishment (Blanford 2011: 212).[10]

In the few months prior to the liberation of the South, the Hezbollah was launching as many as 300 attacks against Israeli forces per month (Daher 2014: 138–41). The ratio of the losses of Hezbollah to those of Israel had also declined considerably from the beginning of the 1990s (ten to one), to nearly one to one at the end of the decade (Daher 2014: 132).

The South of Lebanon was finally freed from Israeli occupation in May 2000, following the withdrawal of the Israeli army. The number of Lebanese civilians dead in the numerous attacks by the Israeli forces and the SLA between the years 1982 and 2000 was around 23,500, in addition to 46,880 injured. The Hezbollah, on its side, lost 1,276 fighters (Blanford 2011: 281). During the same period, the Israeli army suffered the loss of 1,580 men, while 6,485 others were injured, and the SLA's total was 824 dead and 1,439 injured (Daher 2014: 144).

Following the liberation of the South and the withdrawal of Israeli troops in May 2000 (excluding Hezbollah anti-aircraft firing along the border), the Shebaa Farms, a disputed area of land that straddles Lebanon and the Israeli-occupied Syrian Golan Heights, became the exclusive site of official Hezbollah activity. The Hezbollah's military actions nevertheless took on a mostly defensive nature following the withdrawal of the Israeli army. The Hezbollah's leadership had instructed its cadres in the South to automatically retaliate against breaches of the Blue Line,[11] whether by ground, air or sea, including assassinations (Blanford 2011: 281–83).

This largely passive role was to change, however, following Israel's July 2006 invasion of the country. During the invasion, the Hezbollah reported that as many as 250 of its fighters were killed (Israel claimed 530). On its side, the Israeli army lost 120 soldiers and more than forty civilians were killed, while between 300,000 and 500,000 persons from the North of Israel evacuated to the South during the war because of Hezbollah's rockets (Internal Displacement Monitoring Centre 2006). The war itself reinforced the popularity of the Hezbollah as a resistance actor, particularly in the southern areas of the country that are heavily populated by the Shi'a. These areas suffered the most from Israeli attacks, invasions and occupation, and the Hezbollah's resistance enabled it to widen its social base in the Shi'a population even among those that did not adhere to its religious perspective.

One month after the end of the War, on September 22, Hezbollah celebrated *"Al-Nasr al-ilāhi"* (The Divine Victory) in the middle of Dahyeh and hundreds of thousands of people gathered. Hassan Nasrallah declared that it was a strategic, historic and divine victory that had dealt a severe blow to the US President George W. Bush's New Middle East plan. The slogan *"Al-Nasr al-īlāhi"* was later on reformulated in *"Nasr(un) min Allāh"* (A Victory from God) in the party's propaganda in order to instrumentalize this slogan with the family name of Hassan Nasrallah, as part of the cultivation of the leader's image in the Hezbollah's media campaigns.

Following the 2006 Lebanon War, the Israel–Lebanon border witnessed only a few security incidents, most of which occurred between 2013 and 2014, after the outbreak of the Syrian uprising. The Hezbollah retaliated militarily to multiple Israeli incursions. The Islamic movement was attempting to convey a clear message to Israel: despite its involvement in Syria and elsewhere, it was ready to answer any kind of aggression by the Israeli military.

Hassan Nasrallah declared, during the Ashura in November 2014, that Israel should fear the Hezbollah's rockets in the future because "they could reach every part of the Land of Occupied Palestine" (As-Safir 2014). He added that the Hezbollah was never distracted from guarding Lebanon's southern border, contrary to Lebanese and Arab media claims that the Syrian conflict had exhausted the party's capabilities (As-Safir 2014; Khraiche 2014).

Following the January 2015 attack by an Israeli helicopter in the province of Quneitra in Syria, near the Israeli-occupied Golan Heights, on a Hezbollah convoy carrying Jihad Mughniyah and commander Mohamad Issa, known as Abu Issa, killing seven Hezbollah members in all, Nasrallah declared that: "the Islamic resistance is no longer concerned at any such thing as the rules of engagement, we don't recognize them [...] they have come to an end." He added that it was the Hezbollah's right to answer, "whenever, wherever, and in whatever form it finds fit. This is the end of the story" (Al-Ahed News 2015a).

The Hezbollah nevertheless kept the South Lebanon front calm, avoiding clashes with the Israeli army, until it claimed responsibility for a detonated explosive device in the Shebaa Farms area on January 4, 2016. A group named after Samir Qantar, a Hezbollah commander killed in December in an air strike in Syria by Israel, carried out the operation. The Hezbollah leader, Sayyed Hassan Nasrallah, had declared a week before that retaliation would be inevitable. The Israeli state responded by shelling the town of al-Wazzani and other areas, with reports of material damage but no serious injuries (Davison and Al-Khalidi 2016). No escalation nevertheless occurred after these events, while Hezbollah's leader Hassan Nasrallah continued to threaten consequences for Israel in the event that it would launch another war against Lebanon. He declared that no red line would restrain the Hezbollah, adding that the Lebanese party has prepared a target bank of sensitive locations in Israel, including nuclear facilities, biological research centers and petrochemical plants. Nasrallah insisted that Lebanon and the Hezbollah had the right to any defensive weapon to protect Lebanon's existence and sovereignty (Al-Ahed 2016b).

The Arms of the Resistance against Rival Lebanese Actors

The successes of the Hezbollah on the military field against Israel should nevertheless not be interpreted as implying that its arms were directed solely towards the "Zionist enemy." Despite the fact that Hezbollah's official historiography claims that the party adopted a defensive attitude towards other political movements during the Civil War, and its armed activities were solely concentrated on resistance to the Israeli occupation, the historical record indicates that the Hezbollah has been willing to use its weapons against political opponents, including those on the left and other secular forces.[12]

In September 1982, the Lebanese National Resistance Front (LNRF, see Chapter 2) was the target of a wave of assassinations, particularly of its communist leaders in West Beirut. Despite the fact that the LNRF was formed to fight the Israeli occupation, the Hezbollah would criticize it for its secularism, which was called a product of "Maronite pluralism," and because it did not call for an Islamic alternative to gain Lebanese independence from both the Western and Eastern spheres of influence (Charara 2007: 347). Those assassinated included Khalil Naouss (journalist, killed February 20, 1986) Suhail Tawile (February 24, 1986), Hussein Mroue (February 17, 1987), Mehdi Amel (May 18, 1987) Selim Yammout, and Professor Hikmat al-Amin and others in a car bomb against the headquarters of the Lebanese Communist Party (LCP) in Rmeileh (Nassif-Debs 2006; Nash 2008; Hajj Georgiou 2012). These assassinations helped create a climate of fear among the LCP members in regions populated mostly by the Shiʿa, and to a lesser extent among the SSNP members (Charara 2007: 350–56).

Moreover, in November 1983, the Hezbollah—with active Iranian IRGC assistance—on numerous occasions attacked the Lebanese state's remaining presence in the Bekaa Valley, taking control of the *Sheikh Abdallah* barracks, which were the largest and best equipped. It actually became the headquarters of the Pasdaran (Chehabi 2006: 221). The *Sheikh* Abdallah barracks were given back to the army in August 1992 (Daher 2014: 128). The Hezbollah also had numerous violent military conflicts with Amal throughout the middle and end of the 1980s. The most serious battle was in 1988 when both groups sought to establish their dominance in the southern suburbs of Beirut and in South Lebanon. The struggle ended with two negotiated settlements under the auspices of Iran and Syria in February 1989, in which Amal was excluded from the Bekaa and the suburbs of Beirut and the South was divided (Daher 2014: 108–109). The military fights between Amal and the Hezbollah in 1988 and 1989 caused 3,000 deaths, both civilian and fighters (International Center for Transitional Justice 2013). The reconciliation in 1990 allowed a refocus towards the Hezbollah's military resistance in the South, which was undermined considerably by the military confrontation with Amal.

The May 2008 conflict

In May 2008, for the first time since the end of the Lebanese Civil War, the Hezbollah used its weaponry against Lebanese national actors following threats by the March 14 alliance to politically attack key Hezbollah military interests. At that time, the Lebanese government, led by Siniora, passed two decrees aimed at weakening the Hezbollah's military apparatus: first, on May 6, 2008, the government reassigned the head of security at Beirut's airport, Wafiq Shuqayr, a general officer who was accused of being too close to the Hezbollah and of having shared intelligence information with them.[13] Second, the Council of Ministers challenged the legality and constitutionality of the Hezbollah's independent telephone system, which the organization claimed ensured the secrecy of internal communications and the efficiency of its command and control (ICG 2008: 3). The telephone system was believed to have been a cornerstone of the Hezbollah's military performance during the July 2006 Lebanon War with Israel.[14] The Hezbollah's telecommunication network, which has existed since 1995, was never raised as an issue before this event. This last decision was taken despite the fact that the Hezbollah's Deputy Secretary Naim Qassem had warned on May 5 that the Hezbollah would deal with those who interfere with the network as if they were Israeli spies (cited in Blanford 2008). Hassan Nasrallah promptly answered these decisions, describing them as a "declaration of war against the resistance and its weapons for the benefit of America and Israel" and added that: "we will cut the hand that targets the weapons of the resistance" and "we will defend our weapons with our weapons" (Ladki 2008).

These decrees were taken in an atmosphere of heightened social tension, as was discussed earlier. Despite the fact that there was an ongoing general strike at the time, which the Hezbollah officially supported, the organization did not put its efforts behind the labor movement but instead launched a military offensive to repeal the decrees. On May 7, West Beirut was taken over by the Hezbollah and its allies in a well-planned operation. The Hezbollah, with far superior equipment, training and discipline overwhelmed their rivals, the militias from the Future Movement,[15] taking control of West Beirut in less than twelve hours. The Future Movement was forced to shut down its main media offices, which were looted or set ablaze. The various militant groups, including the Hezbollah, were accused of having attacked civilians, destroying cars and shops and proffering anti-Sunni insults (ICG 2008: 2).

Each position taken by the Hezbollah on the Future Movement was directly handed over to the army, demonstrating once more the collaboration and coordination established in the previous years between the two actors. Moreover, the conflict was not confined to Beirut; intense fighting occurred in the Druze areas of Mount Lebanon between

Jumblatt loyalists on the one hand and the Hezbollah militants or allied forces on the other (ICG 2008: 7). In Tripoli, pitched battles opposed the inhabitants of Bab el-Tebbane, a Future Movement dominated Sunni neighborhood, and the inhabitants of Baal Mohsen, populated mainly by Alawites, who are close to a Hezbollah-led coalition of political parties gathered in the March 8 forces (ICG 2008: 7).

The violence ended a week later with over eighty deaths and 250 wounded (Baliani 2008). The Hezbollah had attained its objectives: the government cancelled its two decrees of May 6 and 7. Politically, the events led to the end of two years of paralysis on the Lebanese political scene with the Doha agreement. This agreement between the various Lebanese political forces led to the election of new President General Michel Sleiman, the establishment of a national unity government, adopting the caza (smaller constituencies known as administrative units) as an electoral constituency in conformity with the 1960 law, whereby the cazas of Marjayoun-Hasbaya, Baalbek-Hermel and West Bekaa-Rachaya each remained as a single electoral constituency (Now Media 2008a). The adoption of the electoral law based on the cazas actually ensured better Christian representation and was one of the main demands of the Hezbollah's Christian ally the Free Patriotic Movement (FPM).

The Hezbollah's representatives continued to justify its military action in Beirut against the March 14 led movement. Hussein al-Khalil, the political advisor of Hassan Nasrallah, declared in a press conference that the Hezbollah's intervention was made in order to defend itself from the decision of the government, which was an American plan to disarm the resistance and submit it to Israel's will (Press TV 2008). In addition to this, the Hezbollah member, Ghaleb Abou Zeinab (2008), added that the Hezbollah's military intervention did put an end to the Sunni–Shi'a Fitna by avoiding any outburst. The Secretary General Nasrallah reiterated a similar discourse a few months later in an *iftar* in Nabatieh (Al-Ahed News 2008) and even in May 2012 (Al-Manar 2012b). But contrary to the Hezbollah's claims, these events clearly intensified Sunni–Shi'a tensions. The most prominent Sunni religious authority, the Mufti of the Lebanese Republic, went so far as to characterize the Hezbollah as an occupying force, a clear reference to Israel's earlier occupation (ICG 2008: 2). At the same time, 120 Sunni officers of the Lebanese army sent a collective letter of resignation protesting "the humiliation felt from the military's conduct during the militia's invasion of Beirut." All of the officers later nevertheless retracted and did not resign, except for colonel Amid Hammoud, who became commander of the Future Movement's military wing (Nerguizian 2015: 128).

Following May 2008, the Hezbollah has continued to declare publicly that any actor threatening its armament and its soldiers would face its retaliation. In 2010, Hassan Nasrallah and other Hezbollah members declared that the Islamic movement would "cut off the hand" of anyone who tries to arrest any of its members charged in the assassination of former Prime Minister Rafiq Hariri by the Special Tribunal for Lebanon (STL) (Al-Ahed News 2010).

On January 18, 2011, in another show of strength by the Islamic movement, Hezbollah deployed unarmed militants in Beirut's streets as an attempt to warn the March 14 political forces against renominating Saad Hariri as Prime Minister. This was after the Hezbollah and its allies of the March 8 forces toppled him on January 12 (Choufi 2013; ICG 2014: 17). This show of force, called in Lebanon the "incident of the black shirts," because the Hezbollah members were dressed in black, led Walid Jumblatt, leader of the PSP, to temporarily abandon his alliance with Hariri's Future Movement and join March 8 forces in electing Najib Miqati, who was the Hezbollah's candidate, as new Prime Minister (Choufi 2013; Mouqaled 2013).

These and other examples confirm the Hezbollah's ongoing deployment of its weapons in internal Lebanese politics. Simultaneously, the Hezbollah, in establishing itself as an anti-systemic party opposing the Lebanese state and promising the liberation of Palestine from the "Zionist enemy," has increasingly produced a more moderate propaganda arguing that its weaponry was solely to protect Lebanon and not for external purposes. In 2008, Dr. Ali Fayyad, at the time head of the CCSD, said in regard to Palestine that:

> We (Hezbollah) support the Liberation of Palestine, but we do not want to take their place to free their lands. Hezbollah is firstly a Liberation national movement against the threats and the violence of Israel and to free the Lebanese territories and prisoners.
>
> (Fayyad 2008b)

Ghaleb Abou Zeinab said the same, affirming that: "Our arms are for the liberation of Lebanese lands and the defence of the state and not for Palestine" (Abou Zeinab 2008).

This was also noticed in the Manifesto of 2009 in the section regarding the "Resistance." The Resistance's role is to liberate the Lebanese occupied lands and defend the sovereignty of the country against Israel's threat. There are no words about liberating Palestine.

This changed discourse—away from a resistance focus, towards a pro-Lebanese state orientation—was strengthened especially since the beginning of the uprisings in Syria and with the Hezbollah's increasing military involvement in the conflict. The Hezbollah Secretary General, Sayyid Hassan Nasrallah, acknowledged this evolution in a private meeting in the beginning of 2013 with his cadres, declaring that the party "had changed" and that the group's ultimate priority is to "protect Lebanon" (Al-Akhbar English 2013a). He continued by saying that:

Hezbollah has changed and its priorities have changed based on circumstances [...] There was a time when we used to see Lebanon as a colonial construct that was part of the Ummah [...] That was in our early days, and the country was going through a Civil War. All parties were calling for a Nation that fit their liking [...] Today conditions have changed. We believe that this country is our country, and that the flag of the cedar is our flag that we need to protect, too. At this stage, our priority is to protect the state in Lebanon and to build it.

(Al-Akhbar English 2013a)

The Hezbollah MP, Hassan Fadlallah (2015: 216–18), explained that protecting Lebanon from external threats was the major cause of the Resistance. In addition to Israel threatening Lebanon, he also cites the takfirist groups that want to establish their own emirates. Notably, he argued that the Hezbollah's intervention in Syria against these groups after 2011 was also made in order to prevent the threat of their entering Lebanon.

Conclusion

The Hezbollah's military and security apparatus has been a central and key feature of the Islamic movement since its establishment. This apparatus has served to oppose Israeli's occupation of the South until 2000, and then to create a situation of deterrence against Israel's attacks, especially during the 2006 Lebanon War. The Hezbollah's arms are still justified today for the purpose of liberating the Shebaa Farms still occupied by Israel, and to defend and to protect Lebanon as well, not only against Israel, but increasingly against the *"takfiris* threat" as presented by the Hezbollah's propaganda to legitimize its "pre-emptive war" in Syria (Al-Manar 2013b; ICG 2014: 4), as we will see in Chapter 7. In addition to this military function, the Hezbollah also has a large security apparatus aimed at guaranteeing and managing security in the Shi'a-populated areas. The Hezbollah's security apparatus, as discussed in this chapter and in Chapter 5, is responsible for controlling and even sometimes repressing dissent or opposition against the Islamic Movement.

The Hezbollah's use of its arms materialized through two main aspects. First, the Hezbollah's security apparatus implements tight control over the Shi'a-populated areas, without hesitating to use security or repressive measures to prevent any opposition arising as a serious threat or alternative to the Lebanese Islamic movement. Second, the Hezbollah's military apparatus intervenes outside of Lebanon and particularly in Syria to assist the Assad regime, which is an important political and military supporter of the Hezbollah as the arms produced in Iran are transferred to Lebanon from Syria, which thus maintains its political and military power in Lebanon.

The Hezbollah's armament is also perceived by large sections of the Shi'a popular and middle classes as a form of compensation for historic, political and economic deprivation and a critical instrument of communal leverage in the Lebanese sectarian political system (Gambill 2007: 42). Accordingly, as argued by Saad Ghorayeb (2005), "any plan that seeks to disarm the resistance will be construed as a form of communal disempowerment" for the Shi'a and will be strongly opposed. This feeling was only strengthened with the rise of jihadist forces in the region in the last few years. The Hezbollah's military and security apparatus has been a key and central element in the development of the party. Its purpose today is clearly to guarantee the party's political position and to oppose any threats that would curtail its political interests, while maintaining the status quo of the sectarian political and economic system of Lebanon.

7

Hezbollah and Revolutionary Processes in the Middle East and North Africa Since 2011

The Hezbollah promotes an understanding of world politics as a "clash of civilizations" in which the struggle against the West is based upon a rejection of its values and religious system rather than its exploitative global relations (Saad Ghorayeb 2002: 88). The United States is described as the "Big Satan," Israel as the "Small Satan," and Britain and France as the "evils." The great imperial powers are led by the USA, which represents the first root of vice and the source of all malice on account of its ultimate responsibility for all Muslim catastrophes (Saad Ghorayeb 2002: 90). It is noteworthy that the Hezbollah believes this "clash" goes back to the early origins of Islam in the seventh century (Saad Ghorayeb 2002: 89). Despite this professed hostility towards Western civilization, the Hezbollah's discourse displays a flexibility and pragmatism when it comes to its relationship with Iran.[1]

The Hezbollah's position on foreign actors has its ideological roots in the Islamic Republic of Iran's opposition to what it called "Westoxication" and "Eastoxication." "Westoxication" was considered to be the pathological fascination with everything Western at the expense of the indigenous culture's heritage, while "Eastoxication" was a comparable obsession among intellectuals with Marxist and communist ideologies. The latter were accused of having detached themselves from the masses by negating religion as: "the opiate of the masses and serving the interests of the colonial powers in the Soviet Camp. The solution to both problems was a return to the national self, in other words an Iranian Islamic identity" (Tehranian 1993: 363).

Correspondingly, the Hezbollah viewed its conflict with Israel partly in religious terms rather than as an anti-colonial political struggle. This is also reflected in the way that the Hezbollah continues to blur the line between Zionism and Judaism, presenting these as interchangeable and synonymous. Hezbollah leaders frequently employ anti-Semitic tropes that essentialize Jews and characterize them as evil. *Sheikh* Naim Qassem has written, "the History of Jews has proven that, regardless of the Zionist proposal, they are the people who are evil in their ideas" (cited in Saad Ghorayeb 2002: 174). The former Hezbollah Secretary General Abbas al-Mussawi, who was killed in an Israeli operation, declared that: "according to the *Qur'anic* interpretation of Jewish history, the problem with the Jewish people lies in their religious creed" (cited in Saad Ghorayeb 2002: 174). Hassan Nasrallah has also employed such a discourse on occasion saying, "If we searched the entire world for a person more cowardly, despicable, weak and feeble in psyche, mind, ideology and religion, we would not find anyone like the Jew. Notice I do not say the Israeli" (cited in Saad Ghorayeb 2002: 170). At events organized by the Hezbollah, it is not unusual to see books by the French intellectual Roger Garaudy, who denied the project of Jewish extermination by Hitler and the existence of gas chambers.[2] In February 2006, the Hezbollah leader Hassan Nasrallah described Garaudy as "a great French philosopher," who exposed the "alleged Jewish Holocaust in Germany [...] [Garaudy] proved that this Holocaust is a myth" (MEMRI TV 2006).

Towards other states in the MENA region (except Israel), the Hezbollah has been rather moderate prior to the vast protest movements that emerged in 2010–2011. The struggle against Israel took priority over all other concerns in the international sphere. *Sheikh* Naim Qassem even said that it would be wrong to struggle against autocratic and despotic regimes in the Arab world; instead, popular movements should seek the liberation of Palestine in order to free the Arab regimes and their people (Qassem 2008: 332).

A few months after Israel's war on the Gaza Strip at the end of 2008 and the beginning of 2009, Nasrallah declared that Hezbollah did "not want conflict with the Egyptian regime; regardless of all the accusations they directed against us. We still do not have a battle with the Egyptian regime."[3] He added that Hezbollah does:

> not have a conflict or a problem with anyone, the Arab political system in this or that Arab country, whether democratic, dictatorial, royal

or dynastic, religious or secular, legal or illegal [...] regardless of the description, we do not interfere in such matters.

(Al-Ahed News 2009)

Moreover, Hezbollah does:

not want to engage in feuds with any regime [...] We do not want any bitterness with any Arab regime, we do not want any rivalry with any Arab regime, we clearly do not want to engage in any conflict with any Arab regime, not security wise, politically or militarily, even in the media.

(Al-Ahed News 2009)

Hezbollah and the popular uprisings in the Middle East and North Africa

At first, Hezbollah generally welcomed the revolutionary processes in 2010–2011, particularly in Egypt, Tunisia, Libya, Yemen and Bahrain.

In late February 2011, Hezbollah officials were claiming that the uprisings in the region were part of the resistance project. The Hezbollah deputy, Hassan Fadlallah, declared at a rally,

the uprisings of the Arab population are a real opportunity to regain freedom of decision and to return to the spirit of the Arab position that rejects foreign hegemony [...] all the current problems of the people of the region come from the United States and their political support to totalitarian regimes, which crushed and repressed the will of their peoples [...] once freed from the yoke of dictators and free to decide their future, these people can only support the main cause in the region, that of Palestine.

(Orient le Jour 2011a)

The current Minister of Industry and Hezbollah member Hussein Hajj Hassan, the then Minister of Agriculture, said at another meeting that: "the Arab revolts are part of the project of resistance and urged US allies in the region to reassess their calculations because to depend on the US administration can only lead to further disappointment" (Orient le Jour 2011a). He also insisted that the failing regimes in the region were all allies of the United States, which was a blow to the American system established in the region that had stifled the aspirations of the people (Orient le Jour 2011a).

On March 19, 2011, a massive rally in support of the Arab uprisings was organized by Hezbollah in Dahyeh. Hassan Nasrallah made a speech in which he voiced his support for the Arab people and for their revolutions and sacrifices, especially in Tunisia, Egypt, Bahrain, Libya and Yemen. He made assurances that Hezbollah would stand by those rising up and would be ready to help them. (Notably, not a word was said during his speech about the first demonstrations of the Syrian uprising, which occurred a few days earlier on March 15, and which were subsequently severely repressed.)

Nasrallah condemned the conspiracy theories that were circulating as explanations for the events in the region, and stressed the authenticity of these popular movements:

> We reiterate that these revolutions are the peoples' own wills. Any accusation that claims that America is behind these revolutions, has incited and stirred them, and is leading them represents a false, unjust accusation of these peoples [...] These are regimes that follow America and harmonize with it that have offered and still offer services for the American plot, and that do not constitute any threat to the American policy—which is "Israel" in the Middle East [...] These are true, popular revolutions.
>
> (Al-Ahed News 2011a)

Nasrallah condemned the manner in which the regimes of the region responded to the legitimate popular demands by resorting to repression, murder and humiliation, rather than entering into dialogue with representatives of the revolutions and adopting reforms. He denounced the sectarianism of Bahrain's regime, and expressed gratitude to the Turkish Prime Minister, Recep Tayyip Erdoğan, for his positive stance towards that country's popular movement. At the same time, he accused some in the Arab and Islamic world of remaining silent about the injustices and repression against the Bahraini people, suggesting that this was due to the fact that the majority of them are Shiʿa. He condemned as well the League of Arab States and those governments that sent armies to Bahrain to defend the regime and to crush the popular movement

(Al-Ahed News 2011a). He warned in his speech against: "allowing access to foreign intervention in Arab countries, which will take us back into the era of occupation, direct settlement, division, or else" (Al-Ahed News 2011a).

The Hezbollah's official discourse nevertheless began to shift, particularly with the beginning of the uprising in Syria and its expansion, and to a lesser extent with the rise to power of the Muslim Brotherhood in Egypt and Tunisia and the growing Sunni and Shi'a sectarian tensions in the regions. This was first seen in the Hezbollah officials' warning of foreign plots to sabotage the paths of the region's revolutions (Al-Ahed News 2011b).

In September 2012, Nasrallah explained the different positions of the Hezbollah towards the ongoing events in the region, especially in Syria. He declared that the party's position is based on two decisive criteria: first, the regime's stance on the Palestinian–Israeli conflict; and second, the readiness of the regime to engage in reform (Al-Ahed News 2012).

Regarding Syria, Nasrallah stressed that the Syrian regime is against the Israeli state and has always supported the Palestinian resistance, in addition to supporting the Iraqi resistance. He argued that Syria's stance against the "Zionist enemy" was the reason why the Western and Arab countries were engaged in toppling the country's government. He also noted that: "while the Syrian regime insists on dialogue, the so-called opposition rejects it," and highlighted that: "the opposition demanded the fall of the Syrian regime, but no regime in the world would accept that, especially if it has a vision" (Al-Ahed News 2012).

He further declared that: "when the Syrian crisis started, the weapons flooded into the country, and we started having doubts about the uprising." This ignored the fact that no organized armed resistance occurred in the first months of the Syrian revolutionary process,[4] and the popular resistance was at that time largely peaceful. He added that: "they [Western and Arab countries] want to make Arabs and the Islamic World forget about the Palestinian cause." He explained that before the Syrian crisis, "transformations were in favour of resistance movements, such as the revolutions in Tunisia, Libya, Egypt and Bahrain, and we know the new movements [in Syria] and their stances on the resistance, Palestine and Israel" (Al-Ahed News 2012), which implied support for a settlement with Israel. Hezbollah's post-2011 role in Syria will be dealt with in more detail below.

At the end of 2013 and the beginning of 2014, Hezbollah's earlier enthusiasm for the uprisings had completely fallen away. It focused its efforts on stabilizing the situation in Lebanon and restoring relations with local and foreign political actors—except Saudi Arabia, with whom relations continued to deteriorate against the background of rising tensions between Riyadh and Tehran and the continuing military intervention of the Hezbollah in Syria on the side of the Assad regime.

At the annual conference of the Arab States Broadcasting Union (ASBU) in December 2013, the Lebanese Communication Group (LCG, the umbrella body for the Hezbollah's media, comprising Al-Manar television, Nour radio and its website Al-Manar) apologized to the Bahraini regime for its earlier coverage of the nearly three-year uprising in that country. The LCG promised to be more "objective" and to seek to maintain professional standards, promising to carry out regular evaluations of its editorial policies to ensure compliance with international agreements, in return for allowing the Lebanese media group to continue to broadcast in the island kingdom (Al-Hakim, Baltayeb and Dirani 2013). The Arabic-language news station al-Alam (linked to the IRI) had also substantially reduced its previously intensive coverage of Bahrain (Al-Hakim *et al.* 2013). After LCG's apology was made public, however, the Hezbollah issued a clarification saying that the party leadership was not consulted by the LCG delegation to the meeting in Tunis, and that the decision to issue an apology was made by LCG alone (Al-Hakim *et al.* 2013). The Hezbollah reiterated its support for the struggle of the Bahraini people. Al-Manar's Managing Director, Abdallah Kassir, a former Hezbollah MP, resigned from his post a few weeks later and has left the country for Iran (Ya Libnan 2013b).

This might reveal mere confusion or disagreement inside the Hezbollah's organizational structure, although its decisions are usually well planned and there is strict discipline inside the party. But this episode occurred during the same period as a rapprochement was taking shape between Qatar and the Hezbollah, as confirmed by Hassan Nasrallah in a televised speech of December 2013 in which he announced that he had met with a Qatari delegation. Furthermore, a meeting was held in Lebanon between *Sheikh* Naim Qassem and the new ambassador of Qatar in mid-December 2013. The parties issued a joint statement, stressing that political solutions would be the basis for constructively resolving issues in the interest of the people of the region (Orient le

Jour 2013d). In July 2015, the Hezbollah was nevertheless continuing to support the popular movement in Bahrain in its rhetoric, demanding the release of political prisoners and the beginning of a dialogue with the opposition (Al-Ahed News 2015c).

In June 2016, Bahrain's regime suspended the leading Shi'a opposition group, al-Wefaq National Islamic Society, closing its offices and ordering its assets to be frozen, while revoking a few days later the citizenship of the country's top Shi'a cleric, Ayatollah *Sheikh* Isa Qassim. Qassim is also known as the spiritual father of the now-banned Al-Wefaq, whose leader—*Sheikh* Ali Salman—is serving a nine-year prison sentence (BBC 2016b). Following these developments, Hassan Nasrallah declared that the events in Bahrain were unacceptable, emphasizing the stripping of nationality from *Sheikh* Qassim. He stated that the Bahraini people have remained steadfast in their peaceful resistance, and accused the House of Saud of silencing dialogue in Bahrain. The reason for this, in his view, was the fear that the people of Saudi Arabia would call for a similar dialogue given the chance (Al-Manar 2016b).

With respect to Yemen, the Hezbollah was at first supportive of the 2011 uprising to overthrow the dictator Ali Abdallah Saleh, who finally stepped down in November of that year, after mass protests and an arrangement negotiated by Saudi Arabia and the United States. The negotiated settlement kept the Yemeni regime intact, with the inclusion of some political forces including supporters of the al-Islah party, which is composed of the Yemeni branch of the Muslim Brotherhood, Salafists and tribal leaders in the North (notably the powerful tribe of the al-Ahmar) (Bonnefoy 2015). Saleh nevertheless would still benefit from the allegiance of a significant segment of the security apparatus and army, while he continued to act as Chairman of the General People's Congress, the ruling party at that time. Saleh also, as a result of the deal, enjoyed legal immunity and held onto the riches that he had accumulated as president (a reign of more than 30 years), estimated at more than $60 billion according to a February 2015 UN report (cited in Middle East Monitor 2015a).

Saleh had, from 2004 to 2010, led six brutal wars against the Houthis (a Zaidi sect close to Shiism), with the assistance and support of the Kingdom of Saudi Arabia, accusing the Houthis of loyalty to Iran. The fighting had caused more than 10,000 deaths and displaced over 300,000 people (Internal Displacement Monitoring Centre 2010). Saleh was also a former ally of the Gulf monarchies and the United States in the so-called "war against terrorism."

The Houthis took control of the capital Sanaa in January 2015, but they had already had a significant military presence there since September 2014, with the complicity of Air Force units close to former dictator Ali Abdallah Saleh, pushing for the resignation of the Prime Minister. The Houthis had, since late March 2015, extended their operations to the South of the country. At the end of March 2015, a massive military intervention called "Decisive Storm," led by Saudi Arabia with the participation of nine Arab countries and the support of the United States and England, began under the pretext of opposing the Houthis, also known as Ansar Allah. Some 6,000 people, about half of them civilians, have been killed in Yemen between March 2015 and June 2016, according to the UN (Nichols 2016).

The Hezbollah opposed the Saudi-led military intervention in Yemen and supported the Houthis, despite the Houthis alliance with former dictator Saleh, who had declared in March 2011 that the Arab Uprisings were a media creation of the United States, led from an office in Tel Aviv (Al-Jazeera 2011).

The IRI has also condemned the military intervention in Yemen by Saudi Arabia, and the Iranian Supreme leader Ali Hosseini Khamenei described it as "genocide." Iran has called for a ceasefire and for the start of negotiations with the participation of all Yemeni political factions in order to reach an agreement on a national government (BBC News 2015).

According to various sources, the Houthi forces have been supported, although in a limited way, by the IRI in the form of weapons, money and military training, while a senior Iranian official declared in December 2014 that the Quds Force, the external arm of the Revolutionary Guard, had a "few hundred" military personnel in Yemen who train Houthi fighters (Bayoumi and Ghobari 2015). The Houthis have also received assistance from the Hezbollah, which provided logistical support to the military. The Hezbollah Military Unit 3800 commander, Khalil Harb (see Chapter 6), was spotted in Yemen training Houthi rebels in 2012 (Orléans 2014). On February 24, 2016, the Saudi Arabia owned Al Arabiya news network posted a video of what it claimed was a meeting in the summer 2015 between the Hezbollah commander Abu Saleh and the Houthi forces in Yemen. A Hezbollah commander in an interview with

Foreign Affairs confirmed that the Hezbollah had a presence in Yemen (Amarasingam and Corbeil 2016).

In summer 2015, the Hezbollah continued to condemn Saudi Arabia's military intervention in Yemen, and Nasrallah called on Muslims, Arabs and the Islamic world to say to the Kingdom that enough is enough (Al-Ahed News 2015c). A year later, the Hezbollah remained outspoken on this issue: Hassan Nasrallah declared in May 2016 that the Yemeni people and the Mujahedin in that country have remained steadfast for more than a year against the US-Saudi aggression, which enjoys international and regional support, and that Saudi Arabia had not achieved any of its objectives since the beginning of its military intervention in March 2015 (Al-Ahed News 2016c).

Shifting the view to Egypt, the Hezbollah welcomed the ouster of President Mohamed Morsi in July 2013, as the removal of a regime sympathetic to the Syrian opposition. The new ruler of Egypt, General Abdel Fattah al-Sisi, was viewed positively by the Hezbollah because, according to one official of the party, "those who support him voice support for the Syrian regime" (ICG 2014: 10). In early 2015, Nasrallah actually welcomed the return of Egypt's role in Arab and regional arenas under the presidency of al-Sisi, the former head of Egypt's armed forces, asserting Egypt's importance as a pillar of stability in the region (Al-Mayadeen 2015). This is despite the authoritarianism of al-Sisi's regime, which represses opposition political movements from the Muslim Brotherhood to various democratic and progressive groups and individuals, and maintains a close relationship with Saudi Arabia while enforcing a harsh blockade on the Gaza Strip and criminalizing Hamas. The Hezbollah actually remained silent when Egypt classified Hamas as a terrorist movement in February 2015, and sent Hassan Ezzedine, in charge of Arab Affairs, on an official visit to Cairo in late February 2016 to offer condolences to the family of Mohamed Hassanein Heikal, an Egyptian columnist close to the authorities (Dot Pouillard 2016).

Turning to Iraq, following the seizure of the country's second largest city, Mosul, by ISIS in June 2014, causing 500,000 people to flee, Nasrallah pledged that the Hezbollah was ready to sacrifice five times as many martyrs in Iraq as it had sacrificed in Syria in order to protect shrines, noting that Iraqi holy sites "are much more important" than the Shi'a shrines in Syria (cited in Abi Habib 2014). From that point on, the Hezbollah increasingly maintained a presence in Iraq, contributing to command and coordination in the fight against ISIS. In July 2014, the Hezbollah announced the death of Ibrahim al-Hajj, a veteran of the 2006 Lebanon War against Israel, near Mosul while on a "jihadi mission."

In December 2014, the former Iraqi Prime Minister, Nouri al-Maliki, visited Lebanon and was welcomed by the Hezbollah members. Maliki had resigned in August 2014 after mounting criticism from across the Iraqi political scene—including from Grand Ayatollah Ali al-Sistani—and was appointed to the largely ceremonial position of vice-president. (In summer 2015, popular protests in Iraq would target Maliki for his corruption and authoritarian and sectarian practices, pressuring him to step down.⁵) Maliki met with Nasrallah in Beirut and they discussed regional developments in Syria and Iraq, including the threat posed by ISIS. Al-Manar reported that the "Hezbollah leader and the Iraqi official had identical views regarding the major issues" (Al-Manar 2014).

Nasrallah publicly confirmed in February 2015 that the Hezbollah was in Iraq and that it was engaged in fighting ISIS. Nasrallah called on the countries of the Middle East to join the battle in Syria and Iraq against ISIS:

> We call on the people and governments of the region in order to work together to confront the takfiri threat. We are all capable of defeating this threat and those who stand behind this threat, whether it be Mossad, the CIA, or the British intelligence.
>
> (Al-Ahed News 2015b)

In March 2015, the Secretary-General of the Iraqi Shi'a group Hezbollah al-Nujaba, *Sheikh* Akram al-Kaabi, declared that advisers from the IRGC and mujahedin of Lebanese group Hezbollah were participating in various operations to liberate cities under the occupation of the ISIS (Hashem 2015).

The Hezbollah's official position on the regional popular uprisings had significantly changed since 2011. The early optimism had faded, giving way to hostility towards popular elements. Nasrallah's rhetoric of March 2011 was reversed completely, while Hezbollah's two criteria for support (the regime's stance on the Palestinian–Israeli conflict, and the readiness of the regime to engage in reform) were no longer operative. A return to the pre-uprisings status quo was increasingly the Hezbollah preferred outcome.

The key turning point in the Hezbollah's position towards the events of the region was clearly the beginning of the popular uprising in Syria.

Hezbollah and Syria after 2011

The Hezbollah has long had a close relationship with the Syrian regime, which has only become stronger over the years to become a firm alliance with a deep collaboration between the two actors, especially following the death of Syrian ruler Hafez al-Assad in 2000 and his son Bashar's arrival to power. Hafez al-Assad treated the Hezbollah as a useful tool for strengthening Syria's relations with the IRI, while also exploiting the Hezbollah's attacks to pressure Israel during peace negotiations.

This situation changed under Bashar al-Assad, especially following the withdrawal of the Syrian armed forces from Lebanon in 2005 and the 2006 Lebanon War between Israel and the Hezbollah. The Syrian regime increasingly viewed the relationship with the Hezbollah not as a tactical and temporary alliance, as it had been under Hafez al-Assad, but as a strong and strategic alliance. Bashar al-Assad deepened his collaboration with the group both politically and militarily.

In this manner, the Hezbollah became an important proxy for the Syrian regime in Lebanon. Bashar al-Assad held multiple meetings with Nasrallah, in contrast to his father who saw the Hezbollah Secretary General only twice (Blanford 2011: 290). Furthermore, while Hafez al-Assad had imposed controls on the quantity and variety of arms he allowed the IRI to transfer to the Hezbollah via Damascus airport, Bashar al-Assad opened the arms floodgate, sending greater quantities of weapons and more advanced systems to be dispatched across the border into the Islamic movement's depot (Blanford 2011: 337). The Hezbollah supported the Syrian regime's hegemony in Lebanon until its departure in 2005, and even after Syria's departure, it maintained close alliances with it. In the Hezbollah's new manifesto of 2009, the Syrian regime was described as having recorded:

> a distinctive attitude and supported the resistance movements in the region, and stood beside us in the most difficult circumstances, and sought to unify Arab efforts to secure the interests of the region and challenges. Hence, we [Hezbollah] emphasize the need to adhere to the distinguished relations between Lebanon and Syria as a common

political, security, and economic need, dictated by the interests of the two countries and two peoples, by the imperatives of geopolitics and the requirements for Lebanese stability and facing common challenges.
(Manifesto 2009)

In a recent book, Dr. Hassan Fadlallah (2015: 118–24), a Hezbollah MP, writes that after the Ta'if Agreement, Lebanon was completely controlled by a small number of Syrian officials, with the collaboration of some Lebanese politicians. He accuses the Syrian officials at that time, especially Ghazi Kanaan and Abdel Halim Khaddam,[6] of having pursued their personal interests at the expense of both Lebanon and Syria. Despite his disagreements regarding the domestic Lebanese political scene, Fadlallah nevertheless explains that Syria and the Hezbollah shared a central objective, that is, the capacity to respond militarily to Israel, and that both Presidents Hafez and Bashar al-Assad had always supported the Hezbollah in its military confrontations with Israel. Fadlallah praises the role of Bashar al-Assad in supporting Syria's military assistance to the Hezbollah since the beginning of the 1990s, for example during the Israeli aggression against Lebanon in 1993 and 1996, at which time the Syrian regime supplied missiles to the group (Fadlallah 2015: 118–24).

The eruption of the Syrian uprising in March 2011, and the subsequent military intervention by the Hezbollah in support of the Assad regime, demonstrates that the relationship between the two actors had become a strategic one. In May 2011, during Nasrallah's first speech regarding the situation in Syria, he declared that the overthrow of the regime in Syria is in American and Israeli interests (Al-Muqāwama al-Islāmiyya 2011a). In August of the same year, he said at the occasion of the al-Quds International Day that:

thanks [to] the Syrian leadership the Palestinian cause was preserved and not liquidated as it was the objective of all the US and Western invasions and conspiracies against our region [...] Today some are seeking to break up Syria as part of a new Middle East agenda.
(Al-Muqāwama al-Islāmiyya 2011b)

In early 2012, Nasrallah increasingly accused the West, Israel, "moderate" Arab regimes and even al-Qaida of collaborating to overthrow the Assad regime (Al-Manar 2012a).

Nasrallah reiterated this position much more sharply a few months later, saying that these same parties (the West, Israel and some regional states) sought the downfall of the Assad regime because it supported the resistance, and that these parties are seeking to realize the project of the New Middle East of George W. Bush (Al-Manar 2012b). Nasrallah also accused the USA and Israel on many occasions of using legitimate grievances in Syria as an excuse to destroy the country and the resistance in order to further Israel's control over the Middle East (Al-Akhbar English 2012b).

In May 2013, Nasrallah stated that:

> Syria has been the spine of the resistance, so the resistance can't stand still while that spine is being ruined [...] The US has brought in "al-Qaida" and the other Takfiris organisations from all over the world, paid them money, and offered them all the assistance they needed [...] Obviously, the Takfiris current is dominant among the Syrian opposition, and it is being funded and armed by a number of Arab and regional states [...] If Syria falls in the hands of the USA, Israel, Takfiris, and US instruments in the region, then the resistance will be besieged, and "Israel" will invade Lebanon to impose its conditions and revive its project again. If Syria falls, then Palestine, the Palestinian resistance, Gaza, the West Bank, and the Holy al-Qods (Jerusalem) will be lost and the people of our region will face a dark and cruel era!

> (Al-Ahed News 2013)

Nasrallah also claimed that the Hezbollah's support for the Syrian regime was not only for the Hezbollah and the Shi'a, but also for Lebanon and all its various religious communities against the threats of *Takfiri* forces (Al-Ahed News 2013).

In this context, the Hezbollah has intervened to fight alongside the Syrian regime's armed forces. Since mid-2011, the Hezbollah had been training thousands of Lebanese and Syrian youth in several camps, according to Lebanese journalist Fouad Itani (2014). In October 2011, Nasrallah said in a television interview that reports of the deployment of Hezbollah fighters into Syria were "absolutely untrue" (Blanford 2013a). In May 2012, another senior Hezbollah official also asserted that the Islamic movement did not and would not fight in Syria (ICG 2014: 1).

This was contradicted by some journalists, such as Nicholas Blanford, who wrote: "by early 2012, it was becoming public knowledge within Lebanese Shiʿa circles that some Hezbollah fighters were being sent into Syria" (Blanford 2013a). The Hezbollah's presence was confirmed with the acknowledgement of its first "martyrs" in Syria, as early as June 2012 (Ashkar 2014b). The Hezbollah announced the death of its soldiers while performing their "jihadist duties," a standard phrase used by the group when announcing deaths of fighters in circumstances other than direct combat with Israel (Blanford 2012).

In the middle of 2012, the Hezbollah was increasingly reported to be providing technical and logistical support to Damascus, and helping some of Syria's Shiʿa population to develop self-defense militias (ICG 2014: 1; Orient le Jour and AFP 2014b). The Hezbollah also opened training camps outside the city of Baalbek in the Bekaa Valley, close to the Syrian border, to train youth from various religious sects. While the highest percentage of the trainees in these camps are Shiʿa, their purpose was to develop self-defense militias similar to those in Syria (Al-Monitor 2014).

As reports of the Hezbollah's casualties mounted, especially after the death of Ali Nassif, a senior Hezbollah veteran commander killed near Qusayr in Syria in September 2012 (and whose funeral was attended by *Sheikh* Muhammad Yazbeck), it was becoming increasingly difficult to hide the Hezbollah's involvement in Syria. A few days after Nassif's death, Nasrallah claimed that several Hezbollah fighters who had died in Syria had been fighting as individuals to defend villages close to the border with Lebanon, rather than in the Hezbollah-sponsored operations (Itani 2014; ICG 2014: 1). He added that he did not rule out the possibility that the Hezbollah would join the battle inside Syria (Hersh 2013). By December 2012, videos emerged that allegedly portrayed Hezbollah fighters in southern Damascus, home to a shrine revered by the Shiʿa (Blanford 2013a).

The Hezbollah fighters were increasingly participating in fighting alongside the Syrian army. In spring 2013, the Hezbollah played a key role in a military offensive launched by the regime on Qusayr, then controlled by the Syrian rebels. The city served as a logistical conduit for the anti-Assad revolt, facilitating the movement of weapons and militants between Lebanon and Homs (Blanford 2013b). Roughly 1,200 to 1,700 fighters of the Islamic Movement participated in the battle, most of them seasoned veterans drawn from the Hezbollah's Special Forces (Blanford 2013b). The Hezbollah supporters and sympathizers in Dahyeh celebrated the subsequent victory of the Hezbollah and the Syrian regime forces against rebels. The Hezbollah members offered sweets to locals to mark the victory, and Dahyeh was adorned with Hezbollah flags and banners saying "Qusayr Has Fallen" (Now Media and AFP 2013).

In November 2013, Nasrallah publicly acknowledged the Hezbollah's official presence in Syria and added that: "the presence of Hezbollah fighters on Syrian soil aims at defending Lebanon, the Palestinian cause, and Syria, which defends the resistance" and "as long as there is a purpose for our presence there, we will remain there" (Al-Manar 2013a). In December 2013, he later claimed,

> we are protecting Lebanon [...] If Hezbollah did not fight in Syria, there would have been a Civil War in Lebanon and hundreds of car bombs. We did damage control and diminished the repercussions of the Syrian crisis on Lebanon.
>
> (Al-Manar 2013b)

The Hezbollah's growing military role in Syria took various forms, ranging from veteran Hezbollah fighters commanding squads of Syrian soldiers, essentially acting as Non-Commissioned Officers (NCOs), to supporting the less experienced Syrian regular troops in street fighting in Homs (Blanford 2013b). They also conducted the training of some pro-regime militias known as "popular committees" (Nakhoul 2013), and of some new recruits in the Syrian army (Orient le Jour and AFP 2014b). In February 2014, the Hezbollah sent a large number of its troops to the town of Yabroud, in the Qalamoun Mountains north of Damascus, while maintaining a presence in other regions of Syria such as the outskirts of Aleppo, Idlib, Deraa, Damascus and its suburbs (El-Hassan 2013; ICG 2014: 2). In 2014 and 2015, the Hezbollah established the Syrian Shi'a militia in Syria called Quwat al-Ridha. The Lebanese Islamic movement was responsible for organizing, training and equipping the group's approximately 20,000 members, mostly Syrian Shi'a from the province of Homs (Alipour 2015).

The Hezbollah's intervention in Syria was presented to its supporters and to the Lebanese Shi'a population more generally as an "existential battle" against the Sunni extremists characterized as "*takfiris*" (Orient le Jour and AFP 2014a). This perception among the Shi'a population was reinforced following multiple attacks by jihadist groups[7] who have been targeting Lebanese Shi'a-populated areas and particularly Dahyeh since 2013. Naim Qassem argued that the Hezbollah's intervention in Syria was "necessary and fundamental" (cited in ICG 2014: 21), while the Hezbollah deputy Hussein Mussawi declared that: "the presence of Hezbollah in Syria and Iraq is a duty recommended by God who asks us to support the victims of injustice facing the tyrants" (Orient le Jour 2015c). This discourse was echoed by the Hezbollah soldiers in Syria, as with one 18-year-old fighter who said that he joined Hezbollah to wage jihad in Syria, because it was his religious duty and the duty of every Muslim to fight there. He described what is happening in Syria as, "a repetition of what happened over 1,000 years ago during the battle of Karbalā',"[8] adding that: "the takfiris in Syria were attacking our holy sites, our Mouqadassat, which are our most sacred places, such as the Sayyida Zeinab pilgrimage site. We could not let that happen" (Alami 2016).

At the same time, the Hezbollah continued to present its military intervention in Syria alongside the Assad regime as necessary for the protection of Palestine and the resistance against Israel. In May 2015, on the anniversary of the liberation of South Lebanon, Nasrallah again confirmed that Hezbollah was fighting alongside its:

> Syrian brothers, along with the army and the people and the Syrian popular resistance, in Syria, in Damascus or in Aleppo or in Homs or in Deir Zor or in Hasakeh or in Qalamoun or in Qusayr or in Idlib.
>
> (Al-Ahed News 2015d)

He explained that: "the fight of Hezbollah in Syria was for the defense of everyone, from Syria, Lebanon, Iraq, Yemen, Palestine," adding that the Hezbollah would be willing to expand its operations if necessary (Al-Ahed News 2015d). In summer 2015, Nasrallah accused foreign countries of fueling the violence in Syria by sending fighters, money and weapons, preventing any political solution. He added: "for sure the road to the liberation of Jerusalem passes through Qalamoun, Zabadani, Homs, Aleppo, Deraa, Sweida, and Hasakeh; that's because if Syria [i.e. the Assad Regime] is lost, Palestine would be lost too" (2015 Al-Ahed News 2015f).

In late September 2015, Nasrallah welcomed Russia's direct military intervention in Syria via airstrikes in support of the Assad regime, saying it was the failure of the US-led campaign against the Islamic State that had forced Moscow's hand. At the start of 2016, Hezbollah fighters took part alongside the Syrian army, backed by Russian air strikes and Iranian-supported Shi'a sectarian militias, in the conquest of the city of Aleppo and its countryside, which was previously divided between rebel- and government-held sectors. Collaboration with Russia's military has also been very close in various offensives across Syria since October 2015, with at least two joint Russia–Hezbollah operation rooms in Latakia and Damascus (Katz and Pollack 2015; Maghnayir 2016; Corbeil 2016).

The Hezbollah also played a key role alongside Syrian regime soldiers in the siege of Madaya, a village of 40,000 near the border with Lebanon that was under a blockade from July 2015 to mid-January 2016. At that time residents, saying they received permission from the Syrian government to leave the besieged town, departed after the arrival of an aid convoy (Reuters 2016). Between 30–50 residents died from starvation during this period, or in attempts to escape the blockade that encircled the town (Asher Shapiro 2016; Davis 2016).[9]

In March 2016, Nasrallah reiterated the Hezbollah's support for a political solution in Syria, while continuing to back Bashar al-Assad as president, a major sticking point for the majority of the Syrian opposition (Al-Ahed 2016b). Following the death of the Hezbollah's top military commander Mustapha Badr al-Din, Nasrallah declared during the memorial held in Mustapha Badr al-Din's honor that the Hezbollah will remain in Syria and will send even more fighters and leaders, adding that the party had within it a generation of new leaders ready to fill the void left by those killed. He also said that Hezbollah would continue to fight to defeat and destroy the "USA, Israeli, Takfiri, and Saudi project" in Syria (Al-Ahed 2016d).

As of summer 2016, the Hezbollah has continued to provide crucial support to the Syrian regime's army, alongside Iranian forces and the Russian air force. For example, it participated in the siege of Aleppo's opposition-controlled areas and in the conquest of the Aleppo countryside, and it also had a strong presence in the Damascus countryside, particularly in Qalamoun. On June 20, 2016, Nasrallah acknowledged that twenty-six of Hezbollah's fighters had been killed in the Aleppo region since the beginning of June, but affirmed that this was minor compared to the numbers of "terrorists" killed, more than 600. He went on to say that the Hezbollah would send more fighters to take part in the battle for Aleppo. He concluded by emphasizing that the conquest of Aleppo was a fight to defend Lebanon, Syria, Iraq and Jordan, which a few days earlier had suffered an attack on its border, against the American *Takfiri* project (Al-Manar 2016b).

Estimates of Hezbollah fighters in Syria since 2013 number between 7,000 and 9,000 at any time, including elite fighters, experts and reservists; they are rotated on thirty-day deployments (Alami 2016; Orient le Jour and AFP 2014b; Sullivan 2014). The party has published no official numbers for Hezbollah fatalities in Syria since the beginning of its intervention, but according to various sources over 1,300 of its fighters have been killed and thousands injured as of February 2016 (Corbeil 2016), while the Hezbollah has lost ten senior leaders in Syria, from Fawzi Ayoub in 2014 to Mustapha Badr al-Din in 2016, in addition to important figures such as Samir Qantar and Jihad Mughniyah, both killed in 2015 (Al-Jazeera 2016). The families of the dead fighters in Syria are treated as martyr families, meaning that they gain privileges and receive the highest level of attention from the party, including guaranteed medical care, clothing and schooling (Al-Qods 2014). In addition, each family receives substantial compensation for the loss of their son (Haddad 2015).

The Hezbollah's silence regarding the exact numbers of its losses [10] and the growing death toll has resulted in a feeling of resentment among some families of soldiers killed, in that the status of their sons as martyrs is not acknowledged as similar to that of those who have fallen in the struggle against Israel. Meanwhile, at the beginning of 2016, the Hezbollah cut back on social services provided to its constituency and began recruiting teenagers for the fight in Syria (Corbeil 2016).

According to some Hezbollah soldiers, the war in Syria has nevertheless considerably strengthened the Islamic movement at the military level. One commander explained that it was now militarily stronger than ever before, and had become something resembling a conventional army. He added that the Hezbollah's military involvement in Syria: "has led to an uptick in recruiting, filling the group's ranks with a growing number of young fighters, and years of combat have created a new generation of battle-tested militants" (cited in George 2015). The Hezbollah has also benefited from its collaboration with Russia's military in Syria. "[It is learning] how a world-class army gathers intelligence, makes plans, and executes operations. Working side-by-side with Russian officers is sure to refine Hezbollah's modern military strategy," according to Alexander Corbeil (2016), an analyst with The SecDev Group. And Brig. Gen. Muni Katz, from the Israeli Occupation forces, and Nadav Pollak added that: "working alongside Russian forces will likely enhance the group's ongoing shift toward a more offensive-minded strategy" (Katz and Pollak 2015).

Consequences of Hezbollah's Intervention in Syria: Rising Insecurity, Sectarianism and Regional Political Tensions

The increasing insecurity in Syria and the numerous attacks against the Shiʿa-populated areas was accompanied by intense and growing sectarianism. Despite the denial by the Hezbollah's leadership, the involvement in Syria by the Islamic movement has increased the level of sectarianism and sectarian tensions between the Sunni and Shiʿa communities in Lebanon.

Several events in the last few years have radicalized the Sunni Lebanese population, strengthening especially the Salafists and Sunni jihadists groups. Frustration among Sunnis has stemmed from a number of factors: the assassination of Rafiq Hariri in 2005, which the Assad regime and the Hezbollah were accused of having a hand in; the events of May 2008 mentioned earlier when clashes broke out in Beirut and other parts of the country following the government's decision to shut down the Hezbollah's telecommunication network and remove Beirut airport's security chief Wafiq Shuqayr over alleged ties to the Hezbollah; the fall of the Lebanese National Unity government, led by the Lebanese Sunni leader Saad Hariri, following the resignation of the Hezbollah and its political allies from the cabinet over arguments stemming from a UN investigation into the assassination of Rafiq Hariri; the assassination in 2012 of Brigadier General Wissam al-Hassan, chief of the Intelligence Bureau of the Lebanese Internal Security Forces (one of the two state Security agencies headed by Ashraf Rifi and considered to be an ally of the Hariri Future Movement and Saudi Arabia) (Saab 2012); and finally, the involvement of foreign Shiʿa fighters from the Hezbollah, Iraq and Iran has exacerbated these Sunni grievances.

At the same time, the Hezbollah uses a religious and sectarian Shiʿa discourse among its members to legitimize and justify its military intervention in Syria. Hassan Nasrallah, for example, said that Hezbollah needed to intervene in Syria not only to protect the resistance, but also to defend the Shiʿa villages by sending Hezbollah soldiers to the border. He also stressed the Hezbollah's role in protecting Shiʿa religious symbols like the mausoleum of the Prophet Muhammad's granddaughter, the Shrine of al-Sayyida Zaynab, in Damascus, stating that: "it has been already targeted many times by terrorist groups" (cited in Rida 2013). Sayyid Nasrallah added that this is a very sensitive issue, given the fact that certain extremist groups have announced that if they reach this shrine, they will destroy it (Nashashibi 2014). And reports indicate that the Hezbollah soldiers wore headbands with "O Husayn"[11] written on them (Blanford 2013b).

There has also been an increase in the display of banners, photos and songs glorifying the Shiʿa religious symbols in Shiʿa neighborhoods, which previously appeared almost exclusively during the Ashura. Social media outlets teemed with videos and pages calling for the defense of religious shrines in Syria and praising a young Shiʿa who died in a jihad to protect them (Blanford 2013b). In the Ashura celebrations of 2013, slogans such as "Hal Min Nāsirīn Yansurunā? Labbayki ya Zaynab!" (Is there any supporter to stand up for us? We are all for you, Zaynab!), 'Oh Zaynab! We are all your Abbass!" and "We swear by Hassan and Hussein, Zaynab will not be captured twice!" were raised to call for the defense of the Zaynab shrine that is protected by the Hezbollah and other Shiʿa sectarian groups from possible attacks of opposition armed groups in Damascus (Boumet Beirut 2013).

The growing insecurity in the Shiʿa-populated areas since the Hezbollah's military intervention in Syria and the worsening of sectarianism in Lebanon and the MENA region (to which both Sunni and Shiʿa elements have contributed), in addition to the multiplication of Hezbollah deaths on the Syrian battlefield, have provoked a sense of dissatisfaction among sections of the Lebanese Shiʿa and even in the Hezbollah's popular bases. Vocal criticisms have been limited, probably due to the Hezbollah's control over Shiʿa-populated areas. There are, nonetheless, some indications of growing discontent.

Following the death of a dozen Hezbollah fighters and the wounding of twenty more in an ambush in Sayyida Zaynab outside of Damascus in April 2013, the Hezbollah official *Sheikh* Muhammad Yazbeck, who was offering condolences to a family of one of the deceased, was asked by the mother of a dead fighter for the reason why the Hezbollah was sending their children to Syria when their battle was with Israel (Now Media 2013). In another case, a delegation from the Baalbek region representing the families of fallen Hezbollah fighters met with Yazbeck in June 2013 and told him that they found the Hezbollah's defense of the Syrian regime "flawed and intolerable," an act which, according to the delegation, did not fall within the group's *raison d'être*—resistance to Israel—and one that would widen the Sunni–Shi'a rift in Lebanon (Ya Libnan 2013a). Others in the South of Lebanon, such as the journalist and Hezbollah critic, Ali Amine, echoed similar feelings (Nakhoul 2013).

In Autumn 2013, a rare disgruntlement was also increasing within the Hezbollah leadership itself, according to Hisham Jaber, a Shi'a and retired Lebanese army general. Jaber said that some southern Shi'a families were questioning the wisdom of the Hezbollah's fighting fellow Muslims, even if they are Sunni (Dettmer 2013). In summer 2014, Nasrallah made a rare public appearance in the Bekaa Valley, to visit other Hezbollah soldiers. He also greeted the families of fallen fighters in an effort to assuage the frustration among the Shi'a families who have lost family members in the Hezbollah's military engagements (Naylor 2014).

According to various sources, some of the Hezbollah's allies in Lebanon have also refused to fight in Syria, such as the Palestinian Ansar Allah group forcing its Secretary General to resign. And some members of the Lebanese Resistance Brigades (LRB) were refusing to fight alongside Assad in Syria, prompting the Hezbollah leadership to launch an investigation of its members to determine the reasons behind their refusal (All4Syria 2015).

A majority of the Shi'a population was nevertheless still strongly supportive of, and reliant on, the Hezbollah, despite criticisms by some. No alternative to the Hezbollah has yet been presented by its critics, and many in the Shi'a population believe that in the current situation a weakened Hezbollah would weaken the Shi'a more generally (ICG 2014:12). The Lebanese state and army were not viewed by the Lebanese Shi'a as a representative or as a guarantee of security against jihadist forces. Indeed, the Lebanese Shi'a have continued to join the Hezbollah in increasing numbers, while the party intensifies recruitment and training to satisfy the growing requirements for manpower in Syria (ICG 2015: 8).

As already noted, support for the Hezbollah's intervention in Syria also intensified among the Shi'a population after dozens of attacks and suicide bombings by jihadist groups have targeted the Lebanese Shiʿa-populated areas, including in Beirut, since summer 2013. With the rise of the Islamic State (IS) and the establishment of its caliphate in summer 2014, the Hezbollah's Shiʿa critics grew even more timid. The large majority of the Hezbollah's popular base is now convinced that the movement's survival depends on its ability to assist the Syrian regime to remain in power. This support goes beyond the Hezbollah members, as 78.7 percent of the Lebanese Shiʿa approve of the intervention in Syria according to a 2015 survey by the association Haya Bina, whose founder, Mr. Lokman Slim, is known for its critical stance towards the party (Kostrz 2016).

At the same time, the Lebanese Resistance Brigades (LRB), affiliated with the Hezbollah, were re-energized by the beginning of the Syrian popular uprising in 2011. The LRB's new objective was mainly to act as a sort of adjunct civil guard to the Hezbollah's military force and help to secure its home front, and for a small number to fight in Syria rather than resisting Israel, as was its original official purpose. Some members were reportedly dispatched to party strongholds in north-eastern Lebanon for neighborhood guard duties. Critics among the Hezbollah foes and supporters have accused the LRB of doing the party's "dirty work"; they are "Hezbollah's thugs," said a journalist close to the movement. Some LRB members have been involved in arms trafficking[12] and in street-corner clashes (ICG 2015: 8).[13]

Regionally, the Hezbollah's military involvement in Syria has raised tensions with GCC states led by Saudi Arabia, reflecting also the increasing political animosity between the Saudi kingdom and the Islamic Republic of Iran. At the beginning of 2016, antagonism between these two blocs was very high, following notably the 2015 nuclear agreement between Iran and six world powers which came into effect on January 16, 2016, and which is perceived as a threat by the Saudi leadership.

Saudi Arabia would cut diplomatic ties with Iran in January 2016 after protesters set fire to the Saudi Embassy in Tehran and another diplomatic mission in Iran. They were angry over the Kingdom's execution of the influential Shiʿa cleric, Nimr al-Nimr, a leader of the popular demonstrations against the Saudi kingdom that started in 2011 in the eastern regions of the country populated primarily by the Shiʿa. Nasrallah condemned the execution of *Sheikh* Nimr and launched his sharpest attack yet on the Saudi ruling family, accusing them of seeking to ignite a civil war between Sunni and Shi'a Muslims across the world (Al-Ahed 2016a). He added that the blood of *Sheikh* Nimr would "plague the al-Saud [family] until the Day of Resurrection," prompting cries of "Death to the al-Saud!" among his audience (BBC News 2016a).

Saudi Arabia cancelled $4 billion in military aid to the Lebanese army on February 19, 2016, followed by a warning to its citizens on February 25 not to travel to Lebanon, and in December 2015, the Hezbollah's Al-Manar television channel was removed from the Riyadh-based satellite network Arabsat (Dot Pouillard 2016). In March 2016, the Hezbollah was designated a "terrorist" organization by the GCC and the Arab League, at the initiative of Saudi Arabia.[14] Several GCC states have also declared that they would punish anyone who belongs to the Hezbollah, sympathizes with it, supports it financially or harbors any of its members. Lebanese nationals and others have been deported from Gulf monarchies over suspected links to the group (Bassam and Evans 2016). Hours before the GCC decision on March 2, Nasrallah delivered a televised speech in which he harshly criticized Saudi Arabia for its punitive measures against Lebanon. He repeated his accusations that the Kingdom was directly responsible for car bombings in Lebanon, Syria and Iraq, and denounced Saudi "massacres" in Yemen (Al-Manar 2016a).

On March 22, Nasrallah claimed that the Hezbollah was on the terrorist list due to the wishes of the Saudi ruling family, working under "Israel cover" (Al-Ahed 2016b).[15] Tensions continued to increase between the Hezbollah and Saudi Arabia at the time of writing in early Summer 2016.

Relations between Hamas, the Hezbollah and Iran

The Syrian uprising has been a thorn in the relations between the Palestinian Islamic party Hamas and the Hezbollah. For more than a decade, Hamas' political bureau was based in Syria. Hamas was interested in maintaining its relationship with the Syrian regime, which has supported and welcomed the group when most other Arab regimes closed their doors to them. Hamas also wishes to keep the support of Iran, its largest supporter and supplier of money, weapons and training.

The Hamas leader, Khaled Mish'al, met secretly with Bashar al-Assad three times between January 25 and February 12, 2011. Assad was looking for information about the events that were unfolding in Egypt.

On February 12, 2011, following Mubarak's overthrow, Mish'al met again with Assad, who asked about rumors that the Egyptian Muslim Brotherhood had reached an agreement with the United States. Mish'al assured Assad that the uprising in Egypt was a popular revolt and not an American conspiracy, despite converging interests between the Muslim Brotherhood and the USA in the ousting of Mubarak. He told Assad, "Your foreign policy is excellent. You are loved by your people. But this is not enough; people want reform," and added that "Syria will not be spared by the Arab Spring. Nothing will stop this vogue of protest in the Arab world" (Azm 2012; Barake 2012).

While some senior Hamas officials and cadres have loudly voiced their support for the Syrian revolution, including Ismael Hanieh in a speech delivered at Cairo's Al-Azhar Mosque on February 24, 2012, Hamas officially maintained a neutral position for a long time. The movement has supported the rights of the Syrian people while neither condemning nor directly opposing the Syrian regime. The group has even attempted to mediate the crisis on several occasions, and has encouraged the Syrian President Bashar al-Assad to undertake immediate reforms. Mahmoud Zahar, acting Hamas Foreign Minister at the time, declared that Hamas' position on the revolutions in Libya, Tunisia and Egypt was neutral, and that it has adopted the same policy towards Syria. He added that as Syria hosted Hamas for a long time, the movement had no other choice but neutrality and affirmed that Hamas's confrontation is with Israel's occupation and not the Syrian regime. He concluded by saying that Hamas's "interest lies in harmony between the regime and the people, and for more freedoms. This is what the Syrian government has undertaken. The reforms by Syrian President Bashar al-Assad are a practical response to this question" (Shams 2012).

Popular support for the Syrian revolution among Palestinians in the OPT and the diaspora has nevertheless made it politically impossible for the Hamas leadership to voice clear support for a "political solution" to the conflict, as did the Hezbollah and as was requested by the Syrian regime. The ongoing conflict and increased tensions with the Syrian regime eventually prompted the Hamas leadership in Damascus to leave the country in February 2012 and it is now scattered between several locations, including Gaza, Lebanon, Jordan, Egypt, Turkey and Qatar.

Hamas' relations with the Syrian regime worsened throughout 2012, especially following a speech in Turkey on September 30, 2012, in which Khaled Mish'al voiced his support for the Syrian revolution. In November 2012, Syrian national television was accusing Mish'al of high treason. In addition to this, Hamas military brigades, Izz al-Din al-Qassam, participated in Syria in military confrontations alongside armed opposition forces against the Syrian regime, and shared some of its expertise with the Free Syrian Army brigades, notably in the construction of tunnels in the battle of Qusayr in May 2013 (Seurat 2015: 87).

Hamas' support for the Syrian revolution, however, became less vocal and less clear after summer 2013. For example, in October 2013, Mish'al urged "groups fighting in Syria to direct their rifles towards Palestine," announcing his "support of a peaceful solution in Syria that guarantees the freedom and dignity of people," while adding that "peoples have the right to rise up for their rights, but this must be done through peaceful means," in reference to Syria's armed groups (Asharq al-Awsat 2013). Moreover, following the entry of Jabhat al-Nusra, al-Qaida's branch in Syria, and the Islamic State into the al-Yarmouk Palestinian refugee camp in Damascus in April 2015, the Hamas affiliate in the camp, Aknaf Bayt al-Maqdis, which had been actively fighting the regime since the start of the Syrian revolution, were compelled to collaborate with the Popular Front for the Liberation of Palestine—General Command led by Ahmed Jibril, very well known to be an active supporter of the Syrian regime, while an injured leader of Aknaf Bayt al-Maqdis, Ahmad Zaghmout, was treated in a regime hospital (Lambert 2016).

Relations between Iran and Hamas were also made more difficult because of their differences on Syria, prompting the IRI to diminish its support to Hamas and transfer some of its assistance to rival resistance factions in the Gaza Strip like Islamic Jihad, the PFLP and an armed group affiliated with Fatah (Al-Akhbar English 2013d). But direct contacts and collaboration between Hamas and Iran continued on a political and military level. Relations were also maintained between the Hezbollah and Hamas, and Hamas maintained its offices in the Hezbollah's stronghold in Dahyeh, Beirut, which has been there for nearly two decades despite some tensions between the groups. Moreover, the Hezbollah has not ceased its provision of financial support to Hamas' Al-Quds TV station, which is broadcast into Palestine from one of Dahyeh's wealthier neighborhoods (Charara 2014).

In February 2012, Hanieh traveled to Iran and shared the podium with the Iranian President Mahmoud Ahmadinejad to commemorate the anniversary of the 1979 Islamic Revolution. Following this visit, in March 2012, Mahmoud Zahar met in Iran with Iranian Foreign Minister Akbar Salehi. During this visit, Zahar thanked Iran for its "limitless support" (The Daily Star 2012b). It was then the turn of the Hamas Foreign Minister, Muhammad Awad, to travel to Iran a few months later. In June and July 2013, two meetings were held. First, a delegation headed by Moussa Abu Marzouq came to Lebanon and held private meetings at the Iranian embassy and with Hezbollah officials, notably on the issue of military supply shortages of Hamas' military wing al Qassam. Later, two prominent Hamas leaders also met with Iranian officials in Beirut in the presence of representatives from the Hezbollah, in which the strategic relations between the Palestinian movement and Iran were discussed (Al-Akhbar English 2013d).

According to the Lebanese newspaper *Al-Akhbar*, a meeting in June 2013 between the leaders of Hamas and Iran was held in which a number of issues were settled:

- A resumption of Iranian financial aid to Hamas, though less than pre-crisis amounts;
- An opening of direct channels of communication between Hamas and Hezbollah, particularly over the issue of keeping the Palestinian refugee camps out of the mounting Sunni–Shiʻa tension in Lebanon. Ali Baraka, the Hamas representative in Lebanon, declared that Hamas needed to work with Hezbollah to combat sectarian incitement and to keep Palestinians out of internal Lebanese disputes (Shaheen 2013).
- Preparation for a leadership meeting between Hezbollah and Hamas, after the latter complained that Hezbollah Secretary General Hassan Nasrallah had not received a high-level Hamas delegation in quite some time.

(Al-Akhbar English 2013d)

These meetings suggest that both Hamas and Iran have made efforts to overcome the differences they may have over Syria and to maintain strong relations. Indeed there are common understandings and interests between the two parties that make possible the continuation of good relations despite these and other differences. Today, the IRI is the only power, even more so after Hamas cut ties with the Syrian regime, that is ready and able to provide weapons to the Palestinian Islamic movement, while Hamas' new allies from the Gulf are not ready to provide as much (or any) as the IRI. On the other side, Hamas remains the main military and political power in the Gaza Strip, and Iran's only link to Palestine and to the Muslim Brotherhood, at a time of increasing sectarian discourse across the region against the Shi'a and Iran. However, some sources have claimed that in October 2013, the Hamas leader Khaled Mish'al was not yet ready to make an appearance in Lebanon, where the axis of the Hezbollah, Syria and Iran have a strong presence, because he did not want to upset his Gulf sponsors, Qatar and Saudi Arabia (Khalil 2013b).

In July 2014, during the Israeli War on the Gaza Strip, Hamas' representative in Lebanon, Ussama Hamdan, said that the Palestinian Islamic movement was coordinating on the ground with the Hezbollah (The Daily Star 2014a). In January 2015, senior commanders of Hamas sent their condolences to the Hezbollah Secretary General Nasrallah on the martyrdom of six Hezbollah fighters by an Israeli raid in Syria's Quneitra. In a letter sent to the Lebanese resistance leader, the commander in chief of Hamas' military wing, Muhammad Daif, called on the unity of the resistance against the Zionist enemy (Al-Manar 2015).

This rapprochement was threatened following a summer 2015 Hamas delegation to Saudi Arabia led by Mish'al to meet the newly crowned King Salman. Mish'al's visit was significant given that communications between Hamas and Saudi Arabia had completely ruptured in 2012. The meeting can be explained with reference to the nuclear deal between Iran and the USA, and Saudi Arabia's strategy in response to gather most of the Arab States and various Sunni movements against the IRI, fearing that Iran will emerge empowered by its agreement with Western powers.

This meeting did not however completely halt the process of fragile reconciliation between Hamas and Iran. During an eight-day visit to Iran in February 2016, led by Hamas political bureau members Muhammad Nasr and Ussama Hamdan, to take part in the 37th anniversary of the Islamic Revolution, they met several top Iranian officials including parliament Speaker Ali Larijani and Secretary of the Supreme National Security Council Rear Adm. Ali Shamkhani. Following this, Hamas published a statement declaring that the visit would "usher in a new page of cooperation between Hamas and Iran" (Hashem 2016; Lambert

2016). A few months earlier, in November 2015, a meeting took place in Beirut between the Deputy Secretary General of Hezbollah, *Sheikh Naim Qassem* and a delegation of Hamas leaders, including the senior Hamas political bureau member Moussa Abu Marzouk. During this meeting, Abu-Marzouk condemned the November 2015 suicide attack in Burj al-Barajneh, in Beirut's southern suburbs, while both Hamas and the Hezbollah called this a terrorist attack and stressed that such attacks serve only the Israelis. Both called for support for the ongoing intifada against the Zionist project (Middle East Monitor 2015b).

Hamas is faced with a balancing act. On the one hand, its relations with Iran, which with the assistance of the Hezbollah has provided and continues to provide Hamas with military assistance including weapons and training, in addition to important financial funding. On the other hand, with Saudi Arabia and the GCC, a number of Hamas political leaders reside in Qatar and enjoy relative political security and free movement from one Gulf country to another, which allows the collection of funds donated to charitable institutions affiliated with the movement in the Palestinian territories (Abu Amer 2016). Hamas will likely continue to seek the support of both, with consequences for its relationship with the Hezbollah, the tenuousness of which was on display when Hamas remained silent following the Hezbollah's designation as a terrorist group by the GCC and Arab League in March 2016.

Conclusion

The Hezbollah's international relations are driven by political interests, and not by a principled commitment to solidarity with the oppressed. The Hezbollah's resistance against Israel, which had been at the core of its identity, has been subordinated to the political objectives of the party, its allies and its sponsors Syria and Iran. The weapons of the "Resistance" have been increasingly diverted from the struggle against Israel, and used instead to attack other Lebanese political parties or to prevent the emergence of competitors to the Hezbollah in South Lebanon. The defense of the Resistance is invoked to explain the policies and actions of the party in Lebanon and elsewhere, notably its military intervention in Syria.

The Hezbollah's two decisive criteria (first, the regime's stance on the Palestinian–Israeli conflict; second, the readiness of the regime to engage in reform), from the beginning of the uprisings expressed by Hassan Nasrallah were increasingly put into doubt. Meanwhile, the military and political interventions of the Hezbollah in the various popular uprisings, such as the massive military intervention in Syria and as a military presence in Iraq and Yemen, have confirmed the growing power and influence of the Lebanese movement throughout the region.

The Hezbollah's change of position towards the regional uprisings reveals that its interests and those of its allies are more important in its calculations than the emancipation of the people of the region. The Hezbollah has never called for radical change on a regional level, seeking instead non-confrontational relations with established authoritarian regimes. The Hezbollah's actions today are characterized by its preference to return to the status quo that existed prior to the popular uprisings.

Conclusion

This book has detailed and analyzed the characteristics and evolution of the Hezbollah in relation to the economic and political developments in Lebanese society and in the wider region. The Hezbollah, and Islamic political parties more generally, can be studied using the same theoretical and conceptual tools used to examine other organizations or movements throughout the world. The Hezbollah can be understood in its totality and in its political economic context, in its relations to the sectarian Lebanese political system, to the state, to revolutionary processes in the region, to workers struggles, and to women's rights. Studies often focus on only one or two aspects of the Hezbollah, typically the military, treating the party as somehow separate from the political and social dynamics of the society.

The political economic dynamics of Lebanon and the region have had profound consequences for the development and nature of the Hezbollah. The historical and enduring context for this development is an economy dominated by the service sector, in which trade, finance and tourism have taken a leading position, and inflows of foreign capital have long played a central role. The Hezbollah's growing influence in the Lebanese economy and in the political scene began with its control of the southern suburbs of Beirut in 1989, home to the Shi'a, of which more than 70 percent vote in South Lebanon and in the Bekaa because of the particular Lebanese electoral system in which citizens vote in their place of origin and not of residence. This has been an important route to power at the national level. The southern suburbs lacked basic and necessary services for a population in need, which presented great opportunity. The Hezbollah allied itself with the growing and ascendant Shi'a bourgeoisie, using it as a base for recruitment and fund-raising, and in the process making this class a patron of the new society forming in the suburbs. A huge network of organizations has helped the Islamic movement to consolidate its growing influence and control over large portions of the Shi'a population, which has gained increasing importance in the socio-economic and political structure of Lebanon. The Shi'a majority populated regions in Lebanon have attracted investment from both public and private actors. The large inflow of money to the Hezbollah after Israel's 2006 war against Lebanon only increased the importance of the Hezbollah as a large economic actor. The Hezbollah is known to have purchased large portions of land in South Lebanon and in Beirut, increasingly tying the party to major landowners and to the fast growing Shi'a fraction of the bourgeoisie, mainly concentrated in the construction and trade sectors of the economy.

Over time, these socio-economic and political changes have had important consequences for the party and its policies. The Hezbollah has seen the growing significance inside the party of new higher-middle-class cadres involved in liberal professions, and a weakening of radical and smaller petit bourgeois elements such as the clerics. At the same time, a new fraction of the bourgeoisie linked to the party through Iranian capital and investments was created, while the rest of the Shi'a fraction of the bourgeoisie, whether in Lebanon or in the diaspora, became increasingly intertwined with the Hezbollah. Alongside this increasing economic weight and integration into the political system, the Hezbollah has also been linked to corruption and to the wider use of clientelist practices.

The economic and political strength of the Hezbollah in Lebanon has made the organization an increasingly significant rival to the fraction of the Lebanese bourgeoisie gathered around Hariri and the March 14 Alliance (linked, in turn, to Gulf capital), particularly after Syria's withdrawal from the country in 2005. The political opposition of the Hezbollah to the March 14 forces, which are backed by Western states and Gulf monarchies, should be understood as inter-capitalist rivalry on the national scale, between two blocs linked to different regional and international forces. Despite their rivalries, however, these two blocs have cooperated with one another at points of crisis—as indicated by their similar attitudes towards labor and other social movements, their orientation towards neoliberal reform in Lebanon, and their cooperation in government following the departure of the Syrian army from Lebanon in 2005.

The Sectarian State

The political objectives that initially informed the ideology of the Hezbollah have been subordinated to other priorities. The organization's original radical opposition to the Lebanese sectarian political system has been downplayed following its entry into parliament and participation in government along sectarian lines, in contrast to its continued rhetoric and populist criticism.

The Hezbollah's initial objective was to establish an Islamic regime, despite the near impossibility of such a task given the multi-confessional reality of Lebanese society. From total refusal of involvement in the sectarian system, the organization has been progressively integrated into the system as one of its main actors. The Hezbollah's evolution was linked to various factors, including the change of political leadership in the IRI that sought a more pragmatic policy and improved relations with the Western and Gulf states; the development of the Hezbollah as a mass party that was no longer primarily composed of young radical clerics and individuals who sought to impose a model similar to Iran; and, finally, the Hezbollah's need to protect its armaments and its growing political and economic interests inside Lebanon. The popular base of Hezbollah, which increasingly included the growing Shi'a fraction of the bourgeoisie and the middle classes, especially in Beirut, did not necessarily yearn to live in an Islamic Republic on the Iranian model, and was satisfied with a return to peace and an improvement in political representation. These developments reflected the new political and economic strength of the Shi'a population in the country, achieved after the Ta'if Agreement. Another important feature in this integration into the political system was the withdrawal of the Syrian army from Lebanon, which compelled the party to participate in all Lebanese governments from that point onwards.

In light of these developments, the Hezbollah does not constitute a challenge to the Lebanese sectarian system. On the contrary, it sees this system in much the same way as any other sectarian political party—as a means to serve its own interests. This is particularly important given the various social and political forces that attempt to unify Lebanese popular classes beyond sectarian identities. The Hezbollah has sought to collaborate with other Lebanese elites in opposition to these anti-sectarian forces, despite some political differences, especially during periods of heightened social mobilization.

The Hezbollah's "participatory" engagement with the confessional state reflects both an attempt to moderate (or alleviate) the structural contradictions of Lebanese capitalism (Amel 1986: 337–38) as well as the rivalries that exist within the bourgeoisie between its hegemonic and non-hegemonic fractions. The latter, as Mehdi Amel has noted, reflects:

the consciousness of non hegemonic layers of the bourgeoisie in their (legitimate?) aspiration to occupy hegemonic positions occupied by other fractions, or to rise to their level by identifying where possible with them in the political and economic domain. This non-hegemonic layer of the bourgeoisie wants the end of the hegemonic fraction without removing the domination of the bourgeois class.

(Amel 1986: 339)

This evolution was also linked to the Hezbollah's regional allies, Syria and Iran, both of which supported the party's integration into the Lebanese political scene after the end of the Civil War. At the same time, the Hezbollah's armed apparatus was subordinated to its political interests, in particular the ongoing stability of Lebanon. This has led to increased collaboration with the Lebanese army and security services to prevent military conflict with Israel in the country's South, to collaborate against Salafist and jihadist groups, and finally to guarantee the security of some Shi'a-populated areas. This does not mean that the Hezbollah's military component did not and does not still play a role against Israel's aggression and wars, but the Hezbollah's force is increasingly being used for other purposes, especially after the 2006 Lebanon War.

This can be seen in the transformation of the Hezbollah's orientation towards the uprisings in the Middle East and North Africa. The Hezbollah's so-called solidarity with the oppressed of the world was as we have seen rather rhetoric and was based on the Hezbollah's political interests, which are themselves linked to the IRI and Syria.

Ideology

The Hezbollah promotes the unity of the community and cooperation between classes, as Khomeini used to preach, in which the workers should not ask more than what is given by the bourgeoisie and the bourgeoisie is obligated to be charitable towards the poor. As for other Islamic movements, class struggle is seen as negative because it fragments the community or the Ummah. The solution to poverty is to be found in a return to Islamic values and tradition, or, in the words of the Tunisian

Islamic leader Rached Ghannouchi: "we need to emphasize that poverty, in the eyes of Islam, is linked to unbelief" (1979 cited in Toscane 1995: 28). Likewise, Mustapha Siba'i, the founder of the Muslim Brotherhood in Syria, noted that: "the socialism of Islam leads necessarily to the solidarity of various social categories and not to the war between classes as communism" (1959 cited in Carré and Gérard 1983: 87). As such, Islamic parties seek to re-establish the Ummah, a religio-political entity that would gather all Muslims and transcend the cleavages that divide them today (Toscane 1995: 24).

The Islamization of large sections of the Shi'a population served this objective, splintering and weakening solidarities between the different sects in Lebanon, whereas the Shi'a before the Lebanese Civil War comprised the largest number of members of nationalist and progressive parties that were leading social struggles. The Hezbollah's poor record towards mobilizations around social and worker's issues reflected the party's changing class interests and its opposition towards greater empowerment of the popular classes. The possibility of cross-sectarian mobilization and the development of class-based movements present a potential threat to all the sectarian and bourgeois elements in Lebanon, of which the Hezbollah has become a part. This explains why the Hezbollah has never mobilized its constituency on the basis of socio-economic demands with a cross-sectarian perspective, even while rhetorically supporting the CGTL and/or social demands.

A concern with the social and economic deterioration of Lebanese society was always subordinated to the recognition of the legitimacy of the Hezbollah's armed capacities. The Hezbollah has called on Saad Hariri—on numerous occasions—to collaborate in a government based on the agreements the party had made with his father, Rafiq Hariri.[1] They justified this in the following way: the Hezbollah takes care of the "resistance" against Israel, and Hariri takes care of the economic and social policies of the country, each one not interfering in the affairs of the other (Al-Muntada al-Ishtirākī 2012: 4–8).

The Hezbollah, despite rhetorical and populist criticisms against what it called "savage capitalism," did not develop any alternative. On the contrary, it continues to support capitalism, free markets and neoliberal policies. The Hezbollah's presence in the government has only confirmed the previous policies of earlier Lebanese governments. In this manner, the Hezbollah has become an integral part of the Lebanese bourgeoisie.

Regarding women, the Hezbollah promotes a conservative vision that confers the domination of men and attributes specific roles to women in society, the first and most important being the role of "motherhood" in order to educate future generations with Islamic principles. Women in the Lebanese Islamic movement are not present in decision-making structures. In no way are the patriarchal structures of the society challenged by the party, while women's clothing and behavior must conform to particular norms that are said to preserve her honor and that of the family. The Islamic model is considered to be the only correct path for women, otherwise they are considered to be alien to their own society and under the influence of Western cultural imperialism. As Adam Hanieh has noted: "conservative structures on the role of women are an integral component of broader counterrevolutionary goals" (Hanieh 2013: 172).

Finally, we have seen that Hezbollah's professed solidarity with the oppressed of the world is largely subordinated to its narrower political interests, which are themselves closely linked to those of Iran and Syria. The Hezbollah's military confrontation with Israel has become secondary to the political fortunes of the party and its regional allies. The rhetorical defense of the "axis of resistance" (Hezbollah, Iran, Syria and Hamas) and of the armed apparatus of the party has been used by the Hezbollah to justify the policies and actions of the party, including its military involvement in Syria.

Counter society? Features of Hezbollah's Hegemonic Project

These elements lead to the conclusion that the Hezbollah is not building a counter-society or a counter-hegemonic project per se, as suggested by some, but is more concerned with an effort to win the support of the largest possible section of the Shi'a population, while not presenting a challenge in any way to the dominant political system in its own society or beyond.

To this end, the Hezbollah has pursued Islamization policies in Shi'a-populated regions in multiple ways, including investment in businesses promoting the *hāla islāmiyya*, and social pressure through committees checking the conformity of institutions with the principles of the *hāla islāmiyya*, as well as through the use of its arms. The provision of social services through its huge network of organizations has been instrumental in the spread of Islamic principles among the wider population. When occupying positions of power in ministries or in municipalities, the Hezbollah privileges actors close to its ideology, while reinforcing the exclusion of others. Furthermore, the Hezbollah's armed capabilities have played an important role in the diffusion of the party's political ideas, especially in connection with its military conflict against Israel, which brought huge popularity to the Islamic movement. At the same time, its armed wing also serves other purposes such as the defense of the Islamic movement against any attempts to weaken it, the repression of dissent within the Shi'a population and among other Lebanese actors, and plays the role of the "police" and the "army" to guarantee security in some Shi'a-populated areas.

The Hezbollah has been successful in achieving a level of hegemony among the Shi'a population. This hegemony has involved the development of a twofold nature of class domination, in which, according to Gramsci, the party both "leads the allied classes, and dominates over adverse classes" (cited in Thomas 2009: 163). In this manner, hegemony represents:

> the form of political power exercised over those classes in close proximity to the leading group, while domination is exerted over those opposing it. Consent is one of the means of forging the composite body of a class alliance, while coercion is developed against the excluded other.
>
> (Thomas 2009: 163)

Consent and coercion, in other words, operate together in a dialectical fashion. As Peter Thomas has noted:

> they counterbalance each other in a unity that depends upon the maintenance of a precise, unbalanced equilibrium between its two poles: forces must not appear to predominate too much over consent, but the proper relationship between in reality involves more weight on the side of the former.
>
> (Thomas 2009:165)

The Hezbollah has gained the consent of the popular classes through the mechanism of Islamization and by the domination of the military confrontation against Israel, binding the interests of subaltern classes to the party structure and its interests, while it benefited and relied upon the continuing demobilization of labor movements and other proletarian/working-class forces.

In the words of Bob Jessop, "a hegemonic project can be concerned with various non economic objectives (even if economically conditioned and economically relevant)" (1990 cited in Roccu 2012: 208).[2] In the Hezbollah's case, these non-economic objectives include Islamization and domination of the military confrontation with Israel. However, the Hezbollah ultimately advances the long-term interests of the hegemonic class, which are not the interests of the popular classes but rather those of the rising bourgeoisie with its growing Shi'a fraction.

As Gerratna argues:

> a class that manages to lead, and not only to dominate, in a society based economically on class exploitation, and in which the continuance of such exploitation is desired, is constrained to use forms of hegemony that obscure this situation and mystify this exploitation; it therefore needs a form of hegemony designed to give rise to manipulated consent, a consent of subaltern allies.
>
> (Gerratana 1997 cited in Thomas 2009: 227).

In this manner, Hezbollah's ideology, in which mechanisms of Islamization are predominant, is a "non-organic" philosophy; one that has "maintained the subaltern classes in their subaltern position, glossing over or obscuring the true, fractured nature of the present by speculatively sanctifying it as the only possible present and this as eternity" (Thomas 2009: 209). It is an ideology that attempts to reconcile contradictory and opposing interests.

Alternative Paths

The initial point of departure of this book was that the Hezbollah, and Islamic movements in general, are neither revolutionary nor progressive groups, nor terrorist groups, but are parties led by political interests that can be explained through a materialist approach, and not simply by a focus on ideology. In a Marxist sense, these parties can be identified as actors pulled in two directions—towards radical rebellion against existing society, and towards compromise with it—increasingly widening its ties to the bourgeoisie in connection to their political leaderships and cadres, while attempting to preserve a cross-class base of support. As we have seen, the Hezbollah has evolved from radical rebellion towards compromise and participation within Lebanon's existing political structures. Its project does not present a fundamental alternative to the dominant capitalist and sectarian system in Lebanon. On the contrary, it sustains it, as it does with discrimination against women, Palestinian and Syrian refugees, and so forth. In addition, the provision of services by its networks of organizations does not differ from that of other political and sectarian communities in Lebanon, except in its size and efficiency, by promoting private, sectarian and patronal support or management of social risks (Alagha and Catusse 2008: 132–34). The elites of the Hezbollah deal with the important bourgeois families, tribes and clans in different parts of the country and act as patrons dealing with clients and favoring their own networks, as exemplified by the case of Muhammad al-Khansa Hezbollah, Mayor of Ghobeyri. The party, in many aspects, only strengthens the prevalent dynamics of Lebanese society, those of a social system based on primordial or primary identities (family, sect and sectarian political party) rather than social rights (Le Thomas 2012a: 145).

As Achcar (2013b: 35) argues, it is misleading to consider Islam as merely a "flag and mask" or a rhetorical device, as this overlooks the significant limitations to radicalization of these organizations' membership, and even their mass following, due to their adherence to Islamic fundamentalist doctrines. Indeed, the weakness of Orientalist approaches that view religion as the main tool to analyze these parties, and as the driving force of history in the Middle East, is that they leave out the reality of socio-economic and political dynamics. Following Nilsen's call for, "a theory of social movement that is truly relevant to the needs and knowledge of activist that seek to contribute to what Marx referred to as 'the self clarification [...] of the struggles and wishes of the age'" (Nilsen 2013: 183), I have sought to show the nature and development of the Hezbollah in its totality, in the context of the structures and dynamics within and around the Lebanese Islamic party and in the wider society.

It is beyond the scope of this book to outline a full alternative to the Hezbollah's political program or its socio-economic practices. But it can be said that the preceding analysis suggests that a truly counter-hegemonic project requires a rupture with the sectarian system, a full accounting of the class and social differentiation within Lebanon, and a nuanced appreciation of the regional dynamics as they intersect within Lebanon. Important moments in Lebanese history—notably the labor struggles of the Civil War period, and more recent experiences such as the formation of the UCC, the popular mobilizations of 2015 around the "campaign you stink," the municipal elections of 2016 in which the independent and non-sectarian movement around *"Beirut Madinati"* (Arabic for "Beirut is my city") challenged both the March 8 and 14 forces, securing around 40 percent of the votes in Beirut municipal poll—point towards the possibilities and promise that a non-sectarian approach might take root in the country. In contrast, the Hezbollah fails to provide a vision of modernity that can challenge neoliberal capitalism or the Lebanese sectarian political system. In a region witnessing popular uprisings and intense and rapid political changes, the contradiction between the Hezbollah's proclaimed support for the oppressed, on the one hand, and its orientation towards Lebanese neoliberalism and the country's elite class, on the other, will likely prove increasingly problematic for the leadership of the Lebanese Islamic movement.

Appendix

Shiʿa Fraction of the Bourgeoisie

Table 1   Shiʿa fraction in the Industrial Sector and Members of the Association of Lebanese Industrialists (ALI) 2014, April

Company	Owners	Sector	Location	Role
Foam Mattresses Co. Fomaco SARL	Ussama Helbawi	Furniture	Office: Hadath Factory: Baalbek	President of the association of the industrialists of the southern suburbs of Beirut. He is also President of al-Ahed football club, considered as Hezbollah's club and sponsored by Al-Manar. Member of the board of the ALI.
Maximum Pour Le Commerce et L'Industrie	Hassan Yassine	Textile	Ghobeyri	Member of the board of the ALI.
Kassem Mahfouz and Sons Co. "Mahfouz Stores"	Mr. Bassem Mahfouz	Textile	Office: Ghobeyri Factory: Choueifat	Member of the board of the ALI.
Plastic Chemical Company PCC (SARL)	Khalil Cherry	Chemical products	Office: Beirut, Mar Elias Str. Factory: Ghazieh	Secretary General of the board of the ALI.

Table 2 Other Important Shiʿa Industrialists

Company	Owners	Sector	Location	Role
Helbawi Bros. Co. SARL 1982	Mr. Muhammad Helbawi, Mr. Ali Helbawi and Mr. Hussein Helbawi	Seeds and spices trading.	Burj al-Barajneh	
Moussawi Trading Company SARL	Ali al-Moussawi, Hussein al-Moussawi, Bachir al-Moussawi	Steel works, steel gates, Carrosserie.	Baalbek	
Alfa InterFood Group is a Middle Eastern food company owned by the Group Harb Holding Int. SAL Lebanon	Zein Harb	Produce: Canned food products, under the brand name "Chtoura Gardens."	Factory: Bekaa Office: Haret Hreik	Member of the Union of Lebanese Food Industries' Board. Harb Holding, through Zein Harb, is also member of the Chamber of Commerce, Industry, & Agriculture of Beirut.
Linda Chocolate Factory	Ali Kobayssi	Food and chocolate	Address: Nabatieh	Member of the Union of Lebanese Food Industries.
Dar Bilal For Printing and Publishing Co. SARL	Mr. Ahmad Hussein	Paper and cardboard	Bir Hassan, Jnah	Ex-Secretary General of the board of the ALI (2013).

Table 2   continued

Company	Owners	Sector	Location	Role
Syroliban International Co. SAL (Offshore)	Khalil Zantout, Chairman and CEO of Syroliban International Co. SAL (Offshore).	Sole distributor of Brigestone and Firestone tires in Syria.	.	He is an elected board member of the International Chamber of Commerce in Lebanon. Khalil Zantout has been chosen by the ALI as one of the four prominent industrialists who will establish the model of future industrial city. He is in charge of the industrial city in Nabatieh.

Table 3 Shi'a Fraction of the Beirut Trade Association (BTA)

Company	Owners	Sector	Location	Role
Shar Metal Trading Co. SARL.	Fadi Ali Shahrour	Shar Metal Company (SMC) is the largest ferrous and non-ferrous scrap metal exporters and processors throughout the Middle East region.	Factory: Beirut Office: Jnah, Beirut.	Vice-President of the BTA
Beydoun Fire & Security SARL	Youssef Muhammad Beydoun	Beydoun Fire and Security is a leading provider of fire and security services.	Address: Bir Hassan, Ghobeyri	Member of the BTA. Member of the Union of Security and Safety Professional in Lebanon
Sadco Sami Dandan and Co.	Jamal Sami Dandan	Pharmacy. SADCO is a privately owned company. SADCO was established in 1977 by entrepreneurs with experience in the field of pharmaceutical distribution since 1950.	Address: Bir Hassan, Ghobeyri	Member of the BTA.
	Rashid Hassan Kebbe			Member of the BTA and President of the Barbour Street Merchants Association.

Table 4 Shi'a Fraction of the Chamber of Commerce, Industry, & Agriculture of Beirut (CCIAB)

Company	Owners	Role
Business Projects Company (BPC) is a Lebanese holding company, established in 1978 to develop and hold investments in privately held companies around the world.	Mr. Salah Osseiran, chairman and owner, initially managed BPC from Riyadh, Saudi Arabia before the company transferred headquarters to Beirut, Lebanon in 1995.	President of the Economic Committee of the CCIAB and member of the International Chamber of Commerce, Lebanon.
Abdallah Ali Matar & Sons SARL, a company that engages in real estate and property development, as well as scrap metal trading in Lebanon and Africa.	Mahmoud Matar is the Chairman and General Manager of Abdallah Ali Matar and Sons group.	President of Members Committee of the CCIAB.
Harb Holding International SAL is a holding company, which has subsidiaries that manufacture, pack and distribute all types of assorted foodstuff.	Mr. Zeina Harb, CEO	President of Exhibition Committee of the CCIAB.
• Jyl Food SAL (Offshore) • Big Mills of the South—Al Dick.	Ahmad Hoteit, CEO of both companies and on the board of GS1 company as well.	President of Labour and Social Affairs Committee of the CCIAB. On the board of directors of the Union of agrifood traders of Lebanon and member of the Union of Lebanese Food Industries.

- Star Brands (Procter & Gamble Exclusive Agent in Algeria).
- Lumière Group (High-end lighting fixture distributor in Saudi Arabia, Qatar, Kuwait, UAE, Jordan, Lebanon).
- Hilight (Architectural lighting company)

Wissam Ariss, Founder, Chairman of the Board & CEO of Star Brands.
He is also Co-Founder & Vice-Chairman of the Board Lumière Group.
He is Co-Founder of Hilight (Architectural lighting company).
He is the Chairman of the Board Nestlé Algeria, Partner Founder & Chairman of the Board Star Goods.

President of the Financial Committee of the CIIAB.

Table 5 Shiʿa Fraction of the Banking Sector and Members of the Association of Banks in Lebanon (ABL) 2014, April

Jammal Trust Bank	Mr. Anwar Ali Jammal	The Bank was established in 1963 under the name "Investment Bank" with an initial capital of LL 1 million only. In 1966, Litex Bank took over and increased the capital to LL3 million then ended its services on September 30, 1971. At this time, the entire share capital was purchased by a new group of shareholders who elected an entirely new Board of Directors under the Chairmanship of Mr. Ali Abdullah Jammal. The name was changed to Jammal Investment Bank SAL.	Active member of the ABL
Lebanese Swiss Bank	Tanal Sabah	The bank was originally licensed in Lebanon on 1962. In 1973, it was taken over by Credit Suisse, Zurich, which controlled 99.01 percent of shares under the name of Credit Suisse (Moyen-Orient) SAL. Those same shares were acquired in 1988 by a group of prominent businessmen and bankers headed by the current chairman Tanal Sabah to become Lebanese Swiss Bank SAL.	Member and Treasurer of the ABL

Middle East Africa and Bank (MEAB) is owned by the Hejeij family. Hassan and Kassem Hejeij, the owners of the bank, originally left Lebanon and built a large construction business in Africa. They extended their activities to other businesses, before establishing the bank in 1991. They also own hotels, beach resorts and prime properties in Beirut and the South.

Ali Hejeij. The Hejeij Group Holding SAL also exists.

Brothers Hassan and Kassem Hejeij co-founded MEAB as a family-owned commercial bank in Lebanon in 1991. Today, of 73 active banks in Lebanon, MEAB is the 15th largest bank by deposits.

Member of the ABL

Notes

Introduction

1. Kharafi published an article titled "To Live in Dignity or Die with Pride" that praised the Hezbollah a week before his death in April 2011. He was ranked number seventy-seven in the 2011 Forbes Magazine list of the world's richest people, with a wealth estimated at $11.5 billion, and was closely linked to the Kuwaiti royal family and the brother of the Speaker of *Majlis al-Ummah*, the parliament of Kuwait, Jassem al-Kharafi. Following Kharafi's death, the Hezbollah issued a public statement of condolences for the Kuwaiti people and government.

1. Sectarianism and the Lebanese Political Economy: Hezbollah's Origins

1. Following the Ta'if Agreement (see Chapter 2), the Alawite community was recognized on the political level as a sect in Lebanon, and thus Lebanon is now composed of eighteen officially recognized religious communities.
2. In Mount Lebanon, the breakdown between these different denominations was 156,000 Maronite, 40,689 Greek Orthodox and 16,468 Greek Catholic. Other Christian denominations are also present, such as Armenian Orthodox, Syriac Catholic, Armenian Catholic, Syriac Orthodox, Roman Catholic, Chaldean, Assyrian, Copt and Protestant (Picaudou 1989: 57).
3. A small Jewish community also existed at that period and was an officially recognized community by the Lebanese political system.
4. The notables of the coastal cities (Beirut, Saida, Tripoli and Tyr)—mostly Greek Orthodox and Sunni Muslim—feared economic losses because their direct links to the Syrian hinterland had been severed by annexations to the new Greater Lebanon.
5. The Christian population of Zahle, for example, which had a largely Greek Catholic population, voted in favor of remaining to Syria and against the French Mandate. The establishment of two separate countries could threaten Zahle's intermediate role as a freight hub in the trade between Beirut and Damascus from which it benefited immensely. The city was also a regional agricultural center, providing both Beirut and some regions of Syria with a plentiful supply of food (Issawi 1982: 58).
6. The political parties representing this trend were the Constitutionalist Bloc led by Bechara al-Khuri, a Maronite notable, and composed as well of many

Muslim notables, and the Republican Party created by Riyad al-Solh, a Sunni notable, his cousins, and Aziz al-Hashim, a Maronite notable from Aqra in the region of Jbeil (Traboulsi 2007: 99).

7. We can see this evolution in the Congress of the Coast of 1936 of Muslim Unionists, who reiterated the resolution of the previous Coastal Conference of 1933 that had rejected the separation of Greater Lebanon from Syria. A divergence among the participants regarding the unification of Lebanon with Syria appeared. Sunni leaders, such as Kazim al-Solh and Shafiq Lutfi, refused to sign the resolution reached at the conference. Kazim al-Solh actually considered the issue of unity with Syria as being of secondary importance, if an independent Lebanon would fully adopt Arabism as its national identity (Firro 2006: 751). At the same time, some Muslim personalities advocated, since the mid-1920s, participating in the new state of Greater Lebanon. The first Sunni Muslim to show readiness to share in the management of affairs was Muhammad al-Jisr, who since the 1920s was elected President of the Chamber of Deputies (Salibi 1971: 81).

8. Some authors have claimed that he was assisted in this process by the Lebanese security services, with the objective of undermining the *zu'āma* while moderating the expanding Shi'a proletariat in Beirut's suburbs (Johnson 1986: 149). Traboulsi (2007: 23) claims that he was backed by the Shah of Iran.

9. Palestinian refugees did not enjoy the minimal rights that normally go with the "refugee" status. Palestinians were barred from working in the public sector, where work permits depended on the economy's labor needs and personal connections. The Cairo Agreement signed on November 3, 1969 between the Lebanese government and the PLO Chairman Yasser Arafat redefined the regulations governing refugees in Lebanon, granting notably: Palestinians in Lebanon the right to employment, residence, and movement; to form local committees in the camps; to establish posts of the Palestinian Armed Struggle inside the camps; to give the Palestinians in Lebanon the right to engage in the armed struggle (against Israel); to safeguard and protect the *fidā'īn* path to the Arkub region in the South; to cease/end the propaganda between the two sides [the Palestinians and the Lebanese]; and to release prisoners and confiscated arms. The Lebanese Chamber of Deputies terminated the Cairo Agreement on May 21, 1987 unilaterally, restoring the pre-1969 status towards the Palestinians (Siklawi 2010: 610).

In 2010, only 37 percent of Palestinian refugees of working age were employed. Palestinians face large-scale legal and socio-economic obstacles to working in Lebanon. By law, Palestinians refugees are not allowed to practice their professions in over thirty unions and seventy-two unsyndicated professions, including medical doctors, engineers, nurses and taxi drivers (UNHRC 2013: 6).

10. On Saturday December 6, 1975, following the discovery of four mutilated bodies of members of their organization, the Kataeb entered some

neighborhoods of the center of Beirut and killed dozens of Lebanese Muslims in revenge.

11. According to Asad Abukhalil, Amal and Syria needed each other and shared mutual interests:

> when al-Assad was facing growing sectarian tensions in his own country in the early 1970s, and when Syria's Sunni were increasingly emphasising the non-Islamic nature of Alawism, Imam Moussa Sadr provided the Assad regime with crucial religious and political legitimacy by officially recognising the Alawite as Twelver Shi'a. Sadr also stated his opposition to the rising Islamic movement in Syria. It should be recalled that this fatwa was issued at a time when Sadr was looking for a patron to sponsor his embryonic organisation/militia *Harakat al-Mahrumīn* (later known by the acronym of its military arm, Amal). Assad and Sadr needed one another for their own political purposes. The Assad regime returned the favour to Sadr; Amal was supplied and armed by the As-Saiqah in Lebanon. This pro-Syrian Palestinian organisation undertook to train followers of Sadr. By 1975, Amal had become a Lebanese tool of Syrian policy in Lebanon. Sadr consistently supported Syria's policies and fluctuating alliances in Lebanon, even when those policies were highly unpopular among Lebanese Shi'a.
>
> (Abukhalil 1990: 9)

At the beginning of the Lebanese Civil War, Amal became at this point the major pillar in the formation of the Nationalist Front (Al-Jabha al-Qawmiyya) which was established in December 1975 as the Syrian counterpoise to Kamal Jumblatt's LNM. Amal became inextricably linked to the Assad regime which has used Amal whether in fighting against the Lebanese government led by Amine Gemayel during the years of 1983–1984, culminating in the takeover of West Beirut on February 6 1984, or by unleashing Amal against the Palestinian refugee camps during May–June 1985, April–July 1986 and October 1986–February 1987. Amal became at that time Assad's most important proxy and has enabled Syria to achieve a range of policy objectives in Lebanon (Deeb, M. 1988: 697).

12. The Lebanese Phalanges (al-Kataeb al-Lubnāniyya) was formed in 1936 as a Maronite paramilitary youth organization by Pierre Gemayel, who modeled the party after Spanish Falange and Italian Fascist parties.

13. In August 1978, Sadr disappeared without a trace in Libya after a meeting with Mu'amar Qadhafi.

14. The new invasion of the Israeli army of Lebanon, which reached Beirut, at the beginning of June 1982 was intended principally to evict the PLO and impose Bashir Gemayel, head of the Maronite Christian Phalange party, as President of Lebanon in order to get Lebanon to sign a peace treaty with Israel and bring the country into Israel's sphere of influence (Bensaid 1982).

15. The PLO had almost complete control over certain areas of Lebanon using their own police force, military and economic infrastructure.
16. The al-Dawa party was originally established in Iraq in 1958 and became the main Shiʿa Islamic party in the country. It expanded its field of influence in different countries of the region, notably Saudi Arabia, Lebanon, Kuwait and Bahrain. The organization lauds to overthrow the regimes in power in the objective to establish an Islamic state. A number of them will join the Hezbollah after its creation, such as Muhammad Raad, Abbas al-Mussawi and *Sheikh* Subhi Tufayli. The Lebanese Dawa was disbanded, and its erstwhile members were instructed by party strategists to infiltrate the secular Amal and reform it from within. (Norton 2007: 31). The Lebanese Dawa activists also established a network of secret armed cells, dubbed Qassam, that was based mainly in Beirut, and targeted particularly fighters from the Iraqi Baʿth party, especially after war broke out between Iran and Iraq (Blanford 2011: 35). The Hezbollah Minister Dr. Hassan Fadlallah (2015: 80–81) explains in his book that the Lebanese Dawa was able to constitute an elite of *ulema* and youth, an "avant-garde elite," and to spread their influence in neighborhoods and mosques in the Islamic Shiʿa milieu in the country from the beginning of the 1970s.
17. Hawza is the traditional religious Shiʿa school forming *ulema* (Mervin 2008b: 348).
18. The theory of the *Wilāyat al-Faqīh* is that a guardianship of the jurisprudent or jurisconsult should hold ultimate political power. In 1987, Hassan Nasrallah explained that the authority of this leader is both spiritual and political, and may not be challenged (cited in Lamloum 2008a: 29).
19. The Pasdaran has been used by the Islamic Republic's leadership to suppress internal dissent. Khomeini actively employed the Revolutionary Guards to coerce and, when necessary, crush former political allies as he consolidated power. The Islamic Republic's law made the Revolutionary Guards not only a military organization deterring foreign threats but also a political-military organization tasked with fighting domestic opposition (Alfoneh 2008).
20. Syrian support of the Hezbollah did not always prevent disagreements between the two sides. During the "War of the Camps" (1985–1988), for example, Amal, supported by the Syrian regime, clashed violently with Palestinian organizations, which the Hezbollah supported. Military repression by the Syrian regime against the Hezbollah also occurred on February 24, 1987, when the Syrian army assassinated twenty-seven members of the Hezbollah in the Fathallah military barracks in Basta, West Beirut (Lamloum 2008b: 96).
21. In the beginning of the 1990s, the Pasdaran presence was reduced by about two-thirds, and by 1998 the remainder of the Iranian contingent was withdrawn.
22. Following the death of Khomeini in 1989 and the end of the Iran–Iraq War in 1988, the IRI and segments of the conservative faction softened their

position considerably on the two principles of foreign policy ("Neither East nor West" and the "Export of the Revolution"). The regime's foreign policies have since then been more or less independent of the composition of factions that control the republican institutions and religious supervisory bodies (Rakel 2009: 113). These changes will have consequences on the Hezbollah, as Chapter 2 will discuss.

23. Nabih Berri rejected the Iranian-influenced Islamic national model espoused by some members of Amal. In addition, Hussein al-Mussawi, a member of the Amal Command Council, opposed Berri's presence on the National Salvation Committee (Shanahan 2005: 113). Mussawi also opposed the fact that the leadership was no longer led by clerics (Louër 2008: 59).

24. The name came from the nine representatives elected to speak for the convening parties: three stood for the clerical congregation of the Bekaa, three represented the various Islamic committees, and three spoke for the Islamic Amal's movement (Qassem 2008: 33).

25. Hussein was the grandson of Muhammad who refused to pledge allegiance to Yazīd, the Umayyad Caliph.

26. The level of Iranian financial support today is difficult to determine because it is largely channeled through non-governmental routes. Estimates, however, range from between $100 and $400 million a year. Abdallah Safieddinne, the Hezbollah's representative in Iran, has acknowledged that his organization receives funding directly from the Wilāyat al-Faqīh himself. The Iranian Supreme Leader has sole control of the distribution of these funds to the Hezbollah, and this is why it is largely unaffected by changes of governments in Iran (Norton 2007: 110; Saad Ghorayeb 2012). The Hezbollah nonetheless claims that donations and taxes of rich Shi'a businesspeople and other generous sponsors in the diaspora provide the bulk of financing to the party (Harb 2010: 94). This is quite unlikely: in the beginning of 2015, the Hezbollah had to impose salary cuts on personnel, defer payments to suppliers and reduce monthly stipends to its political allies in Lebanon after increased economic problems in the IRI due to lower oil revenues and international sanctions (Blanford 2015). In addition to this, Hassan Nasrallah declared in a speech in June 2016 that: "Hezbollah's budget, its income, its expenses, everything it eats and drinks, its weapons and rockets, come from the Islamic Republic of Iran," while adding that US sanctions will not impact his group whatsoever (Al-Ahed News 2016d).

2. Hezbollah and the Political Economy of Lebanese Neoliberalism

1. The Ta'if Agreement of October 22, 1989, the fruit of a Saudi, US and Syrian agreement imposed on Lebanese deputies, confirmed Syria's dominant position in Lebanon (Salloukh 2005).

2. Under the Ta'if Agreement, the presidential office now performs a ceremonial and consultative role, with the real power lying in the hands of the Prime Minister (Stewart 1996: 494).

3. These protests were particularly concerned with deteriorating living conditions caused by the rapid rise of the US dollar against the Lebanese Pound.

4. This orientation was partly predicated on a belief that a regional peace agreement would be reached by 1996.

5. Dr. Hassan Fadlallah, a Hezbollah MP, wrote in his book, *Hizb Allāh wa al-Dawla fī Lubnān—al-ru'iyya wa al-massār* (2015: 119), that Ghazi Kanaan was the de facto ruler of Lebanon in the 1990s.

6. In 2008, a decree was passed increasing wages by L£200,000 ($133) for the private sector, but it only benefited the private sector and not the employees of the public sector as the state Shura Council overturned the decree in 2011, citing its illegality (Zaraket 2014).

7. The NSSF provides employees with insurance coverage for sickness and maternity care and it also covers family allowances, end of service pensions and work-related accidents and diseases (Nasnas 2007: 90).

8. On November 11, 2006, two Hezbollah ministers, in addition to three others (two from Amal's movement and one independent) resigned from Siniora's government, protesting what the Hezbollah described as a lack of "power sharing." The Hezbollah was demanding a national unity government in which it would hold with its allies at least one-third—plus one—of the total cabinet seats, which would enable it to veto any important decisions, such as vetoing the upcoming budget on the international tribunal on the assassination of former Lebanese Prime Minister Rafiq Hariri, which it opposed.

9. These workers come mostly from Syria, Egypt, South East Asia and more recently from the Horn of Africa. Syrians work mostly in construction and agriculture, while those from South East Asia are predominant in domestic work (Catusse and Abi Yaghi 2011: 77).

10. The close collaboration between the Lebanese army and the Hezbollah was witnessed again in June 2013 in the military seizure of the mosque and the security compound of the Salafist cleric *Sheikh* Ahmad al-Assir in Saida, following the attack by its followers of a Lebanese army checkpoint, killing sixteen soldiers and wounding thirty-five. Reports emerged of Hezbollah's role alongside the army in the fight against al-Assir's loyalists. On June 24, 2013, Al-Manar TV showed live footage of uniformed soldiers arresting Assir fighters and chanting "Ya Zaynab," a Shi'a religious cry. Future Television, owned by Hariri, showed video footage of fighters in the battle area wearing yellow armbands, presumably identifying themselves as Hezbollah. Again in mid-September 2014, Shi'a residents of the northern Bekaa Valley stated that the Hezbollah assisted the Lebanese army in firing mortar rounds and artillery rockets at the jihadists in the mountains outside Ersal (Blanford 2014b).

11. The General Security Director is also the one who decides on the censorship of movies and on numerous occasions Iranian movies critical of the IRI were banned in Lebanon.

12. The Lebanese Army Intelligence is identified as cooperating with the Hezbollah and the Amal Movement, while the Information Branch, the intelligence arm of the Internal Security Forces (ISF), is seen as being connected with the Future Movement and the March 14 alliance.

13. Gebran Bassil, FPM member and Energy Minister at the time, said, regarding the arrival of Palestinian and Syrian refugees, that: "When we refuse to allow Syrian and Palestinian refugees to replace us, we must devote our refusal by actions and not only by words [...] Lebanon should [not] be the garbage dump for the world's problems" (Ghaddar 2013).

14. Takfirism is a movement that claims that the Muslim *ummah* (the community of believers) has been weakened by deviation in the practice of Islam. Takfirism categorized all non-practicing Muslims as *kafir*s (infidels) and calls upon its adherents to abandon existing Muslim societies, settle in isolated communities and fight all Muslim infidels. *Takfir* is the pronouncement that someone is an unbeliever (*kafir*) and no longer Muslim. This is why individuals or groups that accuse another Muslim or groups of apostasy are referred to as "*takfiri*."

15. "Ziad Abs, and two other key members of the FPM Naim Aoun and Antoine Nasrallah, were expelled from the FPM in July 30, 2016 under the accusation of 'raising the FPM's crises in the media' and 'rebelling against the movement's decisions.'" (Ya Libnan 2016).

16. In February 2016, the Drug Enforcement Administration in the USA, for example, claimed to have busted a money laundering, drug-dealing scheme that linked the Hezbollah to major drug trafficking operations in Latin America (Beauchamp 2016).

17. Before this, Mustapha Siba'i, general secretary of the Syrian Muslim Brotherhoods from 1945 to 1961, had tried to promote a "Socialism of Islam," which led necessarily to the solidarity of various social categories and not to the war between classes as communism. (1959 cited in Carré and Gérard 1983: 87). His book, *Ishtarikiyya al-Islām* (*Socialism of Islam*) published in 1959, symbolized his efforts to articulate this perspective, in which for example he notably put forward the idea that social equality and elimination of poverty, hunger and sickness could be achieved by appealing to the moral obligations of individualism and not to governmental systems or measures such as nationalization, expropriation of capital, limitations on ownership and progressive taxation. Socialism of Islam was put forward by Siba'i as a third way between the materialist systems of capitalism and communism (Teitelbaum 2011: 224). Syrian Muslim Brotherhood members interviewed by the researcher Raphaël Lefèvre, however, described the so-called "radicalism" of Mustapha Siba'i's vision for an Islamic socialism as purely rhetoric (Lefèvre 2013: 53). The Syrian Muslim Brotherhood sought

to undermine the rising influence of Ba'thists and Communists among the Syrian society, with which they were competing, by associating itself with dominant ideological currents such as socialism. A closer look at the program of the Syrian Muslim Brotherhood reveals how little it resembled "socialism," but instead a form of populism that reflected the economic interests of the urban middle and lower-middle classes (Teitelbaum 2011: 220).

18. Abrahamian notes that Khomeini remained constant in his defense of private property throughout his entire political life (Abrahamian 1993: 51).

19. Charbel Nahas is a political personality who was a former Minister of Tele-communication between 2009 and 2011, and then Labor Minister between 2011 and February 2012 in Najib Miqati's second government. He was representing in government the bloc Change and Reform, which is headed by General Michel Aoun. He submitted his resignation to Michel Aoun on February 21, 2012, and officially resigned on February 22, 2012, arguing that all of his colleagues in government were preventing any effective improvement in workers' rights.

20. Ghobeyri has been controlled by the Hezbollah since the end of the Civil War.

21. In the case of the Beirut Mall, al-Khansa was able to choose a percentage of the employees to recruit in order to favor people from Dahyeh, and most probably with links to himself (Deeb and Harb 2013: 71).

22. The bill envisages an increase of about 20 percent of the difference between the old and the current rent during the first year following the implementa-tion of the law. At the end of the initial six years period, the tenant must sign a lease contract with a duration of three years' minimum.

23. Three-quarters of the apartments affected by the new law are in Beirut and Mount Lebanon (Abdallah 2012).

24. The bill did establish a temporary fund to help the poor pay their increased rent, but skeptics fear it is not a long-term solution and will eventually lead to the eviction of thousands of families (Abizeid 2014).

25. The new liberalization law for house rents officially came into force on December 28 2014, but two articles of the new law were invalidated by the Constitutional Council. The law and its implementation are still being discussed in the Administration and Justice Parliamentary Committee.

26. An agreement was reached in the summer 2013 to postpone cannabis field destruction for the time being, because of the clashes between farmers and the security forces (Nazzal 2013).

27. The Federation of Agriculture includes farmers from all regions of the country (the Bekaa, the South, the North and Mount Lebanon) and from all sects. It includes fourteen trade unions, two federations and fifty-eight cooperatives.

28. Noah Zaiter once said "make marijuana and hashish legal for six months and I'll pay down all government debt"—around $36 billion.

3. Lebanese Class Structure under Neoliberalism

1. Parts of this chapter have also appeared in a different form in Joseph Daher, "Reassessing Hizbullah's Socioeconomic Policies in Lebanon," *The Middle East Journal*, Vol. 70, No. 3 (Summer 2016), pp. 399–418.

2. Najib Miqati is the co-founder of the M1 Group, a family-owned holding company registered on the London and Dubai stock exchanges. M1 has interests in various sectors such as telecom, real estate, aircraft financing, fashion and energy. It also operates the British Bank of Lebanon through a license it purchased from the British Bank of the Middle East (Najib Miqati Official Website 2013). The Hariri family is the owner of the Saudi Oger group, one of the largest construction companies in Saudi Arabia, which has financial interests in areas such as banking, telecommunication and real estate. The Hariri family is also a primary shareholder in the company Solidere, awarded control over the reconstruction of downtown Beirut as a center of high-end shopping and leisure activities (Saudi Oger Website 2013).

3. The twelve Alpha Banks are Audi, BLOM, Byblos, Fransabank, Société Générale, Credit Libanaise, BankMed, Beirut, BBAC, Libano-Francaise, First National and Intercontinental. Fifty percent of the Lebanese banking sector's assets are owned by just three of these twelve: Audi, BLOM and Byblos (Traboulsi 2014: 30).

4. Imports are highly monopolized—according to one estimate, just 4 percent of active importing companies are responsible for 90 percent of all imports. The import sector is still largely dominated by Christian-owned conglomerates, which explains the sectarian nature of the debate around a proposal by Rafiq Hariri in 2001 to open up the import market, including abolishing exclusive agencies. The law has still to be implemented due to resistance from Christian-owned conglomerates (Traboulsi 2014: 33).

5. Historically there have existed differences and disagreements between some of these groups, particularly between the BTA and the ALI. These differences have been largely centered on the relative weight of trade and industry, with some business actors arguing for a more open economy, while others have sought better protection for Lebanese industry. Over time, however, these dividing lines have become increasingly blurred as the interpenetration of different sectors has increased. For a discussion of this issue, see Gates 1989.

6. Gulf investors hold 18.6 percent of Audi Bank. These investors include the al-Homaizi family from Kuwait: 6.1 percent, and al-Sabbah Family from Kuwait: 4.8 percent, *Sheikh* Dhiab Bin Zayed al-Nehayan from UAE: 5.10 percent, Abdullah Ibrahim al-Hobayb from the Kingdom of Saudi Arabia: 2.6 percent (Bank Audi 2014).

7. The Saudi-Lebanese Ghassan Shaker, son of one of the bank's founders, owns 5.39 percent of BLOM's shares through Shaker Holding and his wife. Nada Oweini (daughter of former Prime Minister and BLOM founder

Hussein Oweini) owns 5 percent (Traboulsi 2014: 87). Hussein Oweini was the first Saudi-Lebanese to become Prime Minister of Lebanon in 1951 and between 1964 and 1965, and was also a business agent for the Saudi royals between 1923 and 1947. Oweini continued playing this role even while he served as Prime Minister (Mehio 2002).

8. Credit Libanais' ownership is split between EFG Hermes Holding, an Egyptian company whose largest shareholder is from the UAE, and CIH Bahrain Holding owned by Saudi investor, Khaled ibn Mahfouz (Credit Libanais 2014).

9. Much of this investment was facilitated by the Hariri Government's "Foreign Acquisition of Property Law (Law No. 296, 2001)," which abolished discrimination on property ownership by Arab and foreign nationals, and lowered real estate registration fees from 6 percent for Lebanese and 16 percent for foreigners to 5 percent for both categories of investors. In addition, capital gains made by individuals on real estate are exempt from any kind of taxation (IDAL Report 2013: 20).

10. These ongoing connections have been shown by a surprise visit of a delegation of thirteen representatives in March 2013 from Lebanon's main business associations to the number three person in the Saudi royal family, Prince Muqrin Bin Abdul-Aziz, following a threat by Saudi Arabia to pull out billions from Lebanese banks due to statements by the Lebanese Foreign Minister regarding the conflict in Syria (Al-Akhbar English 2013c).

11. The effects of both wars had important consequences on revenue in the region: businesses registered a 91.5 percent decrease in income due to closures or damages to shops. Akkar was also excluded from most national and international emergency funds donated to rebuild and rehabilitate war-stricken areas (Moushref 2008; Carpi 2014).

12. In this context, Sunni-populated regions in the North have witnessed the development of Islamic political movements and Salafi groups, which provide many health and social services, as well as a political presence. In Tripoli, Salafist factions rely on a network of mosques, NGOs and schools, and receive financing from various Gulf monarchies, such as Saudi Arabia, Qatar and Kuwait (Alami 2008). Salafist groups developed considerably in Tripoli in the aftermath of the withdrawal of the Syrian army in 2005. Many Salafists schools and organizations who were closed or had to stop their activities reopened in this period, including the Institute of Guidance and Charity of the Salafist *Sheikh* Shahal, the son of the founder of the Salafist movement in Lebanon (Elali 2012).

13. At the time of independence, the ratio in the Board of Directors was actually five Christians to one Muslim.

14. He also was elected to the municipality of Beirut in 2010 on the list Unity of Beirut supported by March 14 and Amal (Now Media 2010).

15. The Hezbollah's expansion in these areas is partially linked to a growth in religious tourism that caters to both Lebanese and non-Lebanese Arabs and

Muslims, including student groups, academics, political delegations and casual vacationers, who incorporate visits to sites into their trips to Beirut and the Lebanese coast. The description of tourism has evolved among the Hezbollah officials from "jihadi tourism" to "conservative tourism" (*siyyāha muhāfidha*) and to the most recent "purposeful tourism" (*siyyāha hādifa*), all of which contain both ideological and market driven imperatives (Deeb and Harb 2011: 40).

16. Ali Tajjedine and two of his brothers have been accused by the United States Department of the Treasury Office of Foreign Assets Control (OFAC) of providing support to the Hezbollah.

17. Tajco is involved in the building of residential complex, malls, resorts (Al-Nasim Resort), education institutions, Artesian wells, and so on; the majority of these projects are based in Dahyeh and South Lebanon, or in areas with an expanding Shi'a population, such as Choueifat (Tajco Construction and Development 2013).

18. In the pictures of the celebration we can see clearly that Hezbollah Deputies and Ministers are put forward.

19. These include the Psychiatric Hospital, in Khalde, the Beirut Cardiac institute and Ragheb Harb Hospital in South Lebanon close to Nabatieh (client Shahid Association), the Bathoul Hospital and Sohmor Hospital in the Bekaa (client Islamic Health Society) and numerous buildings for al-Mahdi schools.

20. For example, at the opening of the Ceremony Hall of the Martyr Sayyid Muhammad Baqir al-Sadr, the head of the Hezbollah executive council, Hisham Safieddinne, honored and thanked Inmaa, Meamar Engineering and Development company, and Arch Consulting (Al-Mahdi 2012).

21. For example, the municipalities under the control of the Hezbollah or its allies have increasingly used these companies for construction activities. The Wa'd Reconstruction Project, discussed in Chapter 4, also relied heavily on these companies.

22. In addition, regarding the large amount of Hezbollah's employees (see Chapter 5), Gilbert Achcar argues that "even if some of them are of proletarian background, the fact of becoming salaried cadres of such an organisation means a social upgrade, constituting a petty-bourgeois mentality" (cited in Macdonald 2012: 31).

23. The reasons for the superiority of Amal over the Hezbollah in the unions of lawyers is linked to the historic domination and control of Amal over the Faculty of Law—first branch—in Beirut (Mortada 2010).

24. The five deputies with PhDs were Ali Mekdad, Hassan Fadlallah, Nawaf Mussawi, Ali Fayyad and Hussein Hajj Hassan. In terms of business interests, Nawwar Sahili is a board member of the Syrian Lebanese Commercial Bank, Muhammad Raad and Muhammad Fneich are shareholders in the Lebanese Media Group, and Hajj Hassan runs two private schools in Beirut.

25. Ammar has been elected every year since 1992, with the exception of 1996. His uncle, Mahmoud Ammar was also a former Deputy from 1957 to 1992 and close to former Lebanese President Camille Chamoun (Karim 1998: 211).

26. The levels of lower and upper poverty lines were in 2005 respectively of 1.05 percent and 11.37 percent in Nabatieh (more than 95 percent of Shiʿa) and of 0.9 percent and 2.93 percent in Keserwan/Jbeil (composed of 20 percent of Shiʿa) (UNDP 2008b).

27. Charara has been accused of facilitating commercial investments on behalf of the Hezbollah, and of having worked on oil ventures in Iraq with the Hezbollah member Adham Tabaja and the Hezbollah financial supporter Kassem Hejeij, both of whom were previously designated by Treasury. Spectrum Investment Group Holding SAL is a Lebanon-based telecommunications company that provides integrated telecommunications services in the Middle East, Africa and Europe.

28. Both have been accused of being members of the Hezbollah and of transferring funds to the party from Nigeria. In May 2013, they were arrested by the Nigerian's authorities for being in possession of heavy weapons, and other terrorism related activities, but were later released.

29. Wonderland is Abuja (Nigeria)'s biggest and most popular amusement park, while Amigo is one of the largest supermarkets in the Nigerian capital.

30. He was sanctioned for procuring weapons for the Hezbollah and shipping them to Syria.

31. Stars Group Holding network has been accused of covertly purchasing sophisticated electronics and other technology from suppliers across the world for the Hezbollah. Items obtained by the Hezbollah using the Stars Group Holding network have directly supported the group's military capabilities, including the development of unmanned aerial vehicles (UAVs), which have been used most recently to support the Hezbollah's military activities in Syria and to conduct surveillance operations in Israel.

32. The USA increased sanctions in December 2015, by implementing the Hezbollah International Financing Prevention Act of 2015. Under the law, foreign institutions that process transactions for the Hezbollah or entities linked to the group risk being barred from accessing the US financial system. In May 2016, Lebanese banks closed banking accounts of around a dozen individuals with links to the Hezbollah, including the accounts of two Hezbollah MPs.

4. Hezbollah and Shiʿa Civil Society

1. One prominent cadre of the party was, for example, successively director of the party's construction wing, Jihad al-Bina, the party's research unit and its television station. The head of the organization's Shahid association was previously director of Jihad al-Bina. The current mayor of the Ghobeyri

municipality, Muhammad al-Khansa, was at the head of Hezbollah social services. Dr. Hassan Fadlallah, currently an MP, has been occupying various functions in the media wing of the party, working successively in the weekly newspaper of the party *Al-'Ahed*, then the radio station Al-Nour and finally in the television channel Al-Manar.

2. Leaders of both of these organizations were interviewed for this book.

3. Fawwaz Traboulsi (2014: 80) estimated the numbers of employees and full-timers (working for the party) of the Hezbollah at around more than 35,000 working in the various institutions of the party, with Jihad al-Bina accounting for around 10,000 workers.

4. In a study report of *Reuters* on Hezbollah of Samia Nakhoul (2013), Hezbollah is said to pay salaries to 60,000–80,000 people working for charities, schools, clinics and other institutions in addition to its military and security apparatus.

5. Al-Qard al-Hassan has been accused by the US Department of the Treasury of being a cover to manage the Hezbollah's financial activity. The institution is managed by Husayn al-Shami, a senior Hezbollah leader who has served as a member of the Hezbollah's Shura Council and as the head of several Hezbollah-controlled organizations (US Department of the Treasury 2007).

6. The association La Famille was established in 2004 by a few people who presented the idea to one of the officials in the Hezbollah, who in turn gave positive feedback (Now Media 2008b).

7. Information retrieved on Imad Wehbe's personal Facebook account (accessed August 20, 2014).

8. La Famille (2014) states that the purpose of the card is "to ease the economic and social burdens on the life of people, especially the people from the reality of the social situation and living conditions that plague the Lebanese citizen."

9. Fawaz also points out that the residents were not consulted in the composition of the Wa'd board or the architects involved in the construction of their houses.

10. The Hezbollah (in alliance with Amal) was criticized for its clientelist and patronage policies in this regard. Indeed, Riyad al-Assad, an important political figure in the South, declared that the Hezbollah systematically refused reconstruction contracts for his company because of a veto from Nabih Berri (cited in ICG 2007: 7).

11. The *Sheikh* Atif al-Nabulsi, was the one to issue a *fatwa* during the 2005 crisis in the Lebanese government following the suspension of participation of Shi'a ministers to the Siniora Cabinet, forbidding the approval of the nomination of new Shi'a ministers not issued from Amal and the Hezbollah (cited in Daher 2014: 282).

12. Social and entertainment programs, sports programs, programs for children and youth, cultural and religious programs, Lebanese and foreign programs and lastly heads of directors.

13. The series was severely criticized by other forces in Lebanon—including the LCP, the SSNP and Amal Movement—because of its distorted view of the Hezbollah's role. Feminists also attacked the show because of its downplaying of the role of non-military resistance, particularly the direct and indirect support furnished to fighters by women over past decades (Deeb and Harb 2011: 26).

14. Lara Deeb and Mona Harb explain Hezbollah's understanding of culture the following way: "Culture here is a holistic that includes ideas about politics, morality, nature, heritage, space, architecture, design, civic order, education, and taste" (Deeb and Harb 2013: 67–70).

15. Muhammad al-Khansa, the Hezbollah Mayor of Dahyeh, declared on several occasions that "the greatest Jihad is to reach to the people in the framework of social work" (Al-Khansa 2012; Harb 2002: 152).

16. Hamas has also worked to enforce an "Islamic milieu" in the Palestinian Occupied Territories, particularly in the Gaza Strip.

17. Despite this fact, at a political level, the Hezbollah continues to maintain and nurture relations with parties who have different religious bases and identities, for example Hamas, a Palestinian Sunni political movement and an offshoot of the Muslim Brotherhood, or the Free Patriotic Movement (FPM), headed by General Michel Aoun, based in the Christian population, and the Hezbollah's closest ally in Lebanon. In the past few years, and especially following the document of understanding, a political agreement between the Hezbollah and the FPM signed in February 2006, the Hezbollah has made numerous openings to Christians in Lebanon. I witnessed Hezbollah members installing banners celebrating Easter celebrations for Christians in Dahyeh, sending numerous delegations to meet the various Christian religious authorities, and broadcasts on Al-Manar of Christian religious celebrations and church services, including Christmas 2013 where it extensively reported from various churches in Lebanon.

18. Differences continued to arise between the cleric and the Hezbollah and *Wilāyat al-Faqīh*'s followers on political and doctrinal subjects throughout the 1990s and the beginning of the 2000s. In 2003, he launched a strong verbal attack against the IRI, blaming it for arrogantly seeking to monopolize Shi'a religious teaching in Qom (ICG 2003: 13–14). He was not welcome anymore in Hezbollah or Iranian circles. The rivalry was financial as well as social. Fadlallah, as a *"marj'iyya",* received voluntary donations (*"Khoms"*) from his followers and channeled these resources into the social activities of his association *"al-Mabarrāt."* These helped bolster his popular support by running various schools and educational institutions, a radio station (*al-Basha'ir*), mosques, cultural centers, cooperatives, hospitals and subsidy programs for students and orphans. By 2002, Fadlallah's activities were said to be worth $12.6 million (ICG 2003: 13–14). The 2006 Lebanese War witnessed a rapprochement between *Sheikh* Fadlallah and the Hezbollah because of the necessity of unifying against foreign aggression (Mervin

2008b: 283). In 2014, "*al-Mabarrāt*" included twenty schools with 22,000 students (The Daily Star 2014c).

19. Asʿad accused the Hezbollah of feeling "that its military, ideological and political links with Iran are more important than its commitment to Lebanon" (Bathish 2007).

20. See "Imam's speech on the sensitive role played by mothers in the upbringing of their children and consequently in the rectification or degeneration of society" (Khomeini 2001: 81).

21. These social services are provided by the al-Imdad, al-Shahid and al-Jarha Institutions. These three institutions provide welfare services for impoverished families, as well as help to the families of martyrs and the injured.

22. Referring to Imam Hussein, the head of the family and the leader of the Battle (Boumet Beirut 2013).

23. Referring to Sitt Zaynab, Imam Hussein's sister who played a prominent role in managing care-giving tasks, keeping the family together, and ensuring the dissemination of Hussein's message after his martyrdom (Boumet Beirut 2013).

24. Harb (2010: 175) notes that women do not always conform to these codes— some "*multazimāt*," especially younger women, are increasingly favoring dresses with brighter colors.

25. Mona Harb (2010: 191) has listed these as material interests (employment or access to collective service), intellectual interests (the resistance cause and the *Wilāyat al-Faqīh* principle), moral interests (based upon *hāla islāmiyya* and *iltizām*), ludic interests (having access to regular "entertainment" linked to the volunteering and associative sector), and affective interests (to feel fulfilled and satisfied).

26. Here I would disagree with Rula Abisaab, who argues that the Hezbollah promotes a version of "revolutionary Islam" (Abisaab 2006: 255).

5. Hezbollah and the Lebanese Labor Movement

1. These included hunger strikes, marches of Muslim and Christian women, sit-ins in front the parliament, labor strikes against the kidnapping of workers, cultural exhibitions, marches of the handicapped for peace and human rights from Halba to Tyr, and a strike of the CGTL for five days which culminated with demonstrations (Sleibe 1999: 143–44).

2. Adib Bou Habib: "People opposed increasingly the destruction of the society by the militias" (Bou Habib 2012).

3. At the time, the Syrian army—in alliance with some Lebanese politicians— held control of the country's political system.

4. In 1993, the left-backed candidate Elias Abou Rizk, who won the CGTL elections against Antoine Bechara, who had allied with the authorities and the Ministry of Labor (Baroudi 1998). Castro Abdallah (2012), LCP member

and President of the FENASOL, explains that it was Antoine Bechara's move towards an alliance with the state that pushed the left to vote for Elias Abou Rizk.

5. Maroun Khawli, who was executive member of the CGTL at the time in 2002, said, for example, that the Ghassan Ghosn and other members of the leadership acted unilaterally on many issues and "provided cover for solutions suggested by Speaker Nabih Berri for some workers' problems" (Abdul-Hussain 2002b), or that it "was receiving instructions from the nation's politicians" (Abdul-Hussain 2003b).

6. These March 8-aligned members are Ghassan Ghosn (originally SSNP, but today close to Nabih Berri), Hassan Faqih (Amal), Saad al-Din Hamidi Saqr (Al-Jama' al-Islāmiyya), Ali Yassin (Hezbollah), Boutros Saade, (SSNP), Ali Mussawi (Amal), Ahmad Zbidi (Hezbollah), Fawzi Sayyid (Ba'th), Bechara Chai (Independent close to Amal) and Joseph Richa (FPM) (Anon 2012b).

7. These federations include the Federation of Unions of Banks' Employees, the Federation of Print and Media Employees, the National Federation of Chemical Workers, the Federation of Construction Workers and Scaffolders, and the Federation of Independent Trade Unions.

8. 1) Trade Union of workers' hospitals in the Bekaa (187 members registered); 2) Trade Union of workers' vegetable markets in the Bekaa Valley (32 members registered) 3) Trade Union of workers' construction sector and its derivatives in Baalbek (45 members registered); 4) Trade Union of workers and fish farmers in the Bekaa Valley (54 members registered); 5) Trade Union of workers' cooperatives in the Bekaa (92 members registered) (Bedran and Zbeeb 2000: 222–24).

9. Trade Union of workers' cooperatives in Beirut and Mount Lebanon, Trade Union of technicians and professional workers in the domain of electricity in Beirut; Trade Union of workers in the cultivation of vegetables in the South, Trade Union of printing press workers in the South, Trade Union of workers' hospitals in the Bekaa; Trade Union of workers' vegetable markets in the Bekaa Valley, Trade Union of Workers' construction sector and its derivatives in the Bekaa; Trade Union of workers and fish farmers in the Bekaa Valley (Ittihād al-Wafā' 2014a).

10. The Federation of Trade Union of Workers in the Cooperatives, Institutions and Vegetable Markets headed by Omar Subhi Abdallah; and the Federation of Trade Unions of Farmers in Lebanon (known as Inma') headed by Jihad Abbas al-Baluq (for further discussion of the sectarian role of this union, see Chapter 3). In both these federations, all members of the executive council are Shi'a.

11. Federation of Worker and Health Trade Union in the Bekaa, headed by Berbir Othman Hassan.

12. The Loyalty Federation of Transport in Lebanon headed by Abdallah Hamadeh.

13. During Trad Hamadeh's period as Minister of Labor, he granted licenses to a total of twenty-two new trade unions (Khaddaj 2010a).

14. In a 2009 statement, the Unit argued that: "each privatisation should be analysed and studied according to the national interests of the country, whether they are positive or negative, to resolve any controversy around this subject" (*Wahdat al-niqābāt wa al-'ummāl al-markaziyya fī Hizb Allāh* 2009).

15. The main point of contention was the Special Tribunal for Lebanon (STL), which was deemed as unconstitutional and illegal for the Hezbollah and its allies in March.

16. An earlier strike in January 2008 had been called along the same demands. These protests escalated into deadly battles in Beirut's southern suburbs, with roads cut off and taxis refusing to take passengers.

17. A few weeks after the cessation of the hostilities and the formation of a new national unity government, the minimum wage was raised from L£300,000 ($200) to L£500,000 ($333), which was still far from the demands of the workers and as was said previously, it only benefited the private sector and not the employees of the public sector (Zaraket 2014).

18. This demonstration was also not backed by the CGTL, which called for a different mobilization on December 27 that was eventually cancelled. The representative of the Hezbollah in the CGTL, Ali Yassin, stated that the party decided not to support or mobilize for the December 15, action due to its opposition of the CGTL executive. (Interview Ali Taher Yassin, March 2012, Beirut).

19. Personal observations, December 15, 2011.

20. There is no official date for the establishment of the UCC as it is not an official institution, legally speaking. The UCC came to existence after the end of the Lebanese Civil War through the struggles of its two main organizations: Public Primary Schools Teachers League in Lebanon and the Public Secondary Schools Teachers League in Lebanon throughout the 1990s. It was nevertheless the struggle around the salary scale and the increase in wages that made the UCC the main workers' organization in the country at the end of 2011 and the beginning of 2012.

21. Established in 1938.

22. Established in 1980.

23. Article 15 of the labor law forbids any state employee from: "stating or publishing, without the written approval of the head of the directorate, any speech, public statement, or authored work in any subject, or to join professional organisations or unions, or go on strike or instigate others to strike" (Zbeeb 2012b). Moreover, the Lebanese state has always refused to ratify the ILO Convention Number 87 on the trade union liberties, and forbids de facto all members of the public administration to join or create a union. Only the federation of teachers in the private sector is recognized as a federation in the UCC.

24. During the year 2012, the UCC held fourteen strikes, sixty sit-ins, four demonstrations, boycotted exams for two consecutive years and organized two trade union conferences in Beirut (LORWE 2013b: 8).

25. Three private companies were offered a contract to manage the distribution of the electric power (system upgrades, notes indexes and collection of bills).

26. Starting from 1974 and lasting till today, the integration of new staff and the renewal of the retired civil servants was mostly assured through the hiring of precarious workers employed and paid on a daily basis. Since the public administration could not (directly) hire labor force, the employment of daily workers was delegated to subcontractor private companies. Thus, an important percentage of the labor force employed in the public administration and in the national utilities was progressively "externalized" and handed over to subcontractor companies (Civil Society Knowledge Center, Lebanon Support).

27. See Chapter 3.

28. According to Minister Gebran Bassil, 80 percent of the workers belong to non-Christian sects, the majority being Shiʿa, and most of them support Berri (Naharnet 2012). A large section of Christian members of parliament opposed the law because they feared that hiring the part-time workers, most of whom are Shiʿa, would throw off the composition of EDL's so-called sectarian balance (Abizeid 2014).

29. The National Federation of Trade Union of Workers and Employees in Lebanon (FENASOL), through its President Castro Abdallah, was the only trade union to support the strike. I visited the EDL workers' occupation and witnessed Castro Abdallah's presence. In August 2014, daily contract workers and collectors were again launching an open strike in protest against the decision of the EDL board of directors to limit the number of employees provided with full-time jobs to 897 out of the 2,000 workers (The Daily Star 2014b).

30. The demand of the UCC needs to be set in the context of a 120 percent increase in inflation from 1993 to 2012, while public sector wages increased only 55 percent (Wehbe, M. 2013a). It should also be noted that in 2012, the private sector received a salary increase and that parliament also approved legislation doubling the incomes of judges and university professors (Rifai 2014).

31. Lebanon's banks and other powerful business interests represented by the Economic Committees (ECs), were opposing this claim, stating that it would bankrupt Lebanon's economy, drain the cash-strapped treasury, increase inflation and reduce citizens' purchasing power. On April 11, 2014, bankers held a one-day strike against the proposed measure (Abizeid 2014).

32. Hanna Gharib had first tried to form a coalition list, half of which were independent candidates and the other half of candidates with partisan

affiliations with March 8 and 14 forces, but the latter group refused. He was criticized by activists for these maneuvers.

33. One estimate put the number of lapsed Hezbollah members in the UCC at 1,600 out of a total of 2,200 members (Zoghbi 2013).

34. The website of the CGTL indicated the number of forty-eight federations in 2016, as a result of the departure of a few federations of the CGTL to protest against its policies.

35. It should also be noted that the trade union movement as a whole has been largely unsuccessful in attempts to organize women workers, who suffer the most from unemployment, low-paid work and a bias towards the informal economy. Women represent half of the population in the country, but only 21 percent are economically active, (compared to a 73 percent rate for men). There are no women members in the executive committee of 184 trade unions, although the participation of women in unions has increased slightly, thanks partially to the establishment of the Unions Training Centre in 2001, which offers educational programs and supports women's participation in various activities (ILO 2008, Country Brief Advancing women's employment in Lebanon).

6. Hezbollah Military Apparatus

1. For example, in an interview with the Lebanese Newspaper *al-Akhbar*, Hassan Nasrallah declared that the decision to capture the Israeli soldiers had been taken in the Hezbollah's Shura Council months before the operation in July 2006 (Al-Amin, Ileik, Qanso and Zarakat 2014).

2. Al-Sayyid, was the director-general of Lebanon's General Security between 1998 and 2005. He was then imprisoned on suspicion of involvement in the 2005 assassination of the former Prime Minister Rafiq Hariri and then later released due to lack of evidence.

3. For example, the Abdullah Azzam Brigades, a Jihadist group linked to al-Qaida, claimed responsibility for the attack against the Iranian Cultural Center in February 2014 in a posting on Twitter and said it would "continue to target Iran and its party in Lebanon" until the Hezbollah forces are pulled out of Syria (Abu Nasr and Shahine 2014).

4. The head of army intelligence in South Lebanon, General Ali Shahrour, organized a meeting with security officials in Hezbollah and Amal in the region to coordinate security measures for the Ashura's commemoration in November 2013 (Khalil 2013a).

5. Dahyeh was nearly completely closed from November 1–4, 2014 according to local residents, while in the cities of Hermel and Baalbek municipalities, controlled by Hezbollah, published statements asking their "Syrian brothers to stay in their homes and to not go out from Monday 3rd of November until the evening of the day after (Orient le Jour 2014e).

6. The Naksa Day ("day of the setback") is the annual day of commemoration of the defeat of Arab armies in the 1967 Six-Day War, resulting in the occupation of East Jerusalem, West Bank, Gaza Strip, the Syrian Golan Heights and the Egyptian Sinai.
7. The ESA is also known as the Islamic Jihad Organization (IJO) (Levitt 2013).
8. The only exception was the operation led by two members of the Palestinian Islamic Jihad organization in March 2002, and assisted according to the journalist Nicholas Blanford (2011: 310) by the Hezbollah, who crossed the border from Lebanon to Israel and killed five Israelis. Otherwise, the Hezbollah did not hesitate to chase and participate in the arrests by the Lebanese authority of members of small Palestinian factions from Lebanese refugee camps that fired several Katioucha rockets from South Lebanon in March and April 2002 (Harik 2004: 189; Blanford 2011: 313). Even today, the Hezbollah controls the South and especially the areas close to the border and tries to prevent any action that is not under its domination.
9. Kawtharani was also the one who helped secure the release from Iraqi custody of the Hezbollah operative Ali Musa Daqduq, a senior Hezbollah commander who worked closely with one of the Iraqi Shiʻa armed groups called "Asāʼib Ahl al-Haq" and was responsible for numerous attacks against Coalition Force in Iraq (Blanford 2014a; Orléans 2014).
10. The LRB were also re-established in 2006, after having been disbanded following the liberation of the South of Lebanon from Israeli occupation in 2000, to serve different purposes such as including non-Shiʻa partisans in Hezbollah's "reservist resistance" to strengthen the impression of a national resistance rather than a uniquely Shiʻa force and to train Hezbollah's political allies (Blanford 2011: 436). The LRB nevertheless were not expected to play a role in any new military confrontation against Israel and would rather "look after the refugees from the South" according to a Hezbollah soldier (cited in Blanford 2011: 439).
11. The Line of Withdrawal—also called the "Blue Line"—was identified in 2000 by the United Nations in cooperation with Lebanese and Israeli officials for the purpose of confirming the withdrawal of Israel Occupation Forces troops from Lebanese territory in conformity with Security Council Resolution 425. The Blue Line is not the border between Lebanon and Israel.
12. Muhammad Raad, current head of the Hezbollah Deputy bloc in parliament: "We note that the resistance (Hezbollah) tried to affirm since the beginning its national character, of which the target was the Israeli occupation and not other Lebanese" (cited in Charara and Dromont 2004: 120). The Lebanese author, Walid Charara, who is considered close to the Hezbollah, argued that: "Hezbollah's attitudes regarding different protagonists in the Civil War depended mainly on their stand towards Israel" (cited in Charara and Dromont 2004: 120).

13. In particular, Shuqayr was accused of allowing the Hezbollah to operate a system of listening devices and cameras it had set up to monitor runway 17, from where officials fly out and where they land. This directly affected the movement's control over a strategic location that is vital to the flow of people and probably to various types of trafficking (ICG 2008: 3).

14. The Winograd report in Israel highlighted the need to eliminate the Hezbollah's command and control system in which telecommunication played a decisive role (ICG 2008: 3).

15. The Future Movement is a majority Sunni Lebanese political movement, led by the MP Saad Hariri, the younger son of the assassinated former Prime Minister of Lebanon, Rafiq Hariri. The movement is the largest member of the March 14 Alliance. The party was established in 2007.

7. Hezbollah and Revolutionary Processes in the Middle East and North Africa Since 2011

1. According to Norton (2000: 25), in 1999 the Hezbollah's leading officials, including Shura Council and Political Bureau members, had privately explored the possibility of a dialogue with the United States, while contacts between the Hezbollah and European embassies have increased in the last two decades (Qassem 2008: 341).

2. Personal observation during a Hezbollah event in 2012 in Dahyeh, Beirut.

3. During the Gaza War, Nasrallah called on the Egyptian people to take to the streets in their millions and urge the officers of the Egyptian Armed Forces to go to the political leadership and declare their opposition to the policies that assisted in the death of Palestinians. Nasrallah did not call for the overthrow of Mubarak's regime but only for a change in its political stance, particularly the opening of the Rafah border between Gaza and Egypt.

4. The Free Syrian Army was not established before August of 2011 (O'Bagy 2013).

5. Maliki's government (2008–2014) has been accused of sectarian policies against the Sunni population. For example, he refused the integration of the "Sunni awakening" councils, which had fought al-Qaida, in the army; he maintained the anti-Baathist law established after the US invasion against former leaders close to Saddam Hussein, but mainly used by the Iraqi Prime Minister to suppress all Sunni political forces, while accusing leading Sunni politicians of supporting terrorism. The Maliki government has also systematically discriminated against Sunnis in the state public administration.

6. We should note that the Hezbollah's criticisms are targeted at personalities of the Syrian regime that are no longer linked to it and who were put aside. Ghazi Kanaan died in September 2005 in unknown circumstances (the official version is that he committed suicide), while Abdel Halim Khaddam was sacked in the summer of 2005 and relocated to Paris to live in exile.

7. After the fall of the city of Yabroud in January and February 2014, in which the Hezbollah played a leading role in the military fights against Syrian rebel fighters, a suicide bomb targeted Dahyeh which was claimed by Jabhat al-Nusra in Lebanon and the Liwa Ahrar al-Sunna. Both groups said they were avenging Yabroud. "Prepare for the transfer of the battle of Yabroud into Lebanese territory," warned the latter (Nashashibi 2014).

8. The Battle of Karbalā', on October 10, 680, was a military engagement in which a small party led by al-Ḥusayn ibn ʿAlī, grandson of the Prophet Muḥammad and son of ʿAlī, the fourth caliph, was defeated and massacred by an army sent by the Umayyad caliph Yazīd I. The battle helped secure the position of the Umayyad dynasty, but among Shīʿa Muslims (followers of al-Ḥusayn) the 10th of Muḥarram (or ʿĀshūrāʾ) became an annual holy day of public mourning.

9. Hezbollah denied there had been any deaths in the town because of starvation, and accused rebel leaders of preventing people from leaving.

10. The Hezbollah has, for example, enrolled five mukhtars in South Lebanon, five in the Bekaa Valley, and five in Dahiyeh—all of them party affiliates, whose responsibility is to take care of the paperwork for soldiers killed in Syria. The certificates of dead fighters indicate, for example, that the death was the result of an accident (Haddad 2015).

11. The Shiʿaʾs believers regard Ḥusayn (ʿAlīʾs youngest son from his marriage to Fatima, the daughter of the Prophet Muḥammad, and the third Shiʿa Imām), who was killed in the Battle of Karbalāʾ, as a martyr (*shahid*), and count him as an Imām from the Ahl al-Bayt. They view Ḥusayn as the defender of Islam from annihilation at the hands of the new Muawiyah Caliph Yazīd. Ḥusayn is the last Imām following ʿAlī whom all Shiʿa sub-branches mutually recognize. The Battle of Karbalāʾ is often cited as the definitive break between the Shiʿa and Sunni sects of Islam, and is commemorated each year by the Shiʿa Muslims on the Day of ʿĀshūrāʾ. In other words, the significance of wearing "oh Ḥusayn" in the context of the military fights in Syria is to mark their Shiʿa identity against the Syrian Sunni opposition armed groups.

12. In April 2015, Marwan Issa, a LRB member, was found dead in a parking lot of the Ain al-Helweh camp. Marwan Issa was known to engage in arms trafficking inside the camp. One month later, another member of the LRB, Moujahed Balous, was killed in the Ain al-Helweh camp.

13. On July 1, 2015 in the Saadiyat area, 20 kilometers South of Beirut, clashes occurred between members of the LRB and of the Future Movement. In December 2014, the LRB were involved in a shootout with police in the southern city of Saida following the attempted arrest of a wanted Brigade militant. In January 2013, clashes occurred between members of the Popular Nasserite Organization led by ex-MP Osama Saad and the LRB, leaving one person dead and three others wounded in the city of Saida. In the months leading up to the major June 2013 battle between the local Salafist cleric

Ahmad al-Assir and the Lebanese Army, Assir's partisans would regularly clash with LRB members, and in fact just days before the final eruption a smaller, but still heavy, round of fighting involving machine guns and RPGs took place between the two militias.

14. Lebanon and Iraq both objected to the statement and Algeria dissociated itself from it.

15. In May 2016, it was the turn of Egypt-owned NileSat to stop broadcasting the channel.

Conclusion

1. According to the journalist Nicholas Blanford (2011: 360–61), Hariri and Nasrallah met secretly numerous times from mid-2004 until the assassination of Hariri in February 2005. In one of these meetings, Hariri assured Nasrallah would not seek to disarm Hezbollah by force. Dr. Hassan Fadlallah (2015: 139) wrote in his recent book that Rafiq Hariri accepted before his death to maintain Hezbollah's military and organizational strength until the achievement of a settlement with Israel.

2. Roberto Roccu adds, in relation to Jessop's explanation: that: "each accumulation strategy can be related to several alternative hegemonic projects, and on the other hand the success of the latter is dependent on their ability to relate to an existing or prospective accumulation strategy" (Roccu 2012: 72). This is consistent with Gramsci's conception of hegemony, which "must also be economic, must necessarily be based on the decisive function exercised by the leading group in the decisive nucleus of economic activity" (cited in Roccu 2012: 212).

References

Abu Amer, Adnan (2016) "Hamas Drags Feet on Choosing between Iran, Saudi Arabia." *Al-Monitor*, at: www.al-monitor.com/pulse/originals/2016/03/hamas-silence-gulf-decision-hezbollah-terrorist.html#ixzz43e6UaGJp (accessed March 20, 2016).

Abdallah, Castro (2012) National Federation of Trade Union of Workers and Employees in Lebanon (FENASOL) and LCP member, Interview May 2012, Beirut.

Abdallah, Myra (2016) "The Challenges of Anti-Hezbollah Shiites." *Now Media*, at: https://now.mmedia.me/lb/en/reportsfeatures/566691-the-challenges-of-anti-hezbollah-shiites (accessed March 6, 2016).

Abdul-Hussain, Hussain (2002a) "Labor Unions Turn their Fire on Government Policies." *The Daily Star*, September 4, at: www.dailystar.com.lb/News/Lebanon-News/2002/Sep-04/18484-labor-unions-turn-their-fire-on-government-policies.ashx (accessed February 13, 2015).

Abdul-Hussain, Hussain (2002b) "Ghosn: GLC will not be a Tool." *The Daily Star*, September 12, at: www.dailystar.com.lb/News/Lebanon-News/2002/Sep-12/18611-ghosn-glc-will-not-be-a-tool.ashx (accessed February 10, 2014).

Abdul-Hussain, Hussain (2002c) "GLC offers Support for Teachers." *The Daily Star*, November 26, at: www.dailystar.com.lb/News/Lebanon-News/2002/Nov-26/14251-glc-offers-support-for-teachers.ashx (accessed March 2, 2014).

Abdul-Hussain, Hussain (2003a) "GLC Official wants people to Ignore Power Bills." *The Daily Star*, July 22, at: www.dailystar.com.lb/News/Lebanon-News/2003/Jul-22/39271-glc-official-wants-people-to-ignore-power-bills.ashx (accessed February 12, 2015).

Abdul-Hussain, Hussain (2003b) "Dissidents Lash Out at GLC Leadership." *The Daily Star*, September 3, at: www.dailystar.com.lb/News/Lebanon-News/2003/Sep-03/40990-dissidents-lash-out-at-glc-leadership.ashx (accessed February 20, 2012).

Abi Habib, Maria (2014) "Shiite Militias Decamping From Syria to Fight in Iraq." *The Wall Street Journal*, at: www.wsj.com/articles/shiite-militias-decamping-from-syria-to-fight-in-iraq-1403051977 (accessed June 30, 2014).

Abi Yaghi, Marie Noel (2012) "Civil Mobilisation and Peace in Lebanon, Beyond the Reach of the 'Arab Spring'?." *Accord*, Issue 24, at: www.academia.edu/1987158/_Civil_Mobilization_and_Peace_in_Lebanon_in._Elisabeth_Picard_Alexander_Ramsbotham_Reconciliation_reform_and_resilience._Positive_Peace_for_Lebanon_Accord_Publications_Issue_24_London_July_2012 (accessed July 23, 2012).

Abisaab, Rula J. (2006) "The Cleric as Organic Intellectual: Revolutionary Shiism in the Lebanese Hawzas," in H.E. Chehabi (ed.), *Distant Relations: Iran and Lebanon in the Last 500 Years*. London: I.B. Tauris, pp. 231–58.

Abisaab, R.J. and Abisaab, Malek (2014) *The Shi'ites of Lebanon, Modernism, Communism, and Hizbullah's Islamists*. Syracuse, NY: Syracuse University Press.

Abizeid, Marc (2014) "A Guide to Lebanon's Street Protests." *Al-Akhbar English*, at: http://english.al-akhbar.com/content/guide-lebanon's-street-protests (accessed April 17, 2014).

Abla, Zeina (2003) "Confronting the Fiscal Crisis through Privatisation." *Social Watch, Poverty Eradication and Gender Justice*, at: www.socialwatch.org/node/10841 (accessed October 22, 2011).

Abou Habib, Adib (2012) Head of the Printing Press Employees Unions, founder of the Lebanese Observatory of the Rights of Workers and Employees (LORWE) and ex-member of the LCP. Interview April 2012, Beirut.

Abou Rjeili, Khalil and Labaki, Boutros (1994) *Bilan des guerres du Liban, 1975–1990*. Paris: L'Harmattan.

Abou Zaki, Rasha (2012a) "Trāblus: rahla al-mi'a 'ām bahtān 'an ta'ā.," *Al-Akhbar*, May 15, at: www.al-akhbar.com/node/64335 (accessed May 16, 2012).

Abou Zaki, R. (2012b) "Intifāda al-mustā'jirīn." *Al-Akhbar*, May 16, at: www.al-akhbar.com/node/64415 (accessed May 17, 2012).

Abou Zaki, R. (2012c) "Al-Kahrabā'... wa la'āna." *Al-Akhbar*, May 29, at: www.al-akhbar.com/node/94204 (accessed May 29, 2012).

Abou Zeinab, Ghaleb (2008) Political Advisor of Hassan Nasrallah and Hezbollah member. Interview September 2008, Beirut.

Abrahamian, Ervand (1993) *Khomeinism: Essays on the Islamic Republic*. Berkeley, LA: University of California Press.

Abukhalil, Asad (1990) "Syria and the Shiites: Al-Asad's Policy in Lebanon." *Third World Quarterly*, Vol. 12, No. 2, pp. 1–20

Abu Nasr, Donna and Shahine, Alaa (2014) "Hezbollah's 'Mini-Vietnam' in Syria Worsens on Beirut Bombs." *Bloomberg*, at: www.bloomberg.com/news/2014-03-05/hezbollah-s-mini-vietnam-in-syria-escalates-with-beirut-bombs.html (accessed October 30, 2014).

Achcar, Gilbert (1981) "Onze thèses sur la résurgence actuelle de l'intégrisme islamique." *Europe Solidaire*, at: www.europe-solidaire.org/IMG/article_PDF/Onze-thses-sur-la-rsurgence_a3324.pdf (accessed June 13, 2011).

Achcar, G. (2007) "Lebanon and the Middle East Crisis." *International Socialist Review*, at: www.isreview.org/issues/52/achcar.shtml (accessed February 20, 2012).

Achcar, G. (2013a) *Le peuple veut, une exploration radicale du soulèvement arabe*. Paris: Sindbad-Actes Sud.

Achcar, G. (2013b) *Marxism, Orientalism, Cosmopolitanism*. London: Haymarket.

Achcar, G. and Chomsky, Noam (2007) *La poudrière du Moyen Orient*. Paris: Fayard.

Adada, Hani (2015) "Istansābīyya al-āman … al'unf dud muntaqadī al-nizhām." *Al-Modon*, at: www.almodon.com/print/3f9b540d-4039-45e8-a648-9a4779a0938d/9647fe4a-338b-4224-beb1-31b92f2a99ac (accessed December 20, 2015).

Al-Ahed News (2004) "Lā'iha ibnā' Hāra Hrayk," at: http://archive.alahednews. com.lb/alahed.org/archive/2004/3004/file/doc2.htm (accessed March 3, 2012).

Al-Ahed News (2008) "Sayyed Nasrallah: Resistance is Vigilant—Those Plotting to Stop the Resistance Will Fail," at: www.english.alahednews.com.lb/essaydetails. php?eid=5050&cid=449#.VGcP297A1ss (accessed March 20, 2011).

Al-Ahed News (2009) "Sayyed Nasrallah Refutes Egypt Claims, Rejects Enmity with Any Arab State." April 11, at: http://english.alahednews.com.lb/ essaydetails.php?eid=8205&cid=450#.Ueod1xYW134 (accessed September 25, 2012).

Al-Ahed News (2010) "Sayyed Nasrallah Full Speech on Martyr's Day November 11 2010," at: www.english.alahednews.com.lb/essaydetails. php?eid=12621&cid=451#.VGc8sd7A1ss (accessed November 13, 2010).

Al-Ahed News (2011a) "Sayyed Nasrallah on the Ceremony for Consolidation with the Arab Peoples on 19-03-2011." March 19, at: www.english.alahednews. com.lb/essaydetails.php?eid=13713&cid=452#.Vds49CT3Bss (accessed March 22, 2011).

Al-Ahed News (2011b) "MP Fayyad Warns Arab Revolutions to Stay Vigilant on Arrogant Countries' Schemes." November 21, at: www.english.alahednews. com.lb/essaydetails.php?eid=15807&cid=385#.Vds7SyT3Bss (accessed November 23, 2011).

Al-Ahed News (2012) "Sayyed Nasrallah: US Blackmailed Al-Assad, Hand Us Resistance Head … We End Crisis." September 4, at: http://english.alahednews. com.lb/essaydetails.php?eid=20897&cid=513#.Udox-RYW134 (accessed September 6, 2012).

Al-Ahed News (2013) "Al-Sayyīd Nasr Allāh li-jumhur al-muqāwama: a'dakum bil-nasr mujadadān." May 25, at: www.alahednews.com.lb/76648/149/السيد-اعدكم-بالنصر-مجددا #نصر-الله-لجمهور-المقاومة.VHisX97A1ss (accessed October 30, 2014).

Al-Ahed News (2014) "Tunazam haflān takrimiān lil-mu'assassāt al-mutā'qida ma'hā 'la Famille' ma'rad al-Sur." February 18, at: http://media.alahednews. com.lb/galldetails.php?cid=523&items=12 (accessed February 2, 2014).

Al-Ahed News (2015a) "Kalima al-āmin al-'ām li-hizb Allāh al-Sayyīd Hassan Nasr Allāh fī ihtifāl takrīm shuhadā' al-Qunaitra." January 30, at: www. alahednews.com.lb/106672/149#.VfGAbiT3Bss (accessed March 5, 2015).

Al-Ahed News (2015b) "al-kalima al-kāmila li-samāha al-āmin al-'ām li-hizb Allāh al-Sayyīd Hassan Nasr Allāh fī zikra al-qāda al-shuhadā' li'ām 2015." February 16, at: www.alahednews.com.lb/107353/149/#.VfBwkST3Bss (accessed March 20, 2015).

Al-Ahed News (2015c) "al-Sayyīd Hassan Nasr Allāh: al-hadaf al-haqīqī al-3adwān al-Sa'udī 'ala al-īyyaman huwa I'āda al-hayyīmana wa al-wissāiyya

'ala al-īyyaman." April 17, at: www.alahednews.com.lb/109733/149/-السيد
نصر-الله-الهدف-الحقيقي-للعدوان-السعودي-على-اليمن-هو-اعادة-الهيمنة-والوصاية-على-اليمن#.
VfFYviT3Bss (accessed April 30, 2015).

Al-Ahed News (2015d) "Kalima al-Sayyīd Hassan Nasr Allāh fī 'aīd al-tahrīr
kāmila." May 24, at: www.alahednews.com.lb/111167/149/-المقاومة-الله-نصر-السيد
في-أعلى-جهوزيتها-والمشروع-التكفيري-سوف-يدمر-ويسحق-ولن-يبقى-منه#.VeSm4CT3Bss
(accessed August 30, 2015).

Al-Ahed News (2015f) "Kalima al-āmin al-'ām li-hizb Allāh al-Sayyīd Hassan
Nasr Allāh fī maharjān yawm al-quds al-'ālamī." July 10, at: www.alahednews.
com.lb/112961/149/-كلمة-الأمين-العام-لحزب-الله-السيد-حسن-نصر-الله-في-مهرجان-يوم-
القدس-العالمي-2015#.VfLPniT3Bsu (accessed July 15, 2015).

Al-Ahed News (2015g) "Al-Sayyīd Nasr Allāh: al-sa'ūdīyya tatahamul mas'ūlīyya
hāditha mona … mārab tarsam itijā al-hal fil-īyyaman … wa al-hudūr al-rūssī
mū'athir bi-massār ma'araka sūrīyyā … wa narhab bihi." September 26, at:
www.alahednews.com.lb/115781/7/-السيد-نصر الله-السعودية-تتحمل-مسؤولية-حادثة
مؤثر-بمسار-الحضور-الروسي-.و.اليمن-في-الحل-اتجاه-ترسم-مأرب..مني#.VgpazST3Bsu
(accessed September 29, 2015).

Al-Ahed News (2016a) "mawqi' 'al-'ahed' al-īkhbārī yunshur mashāhid fīdīū
hasrīyya wa jadīda lil-āmīn al-'ām li-hizb Allāh Al-Sayyīd Nasr Allāh." March
1, at: www.alahednews.com.lb/119663/149/-فيديو-مشاهد-ينشر-الاخباري-العهد-موقع
حصرية-وجديدة-للأمين-العام-لحزب-الله-السيد-حسن-نصر#.VvF3EyTA1su (accessed
March 20, 2016).

Al-Ahed News (2016b) "Al-Sayyīd Nasr Allāh: kul al-kīyyān al-īsrā'īlī wa ma fīhi
min mafā'il nawaīyya hadaf lanā… wa al-Sa'ūdīyya ta'tal āy taqadam fī al-hal
al-sīyyāssī bi-sūriyyā." March 22, at: www.alahednews.com.lb/122916/149/
السيد-نصر-الله-كل-الكيان-الاسرائيلي-وما-فيه-من-مفاعل-نووية-هدف-لنا..والسعودية-تعطل#.
VvGCsCTA1st (accessed March 22, 2016).

Al-Ahed News (2016c) "kalima samāha al-Sayyīd Hassan Nasr Allāh fī Īhtifāl
hay'a da'm al-muqāwama al-īslāmiyya." May 6, at: www.alahednews.com.
lb/124889/7/#.V20B1CTugdM (accessed June 20, 2016).

Al-Ahed News (2016d) "kalima al-Sayyīd Hassan Nasr Allāh fī zhikra ūsbū'
al-qā'id al-shahīd Mustafa Badr al-Dīn." May 20, at: www.alahednews.com.
lb/125388/149/-كلمة-السيد-نصر-الله-في-ذكرى-أسبوع-القائد-الشهيد-مصطفى-بدر-الدين#.
V21tayTugdM (accessed June 20, 2016).

Al-Ainin, Bahyyat (2008) "Ra'īs niqāba ashāb al-matā'im wa al-muntazahāt
wa al-mu'assassāt al-siyyāhiyya fil-janub 'ala Tabaja: sanaj'lu al-siyyaha um
al-muwassim." Janoubia Online, at: www.janoubiaonline.com/modules.
php?name=News&file=article&sid=417 (accessed December 11, 2012).

Al-Akhbar (2006) " 'Jihād al-Binā'' tanfarad bil-i'mār rithmā tashu al-dawla," at:
www.al-akhbar.com/node/164866 (accessed September 11, 2012).

Al-Akhbar (2011) "Ka's Hāra Hrayk al-rābi'a bi-mushārika thāmaniyya andiyya,"
at: www.al-akhbar.com/node/16689 (accessed April 15, 2012).

Al-Akhbar (2012) "Tashīh al-ujur: al-thālatha thābita," at: www.al-akhbar.com/
node/27465 (accessed August 12, 2012).

Al-Akhbar English (2011) "Thousands Protest against Lebanon Pay Increase," at: http://english.al-akhbar.com/node/2548 (accessed December 15, 2011).

Al-Akhbar English (2012a) "FPM Fumes at Lebanese Electricity Workers' 'Victory,'" at: http://english.al-akhbar.com/content/fpm-fumes-lebanese-electricity-workers-victory (accessed June 15, 2012).

Al-Akhbar English (2012b) "Nasrallah: US Manipulated Syria Grievances," at: http://english.al-akhbar.com/node/9961 (accessed July 18, 2012).

Al-Akhbar English (2013a) "Nasrallah Tells Cadres Hezbollah 'Has Changed,'" January 26, at: http://english.al-akhbar.com/content/nasrallah-tells-cadres-hezbollah-has-changed (accessed January 26, 2013).

Al-Akhbar English (2013b) "Hundreds Rally against Lebanese 'Orthodox Law,'" February 19, at: http://english.al-akhbar.com/content/hundreds-protesters-rally-against-"racist"-lebanese-"orthodox-law" (accessed February 19, 2013).

Al-Akhbar English (2013c) "Lebanon: Economic Committees Pay Saudi Royal a Visit." March 11, at: http://english.al-akhbar.com/content/lebanon-economic-committees-pay-saudi-royal-visit (accessed March 11, 2013).

Al-Akhbar English (2013d) "Hamas Reconsiders Alliances After Fall of Mursi." July 19, at: http://english.al-akhbar.com/content/hamas-reconsiders-alliances-after-fall-mursi (accessed August 1, 2013).

Alagha, Joseph (2006) *The Shifts in Hizbullah's Ideology*. Amsterdam: University of Amsterdam.

Alagha, J. (2007) "Hizbullah's Conception of the Islamic State," in S. Mervin (ed.), *Les Mondes Chiites et l'Iran*. Paris and Beyrouth: Karthala and IFPO, pp. 87–112.

Alagha, J. and Catusse, M. (2008) "Les services sociaux du Hezbollah," in S. Mervin (ed.), *Le Hezbollah: État des Lieux*. Paris: Sindbad, Actes Sud and IFPO, pp. 117–40.

Alami, Mona (2008) "Lebanon: Radical Islam Comes to Town." *Inter Press Service News Agency*, at: www.ipsnews.net/2008/07/lebanon-radical-islam-comes-to-town/ (accessed June 2, 2012).

Alami, Mona (2016) "Meet One of Hezbollah's Teen Fighters." *Al-Monitor*, at: www.al-monitor.com/pulse/originals/2016/01/lebanon-hezbollah-teenagers-jihad-syria.html (accessed January 30, 2016).

Alfoneh, Ali (2008) "The Revolutionary Guards' Role in Iranian Politics." *Middle East Quarterly*, Vol. 15, No. 4, pp. 3–14, at: www.meforum.org/1979/the-revolutionary-guards-role-in-iranian-politics#_ftn1 (accessed January 13, 2014).

Alipour, Farahmand (2015) "Syrian Shiites Take Up Arms in Support of Assad's Army." *Al-Monitor* at: www.al-monitor.com/pulse/originals/2015/08/syrian-shiite-militia.html#ixzz3lQxXNYZE (accessed September 8, 2015).

All4Syria (2015) "hulafā' hizb Allāh fī Saīyydā wa mukhaīyyamātihā īyyrfudūn al-qitāl fī-sūrīyya," at: http://all4syria.info/Archive/234534 (accessed July 30, 2015).

Al-Amal al-Baladi (2013) "No. 14," at: www.amal-baladi.org/uploaded/books/mag14.pdf (accessed February 2, 2014).

Amal al-Ummah TV (2011) "Mashru' al-nahda al-Islāmī ... Khayret Al-Shāter," at: www.youtube.com/watch?v=JnSshs2qzrM (accessed October 26, 2014).

Amarasingam, Amarnath and Corbeil, Alexander (2016) "The Houthi Hezbollah." *Foreign Affairs*, at: www.foreignaffairs.com/articles/2016-03-31/houthi-hezbollah (accessed June 20, 2016).

Amel, M. (1986) *Fil-Dawla al-Tā'ifiyya*. Beirut: Dār al-Farabi.

Al-Amin, Ibrahim, Qanso, Wafic, Ileik, Hassan and Zarakat, Maha (2014) "Atakhaznā qarār al-asr qabl shuhur ... wa tusalal al-mujāhidun marāt 'ada ila Falestīn." *Al-Akhbar*, at: http://al-akhbar.com/node/213547 (accessed September 30, 2014).

Al-Amir Najde, Abd (2012) President of Federation of Public Cars Drivers for Land Transport Unions. Interview April 2012, Beirut.

Amhaz, Sobhi (2016) "Hizb Āllah yafūz bi-īstiftā' ba'lbak—al-hermel." *Al-Modon*, at: www.almodon.com/politics/2016/5/9/حزب-الله-يفوز-بإستفتاء-بعلبك--الهرمل; (accessed May 13, 2016).

Amnesty International (1997) *Lebanon Human Rights Developments and Violations, 1997*, Index number: MDE 18/019/1997.

Andraos, Rana (2012) "Le nouveau projet de loi sur les loyers, détonateur de la crise sociale?." *Orient le Jour*, at: www.lorientlejour.com/article/753165/Le_nouveau_projet_de_loi_sur_les_loyers%2C_detonateur_de_la_crise_sociale_.html (accessed April 5, 2012).

Andraos, R. (2013) "Approuvée! Oui, mais ...." *Orient le Jour*, at: www.lorientlejour.com/article/806752/Grille_des_salaires_%3A_Approuvee_%21_Oui%2C_mais....html (accessed March 23, 2013).

Anon (2012a) with close family ties with Hezbollah members. Interview January 2012, Beirut.

Anon (2012b) member of the CGTL. Interview July 2012, Beirut.

Arch (2014) "Profile," at: www.archco-lb.com/profile.pdf (accessed February 3, 2014).

Asharq al-Awsat (2013) "Syria: Tensions Escalate between Islamist rebels and Hamas," at: https://english.aawsat.com/2013/10/article55319727/syria-tensions-escalate-between-islamist-rebels-and-hamas (accessed January 10, 2015).

Asher Schapiro, Avi (2016) " 'Children Are Eating Leaves Off the Trees': The Nightmare of the Siege of Madaya, Syria," *Vice News*, at: https://news.vice.com/article/children-are-eating-leaves-off-the-trees-the-nightmare-of-the-siege-of-madaya-syria (accessed January 10, 2016).

Ashkar, Hisham (2011) *The Role of the State in Initiating Gentrification: The Case of the Neighborhood of Achrafieh in Beirut* (Master). Lebanese University: Institute of Fine Arts Department of Urban Planning.

Ashkar, H. (2014a) "A Response to the 'End of Rent Control in Lebanon,' or the Deficiencies in Urban Research on Beirut." *Disturbanism, A Blog On Urbanism*, at: http://disturbanism.wordpress.com/2014/06/26/a-response-to-the-end-of-rent-control-in-lebanon-or-the-deficiencies-in-urban-research-on-beirut/ (accessed July 1, 2014).

Ashkar, H. (2014b) "Funerals Hezbollah Fighters Syria 2012–2014." *Mostly Off*, at: https://docs.google.com/a/soas.ac.uk/spreadsheet/ccc?key=0Am1WLKyxQY2 ldEtQQzVBaE5KOU5tSoVIM1pJU2RYRnc&usp=drive_web#gid=0 (accessed October 30, 2014).

Asia Times (2006) "Hezbollah's Lack of Structure its Strength," at: www.atimes.com/atimes/Middle_East/HH11Ak03.html (accessed December 2, 2014).

Association of Banks in Lebanon (2012) "The Lebanese Banking Sector, Pillar of Lebanon's Stability," at: www.abl.org.lb/library/files/ABL%202013%20LBS.pdf (accessed June 13, 2013).

Association of Banks in Lebanon (2014a) "Members Guide," at: www.abl.org.lb/allbankGuide.aspx?pageid=128 (accessed September 3, 2013).

Association of Banks in Lebanon (2014b) "Board of Directors," at: www.abl.org.lb/boardofdirectors.aspx?pageid=20 (accessed September 30, 2013).

Association of Lebanese Industrialists (2014) "Board of Directors," at: www.ali.org.lb/english/board.asp# (accessed March 20, 2014).

Ayub, Nour (2015) "kashāfat al-mahdi fi thalāthinitihā: 76 ālf muntassib." *Al-Akhbar*, at: www.al-akhbar.com/node/234919 (accessed June 6, 2015).

Aziz, Tareq M. (1993) "An Islamic Perspective of Political Economy: The Views of (late) Muhammad Baqir Al-Sadr." *The Ahlul Bayt Digital Islamic Library Project*, at: www.al-islam.org/al-tawhid/vol10-n1/islamic-perspective-political-economy-views-late-muhammad-baqir-al-sadr-tm-aziz-0 (accessed November 4, 2014).

Azm, Yasser (2012) Hamas Official in Lebanon in Charge of Media and Refugee Affairs. Interview January 2012, Beirut, Lebanon.

Al-Azmeh, A. (2003) "Postmodern Obscurantism and the Muslim Question." *Socialist Register*, Vol. 39, pp. 28–50.

Bali, Asli and Salti, Nisreen (2009) "How Lebanon has Weathered the Storm." *Middle East Report*, No. 252, pp. 30–33.

Baliani, Diego (2008) "Lebanon: The Doha Agreement Ends the First Restructuring Phase in the Post Syrian Lebanon." *Centro Militare di Studi Strategici (CeMiSS)*, Year VI, pp. 5–14.

Bank Information Center (BIC) (2012) "The World Bank Group and Lebanon: A Country Study," at: www.bicusa.org/wpcontent/uploads/2013/03/The+World+Bank+Group+and+Lebanon-September+2012.pdf (accessed January 11, 2013).

Bank Audi (2014) "Shareholders," at: www.banqueaudi.com/CorporateGovernance/Pages/shareholders.aspx?pic_url=corpgov (accessed January 20, 2014).

Barake, Ali (2012) Hamas Official Representative in Beirut. Interview January 2012, Beirut, Lebanon.

Baram, Amatzia (1994) "Two Roads to Revolutionary Shi'ite Fundamentalism in Iraq," in M.E. Marty and R.S. Appleby (eds), *Accounting for Fundamentalisms*, *the Dynamic Character of Movements*. Chicago, IL and London: University of Chicago Press, pp. 531–88.

Bargisi, Amr (ed.), Mohameed, Ragab Mohameed, (transcriber) and Pieretti, Damien (translator) (2012) "Khairat al-Shater on 'The Nahda Project' (Complete Translation)." *Hudson Institute*, at: www.hudson.org/research/9820-khairat-al-shater-on-the-nahda-project-complete-translation- (accessed October 26, 2014).

Barrington, Lisa (2016) "Hezbollah Blames Rebel Shelling for Death of Top Commander in Syria." *Reuters*, at: www.reuters.com/article/us-mideast-crisis-hezbollah-blast-idUSKCN0Y506R (accessed May 20, 2016).

Baroudi, Salim E. (1998) "Economic Conflict in Postwar Lebanon: State Labor Relations between 1992–1997." *Middle East Journal*, Vol. 52, No. 4, pp. 531–50.

Baroudi, S.E. (2000) "Sectarianism and Business Associations in Postwar Lebanon." *Arab Studies Quarterly*, Vol. 22, No. 4, pp. 81–107.

Baroudi, S.E. (2001) "Conflict and Co-operation within Lebanon's Business Community: Relations between Merchants' and Industrialists' Associations." *Middle Eastern Studies*, Vol. 37, No. 4, pp. 71–100.

Baroudi, S.E. (2002) "Continuity in Economic Policy in Postwar Lebanon: The Record of the Hariri and Hoss Governments Examined, 1992–2000." *Arab Studies Quarterly*, Vol. 24, No. 1, pp. 63–90.

Al-Barzi, Dalal (2016) "yasārīūn dud al-nisā' wa ma' "Hizb Āllāh." *Al-Modon*, at: www.almodon.com/opinion/2016/7/28/الله-حزب-ومع-ومع-النساء-ضد-يساريون (accessed July 30, 2016).

Bassam, Layla (2014) "Hizb Allāh yakshifu 'an asrār siyyāssiyya wa 'askariyya fī kitāb li-nā'ibihi fī barlamān Hassan Fadl Allāh." *Reuters*, at: http://ara.reuters.com/article/topNews/idARAKBN0JZ0KV20141221 (accessed December 27, 2014).

Bassam, Layla and Evans, Dominic (2016) "Hezbollah says Saudi Arabia, Turkey Obstructing Syria Peace Chances." *Reuters*, at: www.reuters.com/article/us-mideast-crisis-syria-hezbollah-idUSKCN0WN25N?mod=related&channelName=worldNews (accessed March 20, 2016).

Bathish, Hani M. (2007) "New Political Party Offers Shiites a Third Alternative." *The Daily Star*, at: www.dailystar.com.lb/News/Lebanon-News/2007/Jul-12/47640-new-political-party-offers-shiites-a-third-alternative.ashx (accessed January 11, 2014).

Bayoumi, Yara and Ghobari, Mohammed (2015) "Iranian Support Seen Crucial for Yemen's Houthis." *Reuters*, at: www.reuters.com/article/2014/12/15/us-yemen-houthis-iran-insight-idUSKBN0JT17A20141215 (accessed July 30, 2015).

Al-Bayyan (2001) "Idrāb iushalu matār Bayrut wa iulghi 8 rahlāt," at: www.albayan.ae/one-world/8-2001-06-22-1.1174082 (accessed February 13, 2011).

BBC News (2015) "Yemen Crisis: Iran's Khamenei Condemns Saudi 'Genocide,'" at: www.bbc.com/news/world-middle-east-32239009 (accessed July 20, 2015).

BBC News (2016a) "Iran: Saudis Face 'Divine Revenge' for Executing al-Nimr," at: www.bbc.com/news/world-middle-east-35216694 (accessed March 20, 2016).

BBC News (2016b) "Bahrain Revokes Top Shia Cleric Isa Qassim's Citizenship," at: www.bbc.com/news/world-middle-east-36578000 (accessed June 25, 2016).

Beauchamp, Zack (2016) "The DEA says it Just Busted a Hezbollah Operation Laundering Money for Drug Cartels." *Vox World*, at: www.vox.com/2016/2/1/10891370/hezbollah-cartel-dea (accessed February 3, 2016).

Bedran, Ismail and Zbeeb, Muhammad (2000) *Al-ittihād al-'ummali al-'ām fī Lubnān, min yumathil min.* Beirut: Frederich Ebert Stiftung Institution.

Beirut Traders Association (2014) "About Us," at: www.beiruttraders.org/BTA/AboutBTA.aspx (accessed January 20, 2014).

Bejjani, Elias (2009) "Brazilian Samba & Hezbollah's Terrorism." *Canada Free Press*, at: www.canadafreepress.com/index.php/site/comments/brazilian-samba-hezbollahs-terrorism/ (accessed October 12, 2011).

Bensaid, Daniel (1982) "La double défaite de Beyrouth." *Le site de Daniel Bensaid*, at: http://danielbensaid.org/La-double-defaite-de-Beyrouth (accessed October 10, 2014).

Berti, Benedetta and Gleis, Joshua L. (2012) *Hezbollah and Hamas: A Comparative Study*. Baltimore, MD: Johns Hopkins University Press.

Berthélemy, Jean Claude, Dessus, Sebastien and Nahas, Charbel (2007) "Exploring Lebanon's Growth Prospects." *World Bank*, at: www-wds.worldbank.org/servlet/WDSContentServer/WDSP/IB/2007/08/27/000158349_20070827151759/Rendered/PDF/wps4332.pdf (accessed February 12, 2012).

Beydoun, Ahmad (1989) "Bint Jbeil, Michigan suivi de (ou poursuivi par) Bint Jbeil, Liban." *Maghreb Mashrek*, No. 125, pp. 69–81.

Bint Jbeil (2010) "Nabatiyya: 'al-tahāluf'' yatafiqu 'ala Kahīl ra'īssān wa Jāber nā'ibān lahu," at: www.bintjbeil.org/index.php?show=news&action=article&id=28201 (accessed March 30, 2012).

Blanford, N. (2007a) "Hizbullah Builds New Line of Defence." *The Christian Science Monitor*, February 26, at: www.csmonitor.com/2007/0226/p01s02-wome.html (accessed March 30, 2012).

Blanford, Nicholas (2007b) "The Secrets of a Hizballah Renegade." *Time*, April 24, at: www.time.com/time/world/article/0,8599,1613987,00.html (accessed March 12, 2011).

Blanford, N. (2008) "Hezbollah Phone Network Spat Sparks Beirut Street War." *The Christian Science Monitor*, at: www.csmonitor.com/World/Middle-East/2008/0509/p05s01-wome.html (accessed October 30, 2014).

Blanford, N. (2011) *Warriors of God: Inside Hezbollah's Thirty-Year Struggle Against Israel*. New York: Random House.

Blanford, N. (2012) "Hezbollah Role in Syria Grows More Evident." *The Daily Star*, at: www.dailystar.com.lb/News/Politics/2012/Oct-12/191121-hezbollah-role-in-syria-grows-more-evident.ashx#axzz2dVeZJ3yD (accessed October 30, 2014).

Blanford, N. (2013a) "Why Hezbollah has Openly Joined the Syrian Fight." *The Christian Science Monitor*, June 23, at: www.csmonitor.com/World/Middle-East/2013/0623/Why-Hezbollah-has-openly-joined-the-Syrian-fight (accessed October 30, 2013).

Blanford, N. (2013b) "The Battle for Qusayr: How the Syrian Regime and Hizb Allah tipped the Balance." *Combating Terrorism Center*, August 27, at: www.ctc.usma.edu/posts/the-battle-for-qusayr-how-the-syrian-regime-and-hizb-allah-tipped-the-balance (accessed October 30, 2014).

Blanford, N. (2014a) "Why Hezbollah is Playing a Smaller Role in This Iraqi Conflict." *The Christian Science Monitor*, July 14, at: www.csmonitor.com/World/Middle-East/2014/0716/Why-Hezbollah-is-playing-a-smaller-role-in-this-Iraqi-conflict (accessed November 15, 2014).

Blanford, N. (2014b) "Hezbollah Lowers Fighting Age as it Takes on Islamic State (+video)." *The Christian Science Monitor*, August 18, at: www.csmonitor.com/World/Middle-East/2014/0818/Hezbollah-lowers-fighting-age-as-it-takes-on-Islamic-State-video (accessed November 3, 2014).

Blanford, N. (2015) "How Oil Price Slump is Putting a Squeeze on Hezbollah, Iran's Shiite Ally." *The Christian Science Monitor*, at: www.csmonitor.com/World/Middle-East/2015/0104/How-oil-price-slump-is-putting-a-squeeze-on-Hezbollah-Iran-s-Shiite-ally (accessed January 5, 2015).

Blom InvestBank report (2010) "A Decade of Real Estate Demand in Lebanon," at: www.blominvestbank.com/Library/Files/Uploaded%20Files/2010-11-A%20Decade%20of%20Real%20Estate%20Demand%20in%20Lebanon.pdf (accessed February 10, 2014).

Bonnefoy, Laurent (2015) "The Islah Party in Yemen: Game Over?," at: http://muftah.org/islah-party-yemen-game/#.VfK4DiT3Bst (accessed August 30, 2015).

Bou Dagher, Mansour (2008) "Niqāba al-muhandissīn wa intikhābāt 13 nīssān." *Now Media*, at: https://now.mmedia.me/lb/ar/nownewsar/_نقب_لمهندسين_ونتخبت_13_نيسن (accessed June 2, 2012).

Boumet Beirut (2013) "Gendered Ashouraa' in Dahieh," at: http://boumet-beirut.tumblr.com/post/66206697272/gendered-ashouraa-in-dahieh#_ftn9 (accessed November 6, 2013).

Bourdieu, Pierre (1980) *Le sens pratique*. Paris: Editions de Minuit.

Calabrese, Erminia C. (2013) "Al-Ghālibūn Le Hezbollah et la mise en récit de la 'société de la résistance' au Liban." *Revue des mondes musulmans et de la Méditerranée*, No. 134, pp. 171–81, at: http://remmm.revues.org/8339 (accessed March 3, 2014).

Cammett, Melanie (2014) *Compassionate Communalism, Welfare and Sectarianism in Lebanon*. Ithaca, NY and London: Cornell University Press.

Carpi, Estella (2014) "The Everyday Experience of Humanitarianism in Akkar Villages." *Civil Society Knowledge Centre and Lebanon Support*, at: http://cskc.daleel-madani.org/paper/everyday-experience-humanitarianism-akkar-villages (accessed March 26, 2014).

Carré, Olivier and Gérard, Michaud (a pseudonym used by Michel Seurat) (1983) *Les Frères musulmans Égypte et Syrie (1928–1982)*. Paris: Gallimard and Julliard.

Catusse, Myriam (2009) *Tout privatiser ou bātir un Etat (social)? Le système public de sécurité sociale au Liban à la croisée des chemins*, in Congrès Association Française de Science Politique, "Section thématique 23, Les politiques sociales: mutations, enjeux, theories," Grenoble 2009, at: www.congresafsp2009.fr/sectionsthematiques/st23/st23catusse.pdf (accessed November 11, 2010).

Catusse, M. and Abi Yaghi, M.N. (2011) "Non à l'État holding, oui à l'État providence. Logiques et contraintes des mobilisations sociales dans le Liban de l'après-guerre." *Tiers-Monde*, No. 206, pp. 67–93, at: www.cairn.info/revue-tiers-monde-2011-5-page-67.htm (accessed December 3, 2013).

Chaaban, Jad C. and Salti, Nisreen (2009) "The Poverty and Equity Implications of a Rise in the Value-Added Tax: A Micro Economic Simulation for Lebanon." *Economic Research Forum*, at: www.erf.org.eg/CMS/uploads/pdf/1239701735_483.pdf (accessed August 2, 2011).

Chaib, Kinda (2008) "Parcours de militantes," in S. Mervin (ed.), *Le Hezbollah: État des Lieux*. Paris: Sindbad, Actes Sud and IFPO, pp. 287–310.

Charara, Nasser (2014) "Hamās wa hizb Allāh fī mu'ādila harb ghaza." *Al-Monitor*, at: www.al-monitor.com/pulse/ar/originals/2014/07/hezbollah-hamas-repair-ties.html# (accessed September 15, 2014).

Charara, Waddah (2007) *Dawla Hizb Allāh: Lubnān mujtam'ān islāmiyyan*, 5th edn. Beirut: Dar al-Nahār.

Charara, Walid and Dromont, Frederic (2004) *Le Hezbollah, un mouvement islamo-nationaliste*. Paris: Fayard.

Chehabi, Hisham E. (2006) "Iran and Lebanon in the Revolutionary Decade," in H.E. Chehabi (ed.), *Distant Relations: Iran and Lebanon in the Last 500 Years*. London: I.B. Tauris, pp. 201–30.

El-Cheikh, B. and Saghyieh, H. (2013a) "Al-Nabatiyya qil'a 'Hizb Allāh' … Intikāss al-tafā'ul wa saytara 'ala al-mujtama' atfālan wa kibāran, ahiyyā' wa shuhadā' (1 min 3)." *Al-Hayāt*, at: http://alhayat.com/Details/510798 (accessed June 17, 2013).

El-Cheikh, Bissan and Saghyieh, Hazem (2013b) "Al-Nabatiyya qil'a 'Hizb Allāh,' tahdiyyāt al-siyyāssa al-t'āyush fī zaman al-thawra wa al-azma suriyyatayn (3 min 3)." *Al-Hayāt*, at: http://daharchives.alhayat.com/issue_archive/Hayat%20 INT/2013/5/9/النبطية-قلعة-حزب-الله-تحديات-السياسة-والتعايش-في-زمن-الثورة-والأزمة-السوريتين--3من-3.html (accessed June 20, 2013).

Chelkowski, Peter and Dabashi, Hamid (2000) *Staging a Revolution: The Art of Persuasion in the Islamic Republic of Iran*. New York: New York University Press.

Chiit, Bassem (2006) "Lebanon: Anger on the Streets as the Cedar Revolution Wilts." *Socialist Worker*, at: http://socialistworker.co.uk/art/8665/Lebanon%3A+anger+on+the+streets+as+the+Cedar+Revolution+wilts (accessed November 4, 2014).

Chiit, B. (2009a) "Intikhābāt 2009: Mashāhid min al-sirā' al-tabaqī fī Lubnān." *Al-Manshur*, May 13, at: http://al-manshour.org/node/143 (accessed December 3, 2011).

Chiit, B. (2009b) "Divisions confessionnelles et lutte de classe au Liban." *Que Faire?*, at: http://quefaire.lautre.net/Divisions-confessionnelles-et (accessed December 10, 2011).

Chiit, B. (2011) Member of the Socialist Forum, Interview October 2011, Beirut.

Chorev, Harel (2013) "Power, Tradition and Challenge: The Resilience of the Elite Shi'ite Families of Lebanon." *British Journal of Middle Eastern Studies*, Vol. 40, No. 3, pp. 305–23.

Choufi, Firas (2013) "Hezbollah's Black Shirts to Reappear on Beirut Streets?." *Al-Akhbar English*, at: http://english.al-akhbar.com/node/15447 (accessed November 15, 2014).

Civil Society Knowledge Center, Lebanon Support (2016) "EDL Workers," at: http://cskc.daleel-madani.org/party/edl-workers#footnote10_dcaafc2 (accessed June 20, 2016).

Cochrane, Paul (2010) "Who Owns the Banks Revealing the Hands Holding the Real Power in Lebanon." *Executive Magazine*, at: www.executive-magazine.com/business-finance/finance/who-owns-the-banks (accessed January 7, 2013).

Cochrane, P. (2012) "Turning Tragedy into Transformation." *Executive Magazine*, at: www.executive-magazine.com/real-estate-and-development/4951/turning-tragedy-into-transformation (accessed September 8, 2012).

Consultative Center for Studies and Documentation (CCSD) (2008a) *Mu'tamar Bāriss 3, qirā' fil-haythiyyāt wa al-natā'ij wa mulāhazhāt tafsīliyya 'ala barnāmaj al-hukuma.* Beirut: CCSD.

Consultative Center for Studies and Documentation (CCSD) (2008b) *'Aduān Tamuz, al-khassā'ir al-bashariyya wa al-iqtissādiyya wa al-bi'iyya, al-ma'unāt, wa taqwīm 'amaliyyāt i'āda al-i'mār.* Beirut: CCSD.

Consultative Center for Studies and Documentation (CCSD) (2009) *Al-tanmiyya al-iqtissādiyya—al ijtimā'iyya fī Lubnān.* Beirut: CCSD.

Consultative Center for Studies and Documentation (CCSD) (2012) *Conference Reform of Social Policies in Lebanon: From Selective Subsidy Towards Welfare State.* Beirut and Safir Hotel.

Corbeil, Alexander (2016) "Hezbollah is Learning in Russia." *Carnegie Endowment for International Peace*, at: http://carnegieendowment.org/sada/?fa=62896&mkt_tok=3RkMMJWWfF9wsRovva3JZKXonjHpfsX54uou UK6g38431UFwdcjKPmjr1YoFTMB0aPyQAgobGp5I5FEIQ7XYTLB2t60MW A%3D%3D (accessed February 26, 2016).

Corstange, Daniel (2012) "Vote Trafficking in Lebanon." *International Journal of Middle East Studies*, Vol. 44, Issue 3, pp. 483–505.

Credit Libanais (2014) "About Us," at: www.creditlibanais.com.lb/GroupProfile/AboutUs (accessed February 20, 2014).

Daher, Aurélie (2007) "Le Hezbollah et l'offensive israélienne de l'été 2006: Baalbek dans la guerre," in F. Mermier and E. Picard (eds), *Le Liban une guerre des 33 jours*. Paris: La Découverte, pp. 44–50.

Daher, A. (2008) "Al-Tufayli et la «révolte des affamés»," in S. Mervin (ed.) *Le Hezbollah: État des lieux*. Paris: Sindbad, Actes Sud and IFPO, pp. 273–76.

Daher, A. (2012) "Hezbollah face aux clans et aux grandes familles de la Bekaa Nord: les élections municipales de 2004 dans la ville de Baalbeck," in F. Mermier and S. Mervin (eds.), *Leaders et partisans au Liban*. Paris: Karthala, IFPO and IISMM, pp. 419–33.

Daher, A. (2014) *Le Hezbollah, mobilisation et pouvoir*. Paris: PUF.

Daher, Joseph (2016) "Reassessing Hizbullah's Socioeconomic Policies in Lebanon." *The Middle East Journal*, Vol. 70, No. 3, Summer 2016, pp. 399–418.

Dakhlallah, Farah and Matar, Dina (2006) "What It Means to Be Shiite in Lebanon: Al-Manar and the Imagined Community of Resistance." *Westminster Papers in Communication and Culture*, Vol. 3, No. 2, pp. 22–40.

The Daily Star (2010) "Fall in Lebanese Public Debt to GDP Ratio Spurs Rating Upgrades," at: www.dailystar.com.lb/Business/Lebanon/2010/Apr-01/61890-fall-in-lebanese-public-debt-to-gdp-ratio-spurs-rating-upgrades.ashx#axzz3InMF3iVl (accessed February 13, 2012).

The Daily Star (2012a) "Cabinet to Vote on Salary Hike Plans." January 20, at: www.dailystar.com.lb/Article.aspx?id=160242#axzz33Ci7SjuV (accessed January 20, 2012).

The Daily Star (2012b) "Top Hamas Official Visits Tehran." March 15, at: www.dailystar.com.lb/News/Middle-East/2012/Mar-15/166781-top-hamas-official-visits-tehran.ashx#axzz2ZaG9ZBM8 (accessed March 22, 2015).

The Daily Star (2013) "Hezbollah's Seven Assassinated Commanders," at: www.dailystar.com.lb/News/Lebanon-News/2013/Dec-05/239967-hezbollahs-seven-assassinated-commanders.ashx#axzz3JEjntDq5 (accessed November 15, 2013).

The Daily Star (2014a) "Hezbollah, Hamas Coordinating on the Ground: Official." July 12, at: www.dailystar.com.lb/News/Lebanon-News/2014/Jul-12/263640-hezbollah-hamas-coordinating-on-the-ground-official.ashx#ixzz37FNkctpr (accessed July 14, 2014).

The Daily Star (2014b) "EDL Warns of Power Disruption if Protests Continue." August 12, at: www.dailystar.com.lb/News/Lebanon-News/2014/Aug-12/266941-edl-workers-escalate-protest-declare-open-strike.ashx#axzz3AXVjvHw8 (accessed August 12, 2014).

The Daily Star (2014c) "Al-Mabarrat Launches 10-Year Development Strategy." May 6, at: www.dailystar.com.lb/News/Lebanon-News/2014/May-06/255494-al-mabarrat-launches-10-year-development-strategy.ashx#axzz3HYh6LM1w (accessed October 29, 2014).

The Daily Star (2014d) "Hezbollah puts Senior Operative on Trial for Treason." December 19, at: www.dailystar.com.lb/News/Lebanon-News/2014/Dec-

19/281619-hezbollah-puts-senior-operative-on-trial-for-treason.ashx#sthash. gFFIaEpj.dpuf (accessed December 22, 2014).

The Daily Star (2016a) "Gharib Crowned Head of Lebanese Communist Party." April 27, at: www.dailystar.com.lb/News/Lebanon-News/2016/Apr-27/349455- gharib-crowned-head-of-lebanese-communist-party.ashx# (accessed June 20, 2016).

The Daily Star (2016b) "Lebanon Communists Mark Labor Day with Call for Secular State." May 1, at: www.dailystar.com.lb/News/Lebanon-News/2016/ May-01/350097-lebanon-communists-mark-labor-day-with-calls-for-secular-state.ashx?utm_source=Magnet&utm_medium=Related%20Articles%20 widget&utm_campaign=Magnet%20tools (accessed June 20, 2016).

The Daily Star (2016c) "Communists Challenge Hezbollah Claim of Election Sweep in South Lebanon." May 23, at: www.dailystar.com.lb/News/ Lebanon-News/2016/May-23/353439-communists-challenge-hezbollah-claim-of-election-sweep-in-south-lebanon.ashx?utm_source=Magnet&utm_ medium =Recommended%20Articles%20widget&utm_campaign=Magne t%20tools (accessed June 20, 2016).

The Daily Star (2016d) "Lebanon's Authoritarian Class Destroying Country: Gharib." June 19, at: www.dailystar.com.lb/News/Lebanon-News/2016/ Jun-19/357784-lebanons-authoritarian-class-destroying-it-gharib.ashx? utm_source=Magnet&utm_medium=Related%20Articles%20widget&utm_ campaign=Magnet%20tools (accessed June 20, 2016).

The Daily Star (2016e) "EDL Workers Kick Off Two-Day Protest." June 23, at: www.dailystar.com.lb/News/Lebanon-News/2016/Jun-23/358466-edl-workers-kick-off-two-day-protest.ashx?utm_source=Magnet&utm_medium= Related%20Articles%20widget&utm_campaign=Magnet%20tools (accessed June 25, 2016).

Daou, Walid (2011) Member of the Socialist Forum. Interview October 2011, Beirut.

Daou, W. (2013) "Al-Haraka al-niqābiyya wa al'ummāliyya fī Lubnān, Tārikh min al-nidālāt wa al-intissārāt." *Al-Thawra al-Dā'ima*, Issue 3, at: http:// permanentrevolution-journal.org/ar/issue3/brief-history-oflabor-movement-lebanon#footnoteref12_950ex1l (accessed May 2, 2013).

Davison, John and Al-Khalidi, Suleiman (2016) "Hezbollah Targets Israeli Forces with Bomb, Israel Shells South Lebanon." *Reuters*, at: www.reuters.com/article/ us-lebanon-security-israel-idUSKBN0UI1C320160104 (accessed January 10, 2016).

Davis, Charles (2016) "Inside the Syrian Provincial Capital Where 200,000 Face Starvation." *The Daily Beast*, at: www.thedailybeast.com/articles/2016/02/10/ inside-the-syrian-provincial-capital-where-200-000-face-starvation. html?via=mobile&source=email (accessed February 12, 2016).

Deeb, Lara (2003) *An Enchanted Modern: Gender and Public Piety among Islamist Shi'i Muslims in Beirut* (PhD). Emory University.

Deeb, L. (2006) "Lebanese Shia Women Temporality and Piety." *ISIM Review* 18, pp. 32–33.

Deeb, L. (2009) "Emulating and/or embodying the Ideal: The Gendering of Temporal Frameworks and Islamic Role Models in Shi'i Lebanon." *American Ethnologist*, Vol. 36, No. 2, pp. 242–57.

Deeb, L. and Harb, Mona (2008) "Les autres pratiques de la résistance," in S. Mervin (ed.), *Le Hezbollah: État des lieux*. Paris: Sindbad, Actes Sud and IFPO, pp. 227–46.

Deeb, L. and Harb, M. (2009) "Politics, Culture, Religion: How Hizbullah is Constructing an Islamic Milieu in Lebanon." *Middle East Studies*, Vol. 43, No. 2, pp. 198–206.

Deeb, L. and Harb, H. (2011) "Culture as History and Landscape: Hizballah's Efforts to Shape an Islamic Milieu in Lebanon." *Arab Studies Journal*, Vol. XIX, No. 2, pp. 10–41.

Deeb, L. and Harb, M. (2013) *Leisurely Islam: Negotiating Geography and Morality in Shi'ite South Beirut*. Princeton, NJ and Oxford: Princeton University Press.

Deeb, M. (1988) "Shia Movements in Lebanon: Their Formation, Ideology, Social Basis, and Links with Iran and Syria." *Third World Quarterly*, Vol. 10, No. 2, pp. 683–98.

Deghanpisheh, B. (2014) "Special Report: The Fighters of Iraq Who Answer to Iran." *Reuters*, November 12, at: www.reuters.com/article/2014/11/12/us-mideast-crisis-militias-specialreport-idUSKCN0IW0ZA20141112#top (accessed November 13, 2014).

Democracy Now (2006) *Headlines*, at: www.democracynow.org/2006/7/20/headlines (accessed October 29, 2014).

Dettmer, Jamie (2013) "Hezbollah Prepares for Syria Showdown in al-Qalamoun." *The Daily Beast*, at: www.thedailybeast.com/articles/2013/10/29/hezbollah-prepares-for-syria-showdown-in-al-qalamoun.html (accessed November 30, 2013).

Diab, Afif (2012) "'Ala al-jabha: min al-biqa' al-gharbī ila mazāri' shab'ā." *Al-Akhbar*, at: www.al-akhbar.com/node/167211 (accessed September 17, 2012).

Dirani, Ahmad (2012) Independent trade unionist and works at the Lebanese Observatory for the Rights of Workers and Employees (LORWE). Interview April 2012, Beirut.

Dot Pouillard, Nicolas (2016) "Guerre au Hezbollah: le pari incertain de l'Arabie saoudite." *Middle East Eye*, at: www.middleeasteye.net/fr/opinions/guerre-au-hezbollah-le-pari-incertain-de-l-arabie-saoudite-311467344 (accessed March 20, 2016).

Drake, Bruce (2013) "As It Fights in Syria, Hezbollah Seen Unfavorably in Region." *Pew Research Center*, at: www.pewresearch.org/fact-tank/2013/06/07/as-it-fights-in-syria-hezbollah-seen-unfavorably-in-region/ (accessed November 15, 2014).

Dubar, Claude and Nasr, Salim (1976) *Les classes sociales*. Paris: Presses de la Fondation Nationale des Sciences Politiques.

Elali, Nadine (2012) "Lebanese Salafism." *Now Media*, at: https://now.mmedia. me/lb/en/nowspecials/nows_guide_to_lebanese_salafism_ (accessed July 20, 2012).

Executive Magazine (2013) "Half a Percent of Lebanese Adults Own Half the Country's Wealth," at: www.executive-magazine.com/millionaires-own-half-lebanese-wealth/ (accessed November 2, 2013).

Fadlallah, Abd al-Halim (2008) "Athar al-siyyāstayni al-māliyya wa al-naqdiyya 'ala al-tanmiyya fī Lubnān," in CCSD (ed.), *Al-mā'zk al-iqtissādi—al-ijtimā'i fī Lubnān wa khiyyārāt al-badīla*. Beirut: CCSD, pp. 37–67.

Fadlallah, A. al-Halim (2010) "Entretien avec Abd Al-Halim Fadlallah." *Confluences Méditerranée*, No. 76, pp. 113–16, at: www.cairn.info/revue-confluences-mediterranee-2011-1-page-113.htm (accessed June 3, 2012).

Fadlallah, A. al-Halim (2012a) Director of Hezbollah's Development Think Tank, the Consultative Centre for Studies and Documentation (CCSD). Interview January 2012, Beirut.

Fadlallah, A. al-Halim (2012b) Director of Hezbollah's Development Think Tank, the Consultative Centre for Studies and Documentation (CCSD). Interview June 2012, Beirut.

Fadllalah, H. (2015) *Hizb Allāh wa al-Dawla fī Lubnān—al-ru'iyya wa al-massār*. Beirut: Sharika al-matbu'āt lil-tawzi' lil-nashr sh.m.l.

Faour, Muhammad (1991) "The Demography of Lebanon: A Reappraisal." *Middle Eastern Studies*, Vol. 27, No. 4, pp. 631–41.

Farid, Sonia (2011) "Kuwaiti billionaire Nasser al-Kharafi is mourned widely." *Al-Arabiya News*, at: http://english.alarabiya.net/articles/2011/04/19/145958. html (accessed April 23, 2014).

Farrel, Shane (2012) "Hezbollah's Controversial Land Acquisition." *Now Media*, at: https://now.mmedia.me/lb/en/reportsfeatures/hezbollahs_controversial_land_acquisition (accessed January 30, 2012).

Farsoun, Karen and Farsoun, Samih (1974) "Class and Patterns of Association among Kinsmen in Contemporary Lebanon." *Anthropological Quarterly*, Vol. 47, No. 1, pp. 93–111.

Fayyad, Ali (2008a) "Mudakhal: al-iqtissād al-lubnānī bayn wāq' al-azma wa tumuhāt al-hal," in CCSD (ed.), *Al-mā'zk al-iqtissādi—al-ijtimā'i fī Lubnān wa khiyyārāt al-badīla*. Beirut: CCSD, pp.13–18.

Fayyad, Ali (2008b) Hezbollah MP and ex-director of the Consultative Centre for Studies and Documentation (CCSD). Interview August 2008, Beirut.

Fawaz, Mona (2004) "Action et idéologie dans les services: ONG islamiques dans la banlieue sud de Beyrouth," in S. Ben Néfissa, N. Abd al-Fattah, S. Hanafi, and C. Milani (eds), *ONG et Gouvernance dans le Monde Arabe*. Paris and Cairo: Cedej and Karthala, pp. 341–67.

Fawaz, M. (2007) "Beirut: The City as a Body Politic." *Isim Review*, No. 20, pp. 22–23.

Fawaz, M. (2009) "Hezbollah as Urban Planner? Questions To and From Planning Theory." *Planning Theory*, Vol. 8, No. 4, pp. 323–34.

Fawaz, M. (2011) "Hezbollah's Urban Plan. An interview with Mona Fawaz and Nasrin Himada." *Scapegoat*, Issue 1, pp. 8–11 and 27.

Fawaz, M. (2014) "The Politics of Property in Planning: Hezbollah's Reconstruction of Haret Hreik (Beirut, Lebanon) as Case Study." *International Journal of Urban and Regional Research*, Vol. 38, Issue 3, pp. 922–34.

Fawaz, M. and Harb, M. (2010) "Influencing the Politics of Reconstruction in Haret Hreik," in H. Al-Harithy (ed.), *Lessons in Post-War Reconstruction: Case Studies from Lebanon in the Aftermath of the 2006 War*. London: Routledge, pp. 21–45.

Firro, Kais M. (2003) *Inventing Lebanon: Nationalism and the State Under the Mandate*. London and New York: I. B. Tauris.

Firro, K.M. (2006) "Ethnicizing the Shiʿis in Mandatory Lebanon." *Middle Eastern Studies*, Vol. 42, No. 5, pp. 741–59.

Fontana, Benedetto (2008) "Hegemony and Power in Gramsci," in R. Howson and K. Smith (eds), *Hegemony: Studies in Consensus and Coercion*. Abingdon: Routledge, pp. 80–106.

Freedom and Justice Party (2011) "Election Program The Freedom and Justice Party," at: http://kurzman.unc.edu/files/2011/06/FJP_2011_English.pdf (accessed October 22, 2014).

Gambill, Gary (2007) "Islamist Groups in Lebanon." *Middle East Review of International Affairs*, Vol. 11, No. 4, pp. 38–57.

Gates, Carolyn (1989) *The Historical Role of Political Economy in the Development of Modern Lebanon*. Oxford and London: Center for Lebanese Studies and I.B. Tauris.

Gaspard, Fouad (2004) *A Political Economy of Lebanon, 1948–2002: The Limits of Laissez-Faire*. Leiden: Brill.

George, Susannah (2015) "This Is Not Your Father's Hezbollah," *Foreign Policy*, at: https://foreignpolicy.com/2015/01/15/this-is-not-your-fathers-hezbollah/?utm_content=buffer48664&utm_medium=social&utm_source=facebook.com&utm_campaign=buffer (accessed January 17, 2015).

Ghaddar Hanin (2013), "Racism and Indifference; Bassil as an Example." *Now Media*, at: https://now.mmedia.me/lb/en/commentaryanalysis/racism (accessed 20 June 20, 2014).

Ghaddar, Hanin (2014) "I do not have Two Faces … and the Law shall be the Judge." *Now Media*, at: https://now.mmedia.me/lb/en/commentaryanalysis/547158-i-do-not-have-two-faces-and-the-law-shall-be-the-judge (accessed May 15, 2014).

Ghaddar, Hanin (2016) "Hezbollah's Shiite Catch." *Now Media*, at: https://now.mmedia.me/lb/en/commentaryanalysis/566696-hezbollahs-shiite-catch (accessed March 6, 2016).

Gharib, Hanna (2012) the ex-President of Union Coordination committee and of the Union of High School Teachers in Lebanon, LCP member and new Secretary General of the party since April 2016. Interview June 2012, Beirut.

Ghobeyri Municipality (2013) "Qam'a mukhālafāt fī Ghubayrī," at: www.ghobeiry. gov.lb/?p=631 (accessed November 6, 2013).

El-Ghoul, Adnan (2004) "Nasrallah alleges Violent Protests linked to US Embassy." *The Daily Star*, at: http://beirut.indymedia.org/en/2004/05/1343.txt (accessed January 3, 2014).

Habib, Osama (2008) "Fneish wants to Spark Electricity Revival." *The Daily Star*, at: www.dailystar.com.lb/Business/Lebanon/2006/Jun-12/41911-fneish-wants-to-spark-electric-revival.ashx#axzz3AG2uM27W (accessed November 23, 2010).

Hackworth, Jason (2013) "Faith, Welfare and the Formation of the Modern American Right," in F. Gauthier and T. Martikainen (eds), *Religion in the Neoliberal Age, Political Economy and Modes Of Governance*. Aldeshot: Ashgate, pp. 91–108.

Haddad, Rabih (2015) "qatala wa jarha 'Hizb Allah' ... sari lil-ghāiyya." *Al-Modon*, at: www.almodon.com/politics/32eb7aa5-6e7e-4b3e-8245-e6ae017362dd (accessed April 30, 2015).

Haenni, Patrick (2005) *L'Islam de marché, l'autre révolution conservatrice*. Paris: Seuil and République des Idées.

Al-Haf, Hassan (2012) "1992–2001: khatef istiqlāliyya al-haraka al-niqābiyya kayf sār 'al-ītihād al-'oumālī al-'ām' safran 'ala al-shmāl?." *Lebanese Labor Watch*, at: http://lebaneselw.com/node/7975 (accessed January 4, 2016).

Al-Hajj, Faten (2013) "Lebanon Labor Activists Discuss Union Reform." *Al-Akhbar English*, at: http://english.al-akhbar.com/content/lebanon-labor-activists-discuss-union-reform (accessed October 23, 2013).

Al-Hajj, F. (2014a) "Qawā'id al-mu'alimīn wa al-muwazifīn: al-tashīh intihār." *Al-Akhbar*, August 19, at: http://al-akhbar.com/node/213709 (accessed August 19, 2014).

Al-Hajj, F. (2014b) "Hay'at al-tansīq fi muwājaha al-siyyāssīn: lam tatruku lil-saleh mutrahān." *Al-Akhbar*, August 20, at: http://al-akhbar.com/node/213827 (accessed August 20, 2014).

Al-Hajj, George (2012) Head of the Federation of Unions of Banks' Employees. Interview May 2012, Beirut.

Al-Hajj, Hanna S. (2002) "Rijāl Al-Din wa Al-Intikhābāt," in Lebanese Center for Policy Studies (ed.), *Al-Intikhābāt Al-Niyyābiyya fī Lubnān 2000 bayn Al-I'Ada wa al-Taghīr*. Beirut: al-Markaz al-lubnānī lil-dirāssāt, pp. 143–216.

Hajj Georgiou, Michel (2012) "Cette pensée qu'on assassine impunément ...." *Orient Littéraire*, at: www.lorientlitteraire.com/article_details.php?cid=29&nid=3819 (accessed January 14, 2013).

Al-Hakim, Bassem, Baltayeb, Nourredine and Dirani, Zakia (2013) "Lebanon: Hezbollah Media Apologize to Bahrain Regime." *Al-Akhbar English*, at: http://

english.al-akhbar.com/content/lebanon-hezbollah-media-apologize-bahrain-regime (accessed December 11, 2013).

Halawi, Majed (1992) *A Lebanon Defied: Musa al-Sadr and the Shi'a*. Boulder, CO: Westview Press.

Hamadeh, Abdallah (2012) Head of the al-Wala transport federation linked to Hezbollah. Interview June 2012, Beirut.

Hamdan, Adnan (2012) "14 adhar tafuz bi-ri'āssa niqāba al-sayādila wa 6 a'dā' li-majlis al-idāra." *As-Safir*, at: http://m.assafir.com/content/135328866392 1226600/Special (accessed November 22, 2012).

Hamzeh, Ahmad N. (1993) "Lebanon's Hizbullah: From Islamic Revolution to Parliamentary Accommodation." *Third World Quarterly*, Vol.14, No. 2, pp. 321–37.

Hamzeh, A.N. (2004) *In the Path of Hizbullah*. Syracuse, NY: Syracuse University Press.

Hanieh, Adam (2011) *Capitalism and Class in the Gulf Arab States*. New York: Palgrave Macmillan.

Hanieh, A. (2013) *Lineages of Revolt, Issues of Contemporary Capitalism in the Middle East*. Chicago, IL: Haymarket Books.

Harb, M. (2002) "Tatbīqāt muqārana lil-mushārika fī baladatayini: Ghubayrī wa Burj al-Barājna," in Lebanese Center for Policy Studies (ed.), *Al-'amal al-baladī fī Lubnān*. Beirut: al-Markaz al-lubnānī lil-dirāssāt, pp. 125–55.

Harb, M. (2007) "Faith-Based Organizations as Effective Development Partners? Hezbollah and Post-War Reconstruction in Lebanon," in G. Clarke, M. Jennings and T.M. Shaw (eds), *Development, Civil Society and Faith-Based Organizations Bridging the Sacred and the Secular*. New York: Palgrave Macmillan, pp. 240–68.

Harb, M. (2009) "La gestion du local par les maires du Hezbollah au Liban." *Revue Critique Internationale*, No. 42, pp. 57–72, at: www.cairn.info/revue-critique-internationale-2009-1-page-57.htm (accessed May 22, 2012).

Harb, M. (2010) *Le Hezbollah à Beyrouth (1985–2005), de la banlieue à la ville*. Paris and Beyrouth: Karthala and IFPO.

Harb, M. and Leenders, R. (2005) "Know The Enemy: Hizbullah, 'Terrorism' and the Politics of Perception." *Third World Quarterly*, Vol. 26, No. 1, pp. 173–97.

Harb el-Kak, Mona (1996) "Politiques urbaines dans la banlieue sud de Beyrouth." Beirut: Cahiers du CERMOC (Open Edition Books), at: http://books.openedition.org/ifpo/3586#bodyftn12 (accessed June 11, 2013).

Harik, Judith Palmer (1996) "Between Islam and the System: Popular Support for Lebanon's Hizbullah." *Journal of Conflict Resolution*, Vol. 40, No. 1, pp. 41–67.

Harik, Judith Palmer (2004) *Hezbollah: The Changing Face of Terrorism*. London: I.B. Tauris.

Hashem, Ali (2015) "al-quwa al-shī'īyya al-'irāqīyya tu'alin intassārihā 'ala 'dā'esh." *Al-Monitor*, at: www.al-monitor.com/pulse/ar/originals/2015/03/iraq-shiite-hezbollah-nujaba-victory-islamic-state.html (accessed March 25, 2015).

Hashem, Ali (2016) "Hamas and Iran: New Era, New Rules." *Al-Montitor*, at: www. al-monitor.com/pulse/originals/2016/02/iran-hamas-arab-spring-tehran-visit-repair-relations.html (accessed February 20, 2016).

El-Hassan, Jana (2013) "4,000 Hezbollah fighters reach rebel-held Aleppo: FSA." *The Daily Star*, at: www.dailystar.com.lb/News/Politics/2013/Jun-04/219388-4000-hezbollah-fighters-reach-rebel-held-aleppo-fsa.ashx#axzz3HjJLyY5b (accessed October 30, 2014).

Hassan, Nagham (2014) "Hāmel bitāqa al-Amīr: Amīr al-tassuq." *Inbaa Al-Akhbar*, at: www.inbaa.com/التسوق-أمير-أمير-بطاقة-حامل/ (accessed February 21, 2014).

Hazran, Yusri (2010) "The Rise of Politicized Shi'ite Religiosity and the Territorial State in Iraq and Lebanon." *Middle East Journal*, Vol. 64, No. 4, pp. 521–41.

Hersh, Joshua (2010) "Follow the Money." *The National*, at: www.thenational.ae/news/world/follow-the-money (accessed April 2, 2011).

Hersh, J. (2013) "Hezbollah Role in Syria Crisis Looks Poised to Grow." *The Huffington Post*, at: www.huffingtonpost.com/2013/02/22/hezbollah-syria-crisis_n_2741922.html (accessed October 30, 2014).

Hodeib, Mirella (2013a) "Cannabis gets Tacit Green Light—For Now." *The Daily Star*, August 2, at: www.dailystar.com.lb/News/Lebanon-News/2013/Aug-02/226006-cannabis-gets-tacit-green-light-for-now.ashx#ixzz20xKzOT10 (accessed August 5, 2013).

Hodeib, M. (2013b) "General Security on the Rise in Delicate Times." *The Daily Star*, August 23, at: www.dailystar.com.lb/News/Lebanon-News/2013/Aug-23/228366-general-security-on-the-rise-in-delicate-times.ashx#ixzz3JEnpIQsn (accessed November 15, 2014).

Al-Imdad (2014) at: http://alemdad.net/index.php (accessed February 21, 2014).

Indymedia Beirut (2004) "al-jaīsh al-lubnānī īartakab mujazara bi-haq al-'umāl," at: http://beirut.indymedia.org/ar/2004/06/1353.shtml (accessed March 15, 2015).

Al-Inmaa Engineering and Contracting (2013a) "Company Profile," at: www.alinmaa.com.lb/index2.php?id=acompany&name=Company (accessed June 9, 2013).

Al-Inmaa Engineering and Contracting (2013b) "Project Name: Al Mahdi School- Hadath- 411- 2009," at: www.alinmaa.com.lb/index3.php?id=projects&subid=85&name=Al%20Mahdi%20School-%20Hadath-%20411-%202009&cid=specification (accessed June 20, 2013).

Al-Inmaa Engineering and Contracting (2013c) "Project Name: Al Noor Radio Station- Haret Hreik- 2177- 2010," at: www.alinmaa.com.lb/index3.php?id=projects&subid=104&name=Al%20Noor%20Radio%20Station-%20Haret%20Hreik-%202177-%202010&cid=specification (accessed June 21, 2013).

Al-Inmaa Engineering and Contracting (2013d) "Project Name: Maxime Restaurant in Dubai, KSA," at: www.alinmaa.com.lb/index3.php?id=projects&subid=123 (accessed June 22, 2013).

Al-Insaniyyah (2009) "Note: A Discipline Hezbollah." *Al-Insaniyyah*, September 18, at: http://al-insaniyyah.blogspot.ch (accessed February 20, 2013).

Integrated Regional Information Networks (IRIN) (2013) "Ten Ways to Develop Southern Lebanon," at: www.irinnews.org/report/97488/ten-ways-to-develop-southern-lebanon (accessed February 25, 2013).

Internal Displacement Monitoring Centre (2006) "Israel: End of Lebanon Fighting Allows Displaced Israelis to Go Home." *Norwegian Refugee Council*, at: www.refworld.org/pdfid/4517b0344.pdf (accessed October 31, 2014).

Internal Displacement Monitoring Centre (2010) "Yemen: IDPs Facing International Neglect," at: www.internal-displacement.org/assets/library/Middle-East/Yemen/pdf/Yemen-August-2010.pdf (accessed June 3, 2015).

International Center for Transitional Justice (2013) "Lebanon's Legacy of Political Violence, a mapping of serious violations of International Human rights and Humanitarian Law in Lebanon, 1975–2008," at: www.ictj.org/sites/default/files/ICTJ-Report-Lebanon-Mapping-2013-EN_0.pdf (accessed October 30, 2014).

International Crisis Group (ICG) (2003) "Hizbollah: Rebel Without a Cause?," at: www.crisisgroup.org/~/media/Files/Middle%20East%20North%20Africa/Iraq%20Syria%20Lebanon/Lebanon/B007%20Hizbollah%20Rebel%20Without%20A%20Cause.pdf (accessed September 11, 2010).

International Crisis Group (ICG) (2007) "Le Hezbollah et la crise libanaise, Rapport Moyen Orient N°69," at: www.crisisgroup.org/~/media/Files/Middle%20East%20North%20Africa/Iraq%20Syria%20Lebanon/Lebanon/69_hizbollah_and_the_lebanese_crisis_french.pdf (accessed November 11, 2010).

International Crisis Group (ICG) (2008) "Lebanon: Hizbollah's Weapons Turn Inward," at: www.crisisgroup.org/~/media/Files/Middle%20East%20North%20Africa/Iraq%20Syria%20Lebanon/Lebanon/b23_lebanon_hizbollahs_weapons_turn_inward.pdf (accessed November 11, 2010).

International Crisis Group (ICG) (2010) "Lebanon's Politics: the Sunni community and Hariri's Future Current," at: www.crisisgroup.org/~/media/Files/Middle%20East%20North%20Africa/Iraq%20Syria%20Lebanon/Lebanon/96%20Lebanons%20Politics%20-%20The%20Sunni%20Community%20and%20Hariris%20Future%20Current.ashx (accessed February 11, 2011).

International Crisis Group (ICG) (2014) "Lebanon's Hizbollah Turns Eastward to Syria," at: www.crisisgroup.org/~/media/Files/Middle%20East%20North%20Africa/Iraq%20Syria%20Lebanon/Lebanon/153-lebanon-s-hizbollah-turns-eastward-to-syria.pdf (accessed May 30, 2014).

International Crisis Group (ICG) (2015) "Lebanon's Self-Defeating Survival Strategies," at: www.crisisgroup.org/~/media/Files/Middle%20East%20North%20Africa/Iraq%20Syria%20Lebanon/Lebanon/160-lebanon-s-self-defeating-survival-strategies.pdf (accessed September 20, 2015).

Investment Development Authority of Lebanon (IDAL) (2011) "Annual Report 2010," at: http://investinlebanon.gov.lb/Content/uploads/Publication/121211013523594~Annual%20Report%202010.pdf (accessed October 3, 2011).

Investment Development Authority of Lebanon (IDAL) Report (2013) "Invest in Lebanon Guide, Lebanon at a Glance," at: http://investinlebanon.gov.lb/Content/uploads/Publication/130604043814366~Lebanon%20at%20a%20Glance.pdf (accessed March 7, 2014).

Irving, Sarah (2009) "Lebanon's Politics of Real Estate." *Electronic Intifada*, at: http://electronicintifada.net/content/lebanons-politics-real-estate/8412 (accessed January 30, 2011).

Issacharoff, A., Khoury, J. and Pfeffer, A. (2011) "IDF on High Alert as Palestinians Prepare for Naksa Day." *Haarertz*, at: www.haaretz.com/print-edition/news/idf-on-high-alert-as-palestinians-prepare-for-naksa-day-1.365945 (accessed November 30, 2011).

Issawi, Charles (1982) *An Economic History of the Middle East and North Africa.* New York: Columbia University Press.

Itani, Fouad (2014) "Haythu iufashil Nasr Allāh." *Now Media*, at: https://now.mmedia.me/lb/ar/analysisar/559886-حيث-يفشل-نصرالله (accessed August 11, 2014).

Ittihād al-Wafā' (2012) "Al-ittihād al-lubnānī lil-niqābāt al-siyyāhiyya," at: www.syndi-alwafaa.org/article.php?id=33&cid=132 (accessed July 20, 2012).

Ittihād al-Wafā' (2013), "Al-Hāj Hassan ra' itlāq al-ma'rad al-zirā'ī al-sādiss fi Ba'lbak: ma'ān sanabnī wa nuqāwim wa nastashad," at: www.syndi-alwafaa.org/article.php?id=1967&cid=129 (accessed May 8, 2013).

Ittihād al-Wafā' (2014a) "Ta'rīf bil-ittihād," at: www.syndi-alwafaa.org/article.php?id=211&cid=123 (accessed January 12, 2014).

Ittihād al-Wafā' (2014b) "Ittihād al-Walā'," at: www.syndi-alwafaa.org/article.php?id=21&cid=141 (accessed January 20, 2014).

Jaber, Hala (1997) *Hezbollah: Born with a Vengeance.* New York: Columbia University Press.

Jaber Group (2013) "About Us," at: www.jabergroup.com (accessed December 20, 2013).

Jam'iyya al-Ta'līm al-Dīnī al-Islāmī (2012) "Al-Tarbiyya al-dīniyya, al-ta'rīf," at: www.islamtd.org/essaydetails.php?pid=105&eid=17&cid=109 (accessed November 15, 2014).

Janoubia (2012) "Safi al-Dīn: ba'd al-anzima al-'arabiyya fashalet fī rihānihā bil-nīl min mashru' al-muqāwama fil-mintaqa," at: http://janoubia.com/26192 (accessed February 20, 2012).

Al-Jazeera (2011) "Washington tad'u Salih lil-Istijaba li-Sha'bihi," at: www.aljazeera.net/news/arabic/2011/3/2/واشنطن-تدعو-صالح-للاستجابة-لشعبه (accessed June 20, 2013).

Al-Jazeera (2016) "qāda Hizb Āllah al-qutala fī al-mustanqa' al-sūrī," at: www.aljazeera.net/multimedia/infograph/2016/5/15/قادة-حزب-الله-القتلى-في-المستنقع-السوري (accessed June 20, 2016).

Jihad al-Bina Development Association (2013) "nubdha," at: www.jihadbinaa.org.lb/essaydetails.php?eid=4934&cid=734#.VDKGd_2ztss (accessed August 30, 2013).

Jihad al-Bina' Ma'ān nabnī wa nuqāwim (2013) "dafa' al-ta'wīdāt al-īwā'," at: www.tarmeem.org.lb/datapages/rebuild/compensation1.htm (accessed January 20 2014).

Johnson, Michael (1986) *Class and Client in Sunni Beirut, the Sunni Muslim Community and the Lebanese State, 1940–1985.* London: Ithaca Press.

Jorish, Avi (2004) "Al-Manar: Hizbullah TV, 24/7." *The Washington Institute*, at: www.washingtoninstitute.org/policy-analysis/view/al-manar-hizbullah-tv-24-7 (accessed November 15, 2011).

Al-Kantar, Bassam (2013) "A Dreary Labor Day for Lebanon's Ailing Union." *Al-Akhbar English*, at: http://english.al-akhbar.com/content/dreary-labor-day-lebanon's-ailing-union (accessed May 1, 2013).

Katz, Muni and Pollack, Nadav (2015) "Hezbollah's Russian Military Education in Syria." *The Washington Institute for Near East Policy*, at: www.washingtoninstitute.org/policy-analysis/view/hezbollahs-russian-military-education-in-syria (accessed February 26, 2016).

Karim, H. (1998) "Al-intikhābāt al-niyyābiyya fī al-Janub," in Lebanese Center for Policy Studies (ed.) *Al-intikhābāt al-niyyābiyya 1996 wa azma al-dīmuqrātiyya fī Lubnān*, Beirut: al-Markaz al-lubnānī lil-dirāssāt, pp. 199–250.

Kassir, Samir (1994) *La guerre du Liban, de la dissension nationale au conflit regional.* Paris: Karthala.

Khaddaj, A. (2010a) "Politicization of Lebanese Labour Unions Turns Them into Political Tools of Influence." *Al-Shorfa*, June 26, at: http://al-shorfa.com/en_GB/articles/meii/features/main/2010/06/28/feature-01 (accessed June 30, 2014).

Khaddaj, A. (2010b) "Hizbullah Cars Entry into Beirut Airport Continues to Reverberate in Lebanon." *Al-Shorfa*, September 30, at: http://al-shorfa.com/en_GB/articles/meii/features/main/2010/09/30/feature-01 (accessed November 15, 2014).

Khalaf, Samir (1979) *Persistence and Change in 19th Century Lebanon.* Beirut: American University of Beirut Edition.

Khalifa, Sami (2016) "Nasr Āllah wa Badr Al-Dīn fī ma'raka al-Dāhīyya al-baladīyya." *Al-Modon*, at: www.almodon.com/politics/2016/5/15/معركة-الضاحية-البلدية-طريق-القدس-يمر-بالغبيري (accessed May 16, 2016).

Khalil, Amal (2013a) "Hezbollah and Hamas Still Not Ready to Meet Face-to-Face." *Al-Akhbar English*, October 11, at: http://english.al-akhbar.com/content/hezbollah-and-hamas-still-not-ready-meet-face-face?utm_source=feedburner&utm_medium=feed&utm_campaign=Feed%3A+AlAkhbarEnglish+(Al+Akhbar+English) (accessed January 7, 2014).

Khalil, Amal (2013b) "Ashura Threats Heighten South Lebanon Security." *Al-Akhbar English*, November 7, at: http://english.al-akhbar.com/content/ashura-threats-heighten-south-lebanon-security (accessed November 7, 2013).

Al-Khansa, Muhammad (2010) "Ra'īs baladiyya al-Ghubayrī Muhammad Sa'īd Al-Khansā li"al-amāna: 'amalunā lama yanfa' al-nāss." *Al-'Amal al-Baladī*, at:

www.amal-baladi.org/essaydetails.php?eid=87&cid=57 (accessed January 12, 2012).

Al-Khansa, Muhammad (2012) Mayor of Ghobeyri and Hezbollah member, Interview January 2012, Ghobeyri, Beirut.

Khatib, Lina (2014) "Hizbullah's Political Strategy," in L. Khatib, D. Matar and A. Alshaer (eds), *The Hizbullah Phenomenon, Politics and Communication*. London: Hurst and Company, pp. 71–118.

Khatib, Lina, Matar, Dina and Alshaer, Atef (2014) *The Hizbullah Phenomenon, Politics and Communication*. London and New York: Hurst and Oxford University Press.

Khomeini, Ruhollah (2001) *The Position of Women from the Viewpoint of Imam Khomeini*. Teheran: The Institute for Compilation and Publication of Imam Khomeini's Works (International Affairs Division), at: www.iranchamber.com/history/rkhomeini/books/women_position_khomeini.pdf (accessed February 20, 2012).

Khoury, Doreen (2013a) "Lebanon and the Syria Conflict: Between State Paralysis and Civil War." *Heinrich Boll Stiftung*, July 24, at http://lb.boell.org/en/2013/07/24/lebanon-and-syria-conflict-between-state-paralysis-and-civil-war (accessed October 30, 2014).

Khoury, D. (2013b) "Women's Political Participation in Lebanon." *Heinrich Boll Stiftung*, July 25, at: www.boell.de/de/node/277616 (accessed July 25, 2013).

Khoury, Philipp S. (1981) "Factionalism among Syrian Nationalists during the French Mandate." *International Journal of Middle East Studies*, Vol. 13, No. 4, pp. 441–69.

Khraiche, Dana (2012) "Lebanon Pharma Company Denies Involvement in Illegal Meds." *The Daily Star*, at: www.dailystar.com.lb/News/Lebanon-News/2012/Nov-12/194780-lebanon-pharma-company-denies-involvement-in-illegal-meds.ashx#axzz2zcnyV8iM (accessed November 12, 2012).

Khraiche, D. (2014) "Nasrallah: Hezbollah Achieving 'Great Victory' in Syria." *The Daily Star*, at: www.dailystar.com.lb/News/Lebanon-News/2014/Nov-04/276471-nasrallah-says-hezbollah-rockets-can-reach-all-of-israel.ashx#ixzz3I6v1xofM (accessed November 4, 2014).

Kostrz, Marie (2016) "Le Hezbollah maître du jeu libanais." *Le Monde Diplomatique*, at: www.monde-diplomatique.fr/2016/04/KOSTRZ/55214 (accessed May 3, 2016).

La Famille (2014) at: http://lafamille-lb.org/#services (accessed August 20, 2014).

Labaki, Boutros (1988a) *Education et mobilité sociale dans la société multicommunautaire du Liban: approche socio-historique*. Frankfurt: Deutsches Institut fur Internationale Padagogische Forschung.

Labaki, B. (1988b) "L'économie politique du Liban indépendant, 1943–1975," in H.D. Mills and N. Shehade (eds), *Lebanon: A History of Consensus and Conflict*. Oxford: I.B. Tauris, pp. 166–80.

Ladki, Nadim (2008), "Hezbollah says Beirut Government Declares War." *Reuters*, at: http://in.reuters.com/article/2008/05/08/idINIndia-33479120080508 (accessed November 30, 2013).

Lambert, Imogen (2016) "Hamas Announces 'New Page of Cooperation' with Iran." *Al-Araby*, at: www.alaraby.co.uk/english/indepth/2016/2/19/hamas-announces-new-page-of-cooperation-with-iran (accessed February 20, 2016).

Lamloum, Olfa (2008a) "Le Hezbollah au miroir de ses medias," in S. Mervin (ed.), *Le Hezbollah: État des lieux*. Paris: Sindbad, Actes Sud and IFPO, pp. 21–45.

Lamloum, O. (2008b) "La Syrie et le Hezbollah: partenaire sous contrainte?," in S. Mervin (ed.), *Le Hezbollah: État des lieux*. Paris: Sindbad, Actes Sud and IFPO, pp. 93–101.

Lamloum, O. (2009a) "L'histoire sociale du Hezbollah à travers ses medias." *Politix*, No. 87, pp. 169–87, at: www.cairn.info/revue-politix-2009-3-page-169.htm (accessed September 5, 2012).

Lamloum, O. (2009b) "Al-Manār, pilier du dispositif communicationnel du Hezbollah." *Confluences Méditerranée*, No. 69, pp. 61–70, at: www.cairn.info/revue-confluences-mediterranee-2009-2-page-61.htm (accessed May 3, 2012).

Le Thomas, Catherine (2008) "Formation et socialisation: un projet de (contre) société," in S. Mervin (ed.), *Le Hezbollah: État des lieux*. Paris: Sindbad, Actes Sud and IFPO, pp. 147–71.

Le Thomas, C. (2012a) *Les écoles chiites au Liban*. Paris: Karthala-IFPO.

Le Thomas, C. (2012b) "Le paysage scout chiite," in F. Mermier and S. Mervin (eds) *Leaders et Partisans au Liban*. Paris: Karthala, IFPO, IISMM, pp. 285–304.

Lebanese Dentist Association (2014) "Board of Directors," at: www.lda.org.lb/board.aspx (accessed March 15, 2014).

Lebanese Election Data (LEB) (2014) "Registered Voters by Confession," at: http://lebanonelectiondata.org/confessions.html (accessed March 18, 2014).

Lebanese Observatory of the Rights of Workers and Employees (LORWE) (2013a) "Mahmud Haydar: sanuhawil rawābitnā ila niqābāt wa hay'at al-tansīq ila ittihād mustaqil," at: http://lebaneselw.com/content/-محمود-حيدر-سنحوّل-روابطنا إلى-نقابات-و هيئة-التنسيق-إلى-اتحاد-مستقل (accessed May 7, 2013).

Lebanese Observatory of the Rights of Workers and Employees (LORWE) (2013b) "Al-taqrīr al-sanawī al-awal, al-ihtijājāt wa qadāyyā al-'ummāl fī Lubnān 'ām 2012." *Daleel Madani*, at: http://daleel-madani.org/sites/default/files/report-marsad.pdf (accessed November 20, 2013).

Leichtman, Mara L. (2010) "Migration War, and the Making of a Transnational Lebanese Shi'a Community in Senegal." *International Journal Middle East Studies*, Vol. 42, Issue 2, pp. 269–90.

Lefèvre, Raphaël (2013) *The Ashes of Hama: The Muslim Brotherhoods in Syria*. London: C. Hurst and Co.

Leroy, Didier (2015) *Le Hezbollah libanais: De la révolution iranienne à la guerre syrienne*. Paris: L'Harmattan.

Levitt, Matthew (2013) "On a Military Wing and a Prayer." *The Washington Institute*, at: www.washingtoninstitute.org/policy-analysis/view/on-a-military-wing-and-a-prayer (accessed December 13, 2013).

Libcom (2004) "'Leaded/Unleaded'—The Story of the 2004 Beirut General Strike Now Online," at: https://libcom.org/news/article.php/beirut-general-strike-2004-dvd-0106 (accessed January 2, 2014).

Louër, Laurence (2008) *Chiisme et politique au moyen-orient, Iran, Irak, Liban, monarchies du Golfe*. Paris: Autrement.

Lynch, Sarah (2010),"Who is Jamil as-Sayyed?." *Now Media*, at: https://now.mmedia.me/lb/en/reportsfeatures/who_is_jamil_as-sayyed (accessed November 15, 2014).

Macdonald, Samuel C. (2012) *The 2006 War in Lebanon: A Marxist Explanation* (Masters), University of Otago.

Maghnayir, Eljah (2016) "dimashq tas'a li-I'lān al-Lādhiqīyya… 'āwal muhāfazh muharara." *al-Rai Media*, at: www.alraimedia.com/ar/article/special-reports/2016/01/26/652332/nr/syria (accessed June 20, 2016).

Al-Mahdi (2012) "Hafl iftitāh qā'a al-shahīd al-Sayyīd Muhammad Bāqr Al-Sadr," at: www.almahdischools.org/newsite/_ihtifalat.php?filename=201202140913260 (accessed February 20, 2014).

Majed, Rayan (2014) "Failing to Stand Against Domestic Violence." *Now Media*, at: https://now.mmedia.me/lb/en/reportsfeatures/541140-failing-to-stand-against-domestic-violence (accessed March 28, 2014).

Makdissi, Samir (2004) *Lessons of Lebanon: The Economics of War and Development*. London: I.B. Tauris.

Makdissi, Ussama (1996) "Reconstructing the Nation-State: The Modernity of Secularism in Lebanon." *MERIP*, at: www.merip.org/mer/mer200/modernity-sectarianism-lebanon (accessed June 16, 2012).

Makdissi, U. (2000) *The Culture of Sectarianism, Community, History and Violence in Nineteeth-Century Ottoman Lebanon*. Berkeley and Los Angeles, CA: University of California Press.

Mallat, Chibli (1988) "Religious Militancy in Contemporary Iraq: Muhammad Baqer as-Sadr and the Sunni-Shia Paradigm." *Third World Quarterly*, Vol. 10, No. 2, pp. 699–729.

Mallat, Raymond (1973) *Seventy Years of Money Mudding in Lebanon*. Beirut: Aleph.

Al-Manar (2012a) "Al-Sayyīd Nasr Allāh: mutamasikun bil-silāh .. wa sanathā'ru li-mughniyya thārān mucharifān." February 16, at: www.almanar.com.lb/adetails.php?eid=185439 (accessed November 30, 2013).

Al-Manar (2012b) "Kalima al-Sayyīd Nasr Allāh fī ihtifāl 'al-Wa'd al-ajmal' ba'd ikhtitām a'māl 'mashru' Wa'd."' May 11, at: www.almanar.com.lb/adetails.php?eid=234499 (accessed October 3, 2013).

Al-Manar (2013a) "Nuss khitāb al-Sayyīd Nasr Allāh fī zikra 'Ashurā' fī mal'ab al-rāiyya fī al-Dāhiyya al-janubiyya." November 25, at: www.almanar.com.lb/adetails.php?eid=356806 (accessed November 3, 2014).

Al-Manar (2013b) "Nuss muqābila al-amīn al-Sayyīd Nasr Allāh ma' qanā 'OTV' dhumna barnamaj 'balā hasāna."" December 3, at: www.manartv.com. lb/adetails.php?fromval=2&cid=19&frid=21&seccatid=19&eid=667137 (accessed December 6, 2013).

Al-Manar (2014) "Sayyed Nasrallah Receives Maliki: Defeating ISIL 'Inevitable," at: www.almanar.com.lb/english/adetails.php?eid=183720&cid=23&fromval=1&frid=23&seccatid=14&s1=1 (accessed February 2, 2015).

Al-Manar TV (2014), "Sharika Me'amâr lil-handassa," at: http://program.almanar. com.lb/pdetails.php?pid=3647&eid=93641&wid=3177 (accessed January 20, 2015).

Al-Manar (2015) "Hamas Military Chief, Haniyeh Condole Sayyed Nasrallah on Hezbollah Martyrs," at: www.almanar.com.lb/english/wapadetails. php?eid=191794 (accessed January 22, 2015).

Al-Manar (2016a), "al-nas al-kāmil li-kalima al-Sayyīd Nasr Allāh fī ūsbū' al-shahīd al-qa''id 'Alī Ahmad faīyyād." March 6, at: www.almanar.com.lb/ adetails.php?eid=1443891 (accessed March 20, 2016).

Al-Manar (2016b) "al-Sayyīd Nasr Allāh: al-difā' 'an Halab huwa difā' 'an Lubnān wa Sūrīyyā wa al-'irāq." *al-Manar*, June 25, at: www.almanar.com.lb/adetails. php?eid=1443891 (accessed June 25, 2016).

Manifesto 2009 (2009) "The New Hezbollah Manifesto." *Lebanon Renaissance*, at: www.lebanonrenaissance.org/assets/Uploads/15-The-New-Hezbollah-Manifesto-Nov09.pdf (accessed September 13, 2010).

Al-Manshour (2004) "Leaded/Unleaded," at: www.youtube.com/watch?v=fCN9LAfmppM (accessed January 12, 2013).

March 14 Website (2010) "Al-sira al-dhātiyya li-'udu majlis baladiyya Bayrut Fādī 'Ali Shahrur," at: www.14march.org/news-details.php?nid=MjE3MTU3 (accessed January 21, 2014).

Markaz Athār al-Shuhadā' (2014) "min nahnu," at: http://atharshohada.org/ modules.php?name=News&file=article&sid=86 (accessed April 20, 2014).

Marot, Bruno (2012) "The "Old Rent" Law in Beirut: An Incentive or Disincentive for Gentrification?." *Les Carnets de l'IFPO*, at: http://ifpo.hypotheses.org/4376 (accessed October 21, 2012).

Marty, Martin E. (1988) "Fundamentalism as a Social Phenomenon." *Bulletin of the American Academy of Arts and Sciences*, Vol. 42, No. 2, pp. 15–29.

Matabadal, Ashwin (2012) "RadoBank Country Report Lebanon." *Economics RadoBank*, at: https://economics.rabobank.com/PageFiles/6817/Lebanon-201201%20(1).pdf (accessed March 11, 2012).

Al-Mayadeen (2015) "Al-Sayyīd Nasr Allāh lil-Mayyādīn; sārukh 'fāteh 110' tirāz qadīm muqārana bimā numlikuhu al-yawm," at: www.almayadeen.net/ar/ news/lebanon-nTCX90g_DkKCoaQhATmO3A/--السيد-نصر الله-للميادين--صاروخ- فاتح---110طراز-قديم-مقارنة- (accessed January 17, 2015).

Al-Mayadeen (2016) "Hiwār shāmil ma' nā'ib al-āmīn al-'ām li-hizb Allāh al-shaīkh na'īm qāssim 'al-juzzo al-thānī," at: www.almayadeen.net/Programs/

حوار-شامل-مع-نائب-الأمين-العام-لحزب-الله-/Episode/TssmbjTMToWQDYXz,JnkWA
الشيخ-نعيم-قاسم-ال-- (accessed January 10, 2016).

Meamar (2014) "M'amār tahtafilu bil-iubīl al-fudī," at: www.meamar.com.lb/
article.php?id=118&cid=168#.Uo6mvv2ztss (accessed April 22, 2014).

Mehio, Saad (2002) "Prime Minister Alwaleed bin Talal? For What?," *The Daily Star*, at: www.dailystar.com.lb/News/Lebanon-News/2002/Jul-09/35992-prime-minister-alwaleed-bin-talal-for-what.ashx#axzz2sp8JTTPd (accessed January 11, 2012).

MEMRI TV (2006) "Hizbullah Leader Hassan Nasrallah: Implementing Khomeini's Fatwa against Salman Rushdie Would Have Prevented Current Insults to Prophet Muhammad; The Great French Philosopher Roger Garaudy Proved that the Holocaust Is a Myth, Al-Jazeera TV, Al-Manar—February 3, 2006," at: www.memritv.org/clip/en/1023.htm (accessed November 20, 2011).

Merhi, Nada (2012) "La honte au Parlement: le projet de loi sur la protection de la femme revu à la baisse." *Orient le Jour*, at: www.lorientlejour.com/article/748800/La_honte_au_Parlement+%3A_le_projet_de_loi_sur_la_protection_de_la_femme_revu_a_la_baisse.html (accessed March 8, 2012).

Merhi, Zeinab (2012) "Hezbollah's Unorthodox Fans." *Al-Akhbar English*, at: http://english.al-akhbar.com/content/hezbollah's-unorthodox-fans (accessed May 20, 2012).

Mervin, Sabrina (2007) "Débats intelectuels transnationaux," in S. Mervin (ed.), *Les mondes chiites et l'Iran*. Paris and Beyrouth: Karthala and IFPO, pp. 301–26.

Mervin, S. (2008a) "Le lien Iranien," in S. Mervin (ed.), *Le Hezbollah: État des lieux*. Paris: Sindbad, Actes Sud and IFPO, pp. 75–87.

Mervin, S. (2008b) "Muhammad Hussein Fadlallah, du guide spirituel au marja moderniste," in S. Mervin S (ed.). *Le Hezbollah: État des lieux*. Paris: Sindbad, Actes Sud and IFPO, pp. 277–85.

Metal Bulletin Company Database (2013) "Shar Metal Trading Co SARL," at: www.mbdatabase.com/Basic-Information/SharMetalTradingCoSARL/52368 (accessed September 21, 2013).

Mikaelian S. (2015) "Overlapping Domestic/Geopolitical Contests, Hizbullah, and Sectarianism," in J. Al-Habbal, R. Barakat, L. Khattab, S. Mikaelian and B. Salloukh (eds), *The Politics of Sectarianism in Postwar Lebanon*. London: Pluto Press, pp. 155–73.

Middle East Eye (2014) "'Mossad Agent' was in Charge of Security for Hezbollah's Hassan Nasrallah," at: www.middleeasteye.net/news/mossad-agent-was-charge-security-hezbollahs-hassan-nasrallah-128010033#sthash.AH8IPmPo.dpuf (accessed December 28, 2014).

Middle East Monitor (2015a) "Yemen's Saleh Netted $60bn through Corruption." February 25, at: www.middleeastmonitor.com/news/middle-east/17179-yemens-saleh-netted-60bn-through-corruption (accessed September 2, 2015).

Middle East Monitor (2015b) "Hamas and Hezbollah agree to Protect Palestinians in Lebanon." November 23, at: www.middleeastmonitor.com/20151123-

hamas-and-hezbollah-agree-to-protect-palestinians-in-lebanon/ (accessed December 2, 2015).

Mieu, Baudelaire (2009) "L'imam libanais lâché par les Ivoiriens." *Jeune Afrique*, at: www.jeuneafrique.com/Article/ARTJAJA2536-37p076-077.xml5/expulsion-imam-abdul-menhem-kobeissil-imam-libanais-lache-par-les-ivoiriens.html (accessed February 2, 2012).

Mohieddine, Youssef (2012) President of the Federation of Agriculture in Lebanon. Interview May 2012, Chtaura.

Mohsen, Ahmad (2012) "Maqāhi Al-Dāhiyya ba'd al-harb: 'nusf hadātha'... mahajna bil-a'rāf." *Al-Akhbar*, at: www.al-akhbar.com/node/64469 (accessed May 27, 2012).

Al-Monitor (2013) "Hezbollah Again Postpones General Congress," at: www.al-monitor.com/pulse/originals/2013/03/hezbollah-delays-general-congress.html##ixzz2xixPoWnG (accessed March 20, 2013).

Al-Monitor (2014), "Hizb Allāh: Inshā' muqāwama dud 'al-Dawla al-Islāmiyya,'" at: www.al-monitor.com/pulse/ar/contents/articles/originals/2014/08/hezbollah-resistance-arsal-counter-islamic-state-attacks.html (accessed October 30, 2014).

Mortada, Radwan (2010) "'mu'arada' muhāmī Beirut: al-khissāra ma' sibaq al-āsrār," at: www.al-akhbar.com/node/37519 (accessed September 30, 2013).

Mouqaled, Diana (2013) "wizarā' al-qamisān al-sud." *Al-sharq al-awsat*, at: http://classic.aawsat.com/leader.asp?section=3&issueno=12536&article=722109#.VGeN1d7A1su (accessed November 15, 2014).

Moushref, Aicha (2008) "Forgotten Akkar. Socio-Economic Reality of the Akkar Region." *Mada Association*, at: www.policylebanon.org/Modules/Ressources/Ressources/UploadFile/4261_02,03,YYMADA_Forgotten_Akkar_SocioEconomicReality_Jan08.pdf (accessed October 23, 2013).

Al-Mualim, Jihad (2012) Head of the Federation of Workers and Employees in the Bekaa and LCP member. Interview May 2012, Beirut.

Mucci, Alberto (2014) "Hezbollah Profits from Hash as Syria Goes to Pot." *The Daily Beast*, at: www.thedailybeast.com/articles/2014/07/09/hezbollah-profits-from-hash-as-syria-goes-to-pot.html (accessed November 25, 2015).

Al-Muntada al-Ishtirākī (2012) *Tashīh al-ujur wa ist'asa'a al-nizām al-lubnānī*, pp. 4–8.

Al-Muqāwama al-Islāmiyya (2011a) "Maharjān hāshed li-Hizb Allāh fī al-Nabī Shīt fī 'aīd al-muqāwama wa al-tahrīr 2011." May 25, at: www.moqawama.org/essaydetails.php?eid=20819&cid=141#.VHrhTN7A1ss (accessed February 12, 2012).

Al-Muqāwama al-Islāmiyya (2011b) "Al-Amīn al-'ām li-Hizb Allāh: tumuhanā an taqum dawla Falestīn 'ala kāmil turābihā wa mā nushihduhu fī Misr min da'm li-Falestīn mu'ashir 'ala marhala jadīda." August 26, at: www.moqawama.org/essaydetails.php?eid=21598&cid=140#.VHrk6N7A1ss (accessed November 30, 2013).

Murtada, Radwan (2013) "Tafāsīl al-lahzhāt al-latī talet 'amaliyya īghtiyyāl al-shahīd hasān al-laqīs," *Al-Akhbār*, at: www.alhadathnews.net/archives/ 106397 (accessed January 24, 2014).

Al-Mustaqbal (2004) "Tawaqaf al-khadamāt al-Ārdiyya fī al-matār 3 sā'āt, īdrāb wa i'tisāmāt al-yawm fī Bayrūt wa al-manātiq yushārik fīhā al-'umāl wa hay'āt īqtisādiyya wa tarbawiyya," at: www.almustaqbal.com/v4/Article. aspx?Type=np&Articleid=67061 (accessed 8 January 8, 2012).

Naharnet (2012) "Berri-Aoun Differences Linger over EDL Crisis," at: http://m. naharnet.com/stories/en/48391-berri-aoun-differences-linger-over-edl-crisis (accessed January 23, 2013).

Naharnet (2013) "Al-Asaad Claims Receiving Death Threat, Holds Nasrallah and State Responsible for Salman's Murder." June 16, at: www.naharnet.com/stories/ en/87118 (accessed January 11, 2014).

Nahas, Charbel (2012) Ex-Minister of Labor and Telecommunication. Interview July 2012, Beirut.

Najib Miqati Official Website (2013) "Biography," at: www.najib-mikati.net/EN/ NajibMikati (accessed December 13, 2013).

Nakhoul, Samia (2013) "Special Report: Hezbollah Gambles All in Syria." *Reuters*, at: www.reuters.com/article/2013/09/26/us-syria-hezbollah-special-report-idUSBRE98P0AI20130926 (accessed November 5, 2014).

Nash, Matt (2008) "First Shots." *Now Media*, at: https://now.mmedia.me/lb/en/ commentaryanalysis/first_shots (accessed June 14, 2014).

Nashashibi, Sharif (2014) "Hizbollah's Advances in Syria Expose its Fragilties in Lebanon." *The National*, at: www.thenational.ae/thenationalconversation/ comment/hizbollahs-advances-in-syria-expose-its-frailties-in-lebanon#full (accessed March 19, 2014).

Nasnas, Roger (2007) *Le Liban de demain, Vers une vision économique et sociale.* Beirut: Dār An-Nahār.

Nasr, Muhammad (2011) "Mudīr 'ām sharika Arch lil-istishārāt al-handassiyya Walīd Jāber li 'al-amāna': nuqadimu al-istishārāt wa al-dirāssāt al-tawjīhiyya al-awaliyya lil-baladiyyāt majānā." *Al-'Amal al-Baladī*, at: http://amal-baladi. org/essaydetails.php?eid=181&cid=61 (accessed March 1, 2012).

Nasr, Salim (1978) "Backdrop to Civil War: The Crisis of Lebanese Capitalism." *MERIP Reports*, No. 73, pp. 3–13.

Nasr, S. (1985) "La transition des chiites vers Beyrouth: mutations sociales et mobilisation communautaires et espaces urbains au Machreq." *Centre d'études et de recherches sur le Moyen-Orient contemporain (CERMOC)*, (Open Edition Books), at: http://books.openedition.org/ifpo/3417?lang=fr (accessed July 11, 2012).

Nasr, S. (2003) "The New Social Map," in T. Hanf and N. Salam (eds), *Lebanon in Limbo: Postwar Society and State in an Uncertain Regional Environment.* Baden-Baden, Nomos Verlagsgesellschaft, pp. 143–58.

Nassif, Alfred (2012) President of the Federation of Proprietors of Kermel in the Bekaa, and Secretary President of the Federation of Agriculture in Lebanon. Interview July 2012, Chtaura.

Nassif, Samir (2014) "Hassan Fadl Allāh mutasaffihān arshīf 'Hizb Allāh.'" *Al-Akhbar*, at: www.al-akhbar.com/node/221253 (accessed December 27, 2014).

Nassif-Debs, Marie (2006) "Hezbollah en débat. Le point de vue du Parti communiste libanais. Entretien avec Marie Nassif-Debs." *Inprecor*, No. 521–22, at: http://ks3260355.kimsufi.com/inprecor/article-inprecor?id=125 (accessed October 3, 2014).

National News Agency (NNA) (2014a) "Hajj Hassan Congratulates Industrialists on % 50 Decrease Off Exports Tax." April 2, at: www.nna-leb.gov.lb/en/show-news/24454/Hajj-Hassan-congratulates-industrialists-on-50-decrease-off-exports-tax (accessed April 2, 2014).

National News Agency (NNA) (2014b) "Tenants Refuse New Rent Law, Call for a Sitin." April 3, at: www.nna-leb.gov.lb/en/show-news/24592/Tenants-refuse-new-rent-law-call-for-sitin (accessed April 3, 2014).

Naylor, Hugh (2014) "Lebanon's Once-Mighty Hezbollah is Facing Attacks in Syria—and also at Home." *Washington Post*, at: www.washingtonpost.com/world/middle_east/lebanons-once-mighty-hezbollah-is-facing-attacks-in-syria--and-also-at-home/2014/10/27/81cd75a4-9d26-4f9b-b843-9fa0814b2471_story.html (accessed October 30, 2014).

Nazzal, Mohamed (2013) "Lebanese Government Gives 'Blessed' Hashish a Break." *Al-Akhbar English*, at: http://english.al-akhbar.com/content/lebanese-government-gives-"blessed"-hashish-break (accessed September 14, 2013).

Nejm, Tareq (2010) "Kafrtabnīt bayn al-khuruj 'ala Berrī aw 'awda al-mutarudīn ila al-haraka... Hizb Allāh tadkhulu fī tarad al-mu'taridīn." *Farah News*, at: www.farah.net.au/news/id_11921 (accessed April 2, 2012).

Nerguizian A. (2015) "Between Sectarianism and Military Development: The Paradox of the Lebanese Armed Forces," in J. Al-Habbal, R. Barakat, L. Khattab, S. Mikaelian and B. Salloukh (eds), *The Politics of Sectarianism in Postwar Lebanon*. London: Pluto Press, pp. 108–35.

Nichols, Michelle (2016) "Rights Groups urge U.N. to put Saudi Yemen Coalition Back on Blacklist." *Reuters*, at: www.reuters.com/article/us-yemen-security-saudi-un-idUSKCN0YU2IJ (accessed June 10, 2016).

Nilsen, Alf Gunvald (2013) "Contesting the Postcolonial Development Project: A Marxist Perspective on Popular Resistance in the Narmada Valley," in C. Barker, L. Cox, J. Krinsky and A.G. Nilsen (eds), *Marxism and Social Movements*. Leiden: Brill, pp. 167–85.

Nizameddin, Talal (2006) "The Political Economy of Lebanon under Rafiq Hariri: An Interpretation." *Middle East Journal*, Vol. 60, No. 1, pp. 95–114.

Norton, Augustus R. (1987) *Amal and the Shi'a, Struggle for the Soul of Lebanon*. Austin, TX: University of Texas Press.

Norton, A.R. (2000) *Hizballah of Lebanon: Extremist Ideals vs. Mundane Politics*. New York: Council of Foreign Relations Press.

Norton, A.R. (2007) *Hezbollah a Short History*. Princeton, NJ: Princeton University Press.

Noujaim, Sandra (2012) "Qui est derrière les attaques contre les débits d'alcool au Liban-Sud?." *Orient le Jour*, at: www.lorientlejour.com/article/760938/Qui_est_derriere_les_attaques_contre_les_debits_d%27alcool_au_Liban-Sud_.html (accessed May 28, 2012).

Noujeim, S. (2014) "À Baalbeck-Hermel, l'art d'imposer des victoires." *Orient le Jour*, at: www.lorientlejour.com/article/985207/a-baalbeck-hermel-lart-dimposer-des-victoires.html (accessed May 13, 2016).

Noujeim, S. (2016) "La séance plénière trahit la supercherie de la gestion parlementaire." *Orient le Jour*, at: www.lorientlejour.com/article/861423/la-seance-pleniere-trahit-la-supercherie-de-la-gestion-parlementaire.html (accessed April 2, 2014).

Now Lebanon (2012) "Pharm Scandal Rocks Lebanon," at: https://now.mmedia.me/lb/en/nownews/pharm_scandal_rocks_lebanon_ (accessed November 12, 2012).

Now Media (2008a) "The Doha Agreement," at: https://now.mmedia.me/lb/en/reportsfeatures/the_doha_agreement (accessed October 30, 2014).

Now Media (2008b) "al-Āmīr wa Nūr." November 3, at: https://now.mmedia.me/lb/ar/nowspecialar/لأمير_ونور (accessed November 3, 2012).

Now Media (2010) "'Wahda Beirut' takrīssān lil-munāssifa fī Lubnān: Berrī wa al-Tashnāq indimā ... wa 'Awn inkafā nahwa 'al-Mukhtara'," at: https://now.mmedia.me/lb/ar/latestnews2ar/وحد_بيروت_تكريس_للمنصف_في_لبنن_بري_ولطشنق_نضم_وعون_نكفا_نحو_لمختر (accessed January 22, 2013).

Now Media (2011) "Future Movement, Hezbollah Candidate win Dental Association membership," at: https://now.mmedia.me/lb/en/nownews/future_movement_hezbollah_candidate_win_dental_association_membership (accessed February 2, 2012).

Now Media (2013) "Al-Arabiya: Hezbollah Fighters Killed in Ambush outside Damascus." April 9, at: https://now.mmedia.me/lb/en/archive/al-arabiya-hezbollah-fighters-killed-in-ambush-outside-damascus (accessed October 30, 2014).

Now Media (2016) "Anti-Hezbollah News Outlet Comes under Threat," at: https://now.mmedia.me/lb/en/NewsReports/566681-anti-hezbollah-news-outlet-comes-under-threat (accessed March 6, 2016).

Now Media and AFP (2013) "Syria Rebels say They have Lost Battle for Al-Qusayr," at: https://now.mmedia.me/lb/en/nowsyrialatestnews/syria-rebels-say-they-have-lost-battle-for-qusayr1 (accessed October 30, 2014).

Nsouli, Faisal N. (2007) *Privatization in Lebanon, Middle East Airlines* (PhD). Lebanese American University.

O'Bagy, Elizabeth (2013) "The Free Syrian Army." *Institute for the Study of War*, at: www.understandingwar.org/sites/default/files/The-Free-Syrian-Army-24MAR.pdf (accessed October 25, 2014).

Ohrstrom, Lysandra and Quilty, Jim (2007), "The Second Time as Farce, Stories of Another Lebanese Reconstruction." *MERIP*, No. 243, at: www.merip.org/mer/mer243/second-time-farce#_3_ (accessed August 12, 2013).

Orient le Jour (2011a) "Pour le Hezbollah, les soulèvements dans la région s'inscrivent dans le projet de la résistance." February 28, at: www.lorientlejour.com/article/691379/Pour_le_Hezbollah%2C_les_soulevements_dans_la_region_s%27inscrivent_dans_le_projet_de_la_resistance.html (accessed February 2, 2013).

Orient le Jour (2011b) "Le Hezbollah exprime une fois de plus son opposition au statut personnel civil." June 1, at: www.lorientlejour.com/article/706295/Le_Hezbollah_exprime_une_fois_de_plus_son_opposition_au_statut_personnel_civil.html (accessed June 1, 2011).

Orient le Jour (2011c) "Les camps commémorent la naksa dans le calme sous le slogan du droit au retour." June 6, at: www.lorientlejour.com/article/706984/Les_camps_commemorent_la_naksa_dans_le_calme_sous_le_slogan_du_droit_au_retour.html (accessed November 30, 2011).

Orient le Jour (2011d) "Le Hezbollah tente de fermer un débit de boissons à Houla: deux blessés du Parti communiste." July 25, at: www.lorientlejour.com/article/714515/Le_Hezbollah_tente_de_fermer_un_debit_de_boissons_a_Houla+%3A_deux_blesses_du_Parti_communiste.html (accessed July 25, 2011).

Orient le Jour (2011e) "Hausse des salaires: Mikati bat Nahas au vote." December 9, at: www.lorientlejour.com/article/735207/Hausse_des_salaires+%3A_Mikati_bat_Nahas_au_vote.html (accessed December 9, 2011).

Orient le Jour (2012a) "Le gouvernement approuve le réajustement des salaires suivant la formule proposée par le patronat et la CGTL." January 19, at: www.lorientlejour.com/article/740943/Le_gouvernement_approuve_le_reajustement_des_salaires_suivant_la_formule_proposee_par_le_patronat_et_la_CGTL.html (accessed January 19 2012).

Orient le Jour (2012b) "Le Hezbollah pour une loi électorale basée sur la proportionnelle." July 12, at: www.lorientlejour.com/article/767926/Le_Hezbollah_pour_une_loi_electorale_basee_sur_la_proportionnelle.html (accessed July 12, 2012).

Orient le Jour (2012c) "Abs lance le discours électoral aouniste: le Hezbollah 'couve des mafias' et Berry est 'un fromagiste corrompu.'" July 27, at: www.lorientlejour.com/article/770507/Abs_lance_le_discours_electoral_aouniste+%3A_le_Hezbollah_%3C%3C+couve_des_mafias+%3E%3E_et_Berry_est_%3C%3C+un_fromagiste_corrompu+%3E%3E.html (accessed July 27, 2012).

Orient le jour (2012d) "Trafic de médicaments: commission rogatoire contre le frère de Fneich." November 12, at: www.lorientlejour.com/article/787543/

Trafic_de_medicaments+%3A_commission_rogatoire_contre_le_frere_de_Fneich.html (accessed November 14, 2012).

Orient le Jour (2013a) "Le Hezbollah justifie son choix obligé du projet «orthodoxe»." February 25, at: www.lorientlejour.com/article/802349/Le_Hezbollah_justifie_son_choix_oblige_du_projet_%3C%3C+orthodoxe+%3E%3E.html (accessed February 25, 2013).

Orient le Jour (2013b) "Gharib déplore «le long métrage américain» de la grille des salaires." April 25, at: www.lorientlejour.com/article/811345/gharib-deplore-le-long-metrage-americain-de-la-grille-des-salaires.html (accessed April 25, 2013).

Orient le Jour (2013c) "Incident de Bir Hassan: vive indignation du 14 Mars, quasi-silence du 8 Mars." June 11, at: www.lorientlejour.com/article/818590/incident-de-bir-hassan-vive-indignation-du-14-mars-quasi-silence-du-8-mars.html (accessed June 11, 2013).

Orient le Jour (2013d) "L'ambassadeur du Qatar chez Naïm Kassem: le rapprochement se confirme entre Doha et le Hezbollah." December 18, at: www.lorientlejour.com/article/847080/lambassadeur-du-qatar-chez-naim-kassem-le-rapprochement-se-confirme-entre-doha-et-le-hezbollah.html (accessed December 18, 2013).

Orient le Jour (2014a) "Hayek: Le bilan du ministère de l'Agriculture est 'un échec'," at: www.lorientlejour.com/article/848951/hoayek-le-bilan-du-ministerede-lagriculture-est-un-echec-.html (accessed January 3, 2014).

Orient le Jour (2014b) "Khamenei, Facebook et Hussein Moussaoui...," at: www.lorientlejour.com/article/849679/khamenei-facebook-et-hussein-moussaoui.html (accessed January 9, 2014).

Orient le Jour (2014c) "Un journaliste anti-Hezbollah agressé à Saïda," at: www.lorientlejour.com/article/874817/un-journaliste-anti-hezbollah-agresse-a-saida.html (accessed July 6, 2014).

Orient le jour (2014d) "La légalisation des attestations approuvée, le Comité de coordination syndical envisage l'escalade." August 20, at: www.lorientlejour.com/article/881779/la-legalisation-des-attestations-approuvee-le-comite-de-coordination-syndical-envisage-lescalade.html (accessed August 20, 2014).

Orient le Jour (2014e) "Nasrallah: Ce n'est pas vrai que nous voulons entraîner le pays vers le vide...." November 4, at: www.lorientlejour.com/article/894398/nasrallah-ce-nest-pas-vrai-que-nous-voulons-entrainer-le-pays-vers-le-vide.html (accessed November 4, 2014).

Orient le Jour (2015a) "Le dialogue Futur-Hezbollah progresse lentement mais sûrement." January 17, at: www.lorientlejour.com/article/906353/le-dialogue-futur-hezbollah-progresse-lentement-mais-surement.html (accessed January 17, 2015).

Orient le Jour (2015b) "Exit Hanna Gharib." January 26, at: www.lorientlejour.com/article/907999/exit-hanna-gharib.html (accessed July 26, 2015).

Orient le Jour (2015c) " Hussein Moussaoui: Notre présence en Syrie et en Irak est un devoir recommandé par Dieu." July 28, at: www.lorientlejour.com/

article/936480/hussein-moussaoui-notre-presence-en-syrie-et-en-irak-est-un-devoir-recommande-par-dieu.html (accessed July 28, 2015).

Orient le Jour (2015d) "N. Moussaoui revient à la charge: «Nous voulons un vrai président pour le Liban, Aoun»." September 8, at: www.lorientlejour.com/article/943121/n-moussaoui-revient-a-la-charge-nous-voulons-un-vrai-president-pour-le-liban-aoun-.html (accessed September 8, 2015).

Orient le Jour (2015e) "Le soutien du narcotrafiquant Nouh Zeaïter aux soldats du Hezbollah dans le Qalamoun." September 15, at: www.lorientlejour.com/article/944334/le-soutien-du-narcotrafiquant-nouh-zeaiter-aux-soldats-du-hezbollah-dans-le-qalamoun.html (accessed September 16, 2015).

Orient le Jour (2016) "Au Liban-Sud, une crise de confiance entre le Hezbollah et l'électorat chiite." May 19, at: www.lorientlejour.com/article/986725/au-liban-sud-une-crise-de-confiance-entre-le-hezbollah-et-lelectorat-chiite.html (accessed June 20, 2016).

Orient le Jour and AFP (2014a) "Marchands de légumes, commerçants ou étudiants, les hommes du Hezb fiers de combattre en Syrie." April 12, at: www.lorientlejour.com/article/862890/-marchands-de-legumes-commercants-ou-etudiants-les-hommes-du-hezb-fiers-de-combattre-en-syrie.html (accessed April 12, 2014).

Orient le Jour and AFP (2014b) "En Syrie, le Hezbollah a acquis et professe une précieuse expérience antiguérilla." April 16, at: www.lorientlejour.com/article/863267/en-syrie-le-hezbollah-a-acquis-et-professe-une-precieuse-experience-antiguerilla.html (accessed April 16, 2014).

Orléans, Alexander (2014) "Echoes of Syria: Hezbollah reemerges in Iraq." *Institute for the Study of War Updates*, at: http://iswiraq.blogspot.ch/2014/08/echoes-of-syria-hezbollah-reemerges-in.html (accessed November 30, 2014).

Osoegawa, Taku (2013) *Syria and Lebanon: International Relations and Diplomacy in the Middle East*. London: I.B. Tauris.

Osseyran, Hayat N. (1997) *The Shiite Leadership of South Lebanon: A Reconsideration*, (Masters). American University of Beirut.

Owen, Roger (1976) "The Political Economy of the Great Lebanon, 1920–1970," in R. Owen (ed.), *Essays on the Crisis in Lebanon*. London: Ithaca Press, pp. 23–32.

Owen, R. (1988) "The Economic History of Lebanon, 1943–1974: Its Salient Features," in Barakat G. (ed.), *Toward a Viable Lebanon*. London: Croom Helm, pp. 27–41.

Paivandi, Saeed (2006) *Religion et éducation en Iran: l'échec de l'islamisation de l'école*. Paris: L'Harmattan.

Pearlman, Wendy (2013) "Emigration and Power: A Study of Sects in Lebanon, 1860–2010." *Politics & Society*, Vol. 41, No. 1, pp. 103–33.

Perthes, Volker (1997) "Myths and Money: Four Years of Hariri and Lebanon's Preparation for a New Middle East." *Middle East Report*, No. 203, pp. 16–21.

Picard, Elizabeth (1985) "De la 'communauté-classe' à la résistance 'nationale'. Pour une analyse du rôle des Chi'ites dans le système politique libanais (1970–1985)." *Revue française de science politique*, 35e année, No. 6, pp. 999–1028.

Picard, E. (2000) "The Political Economy of Civil War in Lebanon," in S. Heydemann (ed.), *War, Institutions, and Social Change in the Middle East*, Berkeley and Los Angeles, CA: University of California Press, pp. 292–324.

Picaudou, Nadine (1989) *La déchirure libanaise*. Paris: Editions Complexe.

Pompey, Fabienne (2009) "Les Nouveaux Libanais." *Jeune Afrique*, at: www. jeuneafrique.com/Article/ARTJAJA2527p042-044.xmlo/immigration-islam-hezbollah-mosqueeles-nouveaux-libanais.html (accessed February 2, 2012).

Press TV (2008) "The Opposition will Continue Civil Disobedience," at: http:// edition.presstv.ir/detail/55451.html (accessed May 15, 2008).

Al-Qard al-Hassan Association (2014a) at: www.qardhasan.org (accessed February 20, 2014).

Al-Qard al-Hassan Association (2014b) "Al-Ihsāʾāt," at: www.qardhasan.org/ statistics.html (accessed February 21, 2014).

Al-Qard al-Hassan Association (2014c) "Al Jamʿiyya muʾassassa al-qard Hassan," at: www.qardhasan.org/video.html (accessed February 22, 2014).

Qassem, Naim (2008) *Hezbollah, la voie, l'expérience, l'avenir*. Beyrouth: Albouraq.

Qassir, Qassem (2011) "Qussa 'Hizb Allāh' min al-ʿām 1982 ila 2011: hakadha āsbah al-lāʿb al-assassī fī al-lubnānī!." *As-Safīr maʾlumāt*, No. 94, at: www. alorwa.org/content.php?id=300 (accessed March 29, 2012).

Qifa Nakbi (2011) "The Orthodox Gathering's Proposed Electoral System," at: http://qifanabki.files.wordpress.com/2011/12/orthodox-gathering-proposal. pdf (accessed March 3, 2013).

Al-Qods (2014) "Muqātilun fī Hizb Allāh yatrikun kul shīʾ li-khawd 'maʾraka' wujud bi-Suriyyā," at: www.alquds.co.uk/?p=154399 (accessed April 10, 2014).

Qualander, Nicolas (2006) "Hezbollah en débat 'L'anomalie sauvage' du mouvement islamique." *Inprecor*, at: http://ks3260355.kimsufi.com/inprecor/ ~154005898ad322b8a08ac1e0~/article-inprecor?id=123 (accessed October 20, 2011).

Raad, Muhammad (2012) *Speech* at the Conference "Reform of Social Policies in Lebanon: From Selective Subsidy towards Welfare State." Beirut 2012.

Rajaee, Farhang (1993) "Islam and Modernity," in M.E. Marty and R.S. Appleby (eds), *Fundamentalisms and Society, Reclaiming the Sciences, the Family and Education*. Chicago, IL and London: University of Chicago Press, pp. 103–28.

Rakel, Eva P. (2009) "The Political Elite in the Islamic Republic of Iran: From Khomeini to Ahmadinejad." *Comparative Studies of South Asia, Africa and the Middle East*, Vol. 29, pp. 105–25.

Al-Rassoul al-Aazam (2014) "Aqsām al-markaz," at: www.alrasoul-bci.org/ categorypage.php?catid=38 (accessed April 30, 2014).

Rayburn, Joel (2014) *Iraq after America: Strongmen, Sectarians, Resistance*. Stanford, CA: Hoover Institution Press Publication.

Republic of Lebanon, Ministry of Finance (2013) "Debt and Debt Market, A Quarterly Bulletin of the Ministry of Finance, Issue No. 27, Quarter IV," at: www.finance.gov.lb/en-US/finance/PublicDebt/Documents/Quarterly%20 Debt%20Report/2013/Debt%20and%20Debt%20Markets%20QIV%202013. pdf (accessed February 2, 2014).

Reuters (2011) "Egypt Brotherhood Businessman: Manufacturing is Key." *Ahram Online*, at: http://english.ahram.org.eg/~/NewsContent/3/12/25348/Business/ Economy/Egypt-Brotherhood-businessman-Manufacturing-is-key.aspx (accessed December 20, 2011).

Reuters (2016) "Ending the Siege of Madaya," at: www.reuters.com/news/picture/ ending-the-siege-of-madaya?articleId=USRTX221NB (accessed January 15, 2016).

Rida, Nour (2013) "Sayyed Nasrallah: Hizbullah Not Responsible for Drone, Political Settlement Only Solution in Syria." *Al-Ahed News*, at: www.english. alahednews.com.lb/essaydetails.php?eid=22984&cid=445#.VHbqNt7A1ss (accessed December 20, 2012).

Rifai, Marisol (2014) "Au Liban, le corps enseignant au bout du rouleau." *Orient le Jour*, at: www.lorientlejour.com/article/864399/le-corps-enseignant-au-bout-du-rouleau.html (accessed April 24, 2014).

"al-Risāla al-maftūha allati wajjahaha 'Hizb Allāh' ila al-mustad'afīn," (1985). *As-Safir ma'lumāt*, No. 94, pp. 59–71.

Roccu, Roberto (2012) *Gramsci in Cairo: Neoliberal Authoritarianism, Passive Revolution and Failed Hegemony in Egypt under Mubarak, 1991–2010* (PhD), University of London, London School of Economics.

Roy, O. (2002) *L'Islam mondialisé*. Paris: Seuil.

Saab, Bilal Y. (2012) "The Syrian Spillover and Salafist Radicalization in Lebanon." *Combating Terrorism Center*, at: www.ctc.usma.edu/posts/the-syrian-spillover-and-salafist-radicalization-in-lebanon (accessed October 30, 2014).

Saad Ghorayeb, Amal (2002) *Hizbullah Politics and Religion*. London: Pluto Press.

Saad Ghorayeb, A. (2005) "Hizbullah's Arms and Shiite Empowerment." *The Daily Star*, at: www.dailystar.com.lb/Opinion/Commentary/2005/Aug-22/95333-hizbullahs-arms-and-shiite-empowerment.ashx (accessed July 31, 2012).

Saad Ghorayeb, A. (2012) "Hezbollah's Iran Money Trail: It's Complicated." *Al-Akhbar English*, at: http://english.al-akhbar.com/content/hezbollahs-iran-money-trail-its-complicated (accessed July 31, 2012).

Al-Saadi, Yazan (2015) "Electricity Workers in Lebanon, and the Fate of Labour, National Development, and Governance, Civil Society Knowledge Center, Lebanon Support," at: http://cskc.daleel-madani.org/content/electricity-workers-lebanon-and-fate-labour-national-development-and-governance (accessed June 20, 2016).

Sachedina, Abdulaziz A. (1991) "Activist Shi'ism in Iran, Iraq, and Lebanon," in E.M. Marty and R.S. Appleby (eds), *Fundamentalisms Observed*. Chicago, IL and London: University of Chicago Press, pp. 403–56.

As-Safir (2014) "Nasr Allāh: sawārikhnā tutāl kāmel Falestīn al-muhtala," at: http://assafir.com/Article/1/382137 (accessed November 4, 2014).

Saif, Ibrahim (2012) "Al-muwāzana al-lubnāniyya … taghīb al-awlawiyyāt al-muwātin." *Al-Hayat*, at: http://alhayat.com/Details/419038 (accessed July 16, 2012).

Salibi, Kamal S. (1971) "The Lebanese Identity." *Journal of Contemporary History*, Vol. 6, No. 1, pp. 76–81, 83–86.

Salloukh, Bassel (2005) "Syria and Lebanon: A Brotherhood Transformed." *Middle East Report,* No. 236, at: www.merip.org/mer/mer236/syria-lebanon-brotherhood-transformed (accessed July 21, 2013).

Salloukh, B. (2012) "Lebanon, Where Next for Hezbollah: Resistance or Reform?." *Accord*, Issue 25, pp. 100–104, at: www.c-r.org/sites/default/files/Accord25_ Lebanon.pdf (accessed July 23, 2012).

Salloukh, B. (2015) "Sectarianism and Struggles for Socio-Economic Rights" in J. Al-Habbal, R. Barakat, L. Khattab, S. Mikaelian and B. Sallouh (eds), *The Politics of Sectarianism in Postwar Lebanon*. London: Pluto Press, pp. 70–87.

Saudi Oger Website (2013) "Overview," at: www.saudioger.com/overview_ mission.html (accessed December 15, 2013).

Sereni, Jean Pierre (2014) "Le leader d'Ennahda explique ses ambitions pour la Tunisie, de la revolution à la réforme." *Orient XXI*, at: http://orientxxi.info/ lu-vu-entendu/le-leader-d-ennahda-explique-ses,0629 (accessed July 7, 2014).

Seurat, Leila (2015) *Le Hamas et le monde*. Paris: CNRS.

Shaheen, Kareem (2013) "Hamas will Adjust to Egypt, Retain Hezbollah Ties." *The Daily Star*, at: www.dailystar.com.lb/News/Politics/2013/Jul-20/224371-hamas-will-adjust-to-egypt-retain-hezbollah-ties.ashx (accessed July 22, 2013).

Shams, Doha (2012) "Mahmoud Zahar: Hamas Betting on Egypt and Axis of Neutrality." *Al-Akhbar English*, at: http://english.al-akhbar.com/content/ mahmoud-zahar-hamas-betting-egypt-and-axis-neutrality (accessed March 28, 2012).

Shams el-Din, Layla (2012) Al-Manar employee. Interview April 2012, Beirut.

Shanahan, Roger (2005) *The Shi'a of Lebanon: Clans, Parties and Clerics*. London: I.B Tauris.

Shapira, Shimon (2009) "Has Hizbullah Changed? The 7th Hizbullah General Conference and Its Continued Ideology of Resistance." *Jerusalem Center for Public Affairs*, at: http://jcpa.org/article/has-hizbullah-changed-the-7th-hizbullah-general-conference-and-its-continued-ideology-of-resistance/#sthash. vBbycYz4.dpuf (accessed November 16, 2014).

Shar Metal Company (2013) "About Us," at: www.sharmetal.com/about1.html (accessed October 22, 2013).

Sharaf, Raed (2014) "Ma'araka hay'at al-tansīq al-niqābiyya fī 2013: al-hirāk al-markaz." *The Legal Agenda*, at: www.legal-agenda.com/article. php?id=650&lang=ar (accessed February 4, 2012).

El-Shark Online (2012) "14 adhār" tuhaqaq fawzā thamīnā fī intikhābāt niqāba al-siyyādila: hassuna naqībā bi-ziyyāda 131 sawta 'an murashah Hizb Allāh," at: www.elsharkonline.com/ViewArticle.aspx?ArtID=22032 (accessed December 13, 2012).

Al-Sharq al-Āwsat (2004), "Īdrāb 'ām wa massīrāt wa i'tisāmāt fī Lubnān al-yawm li-khafd sa'r al-banzīn wa himāya al-īd al-'āmila al-wataniyya," at: http://archive. aawsat.com/details.asp?article=236210&issueno=9312#.V6Q9UemtgdN (accessed May 15, 2012).

Sherry, Hassan (2014) "Post-War Lebanon and the Influence of International Financial Institutions: A 'Merchant Republic'." Civil Society Knowledge Center, Lebanon Support, at: http://cskc.daleel-madani.org/paper/post-war-lebanon-and-influence-international-financial-institutions (accessed August 5, 2014).

Shibani, Al Hajj Hassan (2013) "al-tajadhābāt al-siyyāssiyya tatajassad fī intikhābāt al-atbā' wa markaz naqīb amam ma'araka 'kassr 'adm'." Al-Liwa', at: http://aliwaa.com/Article.aspx?ArticleId=165007 (accessed May 17, 2013).

Siklawi, Rami (2010) "The Dynamics of Palestinian Political Endurance in Lebanon." Middle East Journal, Vol. 64, No. 4, pp. 597–611.

Slab News (2013) "Ittihād baladiyyāt al-Dāhiyya: li-wuquf a'māl al-binā' aw al-tarmīm aw al-tajdīd qabl al-istihsāl 'ala al-rukhs," at: www.slabnews.com/article/43781/20%أو20%البناء20%أعمال20%لوقف20%الضاحية:20%بلديات20%اتحاد (accessed October 20%الرخص20%على20%الاستحصال20%قبل20%التجديد20%أو20%الترميم) 26, 2013).

Sleibe, Ghassan (1999) Fī al-ittihād kuwa. Beirut: Dar Mukhtarat.

Sleibe, Ghassan (2012) Public Service International Secretary for Arab Countries. Interview May 2012, Beirut.

Stewart, Dona J. (1996) "Society Economic Recovery and Reconstruction in Postwar Beirut." Geographical Review, Vol. 86, No. 4, pp. 487–504.

Sullivan, Marisa (2014) "Middle East Security Report 19, Hezbollah in Syria." Institute for the Study of War, at: www.understandingwar.org/sites/default/files/Hezbollah_Sullivan_FINAL.pdf (accessed December 1, 2014).

Tajamu' al-'Ulamā' al-Muslimīn fī Lubnān (2014), at: http://tajamo.net/ (accessed October 18, 2014).

Tajco Construction and Development (2013) "Our Projects," at: www.tajco.pro/index.php?option=com_content&view=article&id=22&Itemid=114 (accessed August 7, 2013).

Tehranian, Majid (1993) "Islamic Fundamentalism in Iran," in M.E. Marty and R.S. Appleby (eds), Fundamentalisms and Society, Reclaiming the Sciences, the Family and Education. Chicago, IL and London: University of Chicago Press, pp. 341–73.

Teitelbaum, Joshua (2011) "The Muslim Brotherhood in Syria, 1945–1958: Founding, Social Origins, Ideology." Middle East Journal, Vol. 65, No. 2, pp. 213–33.

Terror Control (2014) "Home Page," at: https://stop910.com/en (accessed November 30, 2014).

The International Bank for Reconstruction and Development and The World Bank (2011) "Migration and Remittances: Top countries, Migration and Remittances Factbook 2011," at: https://openknowledge.worldbank.org/bitstream/handle/10986/2522/578690PUB0Migr11public10BOX353782B0.pdf?sequence=1 (accessed February 15, 2013).

The Star (2009) "Madoff-like Scandal Soils Hezbollah's Clean Image," at: www.thestar.com/news/world/2009/09/23/madofflike_scandal_soils_hezbollahs_clean_image.html (accessed April 5, 2012).

Thomas, Peter D. (2009) *The Gramscian Moment: Philosophy, Hegemony and Marxism.* Leiden: Brill.

Toscane, Luiza (1995) *L'Islam un autre nationalisme?.* Paris: L'Harmattan.

Traboulsi, Fawwaz (2007) *A History of Modern Lebanon.* London: Pluto Press.

Traboulsi, F. (2014) "Al-tabaqāt al-ijtimā'iyya fī Lubnān: ithbāt wujud." *Heinrich Boll Stiftung,* at: http://lb.boell.org/sites/default/files/social_classes_in_lebanon.pdf (accessed May 31, 2014).

UNDP (2008a) "Millennium Development Goals, Lebanon Report 2008." *UNDP in Lebanon,* at: www.undp.org.lb/communication/publications/downloads/MDG_en.pdf (accessed March 11, 2011).

UNDP (2008b) "Poverty, Growth and Income Distribution in Lebanon." *UNDP in Lebanon,* at: www.ipc-undp.org/pub/IPCCountryStudy13.pdf (accessed October 12, 2011).

UNDP (2009) "The National Human Development Report 2008–2009: Towards a Citizen's State." *UNDP in Lebanon,* at: www.lb.undp.org/content/dam/lebanon/docs/Governance/Publications/NHDR_Full_Report1_En.pdf (accessed November 11, 2011).

UNHRC (2013) "Syria Needs Analysis Project: Lebanese Baseline Information," at: data.unhcr.org/syrianrefugees/partner.php?OrgId=135 (accessed November 11, 2013).

US Department of the Treasury (2007) "Twin Treasury Actions Take Aim at Hizballah's Support Network," at: www.treasury.gov/press-center/press-releases/Pages/hp503.aspx (accessed October 30, 2015).

US Department of the Treasury (2013) "Action Targets Hizballah's Leadership Responsible for Operations Outside of Lebanon," at: www.treasury.gov/press-center/press-releases/Pages/jl2147.aspx (accessed October 30, 2014).

US Department of the Treasury (2014) "Treasury Sanctions Procurement Agents of Hizballah Front Company Based in Lebanon With Subsidiaries in the UAE and China," at: www.treasury.gov/press-center/press-releases/Pages/jl2562.aspx (accessed October 30, 2015).

US Department of the Treasury (2015a) "Treasury Targets Africa-Based Hizballah Support Network." February 26, at: www.treasury.gov/press-center/press-releases/Pages/jl9982.aspx (accessed May 2, 2016).

US Department of the Treasury (2015b) "Treasury Sanctions Hizballah Front Companies and Facilitators in Lebanon and Iraq." July 10, at: www.treasury.gov/press-center/press-releases/Pages/jl0069.aspx (accessed May 2, 2016).

US Department of the Treasury (2016) "Treasury Sanctions Hizballah Financier and His Company," at: www.treasury.gov/press-center/press-releases/Pages/jl0317.aspx (accessed May 2, 2016).

Verdeil, E. (2008) "Emeutes et électricité au Liban." *Le Monde Diplomatique*, at: www.monde-diplomatique.fr/carnet/2008-01-30-Liban (accessed November 22, 2010).

Verdeil, E. (2009) "Dépolitiser la question électrique au Liban?," *Rumor*, at: http://rumor.hypotheses.org/207 (accessed November 22, 2010).

Vivien, Renaud (2007) "The Paris III Conference on Assistance to Lebanon: Who Aids Whom?." *Mrzine*, at: http://mrzine.monthlyreview.org/2007/vivien310107.html (accessed December 11, 2010).

Wahdat al-niqābāt wa al-'ummāl al-markaziyya fī Hizb Allāh (2008) "Wahdat al-niqābāt wa al-'ummāl al-markaziyya fī Hizb Allāh asdaret wathiqitihā al-sanawiyya: Lubnān dakhala marhala siyyāssiyya jadīda ba'd itifkāq al-Duha." *Moqawama*, at: www.moqawama.org/essaydetails.php?eid=10261&cid=99#.U_NTFv2ztst' (accessed June 19, 2012).

Wahdat al-niqābāt wa al-'ummāl al-markaziyya fī Hizb Allāh (2009) "Nas al-wathīqa wa al-mutalabiyya al-latī asdarethā wahdat al-niqābāt wa al-'ummāl al-markaziyya fī Hizb Allāh." *Moqawama*, at: www.moqawama.org/essaydetails.php?eid=15885&cid=199#.VDQFk_2ztst (accessed June 20, 2012).

Wärn, M. (2012) *A Voice of Resistance: The Point of View of Hizballah—Perceptions, Goals and Strategies of an Islamic Movement in Lebanon.* Stockholm: Department of Political Science, Stockholm University.

Wehbe, Batoul (2011) "Sayyed Nasrallah Condoles Al-Kharafi's Death, Hezbollah Delegation in Kuwait." *Al-Manar*, at: www.almanar.com.lb/english/adetails.php?fromval=3&cid=23&frid=23&seccatid=14&eid=11013 (accessed April 23, 2014).

Wehbe, Muhammad (2012) "Saraf Al-'ummāl bil-jumla wa al-Mufariq." *Al-Akhbar*, at: www.al-akhbar.com/node/182321 (accessed May 2, 2012).

Wehbe, M. (2013a) "Al-khuruj min al-halqa al-mufaragha." *Al-Akhbar*, April 22, at: www.al-akhbar.com/node/181675 (accessed April 22, 2013).

Wehbe, M. (2013b) "Al-Dāhiyya qātira iqtisādiyya a'idān." *Al-Akhbar*, August 19, at: www.al-akhbar.com/node/189107 (accessed August 20, 2013).

Wehbe, M. (2013c) "Ahwāl Al-Dāhiyya: al-tanāqud al-tabaqi dākhil aswār al-ta'ifa." *Al-Akhbar*, August 20, at: www.al-akhbar.com/node/189138 (accessed August 21, 2013).

WikiLeaks (2009) "List of Al-Manar Shareholders Potential Names for Designation?," at: www.wikileaks.org/plusd/cables/07BEIRUT150_a.html (accessed September 15, 2012).

Williams, Daniel (2007) "Hezbollah Expands in North Lebanon, Away from UN Peacekeepers." *Bloomberg*, at: www.bloomberg.com/apps/news?pid=newsarchive&sid=a61ZA5X6NH8E&refer=home (accessed August 8, 2013).

Worth, Robert F. (2009) "Billion-Dollar Pyramid Scheme Rivets Lebanon." *New York Times*, at: http://dealbook.nytimes.com/2009/09/16/billion-dollar-pyramid-scheme-rivets-lebanon/?_php=true&_type=blogs&_r=0 (accessed April 6, 2012).

Ya Libnan (2013a) "Hezbollah Facing Resistance from Within over Its Syria Role." July 7, at: www.yalibnan.com/2013/07/07/hezbollah-facing-resistance-from-within-over-its-syria-role/ (accessed July 20, 2013).

Ya Libnan (2013b) "Al-Manar TV Chief Quits." December 26, at: www.yalibnan.com/2013/12/26/al-manar-chief-quits/ (accessed December 28, 2013).

Ya Libnan (2016) "3 Key Members Expelled from the Free Patriotic Movement, A Party On 'Brink of Internal Collapse,'" at: http://yalibnan.com/2016/07/30/3-key-members-expelled-from-the-free-patriotic-movement/ (accessed 1 August 1, 2016).

Yaghi, Zainab (2012) "Al-Dāhiyya tamhū āthār tamūz." As-Safir, at: http://assafir.com/Article/274887 (accessed May 15, 2012).

Yassin, Ali Taher (2012a) in "Conference Reform of Social Policies in Lebanon: From Selective Subsidy Towards Welfare State." Beirut, 2012.

Yassin, A.T. (2012b) Head of the Federation al-Wafa (linked to Hezbollah) and member of the CGTL's executive committee, Hezbollah member. Interview March 2012, Beirut.

Young, Michael (1998) "Two Faces of Janus: Post-War Lebanon and Its Reconstruction." Middle East Report, No. 209, pp. 4–7, 44.

Zaatari, M. (2011) "Palestinian Refugee Camps Bury Nakba Martyrs." The Daily Star, at: www.dailystar.com.lb/News/Lebanon-News/2011/May-17/138848-palestinian-refugee-camps-bury-nakba-martyrs.ashx#axzz3INSwDJKA (accessed October 30, 2013).

Zaatari, M. (2013) "Palestinian Refugees Burn Hezbollah Aid." The Daily Star, at: www.dailystar.com.lb/News/Local-News/2013/May-31/218980-palestinian-refugees-burn-hezbollah-aid.ashx (accessed October 30, 2014).

Zaraket, Maha (2012) "Tahqīq: al-sāfarāt mahjubāt 'an 'al-Manār." Al-Akhbar, at: www.al-akhbar.com/node/64561 (accessed May 20, 2012).

Zaraket, M. (2014) "Alef bā' silsila al-ratib wa al-rawātib." Al-Akhbar, at: www.al-akhbar.com/node/207145 (accessed May 24, 2014).

Zbeeb, M. (2012a) "A Nation Living Day to Day." Al-Akhbar English, May 31, at: http://english.al-akhbar.com/content/nation-living-day-day (accessed May 31, 2012).

Zbeeb, Muhammad (2012b) "Lebanese Unions: Handcuffing Labor." Al-Akhbar English, 16 August, at: http://english.al-akhbar.com/node/11167 (accessed August 16, 2012).

Zbeeb, M. (2012c) "Lebanon: Budgeting a Free-Falling Economy." Al-Akhbar English, September 13, at: http://english.al-akhbar.com/node/12089 (accessed September 13, 2012).

Zbeeb, M. (2012d) "Bid Farewell to a Lebanese Union Impostor." Al-Akhbar English, December 28, at: http://english.al-akhbar.com/node/14506 (accessed December 28, 2012).

Zeid, Akram (2012) Trade Unionist linked to Hezbollah, Interview July 2012, Beirut.

Zigby Mohammad (2000) *Bullets to Ballots: the Lebanonization of Hizballah* (Masters), McGill University.

Zoghbi, Imad (2013) "massā' lil-tawāfuq 'ala intikhāb naqīb lil-mu'alimīn." *As-Safir*, at: http://assafir.com/Article.aspx?EditionId=2429&ChannelId=58458& ArticleId=445&Author=الزغبي+عماد (accessed July 16, 2013).

Index

Abdallah, Castro: CGTL 230n; EDL 233n; Hezbollah 66; housing rental policy 65–6

Abou Zeinab, Ghaleb: 165–6

Achcar, Gilbert: 2, 88, 206, 226n

Agriculture: Hezbollah's policies 66–71, 144, 171; socio-economic figures 15, 42, 59–60, 67, 70, 80, 208, 221n; trade unions 68–9, 134, 151, 223n

Akkar: 9–10, 14–15, 39, 75–6, 225n

Alawite: Lebanon 165, 216n; Syria 11, 218n

Amal: alliance and collaboration with Hezbollah 1, 46, 52, 121–2, 141–2, 146, 228n; Berri, Nabih 48, 80, 133, 220n; election municipality Beirut 225n; establishment 18, 33–5, 219n, 221n; lawyers 89, 226n; Lebanese Civil War and outcomes 20–1, 23–4, 103, 129, 218n–20n; March 8 139; Minister of Health 141; relation with Lebanese army 222n, 234n; rivalries and competition with Hezbollah 29–33, 92, 229n, trade unions and labour movement: 131–3, 135, 148, 151, 163, 231n

Amel, Mehdi: 22–3, 34–5, 71, 163, 201

Aoun, Michel: 49, 139, 145, 223n, 229n

As'ad (al-), Ahmad: 120–1, 230n

Assad: regime 107, 121, 158, 168, 174, 181, 184–5, 187, 189; revolt 182

Assad (al-), Bashar: 179–80, 185, 191–2

Assad (al-), Hafez: 179–80, 218n

Azmeh (al-), Aziz: 4

Baalbek: 10, 13, 28, 75, 77, 86, 104, 122, 155, 165, 182, 189, 208–9, 231n, 234n

Ba'th: Iraq 219n, 236n, Lebanon 21, 131–3, 231n, Syria 223n

Bassil, Gebran: 145–6, 222n, 233n

Beirut: assassinations 156; association al-Qard al-Hassan 98; "Beirut Madinati" 207; business associations 74, 80, 143; Central Information Unit 107; clashes 2008 164–5, 187; construction 74, 82; East 32, 80; Elissar project 62–3; gentrification 66; Greater 1, 15, 79; Hamas 190, 193–4, 196; Hezbollah's policies and influence 29, 31, 46–7, 52, 62, 87, 96–7, 100–1, 113, 134, 140, 154, 159, 164–6, 178, 190, 193, 196, 199; Mall 62; migration 14; Palestinian 19; region 7, 9, 25, 31; rent control laws 5; rivalries between Amal and Hezbollah 32, 163; role and location 10, 25, 32, 80; sectarian composition 10, 16, 75; social disparities and inequality 15, 20, 33, 39, 75–7, 79, 88, 200; South 21, 33, 35, 52, 60, 75, 77, 88, 104, 111, 137, 146, 163, 198; trade unions and protests 128–31, 137, 142, 146–7, 150–1; University 89; War 2006 155; West 24, 28, 162, 164

Bekaa: agriculture 5, 10, 14; association al-Qard al-Hassan 98; card al-Amir 98; Dawa 30; Hezbollah's influence, institutions and policies 28, 29, 46, 66–7, 69, 71, 82, 85, 87, 104, 107, 111, 113,

219n; Dawa 219n; foreign Shiʿa
fighters 187; Hezbollah 177–8, 184,
186, 191, 197, 227n, 235n;
Hezbollah al-Nujaba 178; Imam
Al-Khuiʾ 120; Inmaa Group 83,
85–6; Iran War 31, 33, 44–5, 219n;
League of Arab states 238n; Maliki
(al-) 178, 236n; Mossul's seizure by
ISIS 177; resistance 173; Sadr (al-),
Muhammad Baqir 26; sectarian
groups and militias 159; ulemas 26;
US/UN-led operation 1990–91 37
Islamic Republic of Iran (IRI):
establishment 3; evolution within
the IRI 44–5, 53, 219n; relation
with Hezbollah 3, 7, 24, 27–9,
31–4, 45–6, 52, 71, 88, 99, 104–6,
109–10, 113, 120, 125, 154, 158,
163, 168–9, 174–6, 179, 185, 187,
190–1, 193–6, 199–201, 203, 220n,
222n, 229n–30n, 234n
Islamization: 2, 53, 55, 94, 122, 202–5
Israel: Arab-Israeli war 35;
assassination 45, 106; Gaza Strip
195; Hezbollah's resistance and
propaganda 1, 6, 29–32, 34, 38,
44–5, 51, 85, 106, 108–9, 111–12,
121, 126, 153–5, 157–62, 164–70,
178–82, 184–7, 189–91, 195, 196,
201–5, 227n, 234n; invasion and
occupation of Lebanon 1, 23–5, 30,
32, 78, 106, 127–8, 167–8, 172–3,
218n; Mufti of Lebanese Republic
165; War 2006 1, 40, 76, 97, 155,
160–1, 164, 178–9, 199, 234n–6n,
238n; Palestinian national
Movement 3, 37, 217n; Zahar,
Mahmoud 192

Jumblatt, Kamal: 20, 135, 218n
Jumblatt, Walid: 165–6

Kataeb (also known as the Lebanese
Phalanges): 20, 21, 129, 217n–18n

Khamenei, Ali Hosseini: Fadlallah,
Muhammad Hussein 120; Iranian
leadership 44–5, link and issues
with Hezbollah 45–6, 114, 119,
125; Yemen 176
Khansa (al-), Muhammad Said: 27,
61–3, 206, 223n, 228n–9n
Khomeini: death 44; Hezbollah's use,
diffusion of ideology and imagery
28–9, 31, 43, 56, 71, 104, 107, 110,
114, 122, 201; political thought
53–4, 122, 201

Lebanese Communist Party (LCP):
elections 46; Lebanese Civil War
21–2, 24, 163; members 65, 128;
protests 129, 139, 145, 147;
secretary general 147; tensions
with Hezbollah 118, 163, 229n–30n
Lebanese Forces (LF): 129
Lebanese National Movement (LNM):
20–4, 129, 218n
Lebanese National Resistance Front
(LNRF) (also known as Jammul):
24, 32, 162
Lebanese Resistance Brigades (LRB):
121, 160, 189–90, 235n, 237n–8n

Mahdi: army 159; Chamsedine 26;
Imam 104, 135; schools 98, 113,
226n; scouts 114, 125
Makdissi, Ussama: 4, 35
Manar TV: 86–7, 106–10, 119, 174,
178, 191, 208, 221n, 228n–9n
Manifesto: "of the nine" 30; "1985" 31,
43, 50; "2009" 47, 50, 52, 167, 179
March 14 coalition: "Beirut Madinati"
207, clashes 2008 6, 140, 163, 165;
Consensual Agreement 143; Future
Movement 236n; Hezbollah rivalry
199, incidents black shirts 166;
Internal Security Forces 222n,
municipality of Beirut 225n; social